OKLAHOMA PLACE NAMES

Oklahoma Place Names

Second Edition, Revised and Enlarged

by George H. Shirk

Foreword by MURIEL H. WRIGHT

UNIVERSITY OF OKLAHOMA PRESS

NORMAN AND LONDON

INTERNATIONAL STANDARD BOOK NUMBER 0–8061–2028–2
LIBRARY OF CONGRESS CATALOG CARD NUMBER: 65–14803

TO THE STAFF OF
The Oklahoma Historical Society

FOREWORD
By Muriel H. Wright

OKLAHOMA MEANS "RED PEOPLE" from the words in the Choctaw language, *okla* meaning "people" and *humma* or *homma* meaning "red."

This name was applied to the Indian Territory in the Choctaw-Chickasaw treaty of 1866 signed in Washington, D.C., by the Choctaw and the Chickasaw delegates and federal commissioners. The treaty provided details for the organization of a territorial government in this as yet unorganized region.

The naming of the proposed territory took place one day when the different delegations from the five Indian nations (or Five Civilized Tribes) were in conference with the United States officials discussing the new territorial organization. The Commissioner of Indian Affairs asked, "What would you call your Territory?" Allen Wright, one of the Choctaw delegates who was translating the Choctaw-Chickasaw treaty under consideration at the moment, immediately replied, "Okla-homa." No one of the Indian delegations present raised any objections, even though their own treaties of 1866 made brief provision for a territorial government. Thereupon the name was written in the Choctaw-Chickasaw treaty, stating that the chief executive of the new territorial organization should be titled "the governor of the Territory of Oklahoma."

The organization of the Indian Territory was not completed under the provisions of the treaties of 1866. The name "Oklahoma," however, became popular and was widely known throughout the country, appearing in several bills providing for the organization of the Indian Territory introduced in Congress, none of which was enacted and approved, during a period of nearly twenty years.

A year after the opening of the 1,880,000 acres of the Unassigned Lands in central Indian Territory to homestead settlement by the "Run of 1889," the western half of the old territory was regularly organized by Congress as "Oklahoma Territory." The eastern half remained the "last Indian Territory," where the five Indian nations allotted their lands in severalty preparatory to closing their old tribal governments. Seventeen years passed before the two territories were organized together and admitted as the state of Oklahoma, the forty-sixth state of the Union, in 1907.

MURIEL H. WRIGHT

Oklahoma Historical Society
Oklahoma City, Oklahoma

PREFACE

Since the publication in October, 1965, of *Oklahoma Place Names*, interest in the fascinating subject of place names has greatly increased throughout the United States and is now something of substantial importance. In 1969 the American Name Society, a group organized in 1951, set in motion the first steps for a nationwide place name survey of the United States. A Survey Commission was organized, and pilot studies were instituted in several states. These studies were undertaken and designed so as to provide a working technique whereby the project could be enlarged to the desired nationwide basis. The Commission is now actively working toward the ultimate goal of the assembly at a national center of all place name information for the entire continental United States.

This circumstance alone perhaps would have warranted the continuous effort since 1965 to revise, to update, and to use all possible effort to eliminate errors in the existing volume. Actually, however, other considerations seem of even greater importance and of more significance.

Toponymy of an area as large as Oklahoma, with its twin territory antecedents, is an ongoing and a never-ending process. Different from the publication of something like, let us say, the multiplication table, the effort is never complete nor is the objective ever entirely achieved. Virgil J. Vogel, in his introduction to *Indian Place Names in Illinois*, was quoted in the introduction to the first edition: "For one who seeks out the true origin and meaning of these names, however, history has been unkind. Egyptologists have perhaps had better success in deciphering hieroglyphics that have endured for five millennia than have those seeking to trace American Indian names first recorded only two or three centuries ago."

Fully aware of those same difficulties, since 1965 the author has covered the same ground and plumbed the same sources again for oversights and additional information. The Oklahoma Press Association continued its superb co-operation, and newspapers in every section of the state published lists of place names for the locality of their circulation area with appeals to readers to come forward with help.

The response was surprising. Even though those identical lists had been published prior to the 1965 volume, as many replies were received to the second series as to the first. Perhaps reader interest had been kindled, or possibly the individual with the needed resource information had not known of the earlier appeal. The greatly expanded list of contributors appearing at the close of this volume gives ample evidence to the success of the efforts of the Oklahoma Press Association and of its members. Without the countless editorial columns and articles featuring the place names of the local area there would not have been enough new material to warrant this revised edition.

I trust that all of the obvious errors, such as Erin Springs in Garvin County, and most of the illusive ones, such as Meers in Comanche County, have by now been detected and eliminated; and it is gratifying that it has required less than a decade to complete the correction or revision of a sufficient number of entries to justify a new and revised edition.

While the need for Oklahoma to be well represented with the Survey Commission of the American Name Society is of significance, the justification for a revised *Oklahoma Place Names* is really the elimination of error.

In his meritorious *American Place-Names*, Dr. George R. Stewart states in his preface: "The study of place-names, comprising several disciplines, is all too conducive to a genial prolixity and the amiable pursuit of hobbies. The linguist, the geographer, the historian, the folk-lorist—each may write upon the subject. The linguist tends to pursue etymology to its depths; the geographer is in danger of producing a gazetteer; the historian devotes a page as to whether a certain pond was named for Joe Smith or his cousin Hank; the folk-lorist endlessly records stories about names. The toponymist, if such a chimera may exist, attempts to co-ordinate the qualities of all four ..."

I hope that *Oklahoma Place Names* is a pleasant and satisfactory mixture of each, and that this volume will be received with equal enthusiasm by those seeking a dictionary and those wanting a gazetteer.

If I am to be accused of more interest in one of the disciplines than in any other, I would perhaps concur that there is greater need in Oklahoma for a volume with emphasis on the origin of the name and the location of the site (and by location I mean both where and when) than in etymology or linguistics. As said before, I feel the entire panorama of Oklahoma history is reflected in its place names.

Long-forgotten plans for a future city, for a railroad center, or for a mercantile enterprise emerge for us today from the limbo of those long-ago ambitions and dreams only through the survival of a place name.

As with other human endeavors in which the form survives long after the substance is lost, so the name alone often remains, perhaps as the name of a cemetery, of a crossroads corner, or of a church or school, with no visible evidence that in the name lies the ghost of the ambitions of the person who first selected that particular appellation for the name of his dream.

History, indeed, has been most unkind to the place names of Oklahoma. The span of merely threescore years has been adequate to remove every living person who may have known the storekeeper whose general store, then far from anywhere, housed a post office for the convenience of the surrounding settlers. Many communities which began as a crossroads store grew and flourished, while others, like the surrounding wild flowers, died and soon vanished forever.

Although of hardy stock, those settlers were not keepers of enduring records. Unless by chance they were landowners whose names were preserved in the land records of some government office, or unless, luckily, some contemporaneous person had enough interest to record the facts, little is left for us to use today in identifying them and their selection of the names they bestowed. Actually, this condition is not improbable, for, after all, there are many among us today who might have difficulty in saying exactly why their parents selected their own given name or "for whom they were named."

I have been told that the first edition of this book placed too much emphasis upon the activities of the Post Office Department and that little real purpose was served by including the dates the post office in question was in operation. While I appreciate the criticism, I have noted that it arises invariably from someone not a resident of Oklahoma and perhaps not familiar with the great importance the activities of the Post Office Department had in the toponymy of the Sooner State.

Considering the recent settlement of Oklahoma, the total number of post offices established in the area constituting the present state is remarkable. The reason for this abundance, particularly in the western half of Oklahoma, is obvious. The land was settled by a rush that overnight transformed empty prairies into future farmsteads, with at least four families to every square mile. Transportation was slow and difficult, and mail service was as important to newly-arrived settlers as it is to soldiers overseas today. The post offices dotting the western prairies every six or eight miles seemed the best way to provide a means of communication for everyone.

Of course, the Post Office Department had no way of knowing where future towns or cities would be located, nor could it tell which of the townsites so hastily laid out would survive. Accordingly, nearly every application for a post office was granted. Moreover, along with the homesteaders came the usual sprinkling of merchants and storekeepers. Each proprietor, in order to ensure the success of his mercantile operation, sought to include a post office as a supplement to his proffered services.

Names for post offices were often selected locally, frequently taking the form of the last name of the postmaster or proprietor of the general store, the first name of a relative, or a name having some relation to a home town in another state. Requested names were sometimes rejected by the Post Office Department, which seems often to have substituted other names arbitrarily.

On this point, the late Charles N. Gould, in his delightful little book, *Oklahoma Place Names*, records a letter he received in 1932 from Joseph B. Thoburn, then curator of the Oklahoma Historical Society: "In '98–'99, while I was in Washington City, I became acquainted with Captain Tuley, then and as late as 1913, connected with the Postoffice Department. He had charge of the establishment of the new postoffices throughout the United States and for three decades, beginning with the early 8o's, all applications for new post-offices passed across his desk. He told me that, not infrequently, residents of newly-developing communities made applications for the establishment of a postoffice without specifying a name. In such events he was wont to make a selection, sometimes honoring a fellow-clerk in the office, and that he had named postoffices for practically all of the kids and babies in his immediate neighborhood in Washington."

While it is true that many post office names were designated in Washington, I am not convinced that this is the reason for such a plenitude of girls' names. It appears to me that such names were selected more often by the townsite developers or by the post office applicants to honor members of their families. May, in Harper County, and Romia, in Bryan County, are cases in point. It is a pity that in most instances there is now no way of finding out who these girls were: persons who might have known are dead, and no records remain. Regrettably, therefore, many towns are destined to live with only the given name of an otherwise anonymous girl, about whose identity we may only speculate.

Although my attention to the activities of the Post Office Department is readily confessed, this book is not a list of the post offices of Oklahoma, and readers are cautioned not to use it as such. Further, dates given for the establishment and the closing of a post office may not be continuous. Quite often, for a variety of reasons, a period of time would elapse when the post office was out of commission and not in operation. These periods of hiatus have been disregarded.

Of even more significance, when the existence of a post office was of short duration or if its listing would contribute nothing to the basic purposes of this volume it was eliminated. Accordingly, it is quite possible to find a reference to a post office of either Oklahoma Territory or Indian Territory that is not included here, although *all* post offices first established since Statehood are included. Conversely, the names of many localities, communities, and railroad stops which never had a post office have been included. Asp, in Noble County (which appears now in *American Place-Names* perhaps because the demise of Cleopatra brings the name within the third category of Dr. Stewart), is an example.

In considering the entries to appear in his *American Place-Names*, Dr. Stewart in his preface bases his selection of the entries to be included on three criteria: (1) widespread knowledge of the place, (2) repetition, or (3) unusualness. Although they are valid for a volume intended to cover the entire continental United States, I have rejected the use of such criteria for Oklahoma. Here my desire to serve the needs of history rather than any other objective has caused me to include most all of the names that have appeared at one time or another in Oklahoma as the designation of a place occupied by people, with less emphasis on other types of nomenclature, such as schools and public works, or natural features such as rivers and mountains.

Oklahoma is rich in interesting combinations of names, such as Romulus and Remus in Pottawatomie County, Long and Short in Sequoyah County, and Alpha and Omega in Kingfisher County. Family names may be found, such as Kenefic for William Kenefic and Clarita for his wife. In the same manner, names of fathers and sons may be found, such as Jones and his son Luther, or Asp and his son Alfred.

The story of the place names on the Santa Fe Railway from Purcell to Ardmore is worth recounting. The engineer in charge of construction was from Pennsylvania, and, in laying out the stations along the road north to Purcell, he adopted the names of places found along the Main Line of the Pennsylvania Railroad west from Philadelphia.

Two special problems, those of spelling and of location, remain.

Generally I have used the spelling of the post office name even if it is different from that of its source; and likewise I continue to use what I believe to be the "correct" spelling, even though highly accepted sources, such as highway maps, may differ. Kenefic, in Bryan County, and Hodgen, in Le Flore County, are examples. In like manner, no effort has been made to call special attention to what appear to be discrepancies, where the post office name is spelled differently from that of the source, such as Fitzlen and Tahona.

The problem of location remains partially unresolved. Townsites were often moved with the advent of a nearby railroad. To an even greater extent, country post offices were moved with the appointment of each new postmaster. For example, the McAlester of 1900 is not the McAlester of today, and the Pond Creek of the Cherokee Outlet is now the town of Jefferson in Grant County, with the modern Pond Creek some miles distant.

Serious consideration was given to including the land call or, as real estate people say, the "legal description" of various villages and post offices; but the realization that a village or post office might have been located in several different places, perhaps even across the line in another county or state, brought an abrupt end to this idea.

With respect to location, there is a mother lode of material in the National Archives awaiting study and compilation. For many years the cartographers of the Post Office Department required postmasters to furnish periodically a report known as "Site Location Report." These forms, which varied slightly in style and content through the years, required the local postmaster to submit accurate details on the precise location of the office, the mileage to surrounding post offices, the names of nearby creeks and other natural land features, along with other details pertaining to site. These reports have been preserved and are now in a separate file for each county in Oklahoma. Because these reports are not arranged in any particular order, and because they do not show the origin of the post office name—although they go back as far as 1885—they were not an aid to this project. They did serve to make me realize that the various country post offices through the years were most peripatetic.

The reader is especially cautioned regarding the designated county of location. In each instance it is the county and the county boundaries as they are presently constituted in Oklahoma that are used herein, even though the place name when in active use was located in a county of another name. For after all, it was the name of the county in which the site was located that was changed, not the location of the site. Since there have been two additional counties created in Oklahoma since Statehood, and since at the time of Statehood a number of additional counties were organized out of areas that comprised only one large Oklahoma Territory county, this distinction is of special significance. For example, Beaver County, Oklahoma

Territory, comprised all of the Oklahoma panhandle, now divided into three counties.

A few words should be said here about the organization of this book and its arrangement. Believing that it would best serve the user if arranged as a gazetteer, and as something to be consulted only, browsed and not read, I feel that one alphabetical listing is the most logical and renders the material most accessible. I have seen other volumes where the material is arranged topically or by some other classification. This of course requires an index; and to me it seems obvious that the arrangement itself should constitute the index.

Dr. Stewart has classified place names by the mechanism of origin as distinguished wholly from the motivation of the namer. Commemoration, for example, such as naming the place after one's home town in another state, is a motivation rather than an origin. He gives ten classifications of origin, and all may be found to apply in Oklahoma.

Keeping before me at all times the distinction between motivation and origin has been of great help in sorting out conflicting information on the origin of place names. Yet, uncertainties arising from conflicting sources will always exist. The origin of Wilburton, the county seat of Latimer County, is perhaps the best example. Gould, in an unpublished manuscript prepared for a second edition of his book, ascribes the name to Elisha Wilbur, president of the Lehigh Valley Railroad; whereas *Oklahoma: A Guide to the Sooner State*, the excellent work of Miss Angie Debo in its first edition, and of Kent Ruth and the staff of the University of Oklahoma Press in its second, ascribes the name to Will Burton, a contractor on the Choctaw, Oklahoma and Gulf Railroad. The problem is the same with Indian names. For example, I have been shown that Catoosa is a Cherokee word referring to "the People of the Light" Clan and also that it is a Cherokee word meaning "new settlement place."

It is with great difficulty that I have avoided the many temptations to include purported origins, which if used would undoubtedly glamorize the place and indeed add spice to the book. Without difficulty, many people can be found who insist that the origin of Enid is merely the word "dine" spelled backwards and had its origin in the word as it was painted above the eating establishment at the railroad depot. As late as 1973 a volume of Oklahoma history includes "another version" of the origin of the name for the Cimarron River, the time-worn story of the cowboy or the trapper whose evening meal was permitted to "simmer on" thus providing the name Cimarron.

I have attempted to give only the origin of the name that appears best sustained by research, even though such research runs counter to the locally accepted view. Henryetta is perhaps the best example, and I adhere without hesitation to the source here given. On the other hand, for the revised volume I have not hesitated to make a radical change from the first edition if such change appears merited. Golden, in McClain County, and Neola, in Caddo County, are examples.

Even though Enid and Cimarron are not here romanticized by the legends, other accounts apparently equally fanciful, such as "walk home us" as the origin of Waukomis in Garfield County (even though the same word appears as a place name in Missouri), are repeated when there seems to be a sound basis for their accuracy.

Errors will continue into this revised edition. The elimination of error is perhaps man's most difficult discipline, because such errors can be those of omission as well as those of commission. I consider those of omission the more venial of the two, and I am thus more eager to eliminate those of commission. Areas of dispute will always remain, and I am certain that some of my conclusions are still open to challenge. The heightened interest in Oklahoma place names spurred by the publication of the first edition has done much to help in the correction of my earlier mistakes; and I am most enthusiastic in the belief that this revised edition will serve a like purpose in that regard.

A word about bibliography. Place name bibliography is now so extensive that an entire volume, *Bibliography of Place-Name Literature*, was published in 1967. Among its many purposes that volume well illustrates the fascination and popular interest in the subject. Arranged by states, the Oklahoma entries in the bibliography are of value and could in one sense of the word serve as a bibliography for this present volume. By way of further example, the bibliography in *American Place-Names* is some seven pages in length. With the ease of accessibility of such extensive listings, an exhausting and comprehensive bibliography on the general subject is pointless here. Accordingly, I have limited my own bibliography to those volumes of especial concern only to Oklahoma.

My gratitude continues for those acknowledged in the first edition, for without their help, that effort would have been impossible. The services of Hugh Corwin, Angie Debo, and Rella Looney have continued, and I feel it essential to thank them again. All members of the staff of the Oklahoma Historical Society have helped me far beyond the call of duty. In addition to those staff members acknowledged previously, the services of Louise Cook, Alene Simpson, and Manon Atkins have been significant and are deeply appreciated.

I continue in deep debt to Muriel H. Wright, long-time editor of *The Chronicles of Oklahoma* and the author of the monumental *A Guide to the Indian Tribes of Oklahoma*. She has again reviewed all material comprising the revised edition for the Indian words and the accuracy of their meanings.

With the publication of the revised edition I pledge that research will continue, and I ask no one believe that now, with this new volume, all has been said and done on the subject. Although fewer in number, gaps yet remain that must be filled.

GEORGE H. SHIRK

Oklahoma City, Oklahoma

CONTENTS

OKLAHOMA PLACE NAMES

OKLAHOMA PLACE NAMES

A

A COUNTY. The original designation for Lincoln County, Oklahoma Territory.

AARON. In Jackson County, 5 miles northwest of Olustee. A post office from January 22, 1899, to January 14, 1905. No longer in existence, it was named for Calvin Aaron, an early-day settler.

ABBIE. In northwestern Woods County, 12 miles north of Freedom. A post office from February 25, 1903, to June 15, 1921. No longer in existence.

ABBOTT. In Pontotoc County near Ada. A post office from January 25, 1909, to February 15, 1910. No longer in existence, it was named for Jourdan A. Abbott, an early-day resident.

ABBOTT. In Pushmataha County, 11 miles north of Antlers. A post office from March 3, 1897, to July 11, 1899. No longer in existence.

ABE. In southwestern Beaver County, 4 miles southeast of Boyd. A post office from July 21, 1904, to November 15, 1907. No longer in existence.

ABNER. In northern Love County, 11 miles southwest of Ardmore. A post office from February 25, 1903, to March 30, 1907.

ACADEMY. In Bryan County, 2 miles northeast of Bokchito. The post office for Armstrong Academy, it was in operation from April 22, 1898, to March 15, 1920.

ACHILLE. In Bryan County, 12 miles south of Durant. Post office established June 30, 1910. The post office name was first Achilla, which was changed to the present designation on August 5, 1910. The name is a corruption of the Cherokee word *atsila*, meaning "fire," and arose from the circumstance that a group of Cherokees settled in the locality as refugees during the Civil War.

ACME. In southwestern Grady County, 3 miles west of Rush Springs. A post office from April 8, 1913, to May 29, 1931, it took its name from Acme Cement Plaster Company.

ACTON. In northern Logan County, 4 miles northeast of Crescent. A post office from November 2, 1895, to December 14, 1903. No longer in existence, it was named for Mary Acton, the first postmaster.

ADA. County seat of Pontotoc County. Record Town for Recording District No. 16, Indian Territory. Post office established July 10, 1891. Named for Ada Reed, daughter of the first postmaster, William J. Reed.

ADAIR. In northern Mayes County, 9 miles north of Pryor. Post office established March 15, 1883. Named for William Penn Adair, Cherokee leader, whose allotment was nearby.

ADAIR COUNTY. County in northeastern Oklahoma. Created at statehood from the eastern portion of Indian Territory Recording District No. 6, it was named for the Adair family, a well-known Cherokee family whose most prominent member was William Penn Adair.

ADAMS. In western Bryan County, 8 miles northwest of Colbert. A post office from August 2, 1901, to August 10, 1910. Site now inundated by Lake Texoma. Named for Nelson F. Adams, early resident.

ADAMS. In eastern Texas County, 10 miles southeast of Hooker. Post office established June 14, 1930. Named for Jesse L. Adams, location engineer for Rock Island Railroad.

ADAMSON. In Pittsburg County, 10 miles east of McAlester. Post office established March 1, 1906. Named for Peter Adamson, mineowner.

ADDIELEE. In northern Adair County, 9 miles north of Stilwell. A post office from August 24, 1914, to May 10, 1943. The name was coined from the given names of Add and Lee Cole, husband and wife, local merchants.

ADDINGTON. In western Jefferson County, 6 miles north of Waurika. Post office established January 8, 1896. Named for James P. Addington, first postmaster.

ADEL. In northwestern Pushmataha County, 12 miles west of Clayton. A post office from June 3, 1907, to November 15, 1954.

ADELAIDE. In Cotton County, 7 miles north of Randlett. A post office from June 23, 1909, to November 30, 1914. No longer in existence.

ADELIA. In Coal County, 7 miles north of Coalgate. A post office from February 18, 1902, to January 31, 1909. No longer in existence.

ADELL. In southern Pottawatomie County, 4 miles northwest of Asher. A post office from March 3, 1892, to August 31, 1905. No longer in existence, it was named for Adell T. Bowles, local Pottawatomie allottee. The community was often referred to as Jefferson.

AFTON. In southwestern Ottawa County. Post office established June 5, 1886. Named for Afton Aires, daughter of Anton Aires, railroad surveyor, who had named his daughter for the Afton River in his native Scotland.

AGATHA. In Latimer County near Wilburton. A post office from June 1, 1903, to July 30, 1904. No longer in existence.

AGAWAM. In Grady County, 12 miles south of Chickasha. A post office from June 18, 1909, to February 28, 1918. Its name, taken from an Indian village in New England, means "fish-curing place."

AGRA. In northern Lincoln County, 13 miles north of Chandler. Post office established December 20, 1902. Its name was coined by the townsite developer from the word agriculture.

AHLOSO. In Pontotoc County, 4 miles southeast of Ada. A post office from November 7, 1904, to June 30, 1917. Until November 7, 1904, the post office name was Ahlora. The name is a Chickasaw word meaning "burnt place."

AHNIWAKE. In Cherokee County, 4 miles west of Tahlequah. A post office from June 16, 1904, to February 28, 1911, named for Ahniwake Hastings, daughter of W. W. Hastings, prominent local resident. The railroad name for this post office was Hastings. On May 13, 1911, this post office was reestablished under the name Gabriel.

AHPEATONE. In western Cotton County, 12 miles west of Walters. A post office from July 22, 1907, to June 30, 1916. No longer in existence, it was named for Ahpeatone (Wooden Lance), great Kiowa chief.

AKINS. In Sequoyah County, 9 miles northeast of Sallisaw. A post office from February 16, 1894, to December 31, 1943. Named for Robert Akins, local mail carrier.

ALAMO. In Major County, 5 miles north of Fairview. A post office from March 13, 1894, to April 2, 1897. No longer in existence. Located on Cottonwood Creek, it takes its name from the Spanish word for cottonwood.

ALAMO. In northern Texas County, 17 miles due north of Guymon. A townsite organized in 1908. No longer in existence.

ALBANY. In southern Bryan County, 11 miles south of Bokchito. Post office established July 10, 1894. Its name comes from Albany, New York.

ALBERT. In Caddo County, 9 miles north of Fort Cobb. Post office established September 1, 1910. On April 14, 1906, a post office named Oney had been discontinued at this approximate location. Named for Albert Baker, townsite owner.

ALBIA. In eastern Craig County, 6 miles southwest of Afton. Post office established July 15, 1899. Name changed to Todd on January 9, 1909.

ALBION. In northern Pushmataha County, 13 miles east of Tuskahoma. Post office established December 6, 1887. Named by John T. Bailey, an Englishman, it bears the Roman name for England.

ALCORN. A switch and loading point on the Rock Island Railroad in Kay County 10 miles southwest of Tonkawa. Named for John Alcorn of Ponca City.

ALDEN. In western Caddo County, 9 miles south of Carnegie. A post office from December 5, 1901, to December 31, 1929. Named for Alden Carpenter, son of Jennie Carpenter, first postmaster.

ALDERSON. In Pittsburg County, 6 miles southeast of McAlester. Post office established March 5, 1890. Named for an employee of the Choctaw, Oklahoma and Gulf Railroad whose full name appears lost.

ALEDO. In southern Dewey County, 13 miles east of Leedey. A post office from May 5, 1899, to February 28, 1954. Its name comes from Aledo, Parker County, Texas.

ALERT. In western Kay County, 8 miles west of Blackwell. A post office from June 7, 1894, to June 29, 1904. No longer in existence. Its name comes from Alert, Riley County, Kansas.

ALEX. In eastern Grady County, 13 miles southeast of Chickasha. Post office established December 2, 1885. Named for William V. Alexander, first postmaster.

ALEXANDRA. In Ellis County, 10 miles northwest of Shattuck. A post office from May 10, 1902, to May 31, 1909. No longer in existence, it was named for Queen Alexandra of England, consort of Edward VII.

ALFALFA. Formerly Boise. In western Caddo County, 7 miles north of Carnegie. Name of post office changed to Alfalfa, December 16, 1908, and discontinued

August 31, 1962. Its name comes from chief local agricultural product.

ALFALFA. In Jackson County, 6 miles northeast of Altus. A post office from May 9, 1903, to February 28, 1905. No longer in existence.

ALFALFA COUNTY. County in northern Oklahoma. Created at statehood from a portion of Woods County, Oklahoma Territory. Named for William H. "Alfalfa Bill" Murray, president of the Oklahoma Constitutional Convention and later governor of Oklahoma.

ALFRED. Present Mulhall, in northern Logan County. Post office established May 18, 1899, and its name changed to Mulhall on June 6, 1890. Named for Alfred Asp, son of Henry E. Asp, Oklahoma City attorney.

ALGER. In Alfalfa County near Cherokee. A post office from June 18, 1898, to March 30, 1901. No longer in existence, it was named for Russell A. Alger, secretary of war under President McKinley.

ALGIERS. In southeastern Osage County near Skiatook. A post office from May 10, 1904, to December 31, 1904. No longer in existence. Its name comes from the city in North Africa.

ALHAMBRA. In northwestern Johnston County, 4 miles north of Mill Creek. A post office from May 5, 1896, to May 31, 1904. No longer in existence. Its name comes from the fortress near Granada, Spain.

ALIGAN. In Muskogee County, 5 miles east of Keefeton. A post office from February 18, 1902, to May 14, 1904. No longer in existence.

ALIKCHI. In western McCurtain County, 6 miles northwest of Wright City. A post office from July 13, 1888, to November 30, 1931. The Choctaw word for "doctor," the name is related to the nearby sulphur springs.

ALINE. In southwestern Alfalfa County, 7 miles north of Cleo Springs. Post office established April 27, 1894. Named for Marie Aline Hartshorn, daughter of Ezra E. Hartshorn, prominent early-day settler.

ALLEN. In the northeastern corner of Pontotoc County, 19 miles northeast of Ada. Post office established April 9, 1892. Named for Allen McCall, son of a deputy United States marshal.

ALLEPPO. In Bryan County, 6 miles north of Durant. A post office from February 6, 1902, to September 30, 1903. No longer in existence. Took its name from the city in northwest Syria.

ALLISON. In southern Bryan County, 7 miles south of Durant. A post office from March 6, 1901, to December 15, 1921. Its name comes from a nearby rural school known as Mount Allison.

ALLMON. In southwestern Ellis County, 7 miles southwest of Ar-

nett. A post office from August 29, 1902, to February 14, 1906. No longer in existence.

ALLUWE. Formerly Lightning Creek. In Nowata County, 8 miles southeast of Nowata. Name of post office changed to Alluwe, June 27, 1883, and discontinued July 31, 1909. The name is a Delaware word meaning "superior" or "better quality."

ALMA. In eastern Stephens County, 20 miles east of Duncan. Post office established February 14, 1906. Named for Alma Peoples, early-day settler.

ALMEDA. In Major County, 7 miles southeast of Cleo Springs. Post office established February 4, 1895, and post office name changed to Bernardi, January 20, 1903.

ALOCAN. In Kiowa County, 9 miles northeast of Roosevelt. A post office from March 25, 1902, to July 14, 1903. No longer in existence.

ALPERS. In northern Carter County, 7 miles northeast of Ratliff City. A post office from July 15, 1918, to November 14, 1931. Named for Dr. H. W. Alpers, local resident.

ALPHA. In Kingfisher County, 10 miles west of Kingfisher. A post office from November 7, 1893, to December 14, 1903. Its name comes from the first letter of the Greek alphabet. A post office named Omega was situated 5 miles west.

ALSFORD. In southeastern Jackson County, 8 miles southeast of Altus. A post office from May 2,

1891, to October 26, 1891. No longer in existence.

ALSUMA. Formerly Welcome. In Tulsa County, 6 miles southeast of Tulsa. Name of post office changed to Alsuma, February 14, 1906, and discontinued June 15, 1926. Named for John Alsuma, local merchant.

ALTO. In extreme northeastern corner of Harper County. A post office from February 25, 1903, to January 31, 1909. No longer in existence.

ALTONA. In the extreme southwestern corner of Kingfisher County. A post office from October 5, 1892, to January 31, 1906. No longer in existence. Its name comes from Altona, a river port near Hamburg, Germany.

ALTUS. County seat of Jackson County. Post office established October 27, 1890. From July 10, 1901, to May 14, 1904, the post office name was Leger. Its name comes from the Latin word meaning "high." The original town, Frazier, was built along low ground, and when it was destroyed by high water, the residents moved the new location to higher land.

ALVA. County seat of Woods County. Post office established August 25, 1893. Named for Alva Adams, railroad attorney, who later was governor of the state of Colorado.

ALVARETTA. In southeastern Alfalfa County, 3 miles south of Goltry. A post office from March 22, 1894, to October 15, 1904.

Named for Alvaretta Wrigley, daughter of M. W. Wrigley, first postmaster.

AMABALA. In southern Okfuskee County, 5 miles northeast of Wetumka. A post office from December 13, 1900, to February 28, 1907. No longer in existence. The name is a coined word, Alabama spelled backwards.

AMBER. In Grady County, 8 miles northeast of Chickasha. Post office established November 5, 1903. Took its name from the amber color of the surrounding countryside.

AMBRIC. A stop and switch on the Rock Island Railroad, 3 miles west of Oklahoma City, but now in the city limits. Took its name from the American Brick Company.

AMERICA. In southeastern McCurtain County, 7 miles southeast of Haworth. A post office from July 24, 1903, to February 15, 1944. Named for Mrs. America Stewart, wife of Tom Stewart, local resident.

AMES. Formerly Hoyle. In southeastern Major County. Post office name changed to Ames, January 4, 1902. Named for Henry S. Ames of St. Louis, secretary-treasurer of the Denver, Enid and Gulf Railroad.

AMORITA. In northern Alfalfa County, 12 miles northeast of Cherokee. Post office established January 8, 1902. Named for Amorita Ingersoll, wife of the president of the Choctaw, Oklahoma & Gulf Railway.

AMOS. In southern Marshall County, 10 miles south of Kingston. A post office from May 31, 1901, to September 14, 1907. No longer in existence, it was named for Amos Goodling, prominent Choctaw.

AMY. In eastern Hughes County, 6 miles north of Stuart. A post office from June 20, 1902, to June 29, 1907. No longer in existence.

ANADARKO. County seat of Caddo County. Post office established April 22, 1873. The name is a corruption of the Caddo word *Na-da-ko*, the name of one of the Caddoan tribes.

ANDERSON. In Pottawatomie County, 3 miles southeast of Macomb. A post office from April 27, 1892, to January 31, 1905. No longer in existence, it was named for Thomas Anderson, first postmaster.

ANGA. In Greer County, 12 miles west of Mangum. A post office from June 7, 1905, to August 31, 1906. No longer in existence.

ANGORA. In Roger Mills County, 6 miles west of Leedey. A post office from February 10, 1902, to April 30, 1914. No longer in existence. Named by Effie Wagner, first postmaster, for a herd of Angora goats owned by Jim Burch, local resident.

ANITA. In Ellis County near Arnett. A post office from May 9, 1905, to February 14, 1906. No longer in existence. Named for Anita Neher, daughter of J. E. Neher, first postmaster.

ANNA. In northern Logan County, 5 miles northwest of Coyle. Post office established January 24, 1900, and its name changed to Pleasant Valley, February 29, 1904. Named for Anna Campbell, daughter of G. W. Campbell, local early-day resident. Another post office named Anna was in operation at a nearby location from March 8, 1905, to February 28, 1907.

ANNETTE. In western Coal County, 5 miles southwest of Tupelo. A post office from April 26, 1882, to October 31, 1899. No longer in existence.

ANTELOPE. In Logan County, 6 miles northeast of Guthrie. A post office from March 13, 1891, to December 2, 1891. Took its name from nearby Antelope Creek.

ANTELOPE. In northwestern Roger Mills County, 14 miles northwest of Roll. A post office from November 20, 1893, to March 31, 1908. No longer in existence. From 1895 to 1899, the post office operated as Grangerville, Texas. Took its name from nearby Antelope Hills.

ANTHON. In northern Custer County, 12 miles northwest of Custer City. A post office from May 15, 1903, to May 31, 1922. No longer in existence. Named for Anthon Hoelker, long-time local resident.

ANTIOCH. In Garvin County, 10 miles west of Pauls Valley. A post office from September 6, 1895, to

May 14, 1932. Its name comes from the city in Middle East.

ANTLERS. County seat of Pushmataha County. Record Town for Recording District No. 24, Indian Territory. Post office established August 26, 1887. Probably took its name from the antlers of a deer nailed up at a nearby spring, indicating a camping place.

ANTRIM. In Noble County, 11 miles southwest of Perry. A post office from May 3, 1898, to October 15, 1904. No longer in existence. Its name comes from county Antrim, Ulster, Ireland.

ANVIL. In southern Lincoln County, 6 miles northeast of Meeker. A post office from April 9, 1892, to March 15, 1904. No longer in existence, it took its name from a nearby anvil-shaped rock, a landmark well known yet today.

APACHE. In southern Caddo County. Post office established September 3, 1901. The word Apache is probably from *apachu,* the Zuñi word for "enemy."

APPALACHIA. In southeastern Pawnee County, adjoining Keystone. A post office from January 18, 1905, to January 1, 1906. Once the subject of widespread real estate promotion, the town has entirely disappeared. The name was coined for association with the Appalachian Mountains.

APPERSON. In western Osage County, 4 miles northwest of Burbank. A townsite established in August, 1920. It was named for the Apperson automobile.

APPLE. In Choctaw County, 5 miles west of Spencerville. A post office from July 11, 1919, to January 31, 1924.

APPLETON. In eastern Texas County, 8 miles northeast of Hardesty. A post office from July 9, 1906, to September 30, 1907. No longer in existence. Its name comes from Appleton, Wisconsin.

APUKSHUNNUBBEE. One of the three districts of the Choctaw Nation. Presided over by a district chief. Named for a prominent Choctaw tribal chief.

AQUILLA. In northern Dewey County, 6 miles south of Mutual. A post office from September 13, 1901, to March 15, 1902. No longer in existence. Its name comes from the constellation "Eagle."

ARA. In Stephens County, 3 miles north of Velma. Post office established March 24, 1894, and name changed to Claud, January 1, 1927. Named for Ara Lawrence, early-day resident.

ARAPAHO. County seat of Custer County; also county seat of predecessor county in Oklahoma Territory. Post office established March 23, 1892. Its name, taken from the Arapaho tribe of Indians, means "blue-sky men" or "cloud men."

ARBEKA. In extreme northeastern corner of Seminole County. A post office from September 10, 1883, to December 14, 1907. Taken from

Abi'hka, an ancient Creek town on the upper Coosa River in Georgia, the word means "peace town" or "a place where justice was received."

ARBOR. In western Greer County, 5 miles north of Jester. Post office from December 23, 1902, to April 2, 1906. No longer in existence.

ARBUCKLE. In southern Garvin County, 9 miles west of Davis. A post office from August 20, 1884, to January 15, 1906. Took its name from old Fort Arbuckle, on which site it was located.

ARBUCKLE. Formerly Crusher. In southeastern Murray County, 4 miles south of Dougherty. Name changed to Arbuckle, August 21, 1911, and post office name changed to Big Canyon, March 2, 1922. Took its name from surrounding Arbuckle Mountains.

ARBUCKLE MOUNTAINS. Mountain range in south-central Oklahoma caused by an igneous intrusion exposing pre-Cambrian formations. Named for Brigadier General Matthew Arbuckle.

ARCADIA. In northeastern Oklahoma County adjoining Oklahoma City. Post office established August 2, 1890. The word means ideal rustic contentment.

ARCH. In eastern Pittsburg County, 6 miles southwest of Hartshorne. A post office from December 15, 1909, to January 15, 1929. Took its name from a nearby arch-shaped land feature.

ARCHER. In Mayes County, 5 miles southeast of Pryor. A post office from September 18, 1912, to June 30, 1916. No longer in existence, it was named for Edwin Archer, son-in-law of Joseph Vann.

ARCHIBALD. In Pittsburg County, 5 miles northwest of McAlester. A post office from May 10, 1901, to February 28, 1910. No longer in existence, it was named for Thomas Archibald, first postmaster.

ARCO. In Woods County, 8 miles southeast of Waynoka. A post office from June 27, 1901, to August 14, 1905. No longer in existence.

ARDMORE. County seat of Carter County. Record Town for Recording District No. 21, Indian Territory. Post office established October 27, 1887. Its name comes from Ardmore, Pennsylvania, a town along the Main Line of the Pennsylvania Railroad.

ARK. In Love County, 5 miles northeast of Marietta. A post office from December 12, 1895, to November 22, 1912. No longer in existence.

ARKANSAS RIVER. A principal river of Oklahoma. All of the state, except the southern portion drained by the Red River, is within its drainage system. A major avenue of early commerce. The word is from the early French reference to the Quapaw, *Akansea,* taken from the Siouan *Ak-a-ko-ze,* which may be rendered as "South Wind People."

ARKOMA. In northeastern Le Flore County, 1 mile southwest of

Fort Smith. Post office established April 8, 1914. The name was coined from Arkansas and Oklahoma.

ARLINGTON. In Lincoln County, 6 miles north of Prague. A post office from June 23, 1892, to July 31, 1906. Its name comes from Arlington, Virginia.

ARMSTRONG. In Bryan County, 2 miles northeast of Bokchito. A post office from April 26, 1882, to October 30, 1883. On April 22, 1898, a post office named Academy was established at the same location. The post office was situated at Armstrong Academy.

ARMSTRONG. In Bryan County, 5 miles north of Durant. A post office from February 15, 1896, to March 31, 1920. Named for Frank C. Armstrong, a member of the Dawes Commission.

ARMSTRONG ACADEMY. In Bryan County, 2 miles northeast of Bokchito. The academy was founded in 1844 by the Baptist Mission Society. Named for Captain William Armstrong, Choctaw agent. Known as *Chata Tamaha*, it was for 20 years the capital of the Choctaw Nation. A post office of this name was in existence here from November 19, 1850, to August 27, 1869, and subsequent post offices named Armstrong and Academy, respectively, were in operation at this site. The academy buildings were destroyed by fire in 1919.

ARNETT. County seat of Ellis County since August 26, 1908. Post office established June 20, 1902.

Named for A. S. Arnett, a minister of Fayetteville, West Virginia, by William G. Brown, first postmaster.

ARNETT. A rural community in Harmon County, 5 miles northwest of Hollis.

ARNETTVILLE. In Noble County, 3 miles north of Perry. See Liberty.

ARNO. In southwestern Creek County near Stroud. A post office from October 11, 1913, to April 15, 1916. No longer in existence, it was named for Arno R. Nauman, first postmaster.

ARNOLD. In Hughes County, 5 miles south of Holdenville. A post office from August 22, 1908, to November 15, 1909. No longer in existence.

ARNOLD. In northwestern Noble County, 4 miles southeast of Billings. Post office established November 27, 1893, and named for John D. Arnold, first postmaster. Name changed to Whiterock, December 14, 1894.

ARNOLDVILLE. In Love County, 4 miles west of Marietta. A post office from February 12, 1885, to April 2, 1889. No longer in existence, it was named for Samuel and Kenneth Arnold, brothers, early-day residents.

ARONDALE. In Osage County near Hominy. A post office from September 15, 1921, to July 15, 1935. No longer in existence. An oil field boom town, it was named for Aaron Steele, oil field superintendent.

ARPELAR. In Pittsburg County, 12 miles west of McAlester. A post office from February 25, 1903, to June 30, 1934. Named for Aaron Arpelar, county judge of Tobucksy County, Choctaw Nation.

ARRILLA. In southeastern Texas County, 7 miles southeast of Hardesty. A post office from July 8, 1907, to March 15, 1908. No longer in existence, it was named for Arrilla Silsbee, a relative of the first postmaster.

ARTESIAN. In Okfuskee County near Pharoah. A post office from March 25, 1914, to June 15, 1915. No longer in existence.

ARTHUR. In Stephens County, 15 miles east of Duncan. A post office from May 14, 1890, to September 29, 1934.

ASHER. Formerly Avoca. Located in southern Pottawatomie County. Post office name changed to Asher, November 26, 1901. Named for G. M. Asher, townsite developer.

ASHLAND. In southwestern Pittsburg County, 11 miles northwest of Kiowa. Post office established October 1, 1902. The name was selected by the Post Office Department in preference to Pearl City, the name requested by the local residents.

ASHLEY. Formerly Short Springs. In western Alfalfa County, 9 miles east of Alva. Post office name changed to Ashley, September 24, 1897, and discontinued April 4, 1898. Named for Frank Ashley, pioneer local resident.

ASP. In Noble County, 7 miles southwest of Perry. Townsite established about 1902. Named for Henry E. Asp, prominent Oklahoma City attorney.

ASPHALTUM. In Jefferson County, 7 miles northwest of Ringling. A post office from April 26, 1905, to October 15, 1931. The word is a variant for asphalt, a commodity produced nearby.

ATHENS. In Greer County, 11 miles west of Mangum. A post office from May 17, 1905, to August 31, 1906. No longer in existence. Its name comes from Athens, Ohio.

ATLAS. In Choctaw County, 11 miles northwest of Hugo. A post office from December 12, 1902, to April 30, 1909. No longer in existence.

ATLEE. In Jefferson County, 6 miles south of Ringling. A post office from July 10, 1891, to December 31, 1929. The community was originally known as Butcher Knife because an early-day settler, Frank Tucker, always carried a large knife in his belt.

ATOKA. County seat of Atoka County. Record Town for Recording District No. 23, Indian Territory. Post office established January 23, 1868. It was named for Captain Atoka, for whom the county was later named.

ATOKA COUNTY. A county in southeast-central Oklahoma. Created at statehood and, in general, comprises Indian Territory Recording District No. 23. Named for

13

Captain Atoka, a Choctaw ball-player. The name is from the Choctaw word *hitoka* or *hetoka*, meaning "ball ground."

ATWOOD. Formerly Newburg. In Hughes County, 5 miles west of Calvin. Post office name changed to Atwood, December 3, 1909. Named for C. C. Atwood, townsite owner.

AUBURN. In Alfalfa County, 7 miles southwest of Cherokee. A post office from August 7, 1894, to August 31, 1903. No longer in existence. Its name comes from Auburn, Logan County, Kentucky.

AUGUSTA. In Alfalfa County, 1 mile west of Carmen. A post office from July 13, 1895, to December 15, 1912.

AURORA. In southwestern Pottawatomie County, 2 miles west of Trousdale. A post office from June 23, 1898, to August 14, 1905. No longer in existence. Its name comes from Aurora, Illinois.

AUSTIN. In eastern Hughes County near Stuart. A post office from August 7, 1911, to August 15, 1913. No longer in existence.

AUSTIN. In Washington County, 5 miles northeast of Ramona. A post office from March 23, 1895, to October 31, 1900. No longer in existence, it was named for Austin Tyner, son of George W. Tyner, first postmaster.

AUTRY. Present Morrison, in southeastern Noble County. Post office established October 14, 1893,

and name changed to Morrison, February 27, 1894.

AUTWINE. Formerly Pierceton. In central Kay County, 4 miles northeast of Tonkawa. The townsite name was Virginia. Post office name changed to Autwine, March 5, 1903, and discontinued June 30, 1922.

AUXIER. In the northeastern corner of Washita County, 6 miles south of Weatherford. A post office from October 16, 1896, to March 31, 1904. No longer in existence, it was named for Samuel W. Auxier, first postmaster.

AVANT. In eastern Osage County, 7 miles southeast of Barnsdall. Post office established August 28, 1906. Named for Ben Avant, prominent Osage Indian.

AVARD. In Woods County, 10 miles southwest of Alva. A post office from June 1, 1895, to November 22, 1963. Named for Isabell Avard Todd, the wife of Frank Todd, first postmaster.

AVERY. In northeastern Lincoln County, 7 miles south of Cushing. The townsite name is Mound City. A post office from September 16, 1902, to July 26, 1957. Named for Avery Turner, an official of the Santa Fe Railroad.

AVIS. In western Harper County near Laverne. A post office from May 3, 1898, to October 31, 1899. No longer in existence.

AVOCA. Present Asher, in Pottawatomie County. Post office established August 4, 1894, and name changed to Asher, November 26, 1901. Another post office named Avoca, situated 2 miles north of Asher was in operation from February 10, 1902, to October 31, 1906. Probably inspired by Thomas Moore's poem "Sweet Vale of Avoca," its name comes from a river in Ireland.

AVONDALE. Present Kendrick, in Lincoln County. Post office established October 13, 1902, and name changed to Kendrick, January 21, 1903. Took its name from Avondale, County Lanark, Scotland.

AYDELOTTE. In Pottawatomie County, 6 miles north of Shawnee. Named for J. M. Aydelotte, railroad employee. The name for the townsite, developed in 1903, was Hansmeyer.

AYLESWORTH. In Marshall County, 6 miles east of Kingston. A post office from June 6, 1903, to October 15, 1943. Named for Allison Aylesworth, Dawes Commission official.

B

B COUNTY. The original designation for Pottawatomie County, Oklahoma Territory.

BABBS SWITCH. In Kiowa County, 6 miles south of Hobart. Scene of tragic schoolhouse fire in which 36 people lost their lives, December 24, 1924. Named for Edith "Babbs" Babcock, who delivered the

first load of wheat to the elevator at the switch.

BACHE. In Pittsburg County, 7 miles east of McAlester. Post office established February 26, 1903. Named for Franklin Bache, mining operator.

BACONE. In Muskogee County, immediately northeast of Muskogee. Post office established March 7, 1888. Named for Almon C. Bacone, Baptist missionary.

BADO. In Major County, 14 miles southwest of Fairview. A post office from February 19, 1901, to February 14, 1905.

BAILEY. In southeastern Grady County, 12 miles northeast of Marlow. A post office from June 25, 1892, to September 30, 1932. Named for J. J. Bailey, wagon master on stage line to Fort Sill.

BAIN. In eastern Kay County, 7 miles northeast of Ponca City. A post office from May 16, 1899, to April 30, 1902. No longer in existence. Named for Daniel Bain, townsite owner.

BAIRD. In eastern Cotton County, 12 miles west of Duncan. A post office from December 5, 1901, to June 30, 1932. Named by John W. Scoggins, first postmaster, for his wife's family name.

BAIRD. In Le Flore County near Heavener. A post office from January 28, 1892, to August 25, 1898. Named for Wilson D. Baird, first postmaster.

BAKER. In Lincoln County, 6 miles northwest of Stroud. A post office from May 10, 1892, to April 30, 1904. No longer in existence, it was named for Timothy Baker, local early-day resident.

BAKER. Formerly Bakersburg. In northeastern Texas County, 10 miles east of Hooker. In honor of Reuben F. Baker of Hooker, Oklahoma, the name of the post office was changed to Baker, August 15, 1953.

BAKERSBURG. In northeast Texas County, 10 miles east of Hooker. Post office established June 5, 1931, and name changed to Baker, August 15, 1953. Named for Reuben F. Baker of Hooker, Oklahoma.

BAKER STATION. In Kingfisher County, 4 miles south of Hennessey. An important station on the Chisholm Trail. Laid out as a townsite, named Baker City, in 1890. No longer in existence.

BAKKE. In Cimarron County, 6 miles northwest of Keyes. Post office established November 16, 1907, and name changed to Esbon, March 29, 1909. Named for Nels H. Bakke, early-day resident.

BALDHILL. In northeastern Okmulgee County, 7 miles north of Morris. A post office from August 29, 1896, to October 15, 1908. Took its name from prominent nearby land feature.

BALDWIN. Present Ryan, in Jefferson County. Post office established June 7, 1881, and named for Truman Baldwin, first postmaster. The post office was named Sugg from March 14, 1888, to January 23, 1890. On June 7, 1892, the post office name of Baldwin was changed to Ryan.

BALKO. In southern Beaver County, 15 miles southwest of Beaver. Post office established March 14, 1904. Generally believed to be named for Bob Coe, early-day settler.

BALL. In northeastern corner of Canadian County, 5 miles south of Cashion. Post office from April 17, 1891, to December 14, 1903. No longer in existence, it was named for Wilson H. Ball, first postmaster.

BALLAIRE. In Harper County, 7 miles west of Buffalo. Post office established June 27, 1903, and name changed to Doby Springs, January 13, 1908.

BALLARD. In northeastern Adair County, 7 miles north of Westville. A post office from May 13, 1896, to July 15, 1916. Took its name from nearby Ballard Creek, which had been named for a slave, Ballard.

BALMAT. In Ellis County, 5 miles northeast of Arnett. Post office from February 15, 1903, to September 30, 1905. No longer in existence.

BANNER. Formerly Cereal. In Canadian County, 5 miles west of Yukon. Name of post office changed to Banner, November 4, 1911, and discontinued March 31, 1954. Took its name from nearby Banner School.

BANNER. Present post office of Elmore City, in Garvin County. The original post office name Elmore was changed to Banner, September 7, 1910; its name, in turn, was changed to Elmore City, March 4, 1911.

BANTY. In northeastern Bryan County, 5 miles north of Bennington. A post office from July 31, 1901, to July 5, 1949.

BANZET. In northern Craig County, 8 miles northwest of Welch. A post office from June 28, 1922, to September 30, 1937. Named for Sam E. Banzet, early-day settler.

BAPTIST. In eastern Adair County, 3 miles north of Westville. A post office from March 9, 1881, to November 15, 1912. Took its name from Baptist Mission, an earlier post office at approximately the same site.

BAPTIST MISSION. In eastern Adair County, 3 miles north of Westville. Established in 1839, it was a post office from July 5, 1850, to June 22, 1866. Site of the publication of *Cherokee Messenger*, 1844, the first periodical published in Oklahoma. In 1881 the post office was re-established under the name Baptist.

BARBER. In eastern Cherokee County, 14 miles southwest of Stilwell. A post office from September 16, 1909, to February 15, 1954.

BARDEN. In northern Texas County, 18 miles northwest of Hooker. A post office from June 25, 1906, to September 30, 1912. No longer in existence.

BARKIS. In Greer County, 3 miles southwest of Jester. A post office from June 7, 1904, to February 29, 1908. It was named for a fictional character of Charles Dickens.

BARNARD. In Hughes County, 10 miles northeast of Holdenville. A post office from May 17, 1902, to December 31, 1912. Named for Timothy Barnard, early-day Creek leader.

BARNES. In southwestern Major County, 5 miles northeast of Seiling. A post office from December 9, 1897, to December 15, 1908. Named for Cassius M. Barnes, fourth governor of Oklahoma Territory.

BARNEY. In Major County, 13 miles southwest of Orienta. A post office from June 12, 1902, to April 15, 1925. No longer in existence. Took its name from nearby Barney Creek.

BARNITZ CREEK. Located in Custer County. Named for Captain Albert Barnitz, Seventh Cavalry, a participant in the Battle of the Washita, November 27, 1868.

BARNOSKIE. In Sequoyah County near Vian. A post office from November 15, 1923, to February 28, 1925.

BARNSDALE. In Osage County near Barnsdall. A post office from January 6, 1911, to January 30,

1915. The name is a variant of Barnsdall Oil Company.

BARNSDALL. Formerly Bigheart. In eastern Osage County. Post office name changed to Barnsdall, November 22, 1921. Took its name from Barnsdall Oil Company.

BARON. In eastern Adair County, 5 miles south of Westville. A post office from November 16, 1895, to December 31, 1942. Local name for this community was Barren Fork, from the Barren Fork of the Illinois River, a tributary of the Arkansas River.

BARR. In southwestern Garfield County, 5 miles south of Drummond. A post office from September 1, 1899, to November 15, 1906. Named for Fred Barr, first postmaster.

BARTA. In southeastern corner of Lincoln County. A post office from November 7, 1901, to August 30, 1903. No longer in existence, it was named for Frank Barta, early-day resident.

BARTLESVILLE. County seat of Washington County. Post office established May 6, 1879. Named for Jacob Bartles who established a trading post nearby in 1879.

BARTLETT. Present Dighton, in Okmulgee County. Named for David A. Bartlett, Tulsa oil producer.

BARTLETT. In western Osage County near Fairfax. A post office from December 2, 1908, to June 30, 1910. No longer in existence.

Named for Don Carlos Bartlett, early-day resident.

BARTLEY. In Garvin County, 5 miles east of Pauls Valley. A post office from September 26, 1902, to June 15, 1903. No longer in existence.

BARTON. A rural community in Kiowa County, 5 miles east of Lugert. Named for J. S. Barton, local resident.

BARTON. The original name for Sentinel, Washita County. Townsite plat filed September 23, 1901. Name never in popular usage.

BARWICK. In Bryan County, 5 miles southeast of Durant. A post office from May 23, 1904, to September 30, 1911. No longer in existence.

BASIN. In southern Pawnee County, 2 miles northeast of Mannford. A post office from May 5, 1899, to June 30, 1906. Its name comes from the natural basin in which it is located.

BATCHELDER. In southeastern Kay County, 6 miles east of Ponca City. A post office from February 4, 1895, to October 31, 1903. No longer in existence. Named for Greenleaf W. Batchelder, townsite owner.

BATTIEST. Formerly Ida. In western McCurtain County, 6 miles northwest of Bethel. Post office name changed to Battiest, November 1, 1928. Named for Byington Battiest, Choctaw jurist.

18

BAUM. Formerly Boland. In Carter County, 3 miles east of Gene Autry. Post office name changed to Baum, September 21, 1894, and discontinued March 15, 1918.

BAYOU MANARD. A branch of the Arkansas River. Mouth 3 miles south of Fort Gibson. The site of Civil War Battle, July 27, 1862, fought 6 miles east of Fort Gibson. Named for Pierre Menard, missionary.

BEACH. In northeastern McCurtain County, 5 miles east of Smithville. A post office from April 30, 1903, to August 14, 1909. On January 18, 1930, a post office named Beachton was established at approximately the same site. Took its name from nearby Beach Creek.

BEACHTON. In McCurtain County, 5 miles east of Smithville. A post office from January 18, 1919, to March 15, 1930. Took its name from Beach, a post office at approximately the same location, discontinued August 14, 1909.

BEALER. In Cotton County, 9 miles north of Temple. A post office from February 1, 1902, to September 30, 1905. No longer in existence. Named for Joel Bealer Patterson, first postmaster.

BEAR. In Hughes County, 3 miles east and across the Canadian River from Calvin. A post office from December 8, 1911, to May 31, 1924.

BEARDEN. In southwestern Okfuskee County. Post office established July 6, 1896. Named for J.

S. Bearden, prominent local resident.

BEARDIE. In Garfield County, just north of Covington. A post office from November 20, 1896, to April 25, 1898. No longer in existence, it was named for John W. Beardie, first postmaster.

BEAR'S GLEN. A small valley or ravine along the west bank of the Arkansas River, made famous by Washington Irving in *A Tour on the Prairies.* Site of Irving's camp the night of October 15, 1832. In southeastern Pawnee County, 2 miles northeast of Keystone, it has been inundated by the waters impounded by the Keystone Dam.

BEATRICE. In northwestern Beaver County, 14 miles east of Tyrone. A post office from August 12, 1904, to March 14, 1908. No longer in existence, its name comes from Beatrice, Nebraska.

BEAVER. County seat of Beaver County, as well as county seat of Beaver County, Oklahoma Territory. Post office established April 5, 1883. Took its name from the Beaver River on which the town is located.

BEAVER COUNTY. The eastern county of the Oklahoma Panhandle. Present county created at statehood from the eastern one third of Beaver County, Oklahoma Territory, which comprised the entire Oklahoma Panhandle. Took its name from the Beaver River.

BEAVERS BEND. A state park 6 miles north of Broken Bow. Named for John T. Beavers, a Choctaw intermarried citizen.

BEAVERSVILLE. In McClain County, 1 mile northwest of Byars, on the site of old Camp Arbuckle. When the post was abandoned by the military in 1851, the buildings were occupied by the Delaware Indians. Named for Black Beaver, well-known Indian scout.

BEBEE. In Pontotoc County, 7 miles northwest of Ada. A post office from September 15, 1896, to February 15, 1928. Named for Frank Bebee, official of the Post Office Department.

BECKHAM COUNTY. A county in southwestern Oklahoma. Created at statehood from portions of Greer and Roger Mills counties, Oklahoma Territory. Named for Governor J. C. Beckham of Kentucky.

BECKWITH. In southern Delaware County, 7 miles east of Kansas. A post office from May 24, 1895, to November 2, 1898. In 1889 a post office named Hilderbrand had been discontinued at this approximate location, and in 1900 a post office named Flint was established at the same site. Named for Richard Beck, first postmaster.

BEDFORD. In Pawnee County, 8 miles east of Pawnee. A post office from June 28, 1894, to October 15, 1904. No longer in existence. Named for John B. Bedford, first postmaster.

BEE. In Johnston County, 10 miles southeast of Tishomingo. A post office from April 5, 1889, to June 15, 1918. Named for Dee Taylor, daughter of local pioneer family, but the spelling changed by the Post Office Department.

BEEF CREEK. Present Maysville, in Garvin County. Post office established June 17, 1878, and its name changed to Maysville, September 19, 1902. Took its name from nearby Beef Creek, a tributary of the Washita River.

BEEMENT. In northwestern Dewey County, 6 miles southeast of Mutual. A post office from June 18, 1898, to October 31, 1911. No longer in existence.

BEGGS. In northwestern Okmulgee County, 10 miles northwest of Okmulgee. Post office established September 15, 1900. Named for C. H. Beggs of St. Louis, vice president of the Frisco Railroad.

BEIRUT. In Seminole County near Bowlegs. A post office from January 23, 1928, to April 15, 1935. No longer in existence, its name comes from Beirut, the capital of Lebanon.

BELAND. Formerly Chase. In Muskogee County, 8 miles southwest of Muskogee. Post office name changed to Beland, June 19, 1908, and discontinued October 30, 1926.

BELFORD. In Osage County, 5 miles southeast of Ralston. A post office from September 3, 1907, to March 31, 1915. No longer in existence, it was named for Irene Belford, first postmaster.

BELL. In Le Flore County, 12 miles south of Wister. A post office from April 13, 1891, to September 23, 1897. No longer in existence, it was named for George W. Bell, county judge of Jack's Fork County, Choctaw Nation.

BELLE. In extreme northwestern Custer County, 5 miles southeast of Leedey. A post office from March 4, 1902, to January 2, 1907. No longer in existence.

BELLE. In Seminole County near Wewoka. A post office from March 1, 1910, to December 31, 1913. No longer in existence.

BELLEMONT. In northeastern Pottawatomie County, 5 miles southwest of Prague. A post office from September 7, 1892, to July 14, 1905. The name was coined from the given name of Isabell Baker, wife of W. S. Baker, first postmaster, and "mount," referring to the elevated site.

BELLEVILLE. In northwestern Grant County, 15 miles northwest of Medford. A post office from June 26, 1895, to October 27, 1898. No longer in existence. Named by Charles F. Grier, first postmaster, for Belleville, Illinois, his wife's birthplace.

BELLVIEW. In Custer County, 6 miles east of Arapaho. A post office from June 12, 1900, to July 30, 1904. No longer in existence.

BELLVUE. In Creek County, 5 miles north of Bristow. A post office from February 25, 1913, to August 31, 1916. Took its name from Bellvue School, organized in 1909, and named by P. T. Fry, county superintendent, for the exceptional view.

BELMINA. In eastern Sequoyah County, 8 miles northwest of Fort Smith. A post office from April 11, 1918, to October 30, 1920. No longer in existence.

BELTON. In Johnston County, 8 miles northeast of Tishomingo. A post office from October 3, 1895, to January 30, 1915. No longer in existence.

BELTON. Formerly Pollock. In northwestern Lincoln County, 6 miles southeast of Langston. Post office name changed to Belton, November 20, 1893, and discontinued February 26, 1895. No longer in existence.

BELVA. In eastern Woodward County, 8 miles southwest of Waynoka. A post office from August 16, 1900, to March 31, 1960. Named for the daughter of a section foreman on the Santa Fe Railway.

BELZONI. In southern Pushmataha County, 10 miles southeast of Antlers. A post office from October 20, 1905, to October 31, 1954. Named for G. B. Belzoni, Italian explorer and archaeologist.

BENGAL. In eastern Latimer County, 7 miles south of Red Oak. Post office established January 24, 1890. Its name comes from a state in eastern India.

BENGE. In eastern Sequoyah

County, 5 miles northwest of Fort Smith. A post office from October 1, 1897, to February 15, 1913. No longer in existence, it was named for George W. Benge, Cherokee jurist.

BENNETT. In Muskogee County, 3 miles southwest of Warner. A post office from June 4, 1895, to July 30, 1904. No longer in existence, it was named for Leo E. Bennett, editor of the *Muskogee Phoenix*.

BENNINGTON. In eastern Bryan County, 21 miles east of Durant. Named by Dr. Thomas H. Stark, descendant of General John Stark, for the battle of Bennington, Vermont. Bennington had been named for Gov. Bennington Wentworth of New Hampshire. Post office established August 7, 1873.

BENOLA. Formerly Keota. In northwestern Cimarron County, 10 miles northeast of Kenton. Name changed to Benola, February 7, 1906, and discontinued May 31, 1908. No longer in existence.

BENTLEY. In southern Atoka County, 12 miles south of Atoka. A post office from June 1, 1903, to August 30, 1963. Named for Professor Alva Bentley, territorial educator.

BENTON. In Beaver County, 12 miles southeast of Beaver. A post office from September 13, 1886, to October 14, 1899. No longer in existence.

BENVILLE. In Canadian County, 9 miles southwest of El Reno. A post office from April 10, 1894, to December 29, 1896. No longer in existence, it was named for Benson Gilliland, first postmaster.

BERG. Original townsite name for Navina in Logan County. Townsite plat was filed May 28, 1900, and on August 29, 1903, the plat was refiled under the name Navina. Named for John Berg, townsite owner.

BERG. In eastern Seminole County, adjoining Wewoka. A post office from March 22, 1912, to March 31, 1915.

BERLIN. Formerly Doxey. In southern Roger Mills County, 10 miles north of Sayre. Post office name changed to Berlin, September 2, 1896, and discontinued May 5, 1967. Its name comes from Berlin, Germany.

BERNARDI. In Major County, 7 miles southeast of Cleo Springs. A post office from April 20, 1896, to September 30, 1901. On January 20, 1903, the name of the nearby post office of Almeda was changed to Bernardi, an office which was, in turn, discontinued August 15, 1910.

BERNICE. Formerly Needmore. In northwestern Delaware County, 6 miles south of Afton. Post office name changed to Bernice, February 12, 1913, and discontinued July 31, 1960. Named for Bernice Lundy, daughter of prominent local family.

BERRY. In northern Cleveland County, 6 miles east of Moore. A post office established June 22, 1892, and name changed to Morgan, April 24, 1901. Named for George G. Berry, early-day resident.

BERRYHILL. A community in Tulsa County, now within the city limits of Tulsa. Named for Tom Berryhill, local resident.

BERTRAND. In southern Cimarron County, 4 miles southeast of Felt. A post office from March 17, 1906, to October 31, 1918. No longer in existence, its name comes from Bertrand, Kansas.

BERTRAND. In eastern Major County, 5 miles north of Ames. A post office from August 15, 1894, to November 31, 1895. No longer in existence, its name comes from Bertrand, Kansas.

BERWYN. Formerly Dresden. In Carter County. Post office name changed to Berwyn, September 1, 1887, and name changed to Gene Autry, January 1, 1942. Its name comes from Berwyn, Pennsylvania.

BESSIE. Formerly Stout. In Washita County, 6 miles north of Cordell. Post office name changed to Bessie, May 22, 1903. Took its name from the "Bess Line," the popular name for the Blackwell, Enid and Southwestern Railroad.

BETHANY. In Ellis County, 5 miles southwest of May. A post office from August 6, 1903, to November 15, 1906. No longer in existence, its name comes from the community adjoining Jerusalem in the Holy Land.

BETHANY. In Oklahoma County, adjoining Oklahoma City on the west. Post office established March 11, 1913. Its name comes from the Biblical community adjoining the city of Jerusalem.

BETHEL. In central Grant County. A post office from March 12, 1895, to November 2, 1895. No longer in existence.

BETHEL. In northern McCurtain County. Post office established January 24, 1900. Its name comes from Bethel in Palestine. The word is Hebrew, meaning "house of God."

BETTINA. In southeastern Beckham County, 10 miles southeast of Delhi. A post office from May 16, 1899, to March 31, 1910. No longer in existence, it was named for Bettina Price, wife of William Price, early-day local resident.

BETTS. A switch stop on the Santa Fe Railway in Osage County, 7 miles west of Pawhuska. Named for C. E. Betts, general auditor of the Santa Fe.

BEULAH. Present Carter, in Beckham County, 10 miles southeast of Sayre. Townsite organized by a Pentecostal group in 1906 and named for the Land of Beulah, a land of rest, in Isaiah 62:4.

BEULAH. Formerly Sequoyah. In Rogers County, 6 miles northeast of Claremore. Post office name changed to Beulah, March 9, 1909, and discontinued June 30, 1913. Named for Beulah Taylor, daughter of the postmaster.

BICKFORD. In Blaine County, 7

miles north of Watonga. A post office from November 2, 1904, to November 30, 1927. Named for H. K. Bickford, early-day resident.

BIDDING SPRINGS. In western Adair County, 9 miles northwest of Stilwell. A post office from October 19, 1912, to June 15, 1928. Took its name from Bitting Springs, named for Dr. Nicholas Bitting, who settled at the location in 1876. The site is now known as Golda's Mill.

BIG CABIN. In southwestern Craig County. Post office established August 21, 1871. Took its name from nearby Big Cabin Creek, named for the large cabin on the Texas Road known as *Planche* Cabin, because it had been constructed of planking rather than the usual logs.

BIG CANYON. Formerly Arbuckle. In southeastern Murray County, 4 miles south of Dougherty. Post office name changed to Big Canyon, March 2, 1922, and discontinued May 31, 1961. Took its name from the large nearby canyon made by the Washita River.

BIGCEDAR. In Le Flore County, 15 miles south of Heavener. Post office established April 3, 1903, and discontinued October 15, 1943. On December 1, 1929, the official spelling of the post office name was changed to Big Cedar.

BIGHEART. Present post office of Barnsdall in Osage County. Post office established January 13, 1906, and name changed to Barnsdall, November 22, 1921. Named for James Bigheart, Osage chief.

BILBY. The railroad name for Wecharty. In Hughes County, 6 miles south of Holdenville, at the site of Fort Holmes. Named for Nicholas V. Bilby, prominent early-day resident.

BILLINGS. In northwestern Noble County. Post office established November 15, 1899. Given his wife's family name by Harry Thompson, Rock Island Railroad townsite agent.

BILLINGSLEA. In Creek County, 9 miles southeast of Depew. Post office established December 6, 1922, but on May 1, 1925, it was moved two miles north and name changed to Gypsy. Named for Frank Billingsley, local oil producer.

BINGER. In Caddo County, 20 miles northwest of Anadarko. Post office established November 5, 1901. Named for Binger Hermann, commissioner of the General Land Office, 1897–1903.

BINKLEY. A switch and loading point on the Frisco Railroad in Lincoln County 6 miles west of Stroud. Named for John W. Binkley, railroad engineer.

BISHOP. In Ellis County, 15 miles southwest of Arnett. A post office from June 30, 1909, to May 31, 1932.

BISMARK. Present Wright City, in McCurtain County. Post office established March 24, 1910, and named for the German chancellor. Name changed to Wright, September 13, 1918.

BISON. In Garfield County, 15 miles south of Enid. Post office established August 31, 1901. Took its name from nearby Buffalo Springs.

BIXBY. In Tulsa County, 15 miles southeast of Tulsa. Post office established July 6, 1899. Named for Tams Bixby, chairman of the Dawes Commission.

BLACK BEAR. A community in Noble County, 6 miles northeast of Perry. Post office named Drace was situated there from April 17, 1894, to October 14, 1905. Took its name from nearby Black Bear Creek.

BLACKBURN. In eastern Pawnee County, 12 miles east of Pawnee. A post office from December 15, 1893, to March 31, 1960. Named for Senator Joseph C. S. Blackburn of Kentucky.

BLACKBURN'S STATION. In southern Pittsburg County, 6 miles south of Blanco. A stage stop on the Butterfield Overland Mail route to California which crossed southeastern Oklahoma, 1858–61. Named for Casper B. Blackburn, local trader.

BLACKGUM. In northwestern Sequoyah County, 10 miles north of Vian. A post office from June 17, 1895, to February 15, 1955. Took its name from the large tree, a well-known member of the dogwood family.

BLACKLAND. In Osage County, 12 miles northwest of Pawhuska. Post office established January 20, 1911, and named for the black soil. On December 14, 1917, post office was moved 3 miles southeast and the name changed to Pearsonia.

BLACK MESA. In northwestern Cimarron County, adjoining Kenton. Caused by a large lava flow, it is the highest point in Oklahoma, elevation 4,978 feet.

BLACKROCK. In Pontotoc County, 11 miles northeast of Ada. Post office established June 27, 1901, and name changed to Steedman, January 19, 1910.

BLACKWELL. In central Kay County. Post office established December 1, 1893, and named for Andrew J. Blackwell, townsite developer. From April 2, 1894, to February 4, 1895, the post office was named Parker.

BLAINE. Formerly Panola. In northern Haskell County, 7 miles northeast of Keota. Post office name changed to Blaine, October 1, 1884, and discontinued September 15, 1919. Named for James G. Blaine, speaker of the House of Representatives and candidate for the Presidency.

BLAINE COUNTY. In west-central Oklahoma, and of the same extent as Blaine County, Oklahoma Territory. Named for James G. Blaine.

BLAIR. Formerly Dot. In Jackson County, 10 miles north of Altus. Post office name changed to Blair,

August 26, 1901. Named for John A. Blair, an official of the Kansas City, Mexico and Orient Railway.

BLAKE. In southwestern Greer County, 12 miles southwest of Mangum. Post office established February 13, 1901. On November 1, 1934, it was moved 2 miles southwest and the name changed to Russell.

BLANCHARD. In western McClain County. Post office established November 27, 1906. Named for W. G. Blanchard, townsite developer.

BLANCK. A rural community in Adair County, 2 miles southwest of Stilwell. Named for Frank A. Blanck of Stilwell.

BLANCO. In southern Pittsburg County, 10 miles northeast of Kiowa. Post office established August 31, 1901. Named for Ramón Blanco y Erenas, governor general of Cuba, 1897–98.

BLAND. In northwestern Creek County near Olive. A post office from April 25, 1910, to May 15, 1912. No longer in existence, it was named for Dr. John C. W. Bland, pioneer doctor of Tulsa.

BLISS. Present Marland, in northeastern Noble County. Post office established November 4, 1898, and name changed to Marland, April 8, 1922. Named for Cornelius N. Bliss, secretary of the interior.

BLOCKER. In northeastern Pittsburg County, 15 miles northeast of McAlester. Post office established April 26, 1905. Named for Eads Blocker, local coal dealer.

BLOOMER. In eastern Garfield County, 5 miles southeast of Garber. A post office from November 6, 1893, to October 31, 1901. No longer in existence, it was named for James F. Bloomer, first postmaster.

BLOOMFIELD. In Dewey County, 5 miles east of Camargo. A post office from July 20, 1899, to December 31, 1912. No longer in existence. Took its name from Bloomfield, Morrow County, Ohio.

BLOOMFIELD. Girls seminary, established in 1853 by the Chickasaw Nation and operated by the Methodist Board of Missions. First site in southern Bryan County near Achille. Moved in 1917 to Ardmore and reopened at that time as Carter Seminary. The name was suggested by the beauty of the prairie flowers blooming nearby.

BLOOMINGTON. In Greer County, 9 miles northwest of Mangum. Post office from June 1, 1892, to April 15, 1909. No longer in existence, its name comes from Bloomington, Illinois.

BLUE. In Bryan County, 9 miles east of Durant. Post office established July 1, 1874. Took its name from the nearby Blue River.

BLUEGRASS. In southeastern Beaver County near Slapout. A post office from September 13, 1886, to October 27, 1898. No longer in existence.

26

BLUEJACKET. In eastern Craig County. Post office established March 3, 1882. Named for Reverend Charles Bluejacket, first postmaster.

BLUFF. In Choctaw County, 6 miles south of Soper. A post office from April 23, 1901, to February 28, 1934. Took its name from a nearby bluff, adjoining the south side of Muddy Boggy River immediately north of its mouth.

BLUNT. In Sequoyah County, 5 miles north of Sallisaw. A post office from May 24, 1905, to October 31, 1914. No longer in existence, it was named for Major General J. G. Blunt.

BLY. In Nowata County, 3 miles northeast of Coody's Bluff. A post office from December 28, 1911, to May 15, 1923. Name "snatched out of the air" by Thomas M. Graham, first postmaster, as one short and easy to remember.

BOATMAN. In Mayes County, 8 miles southeast of Pryor. A post office from August 28, 1922, to December 30, 1965. Named for Joe P. Boatman, local merchant. In 1918 a post office named Chapel was discontinued at this approximate location.

BOB. In southern Love County, 6 miles south of Marietta. Post office established January 23, 1894, and name changed to Bomar, December 30, 1907.

BOGGY. Present post office of Bessie, in Washita County. Post office established May 16, 1895, and name changed to Stout, June 14, 1899. Took its name from nearby Boggy Creek.

BOGGY DEPOT. In Atoka County, 14 miles southwest of Atoka. Post office established November 5, 1849. On March 22, 1872, it was moved 1½ miles south and name changed to New Boggy Depot, which, in turn, on December 26, 1883, was changed to Boggy Depot. Post office discontinued July 31, 1944. Took its name from nearby Boggy Creek, a name derived from the French *vaseux*, meaning "muddy" or "slimy."

BOISE. In western Caddo County, 7 miles north of Carnegie. Post office established February 3, 1902, and name changed to Alfalfa, December 16, 1908. Named for John Boise, of Carnegie.

BOISE CITY. Designated county seat of Cimarron County, September 5, 1908, by proclamation of the governor. Former post office name was Cimarron, but was changed to Boise City, December 23, 1908. Its name comes from Boise, Idaho.

BOKCHITO. In Bryan County, 14 miles east of Durant. Post office established August 11, 1894. The name is a Choctaw word meaning "big creek."

BOKHOMA. Present Idabel, in McCurtain County. Post office established December 15, 1902, and name changed to Idabel, February 3, 1904. The word is Choctaw for "red river."

BOKHOMA. In southeastern Mc-

27

Curtain County, 16 miles southeast of Idabel. A post office from June 16, 1904, to May 30, 1936.

BOKOSHE. In western Le Flore County, 7 miles west of Panama. Post office established September 29, 1886. The word is Choctaw for "little creek."

BOK TUKLO. A county in Apukshunnubbee District, Choctaw Nation. The name is Choctaw for "two creeks," i.e., Lukfata Creek and Yasho Creek.

BOKTUKLO. In central McCurtain County, 7 miles northwest of Idabel. A post office from December 15, 1908, to September 15, 1921. Took its name from Bok Tuklo County, Choctaw Nation.

BOLAND. In Carter County, 3 miles east of Gene Autry. Post office established April 19, 1894, and name changed to Baum, September 21, 1894.

BOLEY. In western Okfuskee County. Post office established July 7, 1903. Named for W. H. Boley, roadmaster for the Fort Smith and Western Railroad.

BOLIN. In northwestern Delaware County. Site now inundated by Grand Lake o' the Cherokees. A post office from January 27, 1890, to August 22, 1893.

BOMAR. Formerly Bob. In Love County, 5 miles south of Marietta. Post office name changed to Bomar, December 30, 1907, and discontinued May 31, 1924. Named for Dr. Edward Bomar of Gainesville, Texas.

BOND. In northwestern Blaine County, 3 miles east of Canton. A post office from August 3, 1894, to July 31, 1906. No longer in existence.

BONTON. Present Ramona, in Washington County. Post office established September 8, 1899, and name changed to Ramona, December 9, 1899. The word is French for "good style."

BOOKERTEE. In Okfuskee County, 3 miles northeast of Weleetka. An important black community, it reached its maximum significance about 1920, and has since entirely disappeared. Named for Booker T. Washington.

BOONE. In Alfalfa County, 7 miles east of Byron. A post office from April 13, 1895, to May 14, 1906. Named for Charles T. Boone, first postmaster.

BORDEAUX. In northwestern Le Flore County near Milton. A post office from March 3, 1910, to February 28, 1911. Its name comes from Bordeaux, France.

BOREN. A switch and loading point on the Santa Fe in northern Washington County, 3 miles south of Caney, Kans. Named for Buck Boren, rancher and cattleman.

BORUM. In Haskell County, 7 miles north of Stigler. Post office established January 27, 1909, and name changed to Floe, September

27, 1909. Named for James H. Borum, first postmaster.

BOSS. In southern McCurtain County, 5 miles southwest of Idabel. A post office from June 1, 1905, to December 15, 1933. Named for Boss Luttrell, landowner and rancher.

BOSTICK. In Major County, 15 miles south of Waynoka. A post office from March 12, 1901, to September 29, 1906. No longer in existence.

BOSWELL. Formerly Mayhew. In Choctaw County, 20 miles west of Hugo. Post office name changed to Boswell, September 30, 1902. Named for A. V. Boswell, engineer and state civic leader.

BOTSFORD. Present Temple, in Cotton County. Post office established January 11, 1902, and name changed to Temple, August 8, 1902.

BOULANGER. In northern Osage County, 19 miles northeast of Pawhuska. A former townsite, established in 1914 and named for Isaac Boulanger, townsite owner.

BOURLAND. In Hughes County, 8 miles southwest of Atwood. A post office from March 29, 1892, to September 7, 1895. No longer in existence. Named for Reuben Bourland, prominent Indian leader.

BOWDEN. In northwestern Creek County, 4 miles north of Sapulpa. A post office from June 9, 1909, to November 1, 1957. Named for Rollandus A. Bowden, Sapulpa merchant.

BOWDENTON. In northwestern Noble County near Ceres. A post office from July 21, 1894, to August 4, 1897. No longer in existence. Named for R. A. Bowden, first postmaster.

BOWER. In northern Pittsburg County, 6 miles southeast of Eufaula. A post office from September 6, 1895, to July 31, 1920.

BOWLEGS. In Seminole County, 7 miles south of Seminole. Post office established April 23, 1927. Named for Billy Bowlegs, Seminole chief.

BOWLES. In Love County, 6 miles west of Marietta. A post office from February 25, 1903, to March 15, 1912. Named for John F. Bowles, first postmaster.

BOWMAN. In northwestern Logan County, 5 miles south of Marshall. A post office from June 25, 1890, to September 15, 1900. No longer in existence. Named for John Bowman, first postmaster.

BOWRING. In northeastern Osage County, 18 miles northeast of Pawhuska. Post office established November 12, 1923. The name was coined from the surnames of two ranchers, Mart Bowhan and Richard Woodring.

BOX. In extreme southeastern corner of Cleveland County. A post office from May 7, 1898, to January 2, 1907. No longer in existence. Named for George Box, first postmaster.

29

BOX. Formerly Roy. In northern Sequoyah County, 6 miles north of Vian. Post office name changed to Box, July 7, 1911, and discontinued February 29, 1928. Named for Henry Box, local resident.

BOYD. In western Beaver County. A post office from December 24, 1887, to April 30, 1964.

BOYER. In southern Pottawatomie County, 3 miles southwest of Asher. A post office from November 8, 1897, to August 31, 1904. Named for Addie Boyer, first postmaster.

BOYNTON. In southwestern Muskogee County. Post office established September 10, 1902. Named for E. W. Boynton, chief engineer of the Shawnee, Oklahoma and Missouri Coal and Railway Company.

BRACE. A townsite established in 1919, in Woods County, 8 miles northwest of Waynoka. Named for Stephen D. Brace, townsite owner.

BRADEN. In northern Le Flore County, 7 miles northeast of Spiro. A post office from September 1, 1890, to June 15, 1939.

BRADLEY. In eastern Grady County, 6 miles northwest of Lindsay. Post office established July 10, 1891. Named for Winters P. Bradley, local stockman and landowner.

BRADY. In Garvin County, 6 miles west of Wynnewood. A post office from June 30, 1892, to August 31, 1929. Named for Monassa Brady, first postmaster.

BRAGGS. Formerly Patrick. In Muskogee County, 12 miles southeast of Muskogee. Post office changed to Braggs, September 10, 1888. Named for Soloman Bragg, local landowner.

BRAIDWOOD. In Le Flore County, 3 miles west of Wister. Post office established July 11, 1891, and name changed to Pocahontas, May 11, 1895.

BRAITHWAITE. A townsite established in 1907 in Washita County, 4 miles west of Bessie. A post office from October 7, 1910, to January 31, 1923. Named for J. S. Braithwaite, an English stockholder of the Kansas City, Mexico and Orient Railway.

BRAMAN. In northwestern Kay County. Post office established April 11, 1898. Named for Dwight Braman, railroad developer.

BRANTLEY. In Roger Mills County, 10 miles southwest of Leedey. A post office from May 25, 1901, to April 30, 1914.

BRAY. In northern Stephens County, 8 miles east of Marlow. Post office established November 24, 1908. Named for Thomas W. Bray, first postmaster.

BRAZIL STATION. In western Le Flore County, 3 miles south of Bokoshe. Post office established April 11, 1879, name changed to Brazil, May 15, 1895, and discontinued May 31, 1913. Took its name from nearby Brazil Creek.

BRECKINRIDGE. In Garfield

County, 7 miles northeast of Enid. A post office from June 15, 1901, to November 22, 1963. Named for Breckinridge Jones, president of the Denver, Enid and Gulf Railway.

BREEDLOVE. In southeastern corner of Sequoyah County. A post office from March 7, 1891, to April 7, 1892. No longer in existence. Named for John W. Breedlove, prominent local resident.

BRENT. In Sequoyah County, 7 miles south of Sallisaw. A post office from May 6, 1896, to May 31, 1929. Took its name from Brent Ferry, a crossing on the Arkansas River.

BRESSIE. In northeastern Noble County, 8 miles east of Bliss. A post office from September 9, 1904, to October 20, 1915. Named for Emma Bressie, first postmaster.

BRIARTOWN. In extreme southern Muskogee County, 7 miles northwest of Stigler. The railroad name for this town was McMurray. Post office established May 15, 1882.

BRICO. A switch and loading point on the Frisco in Kiowa County 5 miles north of Hobart. Established in 1935, the name was coined from Western Brick Company of Clinton.

BRIDGEPORT. In northern Caddo County, 5 miles north of Hinton. Post office established February 20, 1895. Site of stage crossing of the Canadian River. Name came into use because people would wait at the site for low water so that they could cross the river.

BRIDGEWATER. In Ellis County, 7 miles west of Vici. Post office from June 4, 1901, to June 30, 1911. No longer in existence.

BRIGGS. A rural community in Cherokee County, 6 miles east of Tahlequah. Named for John Briggs, local merchant.

BRIGHT. In northeastern Comanche County, 3 miles south of Sterling. A post office from May 22, 1902, to December 15, 1907. No longer in existence.

BRINKMAN. In Greer County, 7 miles north of Mangum. A post office from June 17, 1910, to December 30, 1965. Named for John Brinkman, early-day resident.

BRISTOW. In central Creek County. Post office established April 25, 1898. Named for Senator Joseph L. Bristow of Kansas.

BRITTON. In Oklahoma County. A post office from November 26, 1889, to November 15, 1950. Municipality consolidated with Oklahoma City by Ordinance No. 6351, effective April 1, 1950. Named for Alexander Britton, Washington, D. C., Santa Fe Railway attorney.

BROCK. In Carter County, 7 miles southwest of Ardmore. A post office from September 15, 1896, to October 31, 1954. Named for Smith Brock, prominent Chickasaw.

BROKEN ARROW. In eastern Tulsa County, adjoining Tulsa.

31

Post office established June 9, 1881. Its name comes from a Creek ceremony held following the Civil War, in which an arrow was broken to symbolize a reunion of the two Civil War factions.

BROKEN BOW. In central McCurtain County. Post office established September 23, 1911. Named by the Dierks family for their home in Nebraska.

BROMIDE. Formerly Zenobia. In northeastern Johnston County, 5 miles northwest of Wapanucka. Post office name changed to Bromide, June 8, 1907. Took its name from nearby mineral springs.

BROOKEN. In northwestern Haskell County, 13 miles west of Stigler. A post office from December 15, 1879, to September 30, 1958. Took its name from nearby Brooken Creek.

BROOKSVILLE. In Pottawatomie County, 4 miles southwest of Tecumseh. Another name for the townsite is Sewell. A post office from March 18, 1909, to February 28, 1955. Named for Alfred H. Brooks, first postmaster.

BROWN. In Bryan County, 13 miles northwest of Durant. A post office from July 3, 1913, to July 15, 1927. Named for Robert H. Brown, first postmaster.

BROWN. In Pottawatomie County, 6 miles southwest of Shawnee. A post office from November 1, 1892, to February 14, 1906. No longer in existence. Named for George O. Brown, first postmaster.

BROWN PRAIRIE. Original name of Cravens, in Latimer County. The Post Office Department declined to accept the name for the post office, whereupon Cravens was selected. Named for James Brown, local resident.

BROWNSVILLE. In northern Hughes County near Wetumka. A post office from April 8, 1913, to June 30, 1914. Named for Charity Brown, first postmaster.

BROWNSVILLE. In Marshall County, 8 miles south of Kingston. A post office from March 28, 1890, to June 14, 1902. Named for Odis L. Brown, townsite owner.

BROXTON. In Caddo County, 7 miles northwest of Apache. A post office from February 26, 1903, to June 15, 1906. No longer in existence.

BRULE. Present Buffalo, in Harper County. Post office established June 15, 1899, and name changed to Buffalo, June 6, 1907. Its name comes from the Brulé, a subtribe of the Sioux. The word is French and is a translation of the Brulés' own name for their tribe, which meant "burned thighs," of uncertain origin.

BRUNO. In Atoka County, 4 miles southeast of Atoka. Post office established September 17, 1910, and discontinued March 31, 1925.

BRUSHHILL. In McIntosh County, 7 miles southwest of Checotah. A post office from February 6, 1894, to December 31, 1915. Took its name from a nearby land feature.

BRUSHY. In Sequoyah County, 8 miles northeast of Sallisaw. A post office from May 11, 1900, to October 31, 1910. Took its name from the nearby Brushy Mountains.

BRYAN. In Le Flore County near Victor. A post office from December 12, 1889, to October 7, 1893. Named for Luke W. Bryan, first postmaster.

BRYAN. In Pawnee County, 7 miles southeast of Pawnee. A post office from March 13, 1894, to May 31, 1905. No longer in existence. Named for William Jennings Bryan of Nebraska.

BRYAN COUNTY. A county in southeastern Oklahoma. Created at statehood from an area approximating Recording District No. 25, Indian Territory. Named for William Jennings Bryan.

BRYANT. In extreme southwestern Okmulgee County, 5 miles southwest of Henryetta. A post office from January 10, 1905, to July 31, 1954.

BUB. In southeastern Atoka County near Farris. A post office from June 6, 1921, to September 15, 1922.

BUCK. In Pittsburg County, 2 miles east of Krebs. Often known as Buck Junction. A post office from January 19, 1900, to September 31, 1907.

BUCKHEAD. In southeastern Cleveland County, 6 miles west of Wanette. A post office from March 3, 1893, to November 30, 1906.

BUCKHORN. In Murray County, 6 miles southeast of Sulphur. A post office from June 3, 1890, to August 15, 1910. Took its name from nearby Buckhorn Creek.

BUCKLES. In Garfield County, 6 miles northwest of Garber. A post office from September 14, 1898, to February 28, 1901. Named for J. A. Buckles, editor of the Enid *Eagle*.

BUEHLER. In Tulsa County at the site of present Sperry. A townsite established in 1905 and named for Charles Buehler, local oil producer. In 1907 the Sperry post office was moved to this location.

BUFFALO. County seat of Harper County. Formerly Brule. Post office name changed to Buffalo, June 6, 1907. Took its name from nearby Buffalo Creek.

BUFFALO. In central Texas County near Optima. A post office from March 15, 1888, to August 30, 1902. No longer in existence.

BUFFALO STATION. In southeastern Pittsburg County, 7 miles south of Haileyville. Established in 1867, it was an important stage stop on the post–Civil War mail routes crossing southeastern Oklahoma.

BUGTUSSLE. A rural community in Pittsburg County 9 miles northeast of McAlester, often known as Flowery Mound. The name is a colloquialism meaning a rustic settlement or backwoods area. The boyhood home of Carl Albert, Speaker of the House of Representatives of the United States Congress.

BULLCREEK. In extreme southeastern Rogers County, 9 miles southwest of Chouteau. A post office from February 4, 1896, to September 18, 1897. No longer in existence. Took its name from nearby Bull Creek, a tributary of the Verdigris River.

BUNCH. In southwestern Adair County. Post office established May 26, 1886. Named for Rabbit Bunch, prominent Cherokee.

BURBANK. In western Osage County, 24 miles west of Pawhuska. Post office established December 31, 1907. The name is generally believed to have been taken from a nearby rocky bluff along Salt Creek, covered with cockleburs.

BURDG. In extreme northwestern Grady County. A post office from March 21, 1905, to May 15, 1907. No longer in existence. Named for Willis M. Burdg, first postmaster.

BURFORD. In southern Harper County, 5 miles northwest of Supply. A post office from December 10, 1903, to December 30, 1909. Named for John H. Burford, territorial jurist.

BURFORD. Present Mountain Park, 5 miles north of Snyder, in Kiowa County. Post office established September 26, 1901, and name changed to Mountain Park, February 28, 1902. Named for John H. Burford.

BURGEVIN. In northwestern Le Flore County, 7 miles northwest of Spiro. A post office from January 31, 1890, to November 3, 1898. Named for John T. Burgevin, first postmaster.

BURGOR. In Harper County, 13 miles east of Laverne. Post office established January 31, 1903, and name changed to Tannar, October 25, 1904.

BURKHART. In extreme southwestern Le Flore County near Ludlow. A post office from October 4, 1910, to March 31, 1927. Named for William Burkhart, early settler.

BURLINGTON. In Alfalfa County, 12 miles north of Cherokee. A post office from January 6, 1900, to November 15, 1902. On August 21, 1907, the post office at Drumm, operating at a nearby location, changed its name to Burlington, and has existed to the present time. Its name comes from Burlington, Iowa.

BURLINGTON. In southern Logan County, 5 miles north of Edmond. A post office established January 23, 1890, and name changed to Waterloo, April 9, 1892. Its name comes from Burlington, Iowa.

BURMAH. In southern Dewey County, 7 miles southwest of Putnam. A post office from October 11, 1899, to May 31, 1908.

BURNETT. In Pottawatomie County, 4 miles west of Macomb. A post office from June 8, 1888, to

January 2, 1907. Named for Catherine Burnett, daughter of Abram Burnett, Pottawatomie tribal leader.

BURNEY. In McIntosh County, 5 miles west of Pierce. A post office from July 29, 1896, to November 30, 1907.

BURNEY ACADEMY. Established in 1859 by the Chickasaw Nation as a school for girls. In 1887, the institution changed its name to Chickasaw Orphan Home and Manual Labor School. A post office was located there from July 3, 1860, to June 22, 1866, although it was probably not in continuous operation because of the Civil War. Site in Marshall County, 2 miles southeast of Lebanon. Named for David C. Burney, prominent Chickasaw.

BURNEYVILLE. In Love County, 10 miles west of Marietta. Post office established May 5, 1879. Named for David C. Burney.

BURNS. In Washita County, 10 miles northwest of Cordell. A post office from April 21, 1894, to October 15, 1904. Named for Sarah Burns, first postmaster.

BURNS FLAT. In Washita County, 10 miles northwest of Cordell. A post office established February 28, 1936. Took its name from the former post office of Burns, located immediately to the south.

BURROW. In Coal County, 5 miles northwest of Clarita. A post office from September 26, 1908, to June 15, 1926. Post office

was located in Pontotoc County until March 4, 1918. Named for Henry Burrow, early settler.

BURSE. In northeastern Bryan County, 7 miles northwest of Boswell. A post office from December 15, 1902, to August 31, 1912.

BURSON. In eastern Haskell County near Keota. A post office from November 23, 1899, to January 31, 1901. Named for William I. Burson, first postmaster.

BURT. In Grady County, 12 miles northeast of Marlow. A post office from March 1, 1890, to April 30, 1900. Named for S. E. Burte, local early-day resident.

BURTON. In northern Noble County, in the vicinity of Three Sands. A post office from February 6, 1894, to May 15, 1900. No longer in existence.

BURWELL. Present Ringold, in McCurtain County, 12 miles northwest of Wright City. Post office established October 31, 1906, and name changed to Ringold, May 10, 1911. Named for William P. Burwell, first postmaster.

BURWICK. In Logan County, 5 miles northeast of Guthrie. A post office from January 31, 1891, to December 15, 1900. No longer in existence. Its name comes from Burwick, Maine.

BUSCH. Formerly Crowe in Beaver County. Post office moved to its new location in Beckham County on March 18, 1901, and changed its name to Busch. Post

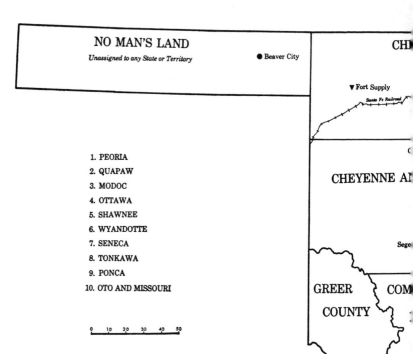

NO MAN'S LAND

Unassigned to any State or Territory   ● Beaver City

CH▮

▼ Fort Supply

Santa Fe Railroad

CHEYENNE A▮

1. PEORIA
2. QUAPAW
3. MODOC
4. OTTAWA
5. SHAWNEE
6. WYANDOTTE
7. SENECA
8. TONKAWA
9. PONCA
10. OTO AND MISSOURI

Sege▮

GREER   COM▮
COUNTY

0 10 20 30 40 50

Indian Territory, 1866–1889
Reproduced from *Historical Atlas of Oklahoma*, by John W. Morris and Edwin C. McReynolds. Copyright 1965 by the University of Oklahoma Press.

office name changed to Elk City, July 20, 1907.

BUSHYHEAD. In northeastern Rogers County, 4 miles southwest of Chelsea. A post office from April 18, 1898, to November 15, 1955. Named for Dennis W. Bushyhead, Cherokee principal chief, 1879–87.

BUTLER. In Custer County, 13 miles northwest of Arapaho. Post office established June 2, 1898. Named for Major General Matthew C. Butler, United States senator from South Carolina, and a general officer in both the Civil and Spanish-American wars.

BUTNER. In eastern Seminole County, 8 miles northeast of Wewoka. A post office from June 1, 1903, to November 30, 1906. Named for Thomas Butner, early-day settler.

BUTTE. In southeastern Dewey County, 6 miles northwest of Fay. A post office from November 30, 1894, to January 31, 1906. It took its name from the buttes along the north bank of the Canadian River.

BUTTE CITY. A townsite established in 1909 in Roger Mills County, 8 miles southwest of Cheyenne. No longer in existence.

BYARS. In eastern McClain County. Post office established April 9, 1903. Named for Nathan H. Byars, local rancher.

BYLLESBY. In Muskogee County, 3 miles east of Muskogee. It was named for H. M. Byllesby of Chicago, who assisted in the financing of the nearby O. G. & E. generating plant.

BYNG. In northern Pontotoc County, 5 miles north of Ada. A post office from December 15, 1917, to January 25, 1957. Named for Sir Julian Byng of the British Army.

BYRD. In Coal County, 9 miles northwest of Coalgate. Post office established March 3, 1892, and named for William L. Byrd, governor of the Chickasaw Nation. Name changed to Owl, July 10, 1894.

BYRD. In Texas County, 7 miles southeast of Hooker. A post office from March 17, 1904, to December 31, 1907. No longer in existence.

BYRNE. In Coal County, 7 miles northwest of Olney. A post office from September 15, 1889, to January 31, 1906. Named for Byrne Statler, early-day resident.

BYRON. In Alfalfa County, 11 miles northeast of Cherokee. Post office established April 27, 1894. Named for Byron Spurrier, a relative of the first postmaster.

C

C COUNTY. Original designation for Blaine County, Oklahoma Territory.

CABANISS. In Pittsburg County, 15 miles northwest of McAlester. A post office from April 18, 1903, to August 15, 1922. Named for

Thomas B. Cabaniss, a member of the Dawes Commission.

CABIN CREEK. In Mayes County, 3 miles north of Pensacola. A post office from July 6, 1868, to August 27, 1869. Two important engagements of the Civil War in Indian Territory were fought nearby, on July 1–2, 1863, and on September 18, 1864. Took its name from Cabin Creek, a tributary of the Neosho River.

CABLE. In Texas County, 6 miles northeast of Midwell. A post office from May 17, 1907, to June 30, 1910. Named for R. R. Cable of Chicago, a director of the Rock Island Railroad.

CACHE. In Comanche County, 12 miles west of Lawton. Post office established January 11, 1902. It took its name from nearby Cache Creek, a tributary of the Red River. The word is French, meaning an underground storage pit.

CACHE. In northwestern Le Flore County near Cowlington. A post office from March 10, 1881, to October 27, 1898. It took its name from nearby Cache Creek, a tributary of the Arkansas River.

CADDO. In northern Bryan County. Post office established December 19, 1872. It took its name from the nearby Caddo Hills, where, according to tradition, an Indian battle was fought in 1808.

CADDO. A county in Chickasaw District, Choctaw Nation. Later part of Chickasaw Nation.

CADDO COUNTY. A county in west-central Oklahoma. In area slightly reduced from the size of the territorial county of the same name. The name is that of an Indian tribe and stems from *ḳaadi* meaning "chief."

CADE. In extreme northeastern Bryan County. A post office from April 1, 1903, to October 31, 1915. Named for Cassius M. Cade, territorial political leader.

CADE. In extreme southeastern Roger Mills County. A post office from July 6, 1899, to April 30, 1902. No longer in existence, it was named for Cassius M. Cade.

CAINVILLE. Present Longdale, in Blaine County. Post office established August 1, 1900, and name changed to Longdale, November 28, 1903. Named for William Cain, first postmaster.

CAIRO. In eastern Coal County, 7 miles northeast of Coalgate. A post office from March 28, 1902, to July 15, 1939. Its name comes from Cairo, Illinois.

CALE. Present Calera, in Bryan County. Post office established November 30, 1889, and name changed to Sterrett, June 20, 1899. Named for George W. Cale, railroad official.

CALERA. Formerly Sterrett. In Bryan County, 6 miles southwest of Durant. Post office name changed to Calera, November 21, 1910. The name is a modification of the former name, Cale.

CALHOUN. Formerly Sutter. In Le Flore County, 8 miles northwest of Poteau. Post office name changed to Calhoun, March 7, 1914, and discontinued November 30, 1934.

CALLOWAY. In southern Atoka County, 9 miles south of Atoka. A post office from March 6, 1901, to February 28, 1911.

CALUMET. In northwestern Canadian County. Post office established April 12, 1893. The word is from the French *chalumet*, shepherd's pipe, and was the name given to the ceremonial pipe used by the Indians.

CALVIN. Formerly Riverview. In central Hughes County. Post office name changed to Calvin, June 24, 1895. Named for Calvin Perry, railroad official.

CAMARGO. In western Dewey County, 8 miles south of Vici. Post office established September 16, 1892. Its name comes from Camargo, Illinois.

CAMBRIDGE. In Kiowa County, 6 miles northwest of Hobart. A post office from May 9, 1903, to February 29, 1904.

CAMEO. In Canadian County, 4 miles south of Calumet. A post office from November 2, 1895, to June 30, 1903. No longer in existence. The word means a stone or shell carved in relief.

CAMERON. In Le Flore County, 8 miles northeast of Poteau. Post office established January 31, 1888.

Named for William Cameron, mining superintendent.

CAMINET. Original name for Higgins. Post office established April 1, 1903, and name changed to Higgins, May 28, 1903.

CAMP. In Texas County, 17 miles northwest of Guymon. A post office from October 26, 1906, to September 30, 1916. No longer in existence. Took its name from nearby Stonebraker Camp, well-known cattle camp.

CAMP ARBUCKLE. In McClain County, 1 mile northwest of Byars. A military encampment established in May, 1850, but abandoned after one year upon the selection of a permanent site farther south to be known as Fort Arbuckle. Named for Brigadier General Matthew Arbuckle.

CAMP AUGER. In southern Tillman County, 9 miles southwest of Grandfield. A post–Civil War military encampment that operated as a satellite of Fort Sill, it was named for Brigadier General C. C. Auger.

CAMPBELL. In northern Logan County, 5 miles northwest of Coyle. Townsite plat filed November 14, 1899, and is now known as Pleasant Valley. Named for G. W. Campbell, local early-day resident.

CAMPBELL. Present Gore, in Sequoyah County. Post office established August 10, 1888, and name changed to Gore, October 22, 1909. Named for Dr. W. W. Campbell, ferry owner at Webbers Falls.

CAMP CREEK. In Sequoyah County near Muldrow. A post office from February 17, 1879, to July 29, 1889. It took its name from nearby Camp Creek, a branch of the Arkansas River, which in turn had been named for an old Cherokee campground.

CAMP GRUBER. A military encampment in eastern Muskogee County. Dedicated July 19, 1942. Named for Brigadier General E. L. Gruber, who died May 30, 1941.

CAMP McCULLAH. A temporary encampment on the wagon road between the Sac and Fox Agency and Darlington; probably located somewhere in the vicinity of present-day Edmond. A post office from February 20, 1880, to August 3, 1880.

CAMP NAPOLEON. A temporary encampment established in 1865 near present-day Verden. Site of a large Indian conference, intended to establish closer relations between the Indians of Indian Territory and the Plains tribes. Named because of the supposed presence of an emissary of Mexican Emperor Maximilian, a puppet of Napoleon III.

CAMP RADZIMINSKI. In Kiowa County, 2 miles northwest of Mountain Park. Established in September, 1858, on Otter Creek as a base of operations against the Indians, it was named for Lieutenant Charles Radziminski.

CAMP RUSSELL. In Logan County, 6 miles north of Guthrie, near south bank of Cimarron River. Established by the military in 1884 as a part of the operations in connection with the Boomer movement, the location continued for a number of years as a community center. Named for Capt. G. B. Russell, 9th Infantry.

CAMP SCHOFIELD. In Kay County, 3 miles east of Chilocco. A temporary military encampment established in September, 1889, for extensive field maneuvers, it was named for John M. Schofield, secretary of war.

CAMP SUPPLY. In western Woodward County, adjoining present-day Fort Supply. Established November, 1868, as a supply base for the Indian campaign of Major General G. A. Custer. Post office established March 17, 1873, and name changed to Fort Supply, June 26, 1889. Post abandoned in 1893, and now a state hospital.

CANADIAN. A district of the Cherokee Nation.

CANADIAN. In Canadian County near Yukon. A post office from March 7, 1891, to October 22, 1895. No longer in existence, it took its name from the Canadian River.

CANADIAN. Formerly South Canadian. In Pittsburg County, 10 miles southwest of Eufaula. Nearby was Canadian Depot, an important supply point during the Civil War. Post office name changed to Canadian, December 11, 1899. It took its name from the Canadian River.

CANADIAN COUNTY. A county in central Oklahoma, comprising the same area as Canadian County, Oklahoma Territory. It took its name from the Canadian River.

CANADIAN RIVER. A principal river system of Oklahoma, the main course of which discharges into the Arkansas River, 30 miles west of the eastern border of the state. The Canadian historically had three branches, the South Fork, the North Fork, and the Deep Fork. The South Fork is now known generally as Gaines Creek, and the main course is popularly called the South Canadian. Although other theories have been advanced, the accepted explanation of the origin of the name is that it is a reference to Canada.

CANADAVILLE. In Rogers County, a few miles southwest of Oologah. A post office from May 28, 1886, to June 13, 1889. No longer in existence, it was named for Montgomery Canada, local merchant and a relative of Green L. Canada, first postmaster.

CANEY. In southern Atoka County. Post office established June 20, 1888. It took its name from Caney Switch on the Katy Railroad, located 1 mile north.

CANEY SWITCH. In southern Atoka County, 1 mile north of present-day Caney. A post office for a short period in 1879, it took its name from nearby Caney Creek, a popular name for streams, referring to cane brakes along the course. At that time the railhead for Fort Sill.

CANTON. In northwestern Blaine County. Post office established May 19, 1905. It took its name from nearby Cantonment, a onetime military post.

CANTONMENT. In Blaine County, 3 miles northwest of Canton. A post office from July 17, 1879, to September 15, 1917. Intended as a supply cantonment, the post was established in 1879 by Colonel Richard I. Dodge but fell into disuse within a decade.

CANTONMENT GIBSON. Original name for the post office at Fort Gibson, Muskogee County, which was established February 27, 1827. Its name was changed to Fort Gibson, September 14, 1842.

CANUTE. In northwestern Washita County. First known locally as Oak. Post office established February 24, 1899. It was named for Canute, king of Denmark.

CANYON. On the Caddo County line, 4 miles southeast of Hinton. A post office from February 6, 1902, to September 30, 1905, it took its name from nearby Red Rock Canyon.

CANYON CITY. In extreme southwestern Canadian County. Townsite plat filed June 1, 1890. No longer in existence.

CAPITOL HILL. Now part of the area of southern Oklahoma City, and originally a separate municipality. A post office from September 5, 1905, to October 31, 1911, on which date it became a substation of the Oklahoma City post office.

The name comes from the circumstance that the area was at one time considered for the location of the state capitol.

CAPLE. In Texas County, 6 miles southeast of Hardesty. A post office from April 13, 1891, to May 31, 1916. Named for William G. Caple, first postmaster.

CAPRON. Formerly Virgel. In northeastern Woods County. Post office name changed to Capron, February 20, 1899. Named for Captain Allyn K. Capron, commander of the territorial detachment in the Spanish-American War.

CARBON. In Pittsburg County, 5 miles east of McAlester. Formerly known locally as Cherryvale. Railroad name was Simpson Station. A post office from February 20, 1899, to November 30, 1933, it took its name from surrounding coal fields.

CARBONDALE. Now within the city limits of Tulsa. A post office from January 22, 1927, to July 31, 1928. The area was the site of a proposed publicly subscribed industrial enterprise. However, the building burned prior to completion, and the project was abandoned. Because of the proposed carbon plant, the site was named for Carbondale, Illinois.

CARDIN. Formerly Tar River. In northern Ottawa County, 1 mile southwest of Picher. Post office name changed to Cardin, January 28, 1920. Named for W. Oscar Cardin, townsite owner.

CARL. In Harmon County, 4 miles north of Madge. A post office from December 29, 1902, to December 31, 1913. No longer in existence, it was named for Carl Armstrong, son of Walter H. Armstrong, first postmaster.

CARLTON. Formerly Hopkins. In Blaine County, 5 miles southeast of Canton. Post office name changed to Carlton, December 1, 1902, and discontinued June 30, 1957. Spelling is often shown as Carleton. Named for Murray Carleton, a financier of the Frisco Railroad.

CARMEL. In Jackson County, 7 miles southwest of Olustee. A post office from February 5, 1898, to June 15, 1910. No longer in existence, it took its name from Carmel, California.

CARMEN. In southwestern Alfalfa County. Post office established September 11, 1901. Named for Carmen Diaz, wife of the president of Mexico.

CARNEGIE. In western Caddo County. Post office established December 28, 1901. Named for Andrew Carnegie.

CARNEY. In northwestern Lincoln County. Post office established April 9, 1892. Named for Carney Staples, townsite developer. The original name of the community was Cold Springs.

CARPENTER. In Roger Mills County, 8 miles north of Elk City. A post office from March 19, 1901, to February 28, 1942. Named for Benjamin Carpenter, local rancher.

CARRIAGE POINT. In Bryan County, 3 miles west of Durant. A post office from March 23, 1869, to February 6, 1871. No longer in existence. The site was at Fisher's Station, an important stop on the Butterfield Overland Mail route prior to the Civil War.

CARRIER. In northwestern Garfield County. Post office established May 22, 1897. Named for Soloman Carrier, merchant.

CARRIZO. Present Kenton, in western Cimarron County. Post office established September 9, 1886, and name changed to Florence, April 9, 1890. The name is a Spanish word for a type of water grass growing along Beaver River.

CARROLL. Formerly Tanner. In Harper County, 13 miles east of Laverne. Post office name changed to Carroll, July 10, 1906, and discontinued June 15, 1907. No longer in existence.

CARSON. In Hughes County, 11 miles southeast of Wetumka. A post office from June 26, 1901, to September 30, 1927.

CARTER. In southeastern Beckham County. Townsite plat was named Beulah. Post office established March 5, 1900, and named for William G. Carter, prominent early-day resident.

CARTER COUNTY. A county of southern Oklahoma created at statehood. Named for a prominent early-day family of which Charles D. Carter was the best-known member.

CARTER NINE. In Osage County, 22 miles northwest of Pawhuska. Post office established August 14, 1928. The name was coined from the name of the Carter Oil Company and the land description, Section 9 of Township 26 North, Range 6 East.

CARTER PARK. A municipality in Oklahoma County, adjoining Midwest City. Townsite laid out in February, 1948, and consolidated with Del City, September 1, 1954. Named for Charles E. Carter and Edward M. Carter, townsite owners.

CARTER SEMINARY. Indian school at Ardmore. Opened in 1917 as an outgrowth of Bloomfield Academy, previously located in southern Bryan County. Named for Charles D. Carter, United States congressman.

CARTERSVILLE. In Haskell County, 4 miles southeast of Keota. First known locally as Hog Town. Post office established January 28, 1891.

CARTHAGE. In Kay County, several miles southeast of Blackwell. A post office from March 29, 1894, to May 20, 1895. No longer in existence, its name comes from Carthage, Missouri.

CARTHAGE. In northwestern Texas County, 5 miles southwest of Elkhart, Kansas. A post office from June 19, 1906, to August 31, 1914.

No longer in existence. Its name comes from Carthage, Missouri.

CARTWRIGHT. In southwestern Bryan County. Post office established April 25, 1940, and named for Wilburn Cartwright, United States congressman and state official.

CARWILE. In southeastern Alfalfa County, 5 miles south of Helena. Post office from June 30, 1894, to April 15, 1905. Named for James D. Carwile, early-day resident.

CARY'S FERRY. In Delaware County, about 5 miles northwest of Grove. A post office from November 5, 1873, to March 9, 1888. Site now inundated by Grand Lake o' the Cherokees. Named for Dan C. Carey, prominent Cherokee and operator of ferry across Grand River.

CASE. In Cleveland County, 12 miles east of Moore. A post office from December 1, 1890, to July 31, 1906. No longer in existence, it was named for Charles P. Case, first postmaster.

CASEY. In Pawnee County, 3 miles northeast of Maramec. A post office from November 23, 1903, to November 21, 1930.

CASHION. In southeastern Kingfisher County. Post office established May 14, 1900, and named for Roy V. Cashion, first Oklahoma Territory soldier killed in Spanish-American War.

CASTLE. In Okfuskee County, 6 miles west of Okemah. Post office established February 25, 1903, and named for Mannford B. Castle, local landowner.

CASTON. Formerly Maxey. In Le Flore County, 3 miles west of Wister. Post office name changed to Caston, November 5, 1887, and discontinued October 8, 1891. On April 18, 1898, a nearby post office named Pocohontas, at Caston Switch, changed its name to Caston; this post office was discontinued August 26, 1898.

CATALE. In Rogers County, 3 miles northeast of Chelsea. A post office from October 6, 1894, to February 15, 1933. The word is Cherokee, meaning "in the valley."

CATAWBA. In Blaine County, 5 miles southwest of Okeene. A post office from October 26, 1893, to August 31, 1902. No longer in existence, it was named for a tribe of Indians, a branch of the Yuchi. The word means "strong people."

CATESBY. In northwestern Ellis County. A post office from February 18, 1902, to January 31, 1970. Named for Catesby ap Roger Jones, hero of the Mexican and Civil wars.

CATHAY. In McIntosh County, 6 miles north of Eufaula. A post office from April 18, 1903, to June 15, 1914. No longer in existence. The name is the poetic word for China.

CATO. In northwestern Kingfisher County, 15 miles east of Okeene. A post office from June 22, 1892, to June 15, 1905. No longer in existence, it was named for the Roman statesman.

CATOOSA. In southwestern Rogers County. Post office established March 27, 1883. It took its name from nearby Catoos Hill. The word is from the Cherokee *gatv gitse* meaning "new settlement place."

CAVALRY CREEK. A tributary of the Washita River near Cordell in Washita County. Named for the Seventh Cavalry.

CAVANAL. In Le Flore County, 3 miles northeast of Wister. A post office from October 10, 1887, to July 15, 1901. It took its name from nearby Mount Cavanal. The word is French, meaning cavernous.

CAVETT. In Oklahoma County, 2 miles southwest of Harrah. A post office from May 24, 1892, to October 27, 1898. No longer in existence, it was named for James S. Cavett, early-day resident.

CAVNAR. In Comanche County, 6 miles east of Fletcher. A post office from August 1, 1904, to November 14, 1905, it was named for John Cavnar, local merchant.

CAYUGA. In Delaware County, 6 miles northeast of Grove. A post office from June 11, 1884, to April 30, 1912. Named for the Cayuga tribe of Iroquois, one of the Five Nations. The word has a meaning, "the place where the locusts were taken out."

CEDAR. A county of Apukshunnubbee District, Choctaw Nation.

Cedar County was the English equivalent of Chuala County.

CEDAR. In western Logan County, 5 miles west of Guthrie. A post office from June 25, 1892, to September 15, 1900, it took its name from a nearby grove of cedar trees.

CEDAR. In Nowata County, 7 miles northeast of Delaware. A post office from April 4, 1902, to August 31, 1918, it took its name from nearby Cedar Creek, a tributary of the Verdigris River.

CEDARDALE. In Woodward County, 12 miles south of Quinlan. A post office from April 13, 1903, to September 30, 1951.

CEEGEE. Present Elgin, in Comanche County. Post office established April 1, 1902, and name changed to Elgin, July 12, 1902. Named for C. G. Jones of Oklahoma City, railroad developer and industrialist.

CELESTINE. In Pittsburg County, 5 miles northeast of Ashland. A post office from November 12, 1896, to March 31, 1915.

CEMENT. In southeastern Caddo County. Post office established June 2, 1902. It took its name from nearby quarrying operations.

CENTER. In Oklahoma County, 8 miles west of Edmond. Post office established March 24, 1890, and name changed to Whisler, June 9, 1890. The name is from the circumstance that the site was in the center of the lands open for settlement April 22, 1889.

CENTER. In Pontotoc County, 6 miles northwest of Ada. A post office from June 9, 1890, to February 15, 1928. The name is from the circumstance that the site was located near the center of Indian Territory.

CENTRAHOMA. Formerly Owl. In Coal County, 8 miles northwest of Coalgate. Post office name changed to Centrahoma, June 11, 1907. The name was coined from the phrase, central Oklahoma.

CENTRALIA. Formerly Lucas. In northwestern Craig County. Post office name changed to Centralia, April 11, 1899. Its name comes from Centralia, Illinois.

CEREAL. In Canadian County, 5 miles west of Yukon. Post office established April 5, 1900, and name changed to Banner, November 4, 1911. It took its name from the type of local agricultural product.

CERES. Formerly McKinney. In Noble County, 6 miles west of Redrock. Post office name changed to Ceres, February 6, 1897, and discontinued May 31, 1915. Named for the Roman goddess of the harvest.

CERROGORDO. In McCurtain County, 18 miles east of Idabel. A post office from May 10, 1923, to September 30, 1958. The name is Spanish, meaning "broad hill."

CESTOS. In northern Dewey County, 10 miles west of Seiling. A post office from November 18, 1898, to December 15, 1923.

CEYLON. In Lincoln County near Stroud. A post office from January 6, 1900, to May 31, 1900. No longer in existence. Its name comes from the island of Ceylon because of the circumstance that with high water in the nearby Deep Fork River the site was always an island.

CHADDICK. In Oklahoma County, 2 miles west of Nicoma Park. Post office established April 16, 1890, and name changed to Dickson, July 17, 1896. Named for Edwin D. Chaddick, railroad official.

CHADWICK. In Tillman County, 1 mile north of Tipton. A post office from March 25, 1902, to August 31, 1906. No longer in existence.

CHAFFEE. In Mayes County near the site of Pensacola Dam. A post office from June 26, 1897, to July 15, 1910. Named for Ezra A. Chaffee, first postmaster.

CHAGRIS. In western Carter County, 4 miles northwest of Healdton. A post office from April 25, 1896, to February 27, 1909.

CHAMBERS. In Pittsburg County, 5 miles south of McAlester. A post office from January 26, 1904, to November 15, 1910. Located at the site of Perryville, an important settlement prior to the Civil War, it was named for T. H. Chambers, coal mine operator.

CHANCE. In Adair County, 10 miles northwest of Westville. A post office from August 5, 1897, to August 31, 1914, it was named for T. C. Chance, first postmaster.

CHANDLER. County seat of Lincoln County. Post office established September 21, 1891. Named for George Chandler, Independence, Kansas, assistant secretary of the interior under President Harrison.

CHANEY. In Ellis County, 13 miles northwest of Gage. A post office from January 29, 1902, to March 15, 1937. The name was coined from the first letter in the names of six local families, Carey, Hull, Adams, Nichols, Edmonds, and Yarnold.

CHANT. In Haskell County, 2 miles southwest of McCurtain. A post office from July 22, 1903, to April 15, 1910, it was named for H. M. Chant, mining engineer.

CHAPEL. In Mayes County, 8 miles southeast of Pryor. A post office from July 20, 1903, to January 15, 1918, it took its name from nearby Bryan's Chapel, built in 1886.

CHARLESTON. In Harper County, 8 miles southeast of Buffalo. Post office established May 18, 1901, and name changed to Selman, August 24, 1923. Named for Charles J. Eilerts, townsite owner.

CHARLEY. In Grady County, 9 miles west of Rush Springs. A post office from May 3, 1902, to August 15, 1907. No longer in existence, it was named for Charley Carmen, father of the first postmaster.

CHASE. In Muskogee County, 8 miles southwest of Muskogee. Post office established April 9, 1903, and name changed to Beland, June 19, 1908.

CHATTANOOGA. In the southwest corner of Comanche County. Post office established January 31, 1903. Its name comes from Chattanooga, Tennessee.

CHECOTAH. In north-central McIntosh County. Post office established June 17, 1886. Named for Samuel Checote, Creek chief.

CHEEK. In Carter County, 10 miles southwest of Ardmore. A post office from November 19, 1888, to March 15, 1935.

CHELSEA. In northeastern Rogers County. Post office established November 21, 1882. Named by Charles Peach, railroad official, for his home in England.

CHEROKEE. County seat of Alfalfa County. Post office established February 7, 1894. It took its name from the circumstance that the site was in the Cherokee Outlet.

CHEROKEE AGENCY. In Cherokee County, 2 miles northwest of Tahlequah. A post office from January 23, 1840, to May 23, 1849, during which time it was the location of the Cherokee Indian Agency.

CHEROKEE CITY. In northeastern Logan County, 1 mile east of Orlando. Townsite plat filed June 20, 1891. No longer in existence.

CHEROKEE COUNTY. A county in northeastern Oklahoma, created at statehood. It took its name from the Cherokee Nation.

CHEROKEE ORPHAN ASYLUM. In Mayes County immediately east of Salina. A post office established January 10, 1876, and its name changed to Salina, March 10, 1884, at which time it was the location of the Cherokee Orphanage.

CHEROKEE TOWN. In Garvin County, 2 miles east of Pauls Valley, and in the mid-nineteenth century an important settlement. A post office from August 17, 1874, to May 10, 1877. No longer in existence. It took its name from a small community of Cherokee Indians, who had settled nearby as refugees during the Civil War.

CHERRYVALE. Present Southard, in Blaine County. Post office established December 24, 1896, and name changed to Southard, September 6, 1905. Its name comes from Cherryvale, Kansas.

CHESTER. In Major County, 5 miles north of Seiling. Post office established April 8, 1895. It was named for Chester Long, United States senator from Kansas.

CHEYENNE. County seat of Roger Mills County. Post office established April 11, 1892. It took its name from the Cheyenne Indians, on whose reservation it was located. The word means "people of alien speech."

CHICKASHA. Formerly Pensee. County seat of Grady County. Post office name changed to Chickasha, June 20, 1892. Record Town for Recording District No. 19, Indian Territory. Chickasha is the correct spelling of Chickasaw, but the popular pronunciation of the word is incorrect.

CHICKIECHOCKIE. In Atoka County, 3 miles south of Limestone Gap. Post office established June 17, 1891, and name changed to Chockie, February 8, 1904. Named for Chickie and Chockie, the two daughters of Charles LeFlore. Chickie was later Mrs. Lee Cruce, Oklahoma's second First Lady.

CHIGLEY. In Murray County, 6 miles southeast of Wynnewood. A post office from January 24, 1900, to October 31, 1914. Named for Nelson Chigley, prominent Chickasaw.

CHIKASKIA RIVER. A tributary of the Salt Fork River, in Kay County. Chikaskia is Osage for "white spotted deer."

CHILCO. In Pawnee County, 3 miles west of Quay. A post office from March 30, 1894, to June 30, 1905. No longer in existence.

CHILDERS. In Nowata County, 6 miles east of Delaware. A post office from May 10, 1901, to July 15, 1915, it was named for Charles W. Childers, prominent early-day resident.

CHILDER'S STATION. Present Sallisaw, in Sequoyah County. A post office established June 26, 1878, and name changed to Sallisaw, December 8, 1888. Named for John Childers, prominent Cherokee.

CHILOCCO. In northern Kay County. Post office established September 6, 1889, it took its name from the Chilocco Indian School, established by the United States in 1882. Although there are several explanations, the name is probably from the Creek *tci lako* meaning "big deer," a name often applied to the horse.

CHILTON. In Jackson County, 7 miles southeast of Altus. Post office established April 18, 1890, and name changed to Dunbar, March 21, 1892.

CHIQUITA. In Noble County, about 10 miles northwest of Perry. A post office from November 11, 1895, to April 25, 1898. No longer in existence. The word is Spanish, meaning "little girl."

CHISM. In McClain County, 6 miles northeast of Byars. A post office from June 29, 1900, to September 15, 1930. Named for William Chisholm, a son of Jesse Chisholm, whose residence was nearby.

CHLOETA. In Delaware County, 6 miles east of the Pensacola Dam. A post office from April 18, 1898, to January 31, 1914.

CHOATE. In Pittsburg County, 3 miles west of Indianola. A post office from November 6, 1894, to May 31, 1904. Named for George W. Choate, sheriff of Tobucksy County, Choctaw Nation.

CHOCKIE. Formerly Chickiechockie. In Atoka County, 11 miles northeast of Stringtown. Post office name changed to Chockie, February 8, 1904, and discontinued March 15, 1905. On August 3, 1916, a nearby post office, Rich, was renamed Chockie, which, in turn, was discontinued November 30, 1934. Named for Chockie LeFlore, daughter of Charles LeFlore.

CHOCTAW. Formerly Choctaw City. In eastern Oklahoma County. Post office name changed to Choctaw, March 14, 1896. It took its name from the Choctaw Coal and Railway Company.

CHOCTAW AGENCY. Indian agency established 1832 by Francis Armstrong at Skullyville, near present Spiro, Le Flore County. Post office established June 26, 1833. Agency moved to Fort Washita in 1858–59. Location of Walker's Station, a stop on the Butterfield Overland Mail route prior to the Civil War. Because of the removal of the agency, the post office name was changed to Scullyville [*sic*] on August 16, 1860, but was changed back to Choctaw Agency on December 14, 1860, and discontinued October 10, 1871. On December 22, 1871, a post office named Oak Lodge was established at this approximate location.

CHOCTAW CITY. Present Choctaw in eastern Oklahoma County. Post office established February 21, 1890, and name changed to Choctaw, March 14, 1896. Took name from Choctaw Coal and Railway Company.

CHOCTAW COUNTY. A county in southeastern Oklahoma, created at statehood. The tribal name is *Chahta*. Named for the Choctaw Nation of Indians.

CHOSKA. In Wagoner County, 9 miles south of Coweta. A post office from January 27, 1890, to October 31, 1913. The word means "post oak"; the town was named for Polly Postoak, townsite owner.

CHOUTEAU. In southwestern Mayes County. Post office established October 18, 1871. Until October 3, 1941, the official spelling of the post office name was Choteau, although such incorrect spelling was never in popular usage. Named for the well-known family founded by Jean Pierre Chouteau.

CHRISTIE. In Adair County, 8 miles southwest of Westville. A post office from February 28, 1903, to January 31, 1944, it was named for John Christie, townsite owner.

CHRONISTER. In Cherokee County, 9 miles southeast of Tahlequah. A post office from May 31, 1919, to September 14, 1929.

CHUCKAHO. In Lincoln County, 1 mile south of Davenport. A post office from December 5, 1903, to April 30, 1908. No longer in existence, it took its name from nearby Chuckaho Creek, which had been named for Che-ka-ko, a local Sauk Indian.

CHULA. In McCurtain County near Millerton. A post office from May 17, 1902, to May 14, 1904. No longer in existence. The name is the Choctaw word for fox.

CHURCH. In Adair County, 6 miles south of Stilwell. A post office from October 19, 1912, to August 31, 1933.

CHUSTENAHLAH. In southeastern Osage County. Site of an important engagement of the Civil War, fought December 26, 1861, which resulted in a Confederate victory. The name is from the Cherokee, meaning "a shoal in a stream."

CHUSTO TALASAH. On Bird Creek in northern Tulsa County. Usually known as "Caving Banks," it was the site of an important engagement of the Civil War, fought December 9, 1861, which resulted in a Confederate victory.

CIMARRON. Present Boise City in Cimarron County. Post office established July 22, 1907, and name changed to Boise City, December 23, 1908. It took its name from nearby Cimarron River.

CIMARRON. Known originally as Cimarron City. In Logan County, 6 miles east of Langston. Post office established as Cimarron City, August 28, 1889; name changed to Cimarron April 21, 1894, and discontinued August 15, 1901. No longer in existence, it took its name from the nearby Cimarron River.

CIMARRON COUNTY. The westernmost county in Oklahoma. Created at statehood from the western one third of Beaver County, Oklahoma Territory, it took its name from the Cimarron River.

CIMARRON RIVER. A principal river traversing the northern portion of Oklahoma, including the Panhandle, and flowing into the Arkansas River, 15 miles west of Tulsa. Often known as the Red Fork. Although there is some uncertainty regarding the origin of the word, it is generally considered to be of Spanish derivation, from Río de los Carneros Cimarrón, or "River of the Wild Sheep."

CISCO. In McCurtain County, 4 miles west of Idabel. A post office from May 21, 1913, to July 31, 1916. No longer in existence. The name is an Algonquian word for a species of fish.

CITRA. In extreme southwestern corner of Hughes County. A post office from April 10, 1894, to May 29, 1931. The word is a prefix meaning "on this side," and the name is from the circumstance that the site is on the east side of the Choctaw Nation boundary.

CIVET. In Garvin County, 4 miles northeast of Pauls Valley. A post office from February 25, 1903, to January 31, 1925. The name is from the French word *civette*, a species of the cat family.

CLARA. In McIntosh County near Checotah. A post office from April 21, 1910, to March 15, 1916.

CLARDYVILLE. Formerly Isabella. In Pottawatomie County, 5 miles west of Asher. Post office name changed to Clardyville, February 25, 1875, and changed to Oberlin, April 25, 1876. Named for

J. E. Clardy, prominent early-day resident.

CLARE. In Grant County, 6 miles north of Deer Creek. A post office from November 12, 1896, to June 30, 1904. Its name comes from Clare, Kansas.

CLAREMORE. County seat of Rogers County. Record Town for Recording District No. 4, Indian Territory. Post office established June 25, 1874. Named for Clermont, well-known Osage chief.

CLARION. In Major County, 6 miles west of Orienta. A post office from May 26, 1902, to February 15, 1908. No longer in existence.

CLARITA. Formerly Kittie, in southwestern Coal County. Post office name changed to Clarita, January 19, 1910. Named for Clarita Kenefic, wife of William Kenefic, railroad official.

CLARKSON. In the southwestern corner of Payne County. A post office from January 31, 1890, to February 28, 1903. No longer in existence.

CLARKSVILLE. In southern Wagoner County, 8 miles east of Haskell. A post office from March 1, 1894, to September 30, 1916, it was named for Gus C. Clark, first postmaster.

CLAUD. Formerly Ara. In Stephens County, 12 miles northeast of Duncan. Post office name changed to Claud, January 1, 1927, and discontinued July 31, 1947. Named for

Claud Collier, long-time local resident.

CLAUDE. In Custer County, 4 miles southeast of Custer City. A post office from October 7, 1895, to January 30, 1904. No longer in existence.

CLAY. In Alfalfa County, 5 miles southwest of Jet. A post office from February 2, 1894, to April 15, 1902. No longer in existence, it took its name from Clay Creek, a tributary of the Salt Fork of the Arkansas River.

CLAYPOOL. In Jefferson County, 11 miles east of Waurika. A post office from June 28, 1903, to May 15, 1928. Named for John M. Claypool, first postmaster.

CLAYTON. In Payne County, 6 miles northeast of Perkins. A post office from February 21, 1890, to April 14, 1900. No longer in existence, it was named for Clayton Dial, son of Samuel Dial, first postmaster.

CLAYTON. Formerly Dexter. In northern Pushmataha County. Post office name changed to Clayton, April 5, 1907. Its name comes from Clayton, Missouri.

CLEARCREEK. In extreme southeastern Choctaw County. A post office from August 4, 1896, to August 15, 1902. It took its name from nearby Clear Creek, a small branch of the Red River.

CLEAR LAKE. In Beaver County, 15 miles southeast of Beaver. A post office from February 11, 1888, to May 15, 1944.

CLEARVIEW. In Okfuskee County, 8 miles southeast of Okemah. A post office established September 30, 1902. In 1904, an order was issued changing the name of the post office to Abelincoln, but it was rescinded a month later.

CLEBIT. In McCurtain County, 11 miles west of Bethel. Post office established May 7, 1924. Named for John Clebo, sawmill foreman.

CLEMATIS. In Lincoln County, 3 miles south of Davenport. A post office from June 18, 1898, to January 14, 1905. No longer in existence, it took its name from a vine of the crowfoot family, the name of which is derived from the Greek word *klema*, meaning "vine."

CLEMSCOT. In northwestern Carter County. A post office from May 5, 1924, to April 22, 1966. The name was coined from the names of two local residents, Clem Brooks and Scott Sparks.

CLEORA. Formerly Klaus. In Delaware County, 6 miles northeast of Ketchum. Post office name changed to Cleora, November 28, 1900, and discontinued October 15, 1954. Named for Cleora Ann Lunday, relative of Edward Lunday, first postmaster.

CLEO SPRINGS. In north-central Major County. Post office established March 21, 1894. From December 7, 1894, to May 3, 1917, the name of the post office was Cleo.

It took its name from nearby Cleo Springs, which, by tradition, had been named for an Indian maid, Cle-oh-i-to-mo.

CLERMONT. Formerly Rock Island. In Canadian County, 7 miles southeast of Okarche. Post office name changed to Clermont, April 30, 1892, and changed to Racine, June 24, 1895. No longer in existence.

CLEVELAND. Formerly Herbert. In eastern Pawnee County. Post office name changed to Cleveland, April 14, 1894. Named for Grover Cleveland.

CLEVELAND COUNTY. A county in central Oklahoma, constituted from Cleveland County, Oklahoma Territory. Named for Grover Cleveland.

CLIFF. In Marshall County, 3 miles east of Kingston. A post office from March 2, 1891, to July 31, 1916. No longer in existence, it took its name from a large cliff along Little Glasses Creek, a tributary of the Washita River.

CLIFFORD. In Roger Mills County, 2 miles north of Crawford. A post office from July 18, 1904, to January 15, 1912. No longer in existence. Named for Clifford Hensley, son of Sarah L. Hensley, the first postmaster.

CLIFTON. Present Meeker, in Lincoln County. Post office established March 3, 1892, and name changed to Meeker, May 29, 1903. Named for Clifton Scott, nephew

of Dr. A. C. Scott of Oklahoma City.

CLINE. In Beaver County, 10 miles west of Laverne. A post office from May 5, 1894, to March 31, 1913.

CLINTON. In central Custer County. Post office established May 22, 1903. Named for Clinton F. Irwin, territorial jurist.

CLOUD CHIEF. In central Washita County. A post office from March 29, 1892, to December 30, 1964. County seat of H County, Oklahoma Territory. Named for a sub-chief of the Arapaho.

CLOUDY. In central Pushmataha County, 12 miles northeast of Rattan. Post office established October 21, 1911. It took its name from nearby Cloudy Creek, a tributary of Little River.

CLOVERTON. In southeastern Kiowa County, 9 miles northeast of Mountain Park. A post office from March 4, 1902, to December 31, 1908, it took its name from an important local agricultural product.

CLYDE. In Grant County, 7 miles northwest of Medford. A post office from October 14, 1897, to November 15, 1926. Named for Clyde N. Palmer, later publisher of the *Medford Patriot.*

CLYMER. In Woods County, 10 miles northwest of Aline. A post office from April 9, 1895, to August 31, 1906. No longer in existence, it was named for Charles H. Clymer, first postmaster.

COAL COUNTY. A county in southeastern Oklahoma, created at statehood. It took its name from the county's chief economic product, and was formed from part of Tobucksy County, Choctaw Nation.

COALGATE. Designated county seat of Coal County, June 13, 1908, by proclamation of the governor. Formerly Liddle, the post office name was changed to Coalgate, January 23, 1890. It took its name from nearby coal mines.

COALTON. In Okmulgee County, 4 miles north of Dewar. A post office from August 3, 1909, to February 15, 1941, it took its name from nearby coal mines.

COATSWORTH. In northeastern Johnston County, 5 miles east of Connerville. A post office from April 1, 1903, to January 2, 1907. No longer in existence.

COBB. Present Fort Cobb, in Caddo County. Post office established September 20, 1899, and name changed to Fort Cobb, October 31, 1902. It took its name from nearby site of Fort Cobb, former military post, which had been named for Howell Cobb, secretary of the treasury under President Buchanan.

COBB. In Okmulgee County near Morris. A post office from January 3, 1905, to February 28, 1910, it was named for Eli Cobb, first postmaster.

COGAR. In northern Caddo County, 11 miles west of Minco. A post office from March 25, 1902, to September 30, 1954. Named for Nancy Cougar of Kentucky, a friend of the first postmaster.

COHN. A railroad switch and loading point in Pushmataha County on the Frisco Railroad, 9 miles south of Talihina. Named for William Cohn, gravel quarry operator.

COIN. In northeastern Beaver County, 9 miles northwest of Gate. A post office from August 3, 1895, to April 30, 1914. No longer in existence.

COLBERT. In southern Bryan County. Post office established November 17, 1853. Named for Benjamin F. Colbert, leading early-day resident.

COLBERT'S STATION. A stage stop on the Butterfield Overland Mail route to California, which crossed southeastern Oklahoma, 1858–61. Named for Benjamin F. Colbert, prominent Chickasaw tribal leader and operator of Colbert's Ferry, important Red River crossing. A post office named Colbert's Station operated at the site from August 5, 1873, to June 29, 1881.

COLCORD. In southern Delaware County, 8 miles northeast of Kansas. On February 1, 1930, a nearby post office named Row was moved 1 mile south and its name changed to Colcord. Named for Charles F. Colcord, prominent early-day Oklahoma City resident.

COLD SPRINGS. In Kiowa County, 5 miles south of Roosevelt. A post office from November 25, 1903, to September 15, 1909. It was a widely known real estate development, whose promoters supposedly placed ice in a nearby spring to aid the sale of lots. On January 27, 1913, a nearby post office named Mondamin had its name changed to Cold Springs and continued in operation at the new site until March 15, 1956.

COLDWATER. In northwestern Garfield County, 5 miles west of Hillsdale. A post office from February 2, 1894, to May 15, 1905. No longer in existence.

COLE. In McClain County, 7 miles southeast of Blanchard. A post office from April 2, 1912, to August 31, 1954. Named for Preslie B. Cole of McAlester, townsite owner.

COLEMAN. Formerly Ego. In Johnston County, 9 miles northeast of Milburn. Post office name changed to Coleman, September 10, 1910.

COLEMAN. In Pittsburg County, 3 miles west of Haileyville. Post office established April 2, 1903, and name changed to Craig, December 7, 1905. Named for H. L. Coleman, townsite owner.

COLLINS INSTITUTE. Site in Pontotoc County, 3 miles southeast of Frisco. A well-known Chickasaw Indian school in operation from 1885 to 1905. Named for Judson D. Collins.

COLLINSVILLE. In Tulsa County, 20 miles northeast of Tulsa. Post office established May 26, 1897, as Collins. Its name changed to Collinsville, June 16, 1898. Named for Dr. H. H. Collins, prominent early-day resident.

COLONEL. In Custer County, 2 miles east of Moorewood. A post office from August 7, 1902, to July 31, 1907. No longer in existence, it was named for Colonel D. Garvin, first postmaster.

COLONY. In northeastern Washita County. Post office established January 8, 1896. It took its name from the Seger Colony, founded by John Seger.

COLUMBIA. In eastern Kingfisher County, 8 miles northwest of Crescent. A post office from February 21, 1890, to February 28, 1913. No longer in existence, it was named for Columbus Fash, local merchant.

COMANCHE. Formerly Tucker. In southern Stephens County. Post office name changed to Comanche, January 26, 1893. It took its name from the Comanche Indian tribe.

COMANCHE COUNTY. A county in southwestern Oklahoma, created at statehood from a portion of Comanche County, Oklahoma Territory. It took its name from the Comanche Indian tribe. The origin of the word *Comanche* is uncertain, but it is believed to be from the Spanish *camino ancho*, "broad trail."

COMBS. In southwestern Washita County, 5 miles west of Sentinel. A post office from October 5, 1892, to July 30, 1904. No longer in existence, it was named for William H. Combs, first postmaster.

COMMERCE. Formerly North Miami. In northern Ottawa County. Post office name changed to Commerce, June 1, 1914.

COMPTON. In western Noble County, 7 miles south of Billings. A post office from March 30, 1894, to August 31, 1903. No longer in existence, it was named for Miller L. Compton, first postmaster.

CONCEPTION. In southern Oklahoma County. On September 7, 1892, the post office Rosedale in Cleveland County was moved north into Oklahoma County, to what is now S.W. 44th and Meridian in Oklahoma City. Its name then was changed to Conception. Discontinued April 4, 1895. No longer in existence. Its name comes from Conception, Missouri.

CONCHARTY. In Wagoner County, several miles north of Stonebluff. A post office from November 6, 1894, to September 9, 1897. Named for Concharty Micco, a Creek leader and a delegate to the Dawes Commission.

CONCHO. In central Canadian County. Post office established April 20, 1915. The word is Spanish for "shell"; the post office was named for Charles E. Shell, Indian agent.

CONCORD. In eastern Major County, 5 miles west of Drummond. A post office from April 10, 1894, to February 29, 1904. No longer in existence.

CONDITVILLE. In extreme northeastern corner of Stephens County. A post office from October 12, 1921, to February 28, 1929. Named for W. M. Condit, first postmaster.

CONNERVILLE. In northern Johnston County. Post office established August 6, 1897, and named for George B. Conner, first postmaster.

CONQUEST. In Beaver County, 14 miles west of Laverne. A post office from September 17, 1904, to April 21, 1908. No longer in existence.

CONROY. In southern Beaver County, 6 miles southwest of Elmwood. Post office established February 3, 1904, and name changed to Lakemp, July 26, 1909. Named by Dan T. Quinlan, first postmaster, for Kate Conroy, a relative.

CONSER. In Le Flore County, 6 miles southwest of Heavener. A post office from July 7, 1894, to July 15, 1919. Named for Jane Conser, first postmaster.

CONWAY. In eastern Pontotoc County, 7 miles north of Stonewall. A post office from August 22, 1896, to April 30, 1914. Its name comes from Conway, Missouri.

COODY'S BLUFF. In Nowata County, 6 miles east of Nowata. A post office from May 5, 1860, to December 31, 1955, it was named for Richard Coody, first postmaster.

COOK. In eastern Pottawatomie County, 5 miles north of Maud. A post office from April 18, 1894, to November 15, 1904. No longer in existence, it was named for Randolph Cook, first postmaster.

COOKIETOWN. A rural community in Cotton County, 12 miles west of Temple. The name comes from the circumstance that the proprieter of the cross roads store, Marvin Cornelius, about 1928 applied the name to his mercantile establishment.

COOKSON. In southeastern Cherokee County. Post office established April 11, 1895. Named for John H. Cookson, first postmaster.

COOKSVILLE. In Choctaw County, 9 miles northwest of Hugo. On January 28, 1910, a post office named Speer was established at this site, and, thereafter, the name Cooksville fell into disuse. Named for Albert Cook, a Choctaw, townsite owner.

COOLEY. In southwestern Woodward County, 8 miles northeast of Harmon. A post office from April 17, 1902, to November 30, 1917. Named for Beatrice Cooley, early-day resident.

COON. Present Wann, in northwestern Nowata County. Post office established July 26, 1895, and name changed to Wann, October 13, 1899. It took its name from the nearby Coon Creek, a tributary of the Little Verdigris River.

COOPER. In Blaine County, 5 miles northeast of Hitchcock. A post office from August 9, 1892, to January 31, 1906. No longer in existence.

COOPER. In western Osage County, 8 miles north of Burbank. A post office from August 20, 1923, to October 14, 1939, it was named for Edward E. Cooper, early-day resident.

COOPERTON. In Kiowa County, 9 miles east of Roosevelt. Post office established February 1, 1902. Named for Captain George Cooper, a member of the Payne colony and a early-day settler.

COOSA. In eastern Latimer County, 5 miles south of Red Oak. A post office from April 11, 1894, to June 4, 1896. Its name comes from Coosa, a Creek town in Alabama.

COOWEESCOOWEE. A district of the Cherokee Nation, established in 1856 from the western portion of Saline District. The name was John Ross's Cherokee name.

COO-Y-YAH. Present Pryor, in Mayes County. Post office established January 31, 1882, and name changed to Pryor Creek, April 23, 1887. The name comes from the Cherokee word *ḳuwahi yi*, meaning "mulberry grove."

COPAN. Formerly Weldon. In northern Washington County. Post office name changed to Copan, February 27, 1904. Its name comes from a town in Honduras.

COPASS. In extreme northwest corner of Beaver County. A post office from April 22, 1905, to October 15, 1906. Named for James H. Copass, first postmaster.

COPE. Formerly Darthie. In northeastern Johnston County, 2 miles west of Wapanuka. Post office name changed to Cope, February 4, 1902, and discontinued December 31, 1913. Named for Henry T. Cope, first postmaster.

COPELAND. In Atoka County, 8 miles west of Atoka. A post office from February 13, 1904, to July 31, 1912, it was named for William T. Copeland, first postmaster.

COPELAND. A rural community in northern Delaware County, 5 miles northwest of Grove. Known locally as Copeland Switch. Named for D. R. Copeland, early-day resident.

CORA. In northeastern Custer County, 3 miles southeast of Thomas. A post office from June 30, 1894, to May 15, 1903. No longer in existence, it was named for Cora Mathis, daughter of Felix D. Mathis, first postmaster.

CORA. In northwestern Woods County, 14 miles west of Alva. A post office from May 18, 1905, to February 28, 1914. No longer in existence.

CORALEA. In eastern Harmon County, 7 miles northeast of Gould. A post office from January 16, 1893, to March 30, 1907. No longer in existence, it was named for Coralea Meredith, early-day resident.

CORBETT. Formerly Higbee. In extreme southeastern Cleveland County, 7 miles southeast of Lexington. Post office name changed to Corbett, February 19, 1902, and discontinued January 2, 1907. Named for James P. Corbett, first postmaster.

CORDELL. County seat of Washita County. Post office established October 12, 1892. Present town is several miles west of original site; name of present townsite is New Cordell. Named for Wayne W. Cordell, long-time employee of the Post Office Department.

CORETTA. In southeastern Wagoner County, 6 miles north of Muskogee. A post office from February 7, 1891, to January 9, 1893. On November 16, 1900, a post office named Rex was established at this same site.

CORINNE. In southern Pushmataha County, 19 miles east of Antlers. A post office from August 24, 1904, to September 30, 1958, it was named for Corinne LeSeur, local resident.

CORN. In northeastern Washita County. Post office established April 27, 1896, as Korn; spelling changed to Corn, September 26, 1918. Took its name from the cornfield on which the site of the post office was originally located.

CORNER. In extreme southeastern corner of Pottawatomie County, hence the name. A post office from March 4, 1903, to April 30, 1906. No longer in existence.

CORNISH. In eastern Jefferson County, 2 miles southwest of Ringling. A post office from July 10, 1891, to March 15, 1918. Named for John H. Cornish, rancher.

CORUM. In southwestern Stephens County, 8 miles west of Comanche. A post office from March 27, 1902, to August 31, 1904. No longer in existence, it was named for Corum Tucker, son of Rev. G. M. Tucker, early-day minister.

COTTON COUNTY. A county in southwestern Oklahoma organized August 28, 1912, from the southern portion of Comanche County. Officially proclaimed November 18, 1912, by Governor Lee Cruce, it took its name from the county's principal agricultural product.

COTTONWOOD. In Coal County, 2 miles northeast of Coalgate. A post office from April 8, 1914, to December 31, 1914.

COTTONWOOD. In southeastern Sequoyah County, 4 miles southeast of Muldrow. A post office from March 3, 1882, to June 15, 1909. No longer in existence.

COUCH. In western Beaver County near Boyd. A post office from February 12, 1907, to January 15, 1914. No longer in existence, it was named for Joseph W. Couch, first postmaster.

COUCH. In Craig County near Chelsea. A post office from June 23, 1900, to February 16, 1901. No longer in existence, it was named for Marion W. Couch, first postmaster.

COULSON. In McClain County near Rosedale. A post office from September 30, 1902, to December 31, 1908. No longer in existence, it was named for Charles P. Coulson, first postmaster.

COUNCIL. Formerly Council Grove. Post office name changed to Council, December 7, 1894, and discontinued August 15, 1906. A stop on the Rock Island Railroad, the depot was removed in 1934 and the site is now a part of Oklahoma City. Took its name from the prior post office of Council Grove.

COUNCIL GROVE. Now within the city limits of Oklahoma City. Post office established June 11, 1892, and name changed to Council, December 7, 1894. Council Grove was the name of a nearby trading post established in 1858 by Jesse Chisholm.

COUNCIL HILL. In southwestern Muskogee County. Post office established July 3, 1905. Took its name from a well-known land feature, 5 miles west, Council Hill, used by the Creek Indians for ceremonial purposes.

COUNCIL HOUSE. In Pushmataha County, 2 miles north of Tuskahoma. Site of the Choctaw National Council House. A post office from February 6, 1872, to June 30,

1880. The site is yet maintained by the Choctaw Nation.

COUNTY LINE. On the county line between Carter and Stephens counties 3 miles west of Ratliff City. Post office established June 29, 1928.

COURTNEY. Formerly Watkins. In the southwestern corner of Love County. Known locally as Courtney Flats. Post office name changed to Courtney, August 17, 1886, and discontinued August 23, 1957. Named for H. D. Courtney, prominent early-day resident.

COVE. In Delaware County, 3 miles north of Jay. A post office from April 17, 1903, to May 31, 1916. Took its name from a natural cove at the mouth of Drowning Creek, a tributary of Grand River.

COVINGTON. Formerly Tripp. In Garfield County, 8 miles south of Garber. Post office name changed to Covington, February 24, 1903. Named for John H. Covington, prominent early-day resident.

COW CREEK. In extreme northeastern corner of Le Flore County. A post office from September 14, 1912, to July 31, 1913. It took its name from nearby Cow Creek, a tributary of Mountain Fork River.

COWDEN. In eastern Washita County, 7 miles east of Cloud Chief. A post office from January 23, 1901, to January 15, 1908. No longer in existence, it was named for Charles H. Cowden, townsite owner.

COWETA. In Wagoner County, 13 miles southeast of Broken Arrow. Post office established May 24, 1897. It took its name from Koweta Mission, established by the Presbyterian Board of Foreign Missions in 1843 as a school for the Creek Indians. The name is from a Creek town on the Chattahoochee River in Alabama.

COWLINGTON. In northwestern Le Flore County, 12 miles northwest of Spiro. A post office from August 27, 1884, to October 31, 1953, it was named for A. F. Cowling, prominent early-day settler.

COX. In northeastern Caddo County, 2 miles northwest of Cogar. A post office from January 4, 1904, to July 30, 1910. Named for Frank Cox, local resident.

COX CITY. In southeastern Grady County, 16 miles southeast of Rush Springs. A post office from March 23, 1927, to April 10, 1964. Named for Edwin B. Cox of Ardmore, oil producer.

COY. In extreme northwestern corner of Woods County. A post office from September 28, 1904, to June 30, 1930. No longer in existence.

COYLE. In eastern Logan County. Townsite plat filed in 1899 as Iowa City. Post office established May 5, 1900. Named for William Coyle of Guthrie.

CRAFT. In Ellis County, 2 miles north of Arnett. A post office from May 25, 1901, to February 14, 1906. No longer in existence, it was named for Elgy Craft, first postmaster.

CRAIG. In McCurtain County, 2 miles southwest of Eagletown. Named for John Craig, a lumberman.

CRAIG. Formerly Coleman. In Pittsburg County, 3 miles west of Haileyville. Post office name changed to Craig, December 7, 1905, and discontinued March 31, 1919. Named for William Craig, local rancher.

CRAIG COUNTY. A county in northeastern Oklahoma. Created at statehood and named for Granville Craig, prominent Cherokee.

CRATERVILLE PARK. In Comanche County, 5 miles north of Cache. A post office from August 4, 1924, to August 31, 1933. The name was coined with reference to the surrounding Wichita Mountains. Upon the expansion of the Wichita Wild Life Refuge, the park was moved to a new location, 2 miles west of Lugert.

CRAVENS. In Latimer County, 7 miles southeast of Wilburton. A post office from November 3, 1903, to February 15, 1916. No longer in existence. Named for John Cravens, railroad official. The original name of the community was Brown Prairie.

CRAWFORD. In Roger Mills County, 6 miles northwest of Roll. Post office established September 12, 1902. Named for Louis Crawford, early-day rancher.

CRAWFORD COUNTY. A county organized by Arkansas Territory, comprising an area approximately 150 miles long and 40 miles wide in the central part of present-day Oklahoma adjacent to Arkansas. Established October 18, 1820, and Fort Smith designated the county seat. Abolished upon allotment of the land to the Indian nations. Named for William H. Crawford, secretary of the treasury under President Monroe.

CREEK. In Okfuskee County, 9 miles west of Okfuskee. Post office established April 16, 1896, and name changed to Welty, October 12, 1905. Named for the Creek Nation.

CREEK AGENCY. In Muskogee County, northwest of Muskogee. A post office from June 7, 1843, to October 16, 1872, serving the Creek Indian Agency. On January 21, 1852, the post office was moved to the south side of the Arkansas River, about 5 miles southwest of the previous location.

CREEK COUNTY. A county in east-central Oklahoma, created at statehood. Intended to be named Moman County in honor of the mother of Moman Pruiett, the name was changed at the last moment by the Constitutional Convention; in the alphabetical list of counties in the engrossed copy of the constitution, Creek County appears following Mayes County. Named for the Creek Nation. The word is from the term "Ochese Creek Indians," used by the early British settlers.

CREKOLA. In Muskogee County, 6 miles southwest of Muskogee. A post office from July 18, 1907, to February 15, 1921. The name was coined from the words Creek and Oklahoma.

CRESCENT. In western Logan County. Post office established February 21, 1890. It took its name from the crescent-shaped ring of nearby oak timber.

CRETA. Formerly Era. In Jackson County, 7 miles southwest of Olustee. Post office name changed to Creta, February 20, 1904, and discontinued October 31, 1904. It took its name from the Latin word for chalk.

CRINER. In McClain County, 12 miles west of Purcell. A post office from June 2, 1910, to October 15, 1928. It took its name from nearby Criner Creek, a branch of the Washita River, which, in turn, had been named for George A. Criner, early-day rancher.

CRINERVILLE. In Carter County, 6 miles southwest of Ardmore. A post office from November 10, 1885, to October 31, 1887, it was named for John Criner, prominent early-day settler.

CRISTA. In southwestern Jackson County near Olustee. A post office from April 5, 1900, to October 31, 1902. No longer in existence, it was named for William W. Crista, first postmaster.

CRITTENDEN. In Cherokee County, 5 miles west of Tahlequah. A post office from October 8, 1896, to November 30, 1900, it was named for Martha Crittenden, townsite allotee.

CROMWELL. In northeastern Seminole County. Post office established May 17, 1924. Named for Joe I. Cromwell, oil producer.

CROPPER. In Garfield County, 3 miles east of Breckenridge. A post office from January 12, 1900, to January 15, 1908, it was named for James L. Cropper, townsite owner.

CROSBY. Present Hinton, in Caddo County. Post office established April 18, 1902, and name changed to Hinton, July 5, 1902. Named for Herbert D. Crosby, county attorney of I County.

CROSS. In southern Harper County near May. A post office from January 6, 1910, to July 31, 1913. No longer in existence, it was named for John L. Cross, first postmaster.

CROWDER. In Choctaw County, 8 miles southeast of Boswell. A post office from January 18, 1898, to January 15, 1904. Named for Richard C. Crowder, local stockman.

CROWDER. Formerly Juanita. In Pittsburg County, 15 miles north of McAlester. Post office name changed to Crowder, June 4, 1904. Named for Dr. W. E. Crowder, prominent early-day physician.

CROWE. In southeastern Beaver County. Post office established May 10, 1899; its site and name changed to Busch, Roger Mills County, March 18, 1901.

CROWSON. In southeastern Creek County, 10 miles southeast of Bristow. A post office from February 4, 1905, to March 15, 1919, it was named for Jessie P. Crowson, first postmaster.

CRUCE. In Stephens County, 8 miles northeast of Duncan. A post office from June 13, 1910, to August 15, 1932, it was named for Lee Cruce, second governor of Oklahoma.

CRUM CREEK. In Pushmataha County, 14 miles southwest of Tuskahoma. A post office from February 9, 1916, to July 30, 1927. Took its name from nearby Crumb Creek, a branch of the Kiamichi River.

CRUSHER. In southeastern Murray County, 4 miles south of Dougherty. Post office established May 11, 1904, and name changed to Arbuckle, August 21, 1911. Took its name from nearby rock crusher.

CRYSTAL. In southern Atoka County, 18 miles southeast of Atoka. A post office from September 5, 1911, to December 31, 1955. It took its name from nearby Crystal Springs, a well-known camp site.

CRYSTAL. Present Maramec, in Pawnee County. Post office established January 22, 1894, and name changed to Maramec, April 8, 1903. Took its name from nearby Crystal Spring.

CULLEN. In Caddo County, 6 miles northeast of Gracemont. Post office from September 3, 1903, to July 15, 1907. No longer in existence, it was named for Florence Cullen, first postmaster.

CULLIE. In Rogers County, 5 miles north of Catoosa. A post office from May 28, 1909, to July 15, 1912. No longer in existence, it was named for Cullie Fry, early-day resident.

CUMBERLAND. In eastern Marshall County. Post office established March 31, 1894. Named for the Cumberland Presbyterian Church, an organization active in local mission work.

CUPID. In western Harper County, 5 miles southeast of Laverne. A post office from June 20, 1895, to April 5, 1916. No longer in existence.

CURL. In western Blaine County, 3 miles west of Eagle City. A post office established June 4, 1901; post office moved and name changed to Harper, Dewey County, October 25, 1901. Named for G. T. Curl, long-time local resident.

CURLEW. In northwestern Tillman County, 6 miles west of Chattanooga. A post office from September 22, 1902, to October 14, 1904. No longer in existence. Took its name from the curlew, a member of the scolopacidae family.

CURRY. In Pottawatomie County, 3 miles south of Shawnee. A post office from May 27, 1899, to January 15, 1900. No longer in existence, it was named for C. D. Curry, local landowner.

CURTIS. In Woodward County,

14 miles east of Woodward. A post office from October 3, 1894, to October 31, 1952. Named for Nels Curtis, of Piedmont, Kansas.

CURTY. In the southwestern corner of McClain County. A post office from April 5, 1906, to February 28, 1914. No longer in existence.

CUSHING. In southeastern Payne County. Post office established November 10, 1891. Named for Marshall Cushing, private secretary to John Wanamaker, postmaster general.

CUSTER. Formerly Ivanhoe, which had been situated 2 miles south, in the southeastern corner of Beaver County. Post office name changed to Custer, October 28, 1891, and name changed to Madison, June 17, 1904. Named for Major General George A. Custer.

CUSTER. Formerly Graves. In Custer County, 8 miles northeast of Arapaho. Post office name changed to Custer, September 28, 1904. Named for Major General George A. Custer.

CUSTER COUNTY. A county in west-central Oklahoma, comprising the same area as Custer County, Oklahoma Territory. Named for Major General George A. Custer.

CUTHBERT. In extreme northwestern Roger Mills County. A post office from June 7, 1904, to July 31, 1904. Named for Cuthbert Harris, son of Robert Harris, prominent local resident.

CUTTHROAT GAP. Located in extreme northwestern section of the Wichita Wild Life Refuge. Took its name from a savage massacre of a Kiowa village by an Osage hunting party in 1833.

CYRIL. In southeastern Caddo County. Post office established August 9, 1906, and named for Cyril Lookingglass, townsite owner.

D

D COUNTY. Original designation for Dewey County, Oklahoma Territory. Name changed to Dewey County, November 8, 1898.

DACOMA. Formerly Zula. In Woods County, 12 miles southeast of Alva. Post office name changed to Dacoma, October 31, 1904. The name was coined from the words Dakota and Oklahoma.

DAGGETT. A townsite filed October 25, 1900, in Lincoln County, adjoining present-day Davenport. Named for Alfred Daggett, townsite owner.

DAGUE. In northern Texas County, 10 miles northwest of Hooker. A post office from December 27, 1904, to December 31, 1910. No longer in existence.

DAIL CITY. Original townsite name for Mooreland in Woodward County. Townsite plat filed June 10, 1901. Named for J. H. Dail, townsite owner.

DAISY. In northeastern corner of Atoka County. Post office established April 5, 1906. In 1897, a post office named Etna had been discontinued at this approximate location. Named for Daisy Beck, local girl.

DAISY. In Harper County, 5 miles east of Buffalo. A post office from December 2, 1902, to October 14, 1905. No longer in existence.

DALE. In Pottawatomie County, 7 miles northwest of Shawnee. Post office established October 26, 1893. Named for Frank Dale, territorial jurist.

DAMON. In Latimer County, 6 miles southwest of Wilburton. A post office from February 5, 1906, to March 15, 1934. Its name comes from the citizen of Syracuse known in history as the hostage for Pythias.

DANE. In Major County, 7 miles southwest of Fairview. A post office from August 3, 1895, to July 31, 1909.

DANNENBURG. A former rural community in Adair County, 3 miles north of Stilwell. Named for Henry Dannenburg, early-day merchant.

DARCIA. In Pittsburg County, 6 miles northwest of McAlester. A post office from February 5, 1907, to November 16, 1909. Named for John Darcia of Chicago, rancher.

DARLINGTON. In Canadian County, 5 miles northwest of El Reno. Cheyenne-Arapaho Indian Agency established there in 1870. First newspaper in Oklahoma Territory, *Cheyenne Transporter* pub-

lished there in 1879. A post office from April 2, 1873, to July 31, 1918. Named for Brinton Darlington, Quaker Indian agent.

DARROW. In northern Blaine County, 4 miles southwest of Okeene. A post office from May 1, 1905, to June 29, 1918. Named for Seth Darrow, townsite owner.

DARTHIE. In northeastern Johnston County, 2 miles west of Wapanucka. Post office established April 12, 1900, and name changed to Cope, February 4, 1902.

DARWIN. In Pushmataha County, 9 miles west of Antlers. A post office from July 31, 1905, to March 14, 1955.

DAVENPORT. In eastern Lincoln County. Post office established March 29, 1892. Named for her family by Nettie Davenport, first postmaster.

DAVIDSON. Formerly Olds. In southern Tillman County, 11 miles south of Frederick. Post office name changed to Davidson, June 20, 1903. Named for A. J. Davidson of St. Louis, director of the Frisco Railroad.

DAVIS. In Murray County. Post office established March 1, 1890, and named for Samuel H. Davis, prominent early-day resident and merchant.

DAVIS CITY. A townsite in northern Lincoln County, 2 miles west of Agra. Townsite plat filed April 4, 1895. No longer in existence, it was named for Warren B. Davis, townsite owner.

DAWES. In Ottawa County, 6 miles northwest of Miami. A post office from May 29, 1901, to August 31, 1908. Named for Senator Henry L. Dawes of Connecticut, chairman of the Dawes Commission.

DAWSON. Now within the city limits of Tulsa. A post office from February 28, 1895, to October 31, 1949, it was named for Wilbur A. Dawson, first postmaster.

DAY. In southeastern Noble County, 5 miles southwest of Morrison. A post office from July 5, 1899, to November 15, 1905. No longer in existence, it was named for William R. Day, secretary of state under President McKinley.

DAY COUNTY. A county in Oklahoma Territory, abolished at statehood, comprising the northern portion of Roger Mills County and the southern portion of Ellis County. Named for Charles Day, the contractor who built the first courthouse at Ioland.

DAYTON. Formerly Lewis. In Atoka County, 5 miles south of Atoka. Post office name changed to Dayton, January 21, 1909, and name changed to Tushka, June 9, 1909.

DAYTON. In southeastern corner of Grant County. A post office from February 11, 1895, to March 15, 1904. No longer in existence. Its name comes from Dayton, Ohio.

DEE. In western Beckham County, 4 miles west of Erick. A post office from December 5, 1900, to May 30, 1903. No longer in existence.

DEE. In eastern Cimarron County, 6 miles southeast of Keyes. A post office from October 15, 1906, to September 15, 1913. No longer in existence.

DEER CREEK. Formerly Orie. In Grant County, 12 miles east of Medford. Post office name changed to Deer Creek, February 27, 1899. Took its name from nearby Deer Creek, a tributary of the Salt Fork of the Arkansas River.

DEESE. In Carter County, 8 miles northwest of Ardmore. A post office from January 21, 1904, to September 15, 1913, it was named for Robert N. Deese, first postmaster.

DEIGHTON. In southeastern Woodward County, 6 miles northeast of Richmond. A post office from November 24, 1899, to November 15, 1908, it was named for Alfronzo Deighton, early-day resident.

DEL CITY. A municipality adjoining Oklahoma City on the southeast. Townsite name, by plat filed September 19, 1946, is Epperly Heights. Named for Delaphene Campbell, daughter of George Epperly, townsite owner.

DELA. In Pushmataha County, 6 miles southeast of Antlers. A post office from May 12, 1920, to October 31, 1954. Named for Dela M. Whitaker, local schoolteacher.

DELANEY. In Rogers County, 5 miles east of Claremore. A post office from October 27, 1909, to August 31, 1912. No longer in existence.

DELAWARE. A district of the Cherokee Nation, created by the Cherokee National Council on November 6, 1840.

DELAWARE. In Nowata County, 5 miles north of Nowata. Post office established March 19, 1898. Named for the Delaware tribe of Indians.

DELAWARE COUNTY. A county in eastern Oklahoma, created at statehood. It took its name from the Delaware tribe. The tribe, Lenápe in their tongue, received the name Delaware from the De la Warr, or Delaware, River in Pennsylvania.

DELAWARE RIDGE. A prominent land feature in Pontotoc County south of Ada and a well-known landmark on the California Road, surveyed in 1849.

DELENA. In central Ellis County, 8 miles northeast of Arnett. A post office from March 5, 1903, to December 14, 1912. No longer in existence.

DELFIN. In extreme southwestern corner of Cimarron County. A post office from October 10, 1907, to September 15, 1926. No longer in existence, it was named for Delfin Espinosa, local sheep rancher.

DELHI. In Beckham County, 8 miles south of Sayre. Post office established January 16, 1893. Its name comes from the capital city of India.

DELIA. In central Pontotoc County, adjoining Ada. A post office from January 13, 1906, to September 15, 1906. Named for Delia Johnson, wife of Samuel Johnson, early-day resident.

DELNORTE. In southwestern Garfield County near Drummond. A post office from December 14, 1896, to October 15, 1901. No longer in existence.

DELPHINE. In Stephens County, 8 miles northwest of Duncan. A post office from October 29, 1921, to March 31, 1923. Named for Delphine Cahill, wife of Leo P. Cahill, first postmaster.

DELTIS. In Dewey County, 6 miles southeast of Camargo. A post office from March 20, 1900, to January 31, 1907. No longer in existence.

DEMPSEY. In southwestern Roger Mills County, 12 miles southwest of Cheyenne. A post office from June 23, 1903, to November 15, 1913.

DENMAN. A rural community in Latimer County 2 miles east of Red Oak. Named for Herbert Denman, coal mine operator.

DENNIS. Present Erick, in Beckham County. Post office established February 8, 1900, and name changed to Erick, November 16, 1901.

DENNIS. In Delaware County, 6 miles southwest of Grove. A post office from March 25, 1914, to January 31, 1956, it was named for Peter Dennis, local resident.

DENOYA. In western Osage County, 3 miles southwest of Shidler. Known locally as Whizbang. A post office from December 31, 1921, to September 30, 1942, it was named for Joseph F. DeNoya, prominent Osage.

DENT. In southeastern Lincoln County, 2 miles east of Prague. A post office from May 23, 1894, to August 30, 1903. No longer in existence.

DENTON. In northwestern Stephens County, adjoining the Comanche County line. A post office from April 23, 1902, to September 17, 1906. No longer in existence.

DENVER. In Cleveland County, 6 miles east of Norman. A post office from May 24, 1892, to April 14, 1906. Its name comes from Denver, Colorado.

DEPEW. In Creek County, 7 miles southwest of Bristow. The railroad name for this town was Halls. Post office established April 12, 1901. Named for Chauncey M. Depew, United States senator from New York.

DETROIT. In Woodward County, 10 miles south of Woodward. A post office from February 19, 1901, to February 18, 1907. No longer in existence. Its name comes from Detroit, Michigan.

DEVOL. In Cotton County, 6 miles southeast of Grandfield. Post office established November 30, 1907. Named for J. F. DeVol, first postmaster.

DEWAR. In Okmulgee County, 3 miles east of Henryetta. Post office established April 27, 1909. Named for William P. Dewar, official of the Missouri, Oklahoma and Gulf Railroad.

DEWEY. Present Weatherford, in Custer County. Post office established August 10, 1898, and name changed to Weatherford, October 28, 1898. Named for Admiral George Dewey, hero of the Battle of Manila Bay, May 1, 1898.

DEWEY. In Washington County, 4 miles north of Bartlesville. A post office established April 19, 1899. Named for Admiral George Dewey.

DEWEY COUNTY. A county in west-central Oklahoma, comprising the same area as Dewey County, Oklahoma Territory. Named for Admiral George Dewey.

DEWRIGHT. In Seminole County, 7 miles southeast of Maud. A post office from June 24, 1931, to July 15, 1939, it was named for Dewey Wright, first postmaster.

DEXTER. Present Clayton, in Pushmataha County. Post office established March 31, 1894, and name changed to Clayton, April 5, 1907. Named for Dexter Chapman, early-day resident.

DIAL. In southern Greer County,

5 miles northwest of Martha. A post office from June 27, 1890, to September 4, 1890, it was named for D. H. Dial, local early-day resident.

DIAMOND. In southwestern Stephens County, 5 miles west of Comanche. A post office from July 14, 1903, to August 31, 1904. No longer in existence, it was named by a local religious group in honor of its seventy-fifth anniversary.

DIBBLE. In McClain County, 15 miles west of Purcell. Post office established May 22, 1894. Named for John and James Dibble, local ranchers.

DICKSON. Formerly Chaddick. In Oklahoma County, 2 miles west of Nicoma Park. Post office name changed to Dickson, July 17, 1896, and discontinued August 15, 1906.

DIGHTON. In southern Okmulgee County, 6 miles northeast of Henryetta. First known locally as Bartlett. A post office from February 13, 1913, to October 31, 1949. Named for Dighton Harding, son of M. B. Harding, first postmaster.

DILL. Present Lone Wolf, in Kiowa County. Townsite plat filed December 7, 1901. Named for D. S. Dill, attorney and banker.

DILL. In Washita County, 8 miles west of Cordell. Post office established August 9, 1902, and name changed to Dill City, February 1, 1944. Named for D. S. Dill.

DILLARD. In Carter County, 16 miles west of Ardmore. A post office from November 22, 1924, to June 30, 1955. Named for Lee H. Dillard, Choctaw allotee.

DILL CITY. Formerly Dill. Post office name changed to Dill City, February 1, 1944. Its name comes from earlier post office of Dill.

DILLEY. In Garfield County, 4 miles northeast of Covington. A post office from March 2, 1895, to November 15, 1905. Named for Missouri relatives of the husband of the first postmaster, Cora Houghland.

DILLON. Present Eagle City, in Blaine County. Post office established July 26, 1902, and name changed to Eagle City, September 4, 1909. Named for John H. Dillon, early-day county treasurer of Blaine County.

DILTSTON. In Tillman County, 5 miles south of Frederick. A post office from February 15, 1903, to July 30, 1904, it was named for John M. Dilts, first postmaster.

DILWORTH. In Kay County, 10 miles northwest of Newkirk. A post office from March 17, 1917, to March 30, 1929, it was named for Charles A. Dilworth, townsite owner.

DILYA. In northeastern Cimarron County, 6 miles northeast of Keyes. A post office from August 22, 1906, to January 31, 1912. No longer in existence.

DISNEY. In northeastern Mayes County. Post office established May

21, 1938. Named for Wesley E. Disney, member of Congress.

DIX. In Pawnee County, 6 miles southeast of Cleveland. Post office name changed to Dix from Dixie on March 20, 1905, to avoid confusion with another post office named Dixie, and discontinued December 14, 1905.

DIXIE. In Pawnee County, 6 miles southeast of Cleveland. Post office established May 10, 1898. Name changed to Dix, March 20, 1905. Named for Dixie Jordan, local resident.

DIXIE. In southeastern Stephens County, 8 miles northwest of Healdton. A post office from August 19, 1886, to June 15, 1931.

DOAKSVILLE. An important early-day settlement in Choctaw County, adjoining Fort Towson. The Fort Towson post office operated under the name Doaksville from November 11, 1847, to June 12, 1903. Named for Josiah Doak, prominent early-day resident.

DOAN'S CROSSING. In extreme southeastern Jackson County. An important early-day crossing on the Red River. Named for Jonathan W. Doan, who with his nephew, C. F. Doan, in 1874 began extensive trading operations on the Texas side of the crossing.

DOBY. In Cimarron County, 4 miles northwest of Boise City. A post office from February 8, 1908, to April 30, 1914. No longer in existence.

DOBY SPRINGS. Formerly Ballaire. In Harper County, 8 miles west of Buffalo. Post office name changed to Doby Springs, January 13, 1908, and discontinued April 29, 1922. Named for C. C. Doby, townsite owner.

DODGE. Formerly Hill. In northeastern Delaware County, 5 miles east of Grove. Post office name changed to Dodge, November 20, 1901, and discontinued August 15, 1941.

DOE CREEK. In the southwestern corner of Woodward County. A post office from October 2, 1916, to July 15, 1918. No longer in existence.

DOLBERG. In southwestern Pontotoc County, 4 miles west of Roff. A post office from November 18, 1895, to May 14, 1915. Named by E. W. Westhoff for his former home in Germany.

DOMBEY. In western Beaver County, 21 miles west of Beaver. A post office from April 18, 1904, to February 28, 1950. It was named for a character in a novel of Charles Dickens.

DONNELLY. In southern Noble County, about 5 miles south of Perry. A post office from May 2, 1900, to April 30, 1901. No longer in existence, it was named for Frank Donnelly, first postmaster.

DORA. In southwestern Seminole County near Konawa. A post office from July 17, 1906, to December 31, 1909. No longer in existence.

DORA. In eastern Sequoyah County, 6 miles north of Moffett. A post office from December 11, 1918, to November 29, 1919. No longer in existence. The post office had previously been located in Crawford County, Arkansas. Named for Dora Hood, local resident.

DORA. In central Texas County. A post office from October 3, 1906, to June 16, 1907. No longer in existence, it was named for Dora Culbertson, wife of the first postmaster.

DORIS. In western Woodward County, 10 miles southeast of Fargo. Post office established July 6, 1901, and name changed to Keenan, February 18, 1910.

DOT. Present Blair, Jackson County. Post office established September 13, 1893, and name changed to Blair, August 26, 1901. Named for Dot Zinn, daughter of townsite developer.

DOT. In Pontotoc County near Roff. A post office from October 8, 1904, to April 15, 1905. No longer in existence.

DOTSON. In Nowata County, 8 miles east of Lenapah. A post office from October 22, 1901, to September 30, 1903. No longer in existence, it was named for Robert Dotson, first postmaster.

DOUGHERTY. In southern Murray County. First known locally as Henderson Flat. Post office established September 3, 1887. Named for William Dougherty of Gainesville, Texas, a banker.

DOUGLAS. Formerly Onyx. In Garfield County, 5 miles southwest of Covington. Post office name changed to Douglas, February 25, 1903. Named for Douglas Frantz, son of a prominent Enid family.

DOUGLAS. In northeastern corner of Oklahoma County. A post office from May 12, 1894, to June 15, 1900. No longer in existence, it was named for Selwyn Douglas, prominent Oklahoma City civic leader.

DOUTHAT. In Ottawa County, 2 miles south of Picher. Post office established March 17, 1917. Named for Zahn A. Douthat, townsite owner.

DOVER. In central Kingfisher County. Known originally as Red Fork Station. Post office established March 1, 1890. Its name comes from Dover, England.

DOW. In Pittsburg County, 11 miles southeast of McAlester. A post office from December 7, 1898, to February 28, 1964. Named for Andrew Dow, coal producer.

DOWNEY. In Roger Mills County, 2 miles east of Roll. A post office from July 14, 1903, to June 15, 1909. No longer in existence, it was named for James M. Downey, first postmaster.

DOWNS. In Kingfisher County, 1 mile north of Cashion. Post office established August 12, 1889; name changed to Cashion and post office moved to new location May 14, 1900. Named for Charles Downs, early-day surveyor.

DOXEY. Formerly Pior. In Beckham County, 3 miles northeast of Sayre. Post office name changed to Doxey, December 5, 1902, and discontinued May 29, 1931. Name adopted from that of a former town of Doxey located to the northwest.

DOXEY. Present Berlin, in Roger Mills County. Post office established January 23, 1894, and name changed to Berlin, September 2, 1896. Named for Sam Doxie, local rancher.

DOYLE. In Stephens County, 15 miles east of Marlow. A post office from June 29, 1897, to February 28, 1934, it was named for Doyle Harrison, early-day settler.

DRACE. In Noble County, 6 miles northeast of Perry. First known locally as Black Bear. A post office from April 17, 1894, to October 14, 1905, it was named for James A. Drace, prominent Perry resident.

DRAGGER. In southeastern Mayes County, about 5 miles east of Locust Grove. A post office from May 25, 1905, to December 31, 1908. No longer in existence, it was named for Lewis Dragger, first postmaster.

DRAKE. In southern Murray County, 6 miles east of Dougherty. A post office from April 22, 1901, to July 31, 1920. Named for Sam and Block Drake, brothers, local ranchers.

DRESDEN. Formerly Lou and present Gene Autry, in Carter County. Post office name changed to Dresden, November 22, 1883, and to Berwyn, September 1, 1887. Its name comes from Dresden, Germany.

DREW. In Caddo County, 6 miles southeast of Eakly. A post office from March 8, 1902, to August 31, 1906. No longer in existence.

DRIFTWOOD. In Alfalfa County, 8 miles north of Cherokee. A post office from May 12, 1894, to October 31, 1959. Took its name from nearby Driftwood Creek, a branch of Medicine River, a tributary of the Cimarron River.

DRISCOLL. In eastern Woodward County, 6 miles southeast of Quinlan. A post office from September 27, 1898, to January 15, 1914. No longer in existence.

DRUMM. Present Burlington, in Alfalfa County. Post office established June 6, 1906, and name changed to Burlington, August 21, 1907. In July, 1907, plans were formulated to change the name to Wheaton but were not completed. Named for Major Andrew Drumm, prominent rancher.

DRUMMOND. In Garfield County, 10 miles southwest of Enid. Post office established July 17, 1901. Named for Harry Drummond, an official of the Blackwell, Enid and Southwestern Railway.

DRUMRIGHT. In northwestern Creek County. Post office established December 28, 1912. First known locally as Fulkerson. Named for Aaron Drumright, townsite owner.

73

DRYDEN. In Harmon County, 7 miles northeast of Hollis. A post office from June 30, 1892, to January 31, 1919. Named for John Dryden, English poet and dramatist.

DUCKPOND. In Beaver County, about 10 miles south of Beaver. A post office from November 12, 1906, to December 31, 1908. No longer in existence.

DUDLEY. In Lincoln County, 3 miles west of Carney. Townsite plat filed April 11, 1905. No longer in existence.

DUDLEY. In Roger Mills County, about 5 miles west of Moorewood. A post office from October 31, 1904, to July 31, 1907. No longer in existence.

DUKE. In western Jackson County, 12 miles west of Altus. Post office established September 11, 1890. Named for F. B. Duke, territorial jurist.

DULAND. In Choctaw County, 4 miles south of Soper. A post office from November 20, 1919, to December 30, 1922. No longer in existence.

DUNBAR. Formerly Chilton. In Jackson County, 7 miles southeast of Altus. Post office name changed to Dunbar, March 21, 1892, and discontinued June 15, 1905. No longer in existence. Named for the maiden name, Dunn, of the mother of the first postmaster, Joseph C. Penwright.

DUNBAR. In Pushmataha County, 17 miles north of Antlers. A post office from May 5, 1925, to January 15, 1956.

DUNCAN. County seat of Stephens County. Post office established April 7, 1884. Named for William Duncan, intermarried Chickasaw, townsite allotee.

DUNDEE. Local name for McMan, in Carter County. Named for Dundee-Christopher Oil Company, which donated the site for the school.

DUNLAP. In Harper County, 5 miles northwest of Supply. A post office from August 28, 1913, to May 30, 1935. Named for Homer H. Dunlap, of Oklahoma City, townsite owner.

DURANT. County seat of Bryan County. Record Town for Recording District No. 25, Indian Territory. Post office established March 8, 1882. From February 20, 1879, to July 11, 1881, an earlier post office, known as Durant Station, had been in operation at this site. Named for the well-known Choctaw family of which Dickson Durant was the prominent member.

DURHAM. In Roger Mills County, 12 miles northwest of Roll. Post office established May 15, 1902. Named for Dora Durham Morris, first postmaster.

DURWOOD. Formerly Yellow Hills. In Carter County, 7 miles east of Ardmore. Post office name changed to Durwood, September 11, 1891. On April 8, 1913, another post office was established a few miles east in Marshall County and designated New Durwood. Its name was changed to Durwood on October 11, 1913; in 1926, the post office was moved to Carter County. The name was intended to be Deerwood, but through error the Post Office Department established the post office under the name Durwood.

DUSTIN. Formerly Spokogee. In northeastern Hughes County, 12 miles east of Wetumka. Post office name changed to Dustin, May 9, 1904. Named for Henry C. Dustin of Cleveland, Ohio, president of the Fort Smith and Western Railway.

DUTTON. In western Grady County, 6 miles west of Pocasset. Post office from May 5, 1902, to November 15, 1906. No longer in existence. Named for William R. Dutton, at that time postmaster at Anadarko.

DWIGHT. In Pittsburg County, 3 miles northeast of Hartshorne and located at Jones Academy. A post office from October 4, 1895, to February 28, 1913, it was named for Simon T. Dwight, prominent Choctaw.

DWIGHT MISSION. Located in Sequoyah County at Marble City. Established in Indian Territory in 1829 by the American Board of Foreign Missions as a mission to the Western Cherokees. The Board acquired the buildings at Nicksville and converted them for use as a seminary. One of the most important educational efforts in Indian

Territory prior to the Civil War, it was named for Timothy Dwight, president of Yale University.

DYCHE. In extreme northwestern corner of Major County. A post office from November 8, 1913, to October 31, 1914. No longer in existence, it was named for William B. Dyche, first postmaster.

DYKE. In western Blaine County, 2 miles northwest of Eagle City. A post office from August 11, 1894, to September 15, 1906. No longer in existence, it was named for John R. Dyke, first postmaster.

E

E COUNTY. Original designation for Day County, Oklahoma Territory.

EAGLE. A county in Apukshunnubbee District, Choctaw Nation.

EAGLE. In Craig County, 8 miles southwest of Welch. A post office from June 30, 1890, to August 14, 1906. No longer in existence.

EAGLE CHIEF. In southwestern Alfalfa County, 2 miles west of Carmen. Post office established January 17, 1894, and name changed to Augusta, July 13, 1895.

EAGLE CITY. Formerly Dillon. In western Blaine County, 8 miles south of Canton. Post office name changed to Eagle City, September 4, 1909.

EAGLEPOINT. Present Lequire, in southern Haskell County, 9

miles southwest of McCurtain. Post office established April 23, 1901, and name changed to Lequire, December 12, 1906.

EAGLETOWN. In extreme eastern McCurtain County. Site of Stockbridge Mission, established 1836, where Cyrus Byington compiled his monumental *Dictionary of the Choctaw Language*. Post office established July 1, 1834. Prior to December 16, 1892, the official name for the post office was Eagle Town. Named for the many eagles that nested in nearby swamp along the Mountain Fork River.

EAKLY. In Caddo County, 13 miles west of Binger. Post office established March 25, 1902. Named for Akly Montague, daughter of Charles Montague, local early-day resident; the initial letter was added by the Post Office Department.

EARL. In Johnston County, 2 miles northwest of Mannsville. A post office from November 3, 1893, to October 15, 1908. No longer in existence.

EARLSBORO. Formerly Loftis. In Pottawatomie County, 7 miles east of Tecumseh. The townsite plat name is Earlsborough. Post office name changed to Earlsboro, June 12, 1895. Named for James Earls, popular local Negro barber.

EASON. In southwestern Pottawatomie County, 5 miles southwest of Trousdale. A post office from November 20, 1893, to February 15, 1907. No longer in existence, it was named for Lou M. Eason, first postmaster.

EAST ENID. A separate post office from July 29, 1913, to June 30, 1922, and now University Station, Enid.

EASTMAN. In Love County, 9 miles northwest of Marietta. A post office from March 2, 1891, to July 15, 1916, it was named for Charles E. Eastman, prominent Chickasaw.

EAST MUSKOGEE. A separate post office from June 21, 1912, to July 31, 1924.

EATON. In Nowata County, 8 miles east of Lenapah. A post office from October 28, 1892, to January 26, 1928, it was named for William Eaton, local merchant.

ECHO. In Delaware County, 5 miles northwest of Grove. Post office from July 10, 1882, to December 31, 1909. Site now inundated by Grand Lake o' the Cherokees.

ECHOTA. In Adair County, 8 miles west of Stilwell. A post office from July 8, 1921, to December 31, 1937. Its name comes from the traditional capital of the Eastern Cherokees in Georgia.

ECONTUCHKA. In extreme northwestern Seminole County. A post office from September 15, 1881, to November 30, 1907. On October 19, 1899, the post office was established slightly to the west at a new site in the Pottawatomie Nation. The name is the Seminole and Creek word meaning a "surveyed line."

ECTER. In southwestern Beaver County near Gray. Post office established October 22, 1906, and name changed to Plainview, November 7, 1910.

EDDY. Formerly Osborne. In Kay County, 7 miles southwest of Blackwell. Post office name changed to Eddy, January 3, 1901, and discontinued February 22, 1957. Named for Ed E. Peckham, son of E. L. Peckham, railroad developer.

EDEN. In central Payne County. Post office from April 13, 1895, to June 30, 1902. No longer in existence. Its name comes from the Biblical Garden of Eden.

EDGEWOOD. In Garfield County, 6 miles northwest of Billings. A post office from June 21, 1898, to November 15, 1906. No longer in existence. It took its name from the circumstance that the post office was located on the edge of a wooded area.

EDGEWOOD. Present Erin Springs, in Garvin County, 2 miles south of Lindsay. Post office established March 15, 1875, and name changed to Erin Springs, November 3, 1875.

EDITH. In Woods County, 7 miles northwest of Freedom. A post office from June 25, 1920, to May 15, 1940, it was named for Edith M. Vincent, wife of W. W. Vincent, townsite owner.

EDMOND. In northern Oklahoma County. Post office established May 23, 1889. Named for Eddy B. Townsend, rancher.

EDNA. In Creek County, 6 miles southeast of Slick. A post office from February 25, 1903, to September 20, 1957. Name selected arbitrarily by local residents, probably intending to honor Ed Rice, early-day settler.

EDSEL. In eastern Dewey County, 2 miles southwest of Oakwood. A post office from August 26, 1903, to December 31, 1905, it was named for David S. Edsall, early-day settler.

EDWARDS. Present Pittsburg, in Pittsburg County, 3 miles east of Kiowa. Formerly Cowper. Post office name changed to Edwards, September 3, 1903, and changed to Pittsburg, August 27, 1909. Named for J. R. Edwards, coal operator.

EDWARDSVILLE. In Custer County, 3 miles south of Butler. A post office from August 2, 1894, to August 15, 1906. No longer in existence, it was named for John A. Edwards, first postmaster.

EDWIN. In Rogers County in the vicinity of Oologah. A post office from June 1, 1905, to November 30, 1907. No longer in existence, it was named for Edwin Noyes, first postmaster.

EGNEW. In Lincoln County, in the vicinity of Stroud. A post office from June 11, 1892, to May 16, 1895. No longer in existence, it was named for Kate Egnew, first postmaster.

EGO. In Johnston County, 9 miles east of Milburn. Post office established June 7, 1895, and name changed to Coleman, September 10, 1910. Name assigned arbitrarily by the Post Office Department in lieu of Echo, the name requested by the local residents.

EGYPT. In Johnston County, 6 miles north of Milburn. A post office from September 17, 1904, to July 31, 1916. Named for the country in northern Africa.

ELAM. In Tulsa County, 5 miles southwest of Broken Arrow. A post office from September 25, 1901, to September 28, 1906. Named for Elam Hodge, townsite allotee.

ELBA. In northeastern Lincoln County, 3 miles southwest of Avery. A post office from December 28, 1892, to August 30, 1902. No longer in existence. Its name comes from the island of Elba off the northwestern coast of Italy.

ELBERTA. In Stephens County, 12 miles west of Duncan. A post office from November 11, 1903, to October 31, 1908. Name selected by John W. Gray, first postmaster, because of a fine crop of Elberta peaches he had just produced.

ELDON. In Cherokee County, 7 miles east of Tahlequah. A post office from March 20, 1911, to May 30, 1936. Its name comes from Eldon, Illinois.

ELDORADO. In southwestern Jackson County. Post office established September 1, 1890. The name was intended to tell "of the golden quality of the land."

ELDRIDGE. In the southwestern corner of Beaver County. A post office from February 15, 1906, to December 31, 1907. No longer in existence, it was named for Cora A. Eldridge, first postmaster.

ELGIN. Formerly Ceegee. In northeastern Comanche County. Post office name changed to Elgin, July 12, 1902. Its name comes from Elgin, Illinois.

ELGIN. In present Garfield County, 10 miles southeast of Covington. A post office from December 29, 1894, to September 30, 1897. No longer in existence, it was named for W. D. Elgin, local farmer.

ELI. In Cherokee County near Hulbert. A post office from October 5, 1911, to July 31, 1916. Named for Elias B. Dunaway, first postmaster.

ELK. Present Pooleville, in northern Carter County. Post office established January 15, 1890, and name changed to Pooleville, July 20, 1907.

ELK CITY. Formerly Busch. In northeastern Beckham County. Post office name changed to Elk City, July 20, 1907.

ELKINS. In Haskell County, 6 miles east of Keota. A post office from June 16, 1904, to May 31, 1912. No longer in existence, it was named for Anderson R. Elkins, first postmaster.

ELKTON. In Alfalfa County, 8 miles south of Cherokee. A post office from February 3, 1899, to

78

June 30, 1909. No longer in existence.

ELLAVILLE. In Pottawatomie County, 3 miles southwest of Maud. A post office from October 14, 1901, to June 30, 1905. Named for Ella C. Mooney, wife of Dr. Jesse Mooney, prominent local resident. Mrs. Mooney was the first woman to be a registered pharmacist in Oklahoma Territory, being licensed July 1, 1901.

ELLEN. Present Milburn, in Johnston County. Post office established January 18, 1900, and name changed to Milburn, August 17, 1901. Named for Ellen Chapman, daughter of prominent early-day resident.

ELLENDALE. In northeastern Woodward County, 19 miles northeast of Woodward. A post office from September 9, 1901, to November 15, 1917. Name arbitrarily substituted by the Post Office Department for Elmdale, the name requested by local residents.

ELLERVILLE. In northeastern Cherokee County, 9 miles northeast of Tahlequah. A post office from March 25, 1914, to December 31, 1954, it was named for David Eller, early-day resident.

ELLIOTT. In Nowata County, 6 miles north of Lenapah. Also known as Seminole Station and as Howden. A post office from January 4, 1892, to July 31, 1926, it was named for James H. Elliott, early-day resident.

ELLIS. In Lincoln County, 4 miles southeast of Chandler. Post office established September 10, 1900, and on September 23, 1904, the post office was moved several miles west and its name changed to Midlothian. Named for Ellis Tovery, early-day settler.

ELLIS COUNTY. County in western Oklahoma, created at statehood from the northern portion of Roger Mills County and the southwestern portion of Woodward County, Oklahoma Territory. Named for Albert H. Ellis, vice-president of the Constitutional Convention.

ELM. In Custer County, 20 miles west of Thomas. A post office from November 1, 1893, to December 15, 1920.

ELM. In northeastern Logan County, 3 miles northwest of Langston, Post office established March 1, 1890, and name changed to Martin, October 27, 1890.

ELMCREEK. Present Owasso, in Tulsa County. Post office established February 10, 1898, and name changed to Owasso, January 24, 1900. Took its name from nearby Elm Creek, a tributary of Bird Creek.

ELMER. In southeastern Jackson County. Post office established February 18, 1902. Named for Elmer W. Slocum, official of the Kansas City, Mexico and Orient Railway.

ELMIRA. In Logan County, 3 miles east of Guthrie. Townsite plat filed January 20, 1911. Named for Elmira Ridley, local resident.

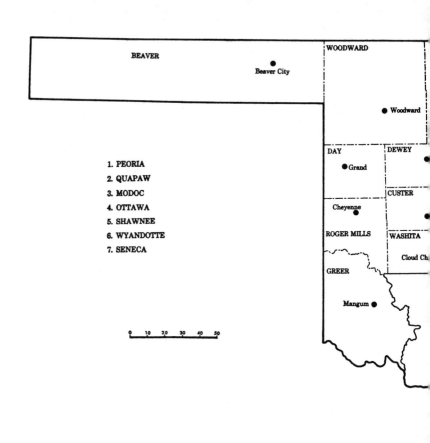

1. PEORIA
2. QUAPAW
3. MODOC
4. OTTAWA
5. SHAWNEE
6. WYANDOTTE
7. SENECA

Oklahoma–Indian Territory, 1900
Reproduced from *Historical Atlas of Oklahoma*, by John W. Morris and
Edwin C. McReynolds. Copyright 1965 by the University of Oklahoma
Press.

ELMORE CITY. In southwestern Garvin County. Post office established June 11, 1890, as Elmore; name changed to Banner, September 7, 1910; and name changed to Elmore City, March 4, 1911. Named for J. O. Elmore, prominent early-day resident.

ELMOT. In Major County, about 11 miles west of Orienta. A post office from December 1, 1903, to March 30, 1912. No longer in existence.

ELMPARK. Present Salt Fork, in Grant County. Post office established July 12, 1895, and name changed to Saltfork, February 4, 1902. It took its name from a nearby grove of elm trees growing along the south bank of the Salt Fork of the Arkansas River.

ELMWOOD. In Beaver County, 15 miles south of Beaver. Post office established January 26, 1888.

EL RENO. County seat of Canadian County. Post office established June 28, 1889. It took its name from nearby Fort Reno and was called El Reno to distinguish it from Reno City, another townsite.

EMAHAKA. On the line between Seminole and Hughes counties, 5 miles south of Wewoka. A post office from January 23, 1895, to July 16, 1906. Site of Emahaka Academy, established in 1893 by the Seminole Nation as a school for girls. The word is a Seminole word, meaning literally "girl's school."

EMANUEL. In Blaine County, 7 miles southwest of Watonga. A post office from March 4, 1904, to March 31, 1906. It was named for Emanuel Newborn, first postmaster.

EMBREE. On the Osage County line, 6 miles west of Ramona. A post office from November 10, 1891, to March 5, 1892.

EMERSON. In Cotton County, 6 miles west of Walters. A post office from January 24, 1908, to November 30, 1914. No longer in existence.

EMET. In Johnston County, 3 miles south of Milburn. A post office from February 18, 1884, to November 30, 1917. Named for Emet Victor, nephew of Douglas H. Johnston, governor of the Chickasaw Nation.

EMMA. In western Beckham County, 8 miles south of Erick. A post office from April 14, 1905, to December 31, 1910.

EMPIRE CITY. In Stephens County, 7 miles southwest of Duncan. A post office from February 4, 1921, to December 31, 1934.

ENEHOE. In Canadian County, 5 miles west of Calumet. A post office from March 3, 1893, to April 14, 1904. The name was coined from the words Cheyenne and Arapaho.

ENFIELD. In Logan County, 6 miles north of Arcadia. A post office from June 22, 1892, to August 15, 1906, it took its name from the Enfield rifle.

ENID. County seat of Garfield County. Post office established August 25, 1893. Although there are a number of versions of the origin of the name, it undoubtedly was taken from *Idylls of the King* by Tennyson.

ENOS. In Marshall County, 9 miles south of Kingston. A post office from June 14, 1915, to December 15, 1930. Assigned arbitrarily by the Post Office Department, the name is a variant for Amos, the name of a post office discontinued at approximately the same site on September 14, 1907.

ENTERPRISE. In Haskell County, 9 miles west of Whitefield. A post office from June 30, 1890, to December 31, 1958. Took its name from the U.S.S. Enterprise, the fifth vessel of the Navy of that name. Commissioned in 1877, the Enterprise saw continuous and distinguished service until her retirement in 1909.

ENVILLE. In Love County, 4 miles west of Lebanon. A post office from June 16, 1904, to January 15, 1935. The name was coined from the phrase "end of the road ville."

EOLA. In Garvin County, 6 miles south of Elmore City. A post office from May 12, 1911, to December 31, 1927.

EOLIAN. In western Carter County. Post office established March 23, 1904, and name changed to Joiner, May 17, 1909. Its name comes from Aeolus, the Greek god of the wind.

ERA. In Jackson County, 7 miles southwest of Olustee. Post office established April 26, 1901, and name changed to Creta, February 20, 1904.

ERAM. In eastern Okmulgee County, 5 miles east of Morris. A post office from June 10, 1913, to July 31, 1950. The name was coined from the first letter of the names of the four children of Ed Oates, local Creek—Eugene, Roderick, Anthony, and Marie.

ERICK. In western Beckham County. Post office established November 16, 1901. Named for Beeks Erick, president of Choctaw Townsite and Improvement Company, the townsite developer.

ERIN SPRINGS. In Garvin County, 2 miles south of Lindsay. Formerly Edgewood. Post office name changed to Erin Springs, November 3, 1875. Named by Frank Murray, local rancher, after his native Ireland.

ERNEST. In Tillman County, 5 miles northwest of Manitou. A post office from July 15, 1902, to January 14, 1905. No longer in existence, it was named for Ernest Adams, son of John W. Adams, first postmaster.

ERVIN. In Choctaw County, 7 miles southeast of Hugo. A post office from March 8, 1904, to July 31, 1922. Named for Edwin E. Ervin, first postmaster.

ERWIN. In Alfalfa County, 2 miles east of Cherokee. A post of-

83

fice from June 11, 1894, to March 16, 1901. Named for Dr. C. E. Erwin of Hazelton, Kansas.

ESBON. In Cimarron County, 6 miles northwest of Keyes. Formerly Bakke. Post office name changed to Esbon, March 29, 1909, and discontinued January 30, 1915.

ESCHITA. Present Grandfield, in Tillman County. Post office established October 31, 1907, and name changed to Grandfield, January 21, 1909. Named for Eschiti, a Comanche medicine man.

ESTELLA. In Craig County, 8 miles northwest of Vinita. A post office from December 28, 1900, to July 31, 1953. Named for Estella Franklin, wife of John Franklin, first postmaster.

ESTELLE. In western Major County, 10 miles northwest of Phroso. Post office established June 27, 1901, and name changed to Hoopville, January 7, 1908.

ESTES. A switch and loading point on the Frisco in Lincoln County 2 miles west of Davenport. Named for David L. Estes, railroad employee.

ESTHER. In northeastern Beaver County, 3 miles west of Knowles. A post office from June 3, 1903, to November 30, 1912. No longer in existence, it was named for Esther Smith, first postmaster.

ETCHEN. In northern Nowata County, adjoining the Oklahoma State line. Post office established March 18, 1909, and name changed to South Coffeyville, April 29, 1909. Named for John P. Etchen, early-day resident.

ETHEL. In southwestern Blaine County, 8 miles north of Hydro. A post office from August 29, 1902, to September 14, 1907. Named for Ethel Moore, daughter of Charles H. Moore, first postmaster.

ETHEL. In Pushmataha County, 6 miles east of Antlers. A post office from April 22, 1901, to August 15, 1933. Named for Ethel Labors, early-day resident.

ETNA. In northeastern Atoka County at location of present Daisy. Originally known as Many Springs, it was the location of the county seat of Jack's Fork County, Choctaw Nation. A post office from August 7, 1884, to August 9, 1897. Named for Etna Hewitt, early-day resident.

ETNA. In southwestern Blaine County, 15 miles northwest of Geary. A post office from August 20, 1898, to October 15, 1913. Its name comes from Mount Aetna in southern Italy.

ETOWAH. In Cleveland County, 11 miles east of Noble. A post office from August 17, 1894, to May 31, 1907. No longer in existence. The name is from a Cherokee settlement in Forsyth County, Georgia.

ETTA. In eastern Cherokee County, 5 miles southeast of Welling. A post office from April 5, 1905, to December 15, 1922, it was named for Etta Willis, wife of Ben Willis, prominent early-day resident.

EUBANK. In southern Texas County, 10 miles southeast of Guymon. A post office from February 12, 1891, to September 15, 1902. No longer in existence, it was named for Jesse L. Eubank, early-day rancher.

EUBANKS. In Pushmataha County, 13 miles north of Antlers. A post office from February 26, 1907, to April 30, 1934, it was named for William Eubanks, local lumberman.

EUCHA. In Delaware County, 5 miles south of Jay. Post office established November 20, 1900. The name is a variant of Ooche, a diminutive of Ochelata, the Cherokee name for Charles Thompson, principal chief.

EUFAULA. County seat of McIntosh County. Record Town for Recording District No. 12, Indian Territory. Post office established February 6, 1874. Its name comes from an old Creek town on the west bank of the Chattahoochee River in Alabama, called *Yufala*, meaning "they split up here and went to other places."

EULA. In central Texas County, 2 miles southeast of Hough. A post office from October 4, 1905, to June 30, 1908, it was named for Eula White, daughter of early-day rancher.

EUREKA. In Le Flore County, 3 miles north of Poteau. A post office

from March 11, 1899, to November 30, 1916.

EVA. In Texas County, 23 miles northwest of Guymon. Post office established July 9, 1906. Named for Eva Hargrove, daughter of Scott Hargrove, first postmaster.

EVANS. In Wagoner County, 3 miles east of Broken Arrow. A post office from November 28, 1904, to February 28, 1911, it was named for A. Grant Evans, president of Henry Kendall College at Muskogee.

EVANSVILLE. In Logan County, 7 miles southwest of Meridian. A post office from May 22, 1894, to July 31, 1906, it was named for James W. Evans, townsite owner.

EVERETT. In Kiowa County, 6 miles south of Hobart. A post office from August 3, 1903, to May 31, 1904, it was named for Everett Pate, long-time Kiowa County publisher.

EXCELSIOR. In northwestern Kingfisher County, 5 miles east of Loyal. A post office from August 19, 1895, to June 30, 1902, it took its name from the nearby Excelsior School. The word is a part of the motto of the state of New York and is from the Latin *excelsus*, meaning "upward" or "high."

EXENDINE. In northwestern Caddo County, 7 miles west of Lookeba. A post office from April 12, 1902, to February 28, 1907, it was named for Jasper Exendine, first postmaster.

EZELL. In southern Woods County, 12 miles southeast of Waynoka. A post office from March 21, 1896, to December 15, 1899, it was named for James Ezell, early-day resident.

EZRA. In Creek County, 6 miles east of Slick. A post office from September 17, 1909, to September 30, 1910. Named for Ezra Freeman, first postmaster.

F

F COUNTY. Original designation for Roger Mills County, Oklahoma Territory. Name changed to Roger Mills County, November 8, 1892.

FAGAN. In Latimer County near Red Oak. A post office from August 17, 1894, to November 16, 1897.

FAIRBANKS. In Major County, 18 miles west of Fairview. A post office from October 17, 1904, to February 28, 1921, it was named for Charles W. Fairbanks, vice president of the United States.

FAIRFAX. In western Osage County. Post office established February 16, 1903. Although there are several versions explaining its origin, the name is probably in honor of Lord Fairfax of Virginia.

FAIRFIELD MISSION. Site in Adair County, 6 miles southwest of Stilwell. Established in 1829 by the American Board of Foreign Missions as a mission for the Western Cherokees. Intended as a day school, the mission was one of the few schools in Indian Territory that did not operate as a boarding seminary. It did not survive the Civil War.

FAIRLAND. In Ottawa County, 9 miles south of Miami. Post office established January 28, 1891. Name intended to denote the surrounding countryside of "tall bluestem grass and prairie flowers."

FAIRMONT. Formerly Luella. In Garfield County, 10 miles southeast of Enid. Post office name changed to Fairmont, December 24, 1902. Named by John Murphy of Enid, probably for Fairmount School in Wichita, Kansas.

FAIRVALLEY. In western Woods County, 5 miles southeast of Freedom. A post office from October 4, 1895, to January 31, 1948.

FAIRVIEW. In Beaver County, 5 miles southwest of Gate. A post office from February 21, 1888, to March 5, 1890. No longer in existence.

FAIRVIEW. In southwestern Logan County, 4 miles west of Seward. A post office from September 1, 1890, to April 11, 1893. No longer in existence.

FAIRVIEW. County seat of Major County. Post office established April 18, 1894. It took its name from its scenic location in a pleasantly wooded valley east of the uplands forming the Glass Mountains.

FALFA. In Latimer County, 8 miles west of Talihina. A post office from June 6, 1919, to March 15, 1923.

FALKEY. In northern Beaver County near Forgan. A post office from March 27, 1906, to January 15, 1916. No longer in existence.

FALLIS. Formerly Mission. In western Lincoln County, 5 miles northwest of Wellston. Post office name changed to Fallis, July 13, 1894, and discontinued April 30, 1970. Named for William H. Fallis, first postmaster.

FAME. In McIntosh County, 5 miles northwest of Eufaula. A post office from June 9, 1894, to July 2, 1965. The name was selected by local residents for the surrounding "famous bottom land" of the valley of the North Canadian River.

FANNIE. In Garfield County, 5 miles southwest of Garber. A post office from December 7, 1893, to March 9, 1898, it was named for Fannie Porter, wife of Charles V. Porter, first postmaster.

FANSHAWE. In western Le Flore County, 10 miles west of Wister. Post office established March 13, 1891.

FARGO. Formerly Oleta. In northeastern Ellis County, 13 miles southwest of Woodward. Post office name changed to Fargo, February 17, 1905. Took its name from Wells, Fargo and Company.

FARMERS. In Le Flore County, 3 miles east of Panama. Railroad name for this town was Adkins. A post office from August 3, 1894,

to November 15, 1909, it was named for P. M. Farmers, local resident.

FARRIS. In southeastern Atoka County, 18 miles southeast of Atoka. A post office established May 17, 1902, it was named for John L. Farris, first postmaster.

FARRY. In northwestern Woods County, 7 miles northeast of Freedom. A post office from May 22, 1889, to September 30, 1952.

FAULKNER. In northwestern Woods County, 16 miles northwest of Alva. A post office from June 13, 1901, to September 29, 1917, it was named for Charles F. Faulkner, first postmaster.

FAWLING. Formerly Harris. In Muskogee County, 9 miles east of Oktaha. Post office name changed to Fawling, March 19, 1890, and discontinued September 17, 1896.

FAWN. In eastern McIntosh County, 8 miles southeast of Checotah. A post office from February 11, 1898, to October 31, 1916.

FAXON. In southwestern Comanche County, 5 miles northeast of Chattanooga. Post office established January 7, 1902. Named for Ralph Faxon, private secretary to Chester Long, United States senator from Kansas.

FAY. In extreme southeastern corner of Dewey County. Post office established April 19, 1894. Named for Fay Fiscos, son of Leander Fiscos, first postmaster.

FEATHERSTON. In northeastern Pittsburg County, 7 miles west of Quinton. A post office from June 23, 1892, to November 29, 1957, it was named for Lucius C. Featherston, early-day rancher.

FELIX. In Mayes County, 4 miles northwest of Locust Grove. A post office from October 2, 1903, to January 31, 1906, it was named for Dr. Felix McNair, local early-day resident.

FELT. In southwestern Cimarron County, 17 miles southwest of Boise City. Post office established July 16, 1926. Named for C. F. W. Felt, chief engineer for the Santa Fe Railway.

FELTBURG. In Pottawatomie County, 6 miles west of Maud. A post office from July 14, 1892, to May 3, 1893. No longer in existence, it was named for Joseph C. Willfelt, first postmaster.

FENNELL. In Choctaw County, 3 miles north of Fort Towson. A post office from September 5, 1911, to April 15, 1916, it was named for Thomas Fennell, Fort Towson postmaster.

FENTRESS. Present Holdenville, in Hughes County. Post office established May 24, 1895, and name changed to Holdenville, November 15, 1895. Named for J. Fentress Wisdom, son of D. M. Wisdom, Indian agent.

FENTRESS. In Okfuskee County, 6 miles south of Okemah. A post office from September 23, 1897, to January 31, 1908. First known locally as Sand Burr. Named for J. Fentress Wisdom, son of D. M. Wisdom, Indian agent.

FERDINANDINA. Site in Kay County, 5 miles northeast of Newkirk on the west bank of the Arkansas River at the mouth of Deer Creek. An important French trading post that flourished during the first half of the eighteenth century, it is generally considered to be the first white settlement in present-day Oklahoma. It is believed to have been named for King Ferdinand VI of Spain.

FERGUSON. In Blaine County, 12 miles north of Watonga. A post office from August 21, 1901, to April 30, 1920, it was named for T. B. Ferguson, governor of Oklahoma Territory.

FERN. In southern Harper County, 14 miles north of Woodward. A post office from March 14, 1904, to July 15, 1914, it was named for Fern LaMunyon, early-day resident.

FEWELL. In eastern Pushmataha County, 18 miles southeast of Clayton. A post office from November 4, 1913, to October 15, 1943, it was named for Ben F. Fewell, first postmaster.

FILLMORE. In eastern Johnston County, 11 miles northeast of Tishomingo. A post office from February 10, 1902, to October 31, 1965. Named for Elias Fillmore, local Chickasaw.

FILSON. In northern Pawnee County, 4 miles southwest of Ralston. A post office from August 3, 1894, to July 14, 1906, it was named for Charles Filson, territorial secretary of state.

FINCH. In southern Bryan County, 2 miles northwest of Colbert. Post office established June 16, 1898, and name changed to Platter, April 11, 1901. For a few months in 1889, a post office named Finchville had been in operation at this same site. Named for Ode Finch, Chickasaw.

FINLEY. In Pushmataha County, 10 miles northeast of Antlers. Post office established April 30, 1903. Named for Sidney W. Finley, local merchant and first postmaster.

FISHER. In Tulsa County, 3 miles west of Sand Springs. A post office from June 27, 1904, to November 15, 1912, it was named for Amos Fisher, Creek allotee, townsite owner.

FISHER'S STATION. In Bryan County, 3 miles west of Durant. A stage stop on the Butterfield Overland Mail route to California, which crossed southeastern Oklahoma, 1858–61. The site is usually known as Carriage Point.

FISHERTOWN. In McIntosh County, 5 miles northeast of Eufaula. A post office from July 10, 1883, to April 25, 1893, it was named for William and George Fisher, brothers, early-day merchants.

FITTSTOWN. In Pontotoc County, 11 miles south of Ada. Post office established June 22, 1935. Named for John Fitts, geologist.

FITZGERALD. Present Fort Supply, in Woodward County. Post office established February 3, 1902, and name changed to Supply, May 12, 1903. Named for P. H. Fitzgerald, townsite promoter.

FITZHUGH. In Pontotoc County, 8 miles southwest of Ada. Post office established June 24, 1898. Named for General Fitzhugh Lee, Confederate hero.

FITZLEN. In northwestern Woods County, 10 miles northwest of Alva. A post office from September 9, 1889, to February 28, 1913, it was named for James E. Fritzlen, early-day resident.

FLAGG. In Woods County, 15 miles west of Alva. A post office from June 17, 1905, to December 31, 1915.

FLANDERS. In extreme northern Craig County. A post office from July 10, 1913, to October 31, 1914. No longer in existence.

FLAT. In central Harper County. A post office from June 25, 1903, to October 15, 1906. No longer in existence, it took its name from character of surrounding countryside.

FLAVIA. In Sequoyah County, adjoining Sallisaw. A post office from July 9, 1910, to December 31, 1912, it was named for Flavia Griffith, daughter of Jackson Griffith, first postmaster.

FLEETWOOD. In southern Jefferson County, 5 miles east of Terral. A post office from December 2, 1885, to July 21, 1961, it was named for H. H. Fleetwood, operator of a ferry on Red River.

FLETCHER. In northeastern Comanche County. Post office established May 10, 1902. Named for Fletcher Dodge, local early-day resident.

FLINT. Present Stilwell, in Adair County. Post office established August 1, 1846; on May 12, 1896, the post office was moved 3 miles north and the name changed to Stilwell. Its name comes from Flint District, Cherokee Nation.

FLINT. A district of the Cherokee Nation, created by the Cherokee National Council on November 6, 1840.

FLINT. In southern Delaware County, 7 miles east of Kansas. A post office from November 7, 1900, to July 31, 1951. In 1898 a post office named Beckwith was discontinued at this same location. Its name comes from Flint District, Cherokee Nation.

FLOE. Formerly Borum. In northern Haskell County, 7 miles north of Stigler. Post office name changed to Floe, September 27, 1909, and discontinued August 31, 1911.

FLORENCE. Present Kenton, in northwestern Cimarron County. Former post office name Carrizo.

Post office name changed to Florence, April 9, 1890, and to Kenton, May 12, 1891. Named for Florence Hubbard, daughter of George W. Hubbard, first postmaster.

FLORENCE. In western Grant County, 19 miles west of Medford. A post office from November 30, 1895, to February 14, 1922. Named for Florence Arnold, mother of an early-day rancher.

FLORIS. In northern Beaver County, 9 miles west of Forgan. The present town of Floris is 3 miles south of the site of the Floris post office, established August 7, 1903, and discontinued September 30, 1925. Named for Floris Derthwick, daughter of Byron S. Derthwick, townsite owner.

FLOWERY MOUND. In Pittsburg County, 9 miles northeast of McAlester. See Bugtussle.

FLOYD. In northern Payne County, 3 miles east of Glencoe. A post office from March 22, 1895, to June 15, 1900. Named for Floyd C. Jessee, first postmaster.

FLY CREEK. In northern Delaware County, 8 miles northwest of Grove. Post office established May 9, 1878, and name changed to Horse Creek, February 12, 1879. Site now inundated by Grand Lake o' the Cherokees. It took its name from Fly Creek, a tributary of Horse Creek, a branch of Grand River.

FLYNN. In northern Lincoln County, 3 miles northeast of Agra.

90

A post office from August 27, 1892, to March 31, 1903. No longer in existence, it was named for Dennis T. Flynn, territorial delegate to Congress.

FOGEL. Formerly Howard. In extreme eastern Le Flore County, 6 miles east of Page. Post office name changed to Fogel, February 25, 1914, and discontinued February 15, 1923. Named for Carrie L. Fogel, first postmaster.

FOLSOM. In Johnston County, 6 miles southeast of Milburn. A post office from July 13, 1894, to March 14, 1955, it was named for David Folsom, prominent Chickasaw.

FONDA. In northeastern Dewey County, 7 miles east of Seiling. A post office from March 5, 1903, to December 30, 1916. The name is the Spanish word for inn.

FORAKER. In northwestern Osage County. Post office established February 13, 1903. Named for Joseph B. Foraker, United States senator from Ohio.

FORD. In northern Pawnee County, 6 miles east of Bliss. A post office from July 6, 1905, to February 29, 1916. No longer in existence, it took its name from a nearby ford across the Arkansas River.

FOREMAN. In Sequoyah County, 5 miles southwest of Muldrow. A post office from October 31, 1898, to August 31, 1936, it was named for Zack Foreman, local merchant.

FOREST PARK. A separate municipality adjoining Oklahoma City on the northeast. Incorporated July 11, 1956. Situated within the western edge of the Cross Timbers, the name comes from the fine growth of blackjack and other oak within the townsite.

FORGAN. In Beaver County, 6 miles north of Beaver. Post office established June 1, 1912. Named for James B. Forgan, at that time a Chicago banker.

FORNEY. In southwestern Blaine County, 12 miles east of Thomas. A post office from June 4, 1901, to July 14, 1903. No longer in existence, it was named for Henry Forney, first postmaster.

FORNEY. In Choctaw County, 5 miles west of Hugo. A post office from September 11, 1903, to March 31, 1904. Named for Forney, Texas, because both communities were in a locality that produced much prairie hay.

FORREST. In Lincoln County, 5 miles south of Chandler. A post office from May 23, 1894, to September 21, 1894. No longer in existence. Named by James G. Cansler, first postmaster, for the surrounding uncleared forest of black jack timber.

FORRESTER. In Le Flore County, 5 miles east of Heavener. A post office from June 8, 1915, to February 14, 1922.

FORT ARBUCKLE. Site in southern Garvin County, 9 miles west of Davis. Established in 1851 and garrisoned until the Civil War;

finally abandoned in 1870. A post office by this name was in operation at the site from August 4, 1853, to October 7, 1875. On August 20, 1884, a post office named Arbuckle was established at this site. The initial point from which all land surveys in Oklahoma except the Panhandle were measured is located 1 mile south. Named for Brigadier General Matthew Arbuckle.

FORT BLUNT. The name applied to Fort Gibson by the Union troops garrisoned there during 1863. Named for Major General J. G. Blunt.

FORT COBB. Site in Caddo County, 1 mile east of present town of Fort Cobb. Established in 1859 and garrisoned until the evacuation of Indian Territory in May, 1861, by Union troops; occupied for a short while following the Civil War. Present post office of Fort Cobb was established under name Cobb in 1899, and name changed to Fort Cobb, October 31, 1902. Named for Howell Cobb of Georgia, secretary of the treasury under President Buchanan.

FORT COFFEE. Site in Le Flore County, 8 miles north of Spiro. A military post established in 1834 at Swallow Rock on the Arkansas River and abandoned in 1838. A post office from April 20, 1835, to September 20, 1838. The buildings thereafter were used as a Choctaw school for boys. Named for General John Coffee of Tennessee.

FORT DAVIS. Site in Muskogee County near present-day Bacone College. Established in 1861 by Brigadier General Albert Pike as Confederate military headquarters for Indian Territory. Destroyed by Union forces under Colonel W. A. Phillips on December 27, 1862. Named for President Jefferson Davis.

FORT GIBSON. Site adjoining present town of Fort Gibson in Muskogee County. Established April 21, 1824, and occupied continuously until 1857; again used as a military post during the Civil War. Known as Fort Blunt in 1863. Finally abandoned as a military post in 1890. Name of first post office at the site, Cantonment Gibson, changed to Fort Gibson, September 14, 1842. Named for Colonel George Gibson, head of the Army Commissary Department.

FORT HOLMES. Site in Hughes County at Bilby. Established as a military post in 1834 at the mouth of Little River, it did not see extended service. Named for Theophilus H. Holmes, who rose to the rank of lieutenant general in the Confederate Army.

FORT McCULLOCH. Site in Bryan County, several miles west of Kenefic. Established in 1862 by Brigadier General Albert Pike, as a Confederate military post on the west side of Blue River at Nail's Crossing. Extensive earthworks remain. Named for Brigadier General Ben McCulloch of Texas, killed at the Battle of Pea Ridge.

FORT NICHOLS. Site in Cimarron County, 2 miles north of Wheeless. A temporary military post established in 1865 by Colonel Kit Carson to protect the travelers on the Santa Fe Trail. Named for Major General William A. Nichols.

FORT RENO. In Canadian County, 2 miles west of El Reno. Post established July, 1875. An army remount station from 1908 until 1949. A post office from February 1, 1877, to May 30, 1907. Named for Major General Jesse L. Reno, killed at Antietam.

FORT SILL. In Comanche County. Established as a military post January, 1869, and occupied continuously since that date. Post office established September 28, 1869, and discontinued August 15, 1917, to become a branch of Lawton post office. Named by Major General P. H. Sheridan for his colleague, Major General Joshua Sill, killed at the Battle of Stone's River.

FORT SPUNKY. In southwestern Rogers County near Catoosa. Not a military post, but a stop on the stage line from Vinita to Tulsa. A post office from January 9, 1880, to February 5, 1883, it took its name from nearby Spunky Creek.

FORT SUPPLY. In western Woodward County, adjoining present town of Fort Supply. Established November, 1868, as a supply base for the Indian campaign of Major General G. A. Custer. Post abandoned in 1893, and now a state hospital. Original post office name

of Camp Supply, changed to Fort Supply on June 26, 1889, and discontinued October 12, 1895. On February 3, 1902, a post office named Fitzgerald was established 1 mile west of the army post; name changed to Supply, May 12, 1903, and to Fort Supply, May 1, 1943.

FORT TOWSON. Established as a military post in 1824 and permanent site selected in 1831. Location of military post was 2 miles northeast of present Fort Towson in Choctaw County. Abandoned by the United States Army in 1854, it was used as the Confederate military headquarters for Indian Territory in 1864–65 and was the site where Brigadier General Stand Watie, the last regularly commissioned Confederate general officer to surrender, laid down his arms June 23, 1865. Named for Nathan Towson, paymaster general of the army. Post office established September 7, 1832; name changed to Doaksville, November 11, 1847; the post office was moved to the present site and name changed to Fort Towson on June 12, 1903.

FORT WASHITA. Site in northwestern Bryan County, adjoining Lake Texoma. Established in 1843 by Zachary Taylor, later United States president. Garrisoned continuously until the evacuation in May, 1861, of Indian Territory by United States troops. Used as a Confederate military post during the Civil War. Site now owned and developed by Oklahoma Historical Society. A post office from November 4, 1844, to May 24, 1880, it took its name from nearby Washita River.

FORT WAYNE. Site in northeastern Adair County. Established in 1838 and abandoned by the military in 1842. Used during the Civil War, it was site of a battle on October 22, 1862. Named for Anthony Wayne, Revolutionary War hero.

FORTY ONE. In western Washita County, 8 miles west of Dill City. Took the name from its location on former State Highway 41.

FOSS. In Washita County, 12 miles southwest of Clinton. Post office established September 15, 1900. Named for J. M. Foss of Cordell.

FOSTER. In western Garvin County, 17 miles west of Wynnewood. Post office established August 12, 1891. Named for Noah Foster, first postmaster.

FOUNTAIN. In northeastern Dewey County, 12 miles east of Taloga. A post office from June 26, 1895, to June 30, 1916, it was named for Albert S. Fountain, first postmaster.

FOURMILE. In northwestern Ottawa County, 3 miles west of Commerce. A post office from August 23, 1882, to October 15, 1892. It took its name from the circumstance that the site was four miles from the Kansas State line.

FOUTS. Present Tryon in Lincoln County. Post office established April 19, 1894, and name changed to Tryon, March 15, 1899. Named for Byron Fouts, early-day resident.

FOWLERVILLE. Present Valliant in McCurtain County. Post office established July 7, 1894, and name changed to Valliant, June 23, 1902. Named for Nathaniel M. Fowler, first postmaster.

FOX. In northwestern Carter County, 8 miles north of Healdton. Post office established January 25, 1894. Named for Frank M. Fox, prominent Chickasaw.

FOYIL. In Rogers County, 10 miles northeast of Claremore. Post office established June 5, 1890. Named for Alfred Foyil, first postmaster.

FRANCIS. Present Vinson, in northern Harmon County. Post office established March 19, 1892, and name changed to Trotter, April 25, 1902. Named for William P. Francis, prominent Greer County rancher and stockman.

FRANCIS. Formerly Newton. In northern Pontotoc County, 7 miles northeast of Ada. Post office name changed to Francis, June 5, 1902. Named for David R. Francis, secretary of the interior under William McKinley.

FRANKFORT. In northwestern Osage County, 10 miles northwest of Foraker. A post office from January 12, 1910, to August 15, 1912, it was named for Frank Murphy, townsite developer.

FRANKLIN. In Cleveland County, 11 miles northeast of Norman. A post office from May 10, 1892, to April 14, 1906, it was named for

Joe Franklin, long-time local resident.

FRANKS. In Pontotoc County, 8 miles southwest of Stonewall. A post office from February 1, 1894, to August 15, 1932, it was named for Frank Byrd, early-day resident.

FRAZER. In Jackson County, 3 miles southwest of Altus. First known locally as Buttermilk Station. A post office from February 18, 1886, to December 31, 1895. No longer in existence, it took its name from the Frazer River, now known as the Salt Fork of the Red River.

FRED. In Grady County, 4 miles south of Chickasha. A post office from January 2, 1884, to August 7, 1894, it was named for Franklin L. Fred, prominent early-day Indian trader.

FREDERICK. County seat of Tillman County. Formerly Gosnell. Post office name changed to Frederick, September 30, 1902. Named for Frederick VanBlarcom, son of J. C. VanBlarcom of St. Louis, railroad developer.

FREEDOM. In western Woods County. Post office established May 18, 1901.

FRIENDS. In Alfalfa County, 3 miles northeast of Cherokee. A post office from October 11, 1899, to July 31, 1901, it took its name from the Stella Friends Academy, where the post office was located.

FRIENDSHIP. In northeastern Washita County, 5 miles southwest of Colony. A post office from Oc-

tober 27, 1904, to November 30, 1907. No longer in existence.

FRISCO. In Canadian County, 3 miles northwest of Yukon. A post office from May 18, 1889, to April 30, 1904. No longer in existence, it was named for a proposed railroad, that, when built, missed the townsite entirely.

FRISCO. In eastern Pontotoc County, 2 miles south of present Stonewall, and at the location of the original townsite of Stonewall. A post office from June 13, 1906, to April 30, 1941. Named by the townspeople under the mistaken impression that a railroad route under construction by the Oklahoma Central Railway was the Frisco Railroad.

FROGVILLE. In southeastern Choctaw County, 9 miles southwest of Fort Towson. A post office from October 29, 1897, to August 15, 1933. Took its name from the great plethora of frogs so large they reputedly "ate young ducks."

FRY. In Tulsa County, 6 miles southwest of Broken Arrow. A post office from May 20, 1896, to June 30, 1909, it was named for Robert Fry, early-day resident.

FRYE. In Sequoyah County, 7 miles northeast of Sallisaw. A post office from October 5, 1911, to April 15, 1914. Named for Charles O. Frye, prominent resident and member of the Oklahoma Constitutional Convention.

FULTON. In extreme southwest

Beaver County. A post office from April 21, 1887, to December 31, 1907. No longer in existence.

FUNSTON. In Woods County, 5 miles southwest of Avard. Post office established May 12, 1900, and name changed to Nira, May 18, 1903. Named for Major General Fred H. Funston of Spanish-American War fame.

FURRS. Present Henryetta, in Okmulgee County. Post office established May 12, 1899, and name changed to Henryetta, August 28, 1900. Named for Albert C. Furr, long-time local resident.

G

G COUNTY. Original designation for Custer County, Oklahoma Territory. Name changed to Custer County, November 8, 1892.

GABRIEL. In Cherokee County, 4 miles west of Tahlequah. A post office from May 13, 1911, to January 31, 1921. On February 28, 1911, a post office named Ahniwake had been discontinued at this same site.

GADDY. In Pottawatomie County, 5 miles west of Shawnee. A post office from April 26, 1901, to October 31, 1904, it was named for J. R. Gaddy, early-day local resident.

GAGE. In Ellis County, 7 miles northeast of Shattuck. Post office established February 5, 1895. Named for Lyman J. Gage, secretary of the treasury under William McKinley.

GAINES. A county in Moshulatubbee District, Choctaw Nation. Named for George S. Gaines, Choctaw trader.

GAINES CREEK. A stream flowing into the Canadian River from the south above its junction with the Arkansas River. Originally known as the South Fork of the Canadian River, it took its name from Gaines County, Choctaw Nation.

GAITHER. In central Okmulgee County. A post office from August 6, 1909, to March 15, 1914, it was named for W. J. Gaither, local resident.

GALENA. In southeastern Woods County, 13 miles southeast of Waynoka. A post office from March 13, 1895, to May 15, 1936.

GALLIENAS. In northwestern Cimarron County, 6 miles northeast of Kenton. A post office from May 14, 1890, to March 31, 1904. No longer in existence, it took its name from nearby Gallienas Creek. The word is Spanish and has reference to the prairie chicken.

GAMET. In northern Woods County, 14 miles northwest of Alva. A post office from June 30, 1904, to December 31, 1914, it was named for William S. Gamet, first postmaster.

GANN. In Sequoyah County, 7 miles southeast of Sallisaw. Post office established March 21, 1896, and name changed to Gans, September 8, 1899. Named for Charles and

Swimmer Gann, brothers, local Cherokees.

GANS. In Sequoyah County, 7 miles southeast of Sallisaw. Post office name changed from Gann to Gans, September 8, 1899. The name is a modification of the former post office name, Gann.

GAP. In Carter County, 3 miles east of Gene Autry. A post office from July 10, 1891, to June 1, 1894. No longer in existence, it took its name from a local land feature through which the Washita River flows.

GARBER. Formerly McCardie. In Garfield County, 16 miles east of Enid. Post office name changed to Garber, April 20, 1894, to honor Martin Garber, long-time local resident.

GARDEN. In southeastern Logan County, 3 miles west of Fallis. A post office from January 19, 1895, to December 15, 1900. No longer in existence.

GARFIELD. In southwestern Cherokee County, 6 miles east of Braggs. A post office from December 16, 1881, to February 13, 1889. Named for President James A. Garfield.

GARFIELD COUNTY. A county in northwestern Oklahoma, comprising the same area as Garfield County, Oklahoma Territory. The names Berry, for Senator James H. Berry of Arkansas, and Hancock, for Major General Winfield S. Hancock, had also been considered for this county. Named for President James A. Garfield.

GARLAND. In Haskell County, 7 miles northeast of Stigler. A post office from May 10, 1892, to June 30, 1914. Named for Joseph G. Garland, Choctaw jurist.

GARLINGTON. Formerly Jurgensen. In central Cimarron County, 7 miles southeast of Boise City. Name changed to Garlington, February 14, 1908, and post office discontinued July 31, 1926. Named for H. C. Garlington, townsite owner.

GARNER. Formerly Thurman. In northern Pittsburg County, 5 miles west of Indianola. Post office name changed to Garner, July 1, 1902, and discontinued November 30, 1906. Named for Edward L. Garner, first postmaster.

GARNETTVILLE. Present Luther, in Oklahoma County. Post office established May 22, 1892, and name changed to Luther, July 26, 1898. Named for Eugene M. Garnett, first postmaster.

GARRETT. In northern Cimarron County, 15 miles north of Boise City. A post office from April 17, 1891, to November 15, 1917, it was named for Martha E. Garrett, first postmaster.

GARRISON. Present Roland, in Sequoyah County. Post office established February 7, 1902, and name changed to Roland, May 18, 1904. Took its name from Garrison Creek, which, in turn, had been named for the garrison road to Fort Smith.

GARVIN. In McCurtain County, 7 miles northwest of Idabel. Post office established February 17, 1894. Garvin was the post office for Wheelock Academy. Named for Isaac Garvin, Choctaw principal chief, 1878–80.

GARVIN COUNTY. A county in south-central Oklahoma, created at statehood. Named for Samuel J. Garvin, prominent citizen of the Chickasaw Nation.

GASWELL. In northwestern Creek County. A post office from December 26, 1906, to December 31, 1915, it took its name from surrounding gas wells.

GATE. In northeastern Beaver County, 23 miles west of Buffalo. Post office name changed from Gate City to Gate, November 24, 1894.

GATE CITY. In northeastern Beaver County, 23 miles west of Buffalo. Post office established April 13, 1886, and name changed to Gate, November 24, 1894. The name is from the circumstance that the location was the entrance, or gate, to the old Neutral Strip.

GATESVILLE. In southern Wagoner County, 5 miles west of Clarksville. A post office from August 2, 1901, to November 30, 1913, it was named for Alfred Gates, first postmaster.

GAY. Formerly Lenton. In Choctaw County, 6 miles southwest of Hugo. Name changed to Gay, April 28, 1908, and post office discontinued December 31, 1932. Named by the first postmaster, William J. Williams, for his home town of Gay, Georgia.

GEARY. In southeastern Blaine County. Post office established October 12, 1892. Named for Ed Geary, whose complete name was Edmund Charles F. C. Guerrier, Indian scout of French descent. In 1898 the site was moved several miles southeast.

GEARY'S STATION. In Atoka County, 6 miles north of Atoka. A stage stop on the Butterfield Overland Mail route to California which crossed southeastern Oklahoma, 1858–61. Named for A. W. Geary, local toll-bridge operator. Site now inundated by Atoka Reservoir.

GEE. In Pushmataha County, 11 miles southeast of Clayton. A post office from May 22, 1909, to November 30, 1911. No longer in existence, it was named for Henry V. Gee, first postmaster.

GENE AUTRY. Formerly Berwyn. In Carter County, 10 miles northeast of Ardmore. Post office name changed to Gene Autry, January 1, 1942, to honor the motion picture actor.

GEORGE. In southwestern Garvin County near Elmore City. A post office from May 27, 1911, to August 15, 1919. Named for George Stewart, local cattleman.

GERLACH. In Woodward County, 3 miles west of Woodward. A switch and loading point on the Santa Fe Railway. Named for John Gerlach, Woodward banker.

GERONIMO. In Comanche County, 7 miles south of Lawton. Post office established March 5, 1903. Named for well-known Apache Indian chief.

GERTRUDE. In Atoka County near Stringtown. A post office from January 11, 1886, to February 1, 1887. No longer in existence, it was named for Gertrude L. Westbrook, first postmaster.

GERTY. Formerly Raydon. In Hughes County, 8 miles southeast of Allen. Post office name changed to Gerty, June 23, 1910, and discontinued April 9, 1965. The name is a variant of the former post office name, Guertie.

GHOST MOUND. A distinctive land feature in western Caddo County, 9 miles south of Hydro. Legend attributes much Indian ceremonial significance to the site.

GIBBON. In northwestern Grant County, 6 miles northwest of Wakita. A post office from March 26, 1896, to February 28, 1945, it was named for William M. Gibbon, first postmaster.

GIBSON. Original townsite name for Gould, in Harmon County. Plat filed October 12, 1908. Named for Samuel L. Gibson, townsite owner.

GIBSON STATION. In southeastern Wagoner County. A post office from March 29, 1872, to August 15, 1933, it took its name from nearby Fort Gibson.

GIDEON. In Cherokee County, 8 miles northwest of Tahlequah. A post office from June 13, 1920, to October 14, 1954. Named for Gideon Morgan, wildlife enthusiast.

GILBERT. A rural community in Grant County, 7 miles southwest of Wakita. Named for Truman H. Gilbert, local rancher.

GILBERT. In Nowata County, 6 miles northwest of Lenapah. A post office from January 13, 1899, to May 25, 1899. Named for Allen Gilbert, who was a prominent early-day rancher.

GILMORE. In Le Flore County, 6 miles east of Poteau. A post office from June 30, 1890, to January 15, 1918, it was named for Rad Gilmore, local mill operator.

GILSONITE. In Murray County, 7 miles east of Davis. A post office from March 31, 1900, to February 27, 1909. The name is that of a variety of asphalt, a commodity mined nearby.

GIP. In central Custer County, 8 miles northwest of Arapaho. A post office from March 16, 1895, to September 15, 1909. No longer in existence. The name is a slang word for gypsum, selenite or alabaster, found in the vicinity.

GLADIE. In eastern Garfield County, 5 miles southeast of Garber. A post office from March 24, 1902, to July 14, 1904. Named for

Gladys Ellis, daughter of George Ellis, first postmaster; the spelling was arbitrarily modified by the Post Office Department.

GLASS MOUNTAINS. A prominent land feature in Major County west of Orienta. The buttes are heavy with selenite, which resembles bits of glass. Sometimes incorrectly shown on maps as the Gloss Mountains.

GLAZE. Present Jones, in Oklahoma County. Post office established May 19, 1896, and name changed to Jones, June 1, 1898. Named for Charles D. Glaze, early-day resident.

GLAZE. In Stephens County near Comanche. A post office from April 21, 1891, to September 8, 1892. No longer in existence, it was named for A. H. Glaze, first postmaster.

GLENCOE. In northern Payne County, 10 miles southwest of Pawnee. Post office established December 6, 1899. Until June 14, 1901, the official name of the post office was Glenco. Its name comes from Glencoe, a glen in Argyllshire, Scotland.

GLENN. In Carter County, 2 miles east of Woodford. A post office from April 20, 1894, to July 15, 1922. Named for Thomas H. Glenn, local resident.

GLENOAK. In western Nowata County, 8 miles east of Bartlesville. A post office from February 13, 1906, to December 15, 1932.

GLENPOOL. In southwestern Tulsa County. Post office established January 31, 1908. Named for Ida E. Glenn, Creek, owner of the land on which the discovery well came in on December 1, 1905.

GLENWOOD. In northeastern Dewey County, 6 miles southwest of Canton. A post office from January 18, 1899, to August 31, 1907.

GLOBE. In Coal County, 10 miles northeast of Stonewall. A post office from November 25, 1896, to October 31, 1912.

GLOVER. In McCurtain County, 10 miles northwest of Broken Bow. A post office from June 26, 1901, to October 31, 1955, it took its name from nearby Glover River.

GOINGSNAKE. In Adair County near Westville. A post office from May 5, 1890, to October 27, 1894. Its name comes from Going Snake District, Cherokee Nation.

GOING SNAKE. A district of the Cherokee Nation, created by the Cherokee National Council on November 6, 1840. Named for Going Snake, prominent leader of the Eastern Cherokees.

GOFF. Present Hayward, in southeastern Garfield County. Post office established January 5, 1899, and name changed to Hayward, May 12, 1903.

GOLCONDA. In extreme northwestern Haskell County. A post office from April 25, 1891, to October 30, 1909. Site now inundated by waters of Eufaula Reservoir.

GOLDA'S MILL. In western Adair County, 9 miles northwest of Stilwell. An important early-day mill, established in 1836 by Thomas Taylor and later operated by Dr. Nicholas Bitting. Named for Golda Hunkifer, present owner.

GOLDBURG. In western Kiowa County, 6 miles north of Lone Wolf. A post office from August 13, 1902, to October 31, 1903, it was named for Thomas H. Gold, first postmaster.

GOLDEN. In extreme northeastern Custer County. A post office from March 4, 1902, to September 15, 1903. No longer in existence. The name was selected by the townsite developer to infer that gold was to be found in the vicinity.

GOLDEN. In extreme southeastern Beaver County. A post office from December 21, 1905, to September 15, 1908. No longer in existence.

GOLDEN. In McClain County, 2 miles south of Byars. A post office from April 9, 1896, to April 21, 1897. No longer in existence. Named for W. T. Golden, local resident.

GOLDEN. In McCurtain County, 8 miles west of Broken Bow. Post office established March 13, 1911. Named for James M. Golden, first postmaster.

GOLDSBY. In McClain County, 6 miles north of Washington. Named for Frank W. Goldsby, prominent early-day resident.

GOLF. In eastern Cimarron County, 7 miles east of Keyes. A post office from June 22, 1907, to August 31, 1910. No longer in existence, it took its name from nearby Golf Creek.

GOLTRY. Formerly Karoma. In southeastern Alfalfa County. Post office name changed to Goltry, January 27, 1904. Named for Charles Goltry, local business leader.

GOODE. In southwestern Okfuskee County, 2 miles south of Paden. A post office from February 18, 1902, to June 15, 1903. No longer in existence, it was named for Charles H. Goode, first postmaster.

GOODLAND. In Choctaw County, 4 miles north of Hugo. A post office from August 21, 1871, to February 28, 1902. No longer in existence.

GOODLAND. In Choctaw County, 3 miles south of Hugo. A post office from April 5, 1915, to July 31, 1944, located at Goodland Indian orphanage. The institution was founded in 1848, and has been continuously in service since that date.

GOODMAN. In southeastern Cotton County, 3 miles southwest of Hastings. A post office from March 4, 1902, to March 31, 1904, it was named for Soloman P. Goodman, first postmaster.

GOODNIGHT. In eastern Logan County, 5 miles east of Coyle. A post office from February 23, 1900, to October 31, 1949, it was named for Calvin U. Goodnight, townsite owner.

GOODWATER. In McCurtain County, 12 miles east of Idabel. A post office from December 19, 1894, to February 28, 1959, it took its name from nearby Goodwater Creek, a tributary of Little River.

GOODWELL. In southern Texas County. Post office established June 16, 1903. Its name comes from the good quality of the water well drilled by the Rock Island Railroad at the townsite.

GOODWIN. In western Ellis County, 12 miles west of Arnett. A post office from October 31, 1901, to September 30, 1916. Original townsite name was Holstein. Named for George L. Goodwin, assistant treasurer of the Santa Fe Railway.

GORDON. In Latimer County, 9 miles southeast of Wilburton. A post office from March 5, 1894, to December 14, 1901, it was named for James H. Gordon, McAlester attorney.

GORE. Formerly Campbell. In western Sequoyah County. Post office name changed to Gore, October 22, 1909. Named for Senator Thomas P. Gore.

GOSNELL. Present Frederick, in Tillman County. Post office established November 5, 1901, and name changed to Frederick, September 30, 1902. Named for Robert L. Gosnell, townsite owner.

GOTEBO. Formerly Harrison. In northern Kiowa County, 6 miles west of Mountain View. Post office name changed to Gotebo, February 25, 1904. Named for the chief of a minor band of the Kiowa Indians.

GOULD. In central Harmon County. Post office established February 8, 1909. Original townsite name was Gibson. Named for John A. Gould, first postmaster.

GOW. A switch and loading point on the Frisco in Lincoln County, 4 miles west of Chandler. Named for Francis C. Gow, railroad employee.

GOWEN. In western Latimer County. Post office established January 13, 1894. Named for Francis I. Gowen, Philadelphia attorney.

GOZA. In northwestern Stephens County, 8 miles west of Marlow. A post office from June 16, 1926, to August 31, 1932, it was named for James Goza, local resident.

GRACEMONT. Formerly Ison. In central Caddo County. Post office name changed to Gracemont, September 30, 1904. The name was coined from Grace and Montgomery, the names of two friends of the first postmaster, Alice L. Bailey.

GRADY. In southeastern Jefferson County. Post office established June 16, 1890. Named for Henry W. Grady.

GRADY COUNTY. A county in central Oklahoma, created at statehood. Named for Henry W. Grady, editor of the Atlanta *Constitution*.

GRAHAM. In northwestern Carter County. Post office established June 16, 1891.

GRAINOLA. Formerly Salt Creek. In northwestern Osage County, 6 miles northwest of Foraker. Post office name changed to Grainola, March 28, 1910. The name is a coined word.

GRANADA. In southern Beaver County near Balko. A post office from September 30, 1904, to November 15, 1907. No longer in existence, it was named for the city in Spain in which the Alhambra is located.

GRAND. In southern Ellis County, 11 miles south of Arnett. The county seat of Day County, Oklahoma Territory, from March 8, 1895, until statehood, and the county seat of Ellis County from statehood to August 26, 1908. A post office from November 4, 1892, to September 30, 1943, it was named for Grandville Alcorn, son of Robert Alcorn, county judge.

GRANDFIELD. Formerly Eschita. In southeastern Tillman County. Post office name changed to Grandfield, January 21, 1909. Named for Dr. Charles P. Grandfield, assistant postmaster general under President Taft.

GRAND LAKE TOWNE. A resort community in Mayes County, 2 miles south of Ketchum. Took its name from nearby Grand Lake o' the Cherokees.

GRAND RIVER. Formerly Prairie City. Present Wyandotte, in Ottawa County. Post office name changed to Grand River, December 1, 1876, and changed to Wyandotte, October 3, 1894. It took its name from nearby Grand River.

GRAND SALINE. Near Salina, in Mayes County. A post office from February 23, 1849, to August 24, 1866, and an important early-day settlement. It took its name from the extensive salt works nearby.

GRAND VALLEY. In southeastern Texas County, 9 miles southeast of Hardesty. A post office from June 23, 1888, to December 31, 1930, it took its name from nearby valley of Palo Duro Creek.

GRANDVIEW. In Muskogee County, 6 miles south of Muskogee. Post office established May 5, 1906, and name changed to Crekola, July 18, 1907.

GRANITE. In eastern Greer County. Post office established December 6, 1889. It took its name from the large formations of granite in nearby Wichita Mountains.

GRANT. In southern Choctaw County. Post office established January 31, 1889. Named for President Ulysses S. Grant.

GRANT COUNTY. A county in north-central Oklahoma, comprising the same area as Grant County, Oklahoma Territory. The name Simpson, for Jerry Simpson of Kansas, was also considered as a name for this county. Named for President Ulysses S. Grant.

GRANTHAM. In Marshall County, 6 miles east of Madill. A post office from August 19, 1896, to November 30, 1903. No longer in existence, it was named for Robert L. Grantham, first postmaster.

GRANTON. In Major County, 11 miles northwest of Fairview. A post office from August 25, 1898, to May 31, 1921.

GRAVES. Present Custer, in Custer County. Post office established January 22, 1894, and name changed to Custer, September 28, 1904. Named for Phillip Graves, first postmaster.

GRAY. In southwestern Beaver County. A post office from January 13, 1906, to April 30, 1964. Named for Cora F. Gray, first postmaster.

GRAY. In Kay County, 6 miles northwest of Newkirk. Post office established June 29, 1900, and name changed to Middleton, July 30, 1900.

GRAY HORSE. In Osage County, 5 miles southeast of Fairfax. A post office from May 5, 1890, to December 31, 1931. Named for Gray Horse, or *Ko-wah-ho-tsa*, an Osage medicine man.

GRAYSON. Formerly Wildcat. In southeastern Okmulgee County, 11 miles southeast of Okmulgee. Post office name changed to Grayson, February 20, 1902, and discontinued April 30, 1929. Named for George W. Grayson, Creek tribal leader.

GREASY. In extreme southwestern

Adair County. A post office from April 29, 1920, to October 15, 1921. No longer in existence, it took its name from Greasy Creek, so named because of a local lard-rendering operation.

GREENBRIER. In Mayes County, 5 miles south of Salina. A post office from September 1, 1900, to April 30, 1914. Named for Joseph Lynch Martin, known as "Greenbrier Joe," son of Judge John Martin, chief justice of the Cherokee Nation.

GREENFIELD. In Blaine County, 8 miles northwest of Geary. Post office established September 27, 1901. Named for Henry Greenfield, first postmaster.

GREEN HILL. In northern Le Flore County. Post office established February 15, 1881, and name changed to Grover, February 12, 1886.

GREENLAND. In central Payne County. A post office from June 17, 1895, to June 24, 1897. No longer in existence, it took its name from the surrounding countryside.

GREENLEAF. In southwestern Cherokee County, 7 miles east of Braggs. A post office from December 8, 1910, to February 28, 1925, it took its name from nearby Greenleaf Creek, a tributary of the Arkansas River.

GREENOUGH. A rural community, 10 miles northwest of Forgan in Beaver County.

GREENUP. In Pawnee County, 6

104

miles north of Jennings. A post office from December 21, 1903, to February 14, 1906. No longer in existence, it was named for S. W. Greenup, early-day cattleman.

GREENVILLE. Formerly Orinne. In Love County, 6 miles north of Marietta. Post office name changed to Greenville, December 4, 1902, and discontinued January 31, 1909. Named for Irvine P. Green, first postmaster.

GREENWOOD. In northeastern Ellis County, 6 miles southwest of Fort Supply. A post office from February 19, 1901, to October 26, 1906. No longer in existence.

GREENWOOD. In southwestern corner of Johnston County. A post office from April 17, 1896, to July 8, 1898. No longer in existence.

GREER. In Harmon County at the approximate site of present-day Gould. A post office from October 10, 1891, to August 31, 1909. Its name comes from Greer County, in which the site was located prior to statehood.

GREER COUNTY. A county in southwestern Oklahoma, comprising a portion of Greer County, Oklahoma Territory. Named for John A. Greer, lieutenant governor of Texas.

GREGG. In eastern Cotton County, 5 miles north of Temple. A post office from October 14, 1901, to August 31, 1904. No longer in existence, it was named for Vern E. Gregg, first postmaster.

GRESHAM. In southwest Cimarron County, 6 miles west of Felt. A post office from July 7, 1906, to October 13, 1913. No longer in existence, it was named for Elias A. Gresham, local resident.

GRIEVER. In Major County, 16 miles west of Orienta. A post office from April 10, 1901, to November 30, 1907. No longer in existence. Took its name from nearby Griever Canyon.

GRIFFIN. In central Atoka County. A post office from July 26, 1907, to September 30, 1920. No longer in existence, it was named for Wade H. Griffin, first postmaster.

GRIGGS. In southeastern Cimarron County. Post office established June 13, 1906. Named for J. W. Griggs, rancher.

GRIMES. In southern Roger Mills County. A post office from March 1, 1901, to November 26, 1971. Named for William Grimes, territorial secretary of state.

GRITTS. In southern Muskogee County, 4 miles southwest of Webbers Falls. A post office from March 21, 1896, to October 30, 1909. No longer in existence, it was named for Franklin Gritts, local merchant.

GRIZZLE. In Tillman County, 4 miles southwest of Hollister. A post office from May 17, 1902, to July 30, 1904. No longer in existence, it was named for Millard F. Grizzle, first postmaster.

GROVE. In northern Delaware

105

County. County seat of Delaware County from statehood to January 3, 1912. Post office established December 27, 1888. It took its name from nearby Round Grove, well-known landmark and Civil War site.

GROVER. Formerly Green Hill. In northern Le Flore County. Post office name changed to Grover, February 12, 1886, and discontinued February 25, 1888.

GROW. In northeastern Roger Mills County, 9 miles northwest of Leedey. A post office from May 22, 1900, to November 30, 1918. Name selected by Charlie Dunagan, first postmaster, because he believed there was "plenty of room for the town to grow."

GUERTIE. Present Gerty, in Hughes County, 8 miles southeast of Allen. First known locally as Buzzard Flop. Post office established June 15, 1894, and name changed to Raydon, December 16, 1907. Named for Guertie Raydon, daughter of James S. Raydon, first postmaster, it had the spelling of its name changed by the Post Office Department to prevent confusion with Guthrie.

GUILD. In southeastern Lincoln County, 4 miles north of Prague. Post office established December 14, 1896, and name changed to Willzetta, July 2, 1904. Named for Lee Guild, early-day settler.

GUILEY. Formerly Richland. In western Kay County, 10 miles west of Blackwell. Post office name changed to Guiley, September 10, 1894, and discontinued February 28, 1902. Named for John D. Guiley, first postmaster.

GUNTER. In western Sequoyah County near Gore. A post office from March 29, 1882, to August 8, 1882. No longer in existence, it was named for William Gunter, prominent Cherokee.

GUNTON. In Marshall County, 10 miles northwest of Madill. Post office established December 16, 1903, and name changed to Simpson, March 23, 1904.

GUTHRIE. Capital of Oklahoma Territory and capital of the state of Oklahoma until June 11, 1910. County seat of Logan County, as well as its predecessor territorial county. Post office established April 4, 1889. Named for John Guthrie of Topeka, Kansas, jurist.

GUY. In northern Dewey County, 4 miles northeast of Taloga. A post office from August 6, 1896, to December 31, 1902. No longer in existence.

GUYMON. County seat of Texas County. Post office established June 29, 1901. Named for E. T. Guymon of Liberal, Kansas, president of local townsite company.

GWENNDALE. In Craig County, 5 miles west of Vinita. A post office from May 10, 1892, to March 31, 1904. No longer in existence.

GYPSY. Formerly Billingslea. In Creek County, 8 miles southeast of Depew. Post office name changed to Gypsy, May 1, 1925, and discontinued November 30, 1955. Named for Gypsy Oil Company.

H

H COUNTY. Original designation for Washita County, Oklahoma Territory. Name changed to Washita County, November 8, 1892.

HACKBERRY. Present Sharon, in Woodward County. Post office established June 17, 1895, and name changed to Sharon, February 24, 1912. It took its name from a hackberry grove on the N. Z. Rouse farmstead.

HADDON. In Comanche County, 13 miles southeast of Lawton. A post office from February 26, 1902, to September 29, 1906. No longer in existence, it was named for Julian W. Haddon, first principal of the Fort Sill Indian School.

HADLEY. In northwestern Cherokee County, 15 miles northwest of Tahlequah. A post office from July 20, 1903, to November 15, 1915.

HAGAR. In Pottawatomie County, 3 miles south of Meeker. A post office from October 4, 1895, to January 31, 1908. No longer in existence, it was named for Robert H. Hagar, long-time local resident.

HAILEYVILLE. In eastern Pittsburg County. Post office established April 20, 1901. Named for Dr. Daniel M. Hailey, prominent resident of the Choctaw Nation.

HALEY. In northeastern Grady County, 5 miles south of Tuttle. Post office established May 17, 1910, and name changed to Sooner, April 9, 1913.

HALFWAY. In southwestern Ottawa County. A post office from July 17, 1895, to November 14, 1896. No longer in existence. The location was halfway between the Missouri State line and Vinita.

HALIFAX. Present Newalla, in Oklahoma County. Post office established September 3, 1903, and name changed to Newalla, June 24, 1904.

HALL. In Cleveland County, 6 miles southeast of Noble. A post office from March 7, 1891, to November 15, 1906. Named for Carrie Hall, first postmaster.

HALL PARK. A separate municipality incorporated August 26, 1960, in Cleveland County and adjoining Norman on the northeast. Named for Ike Hall, townsite developer.

HALLEMAN. In Pittsburg County, 10 miles south of McAlester. A post office from July 13, 1898, to March 31, 1904. No longer in existence.

HALLETT. In Pawnee County, 4 miles north of Jennings. Post office established May 19, 1905. Named for Lieutenant Charles H. Hallett, of Company K, Nineteenth Kansas Cavalry.

HALLREN. In southwestern corner of Woodward County. A post office from December 27, 1904, to January 31, 1910. No longer in existence, it was named for Betty Hallren, first postmaster.

HAMBURG. In northwestern Roger Mills County, 8 miles north of Reydon. A post office from August 28, 1900, to December 31, 1929. Its name comes from Hamburg, Germany.

HAMDEN. In northern Choctaw County, 7 miles southeast of Antlers. A post office from March 31, 1894, to May 15, 1924.

HAMILTON. In Beaver County, 3 miles northwest of Forgan. Post office established February 12, 1907, and name changed to Hatten, June 27, 1910.

HAMMON. In eastern Roger Mills County. Post office established June 30, 1894. Named for J. H. Hammon, Indian agent.

HAMPTON. In western Okfuskee County. A post office from December 10, 1906, to August 31, 1908. No longer in existence, it was named for Isaiah B. Hampton, first postmaster.

HAMPTON. In northeastern Osage County, 5 miles west of Copan. A post office from October 5, 1892, to October 25, 1897. No longer in existence, it was named for William A. Hampton, first postmaster.

HAMTON. In eastern Jackson County, 5 miles north of Headrick. A post office from April 25, 1891, to October 6, 1891. No longer in existence, it was named for William G. Ham, first postmaster.

HANCE. In Okmulgee County, 10 miles west of Okmulgee. Post office established May 1, 1909, and name changed to Nuyaka, October 14, 1912. Named for John D. Hance, local merchant.

HANDLEY. In Lincoln County, 6 miles southeast of Chandler. A post office from December 15, 1898, to March 14, 1906. No longer in existence, it was named for John A. Handley, first postmaster.

HANEY. In northern Seminole County, 10 miles northeast of Seminole. A post office from February 17, 1908, to November 30, 1916. Named for Rev. Willie Haney, prominent Seminole.

HANNA. Formerly Hasson. In southern McIntosh County, 18 miles southwest of Eufaula. Post office name changed to Hanna, August 24, 1904. Named for Hanna Bullett, daughter of long-time local resident.

HANSMEYER. In Pottawatomie County, 6 miles north of Shawnee. Townsite plat filed May 14, 1903. The location is usually known by the railroad name of Aydelotte. Named for William H. Hansmeyer, townsite owner.

HANSON. In Sequoyah County, 6 miles east of Sallisaw. A post office from July 13, 1888, to November 30, 1954.

HARDEN CITY. In Pontotoc County, 11 miles south of Ada. Post office established May 7, 1937. Named for Andrew Harden, longtime local resident.

HARDESTY. In southwestern Texas County. Post office established August 3, 1887. The location of the original Hardesty post office was 4 miles northeast of the present townsite. Named for A. J. Hardesty, Dodge City rancher.

HARDIN. Present Hobart, in Kiowa County. Post office established July 21, 1889, and name changed to Speed, February 20, 1901.

HARDWOOD. In southern Coal County, 6 miles southwest of Olney. A post office from April 20, 1914, to October 31, 1923. Took its name from local timber product.

HARDY. In northeastern Kay County. A post office from February 24, 1906, to January 31, 1940, it was named for William Hardy, townsite developer.

HARJO. In Pottawatomie County, 4 miles south of Earlsboro. A post office from June 24, 1921, to August 31, 1954. The name is a Creek word meaning "crazy."

HARLAND. In southern Ottawa County, 7 miles southeast of Fairland. A post office from December 10, 1888, to May 4, 1893. No longer in existence, it was named for Albert W. Harland, first postmaster.

HARMON. In Ellis County, 11 miles east of Arnett. Post office established April 4, 1906. Named for Judson C. Harmon.

HARMON COUNTY. A county in extreme southwestern Oklahoma. Created from a portion of Greer County by special election held May 22, 1909. Named for Judson C. Harmon, governor of Ohio and later United States secretary of state.

HARNEY. Present Woodville, in Marshall County. Post office established November 8, 1881, and name changed to Woodville, July 9, 1888. Named for Sison Harney, local Chickasaw.

HARPER. Formerly Curl in Blaine County. Site in eastern Dewey County, 7 miles northeast of Eagle City. Post office location and name changed to Harper, October 25, 1901, and discontinued December 31, 1911. Named for James A. Harper, early-day resident.

HARPER COUNTY. A county in northwestern Oklahoma, created at statehood from a portion of Woodward County, Oklahoma Territory. Named for Oscar G. Harper, a clerk of the Oklahoma Constitutional Convention.

HARPERVILLE. In Noble County, a few miles northeast of Billings. A post office from May 3, 1894, to October 31, 1900. No longer in existence.

HARRAH. Formerly Sweeney. In eastern Oklahoma County. Post office name changed to Harrah, December 22, 1898. Named for Frank Harrah, merchant and business leader.

HARRINGTON. In western Roger Mills County, 15 miles southwest of Cheyenne. A post office from April 30, 1903, to November 15, 1911. No longer in existence, it was named for John G. Harrington, first postmaster.

HARRIS. In McCurtain County, 11 miles southeast of Idabel. Post office established May 22, 1894. Named for Henry C. Harris, Choctaw jurist and nephew of Peter P. Pitchlynn, Choctaw principal chief.

HARRIS. In Muskogee County, 9 miles east of Oktaha. Post office established July 28, 1884, and name changed to Fawling, March 19, 1890. Named for Bird Harris, prominent Creek.

HARRIS. In Pottawatomie County, 2 miles north of Tecumseh. Townsite plat filed April 11, 1907. Named for Josiah G. Harris, townsite owner.

HARRISBURG. In Stephens County, 10 miles southeast of Duncan. A post office from April 2, 1900, to December 31, 1920.

HARRIS MILL. A well-known mill on Rock Creek in extreme eastern McCurtain County. On April 5, 1859, the name of the nearby post office of Mineral Hill was changed to Harris Mill and moved to this location. Post office discontinued July 2, 1866, but there is no evidence that the office was in operation after the outbreak of the Civil War. Named for William R. Harris, mill owner.

HARRISON. Present Gotebo, in northeastern Kiowa County. Post office established August 17, 1901, and name changed to Gotebo, February 25, 1904. Named for President Benjamin Harrison.

HARRISON. Present Shady Point, in Le Flore County. Post office established September 17, 1891, and name changed to Shady Point, December 11, 1894. Named for William H. Harrison, attorney and Choctaw leader.

HARRISON. In Sequoyah County, 3 miles southwest of Sallisaw. A post office from March 9, 1908, to December 31, 1912. No longer in existence, it was named for John Harrison, local resident.

HARRISTON. Original townsite name for Loveland in Tillman County. Plat dated July 27, 1908. Named for G. V. Harris, townsite owner.

HART. In Pontotoc County, 3 miles southwest of Vanoss. A post office from June 28, 1894, to September 30, 1920, it was named for John A. Hart, first postmaster.

HARTSHORNE. In eastern Pittsburg County. Post office established March 5, 1890. Named for Dr. Charles Hartshorne, railroad official.

HARTVILLE. In southeastern Texas County. A post office from March 7, 1907, to May 31, 1908. No longer in existence, it was named for Rose A. Hart, first postmaster.

HARTZELL. In Oklahoma County, 3 miles east of Witcher. A post office from January 27, 1893, to April 2, 1906, it was named for John H. Hartzell, first postmaster.

HARVEY. In Lincoln County, 9 miles northeast of Chandler. A post office from December 8, 1891, to May 31, 1900. No longer in existence, it was named for W. L. Harvey, county judge of Lincoln County.

HASKELL. Formerly Sawokla. In northwestern Muskogee County. Post office name changed to Haskell, June 20, 1904. Named for Charles N. Haskell.

HASKELL COUNTY. A county in eastern Oklahoma, created at statehood. Named for Charles N. Haskell, a member of the Oklahoma Constitutional Convention and the state's first governor.

HASKEW. In northern Woodward County, 8 miles southwest of Freedom. A post office from July 9, 1902, to October 15, 1921. Named for William L. Haskew, prominent rancher.

HASSON. Present Hanna in southern McIntosh County. Post office established September 22, 1902, and name changed to Hanna, August 24, 1904.

HASTINGS. A rural community in Cherokee County, 4 miles west of Tahlequah. From 1904 to 1911 a post office named Ahniwake was located at the site. Named for W. W. Hastings, long-time local resident.

HASTINGS. In western Jefferson County, 9 miles northwest of Waurika. Post office established March 12, 1902. Its name comes from Hastings, Nebraska.

HATCHETT. In southeastern Blaine County, 7 miles southeast of Watonga. A post office from May 2, 1903, to January 2, 1907. Named for William L. Hatchett, first postmaster.

HATOBI. Present Smithville, in northeastern McCurtain County. Post office established September 13, 1886, and name changed to Smithville, May 1, 1890. The name is from a Choctaw word *hatak-abi*, meaning "warrior man."

HATTEN. Formerly Hamilton. In Beaver County, 3 miles northwest of Forgan. Post office name changed to Hatten, June 27, 1910, and discontinued April 15, 1913. Named for Jarriott P. Hatten, first postmaster.

HAWLEY. In western Grant County, 6 miles north of Nash. A post office from March 13, 1894, to January 31, 1908. No longer in existence, it was named for John H. Hawley, first postmaster.

HAWORTH. Formerly Norwood. First known locally as Harrington. Post office name changed to Haworth, November 17, 1906. In southeastern McCurtain County, 10 miles east of Idabel. Named for John Haworth, railroad surveyor.

HAYDEN. In Nowata County, 10 miles southeast of Nowata. A post office from October 29, 1890, to

October 15, 1936. Named for Henry C. Hayden, first postmaster.

HAYNES. In Wagoner County, 5 miles north of Muskogee. A post office from January 5, 1904, to May 15, 1914.

HAYSTACK MOUNTAIN. A prominent and well-known land feature, distinctive in shape, in northwestern Greer County, 8 miles northwest of Willow.

HAYWARD. Formerly Goff. In southeastern Garfield County 5 miles southeast of Covington. First known locally as Ladysmith. Post office name changed to Hayward, May 12, 1903, and discontinued December 6, 1963. Named for Samuel A. Hayward, townsite developer.

HAYWOOD. In Pittsburg County, 11 miles southwest of McAlester. The railroad name was Barnett. Post office established September 20, 1904. Named for Bill Haywood, prominent socialist.

HAZEL. In western Seminole County, 6 miles north of Konawa. A post office from July 31, 1905, to March 24, 1943. Named for Hazel Whalen, daughter of R. C. Whalen of Ada, an official of the Oklahoma City, Ada and Atoka Railway.

HAZZARD. In northern Caddo County, 5 miles southwest of Hinton. A post office from January 11, 1902, to May 15, 1905. No longer in existence, it was named for William R. Hazzard, first postmaster.

HEADRICK. In eastern Jackson County. Post office established April 21, 1902. Named for T. B. Headrick, townsite owner.

HEALDTON. In western Carter County. Post office established February 26, 1883. Named for Charles H. Heald, prominent resident.

HEALY. In eastern Texas County, 8 miles northeast of Hardesty. A post office from May 5, 1904, to July 31, 1908. Named for George and Frank Healy, brothers and local ranchers.

HEASTON. In Canadian County, 8 miles southwest of El Reno. A post office from February 14, 1896, to June 15, 1907. No longer in existence.

HEAVENER. In Le Flore County, 12 miles south of Poteau. Post office established May 12, 1896. Named for Joseph Heavener, local merchant.

HEBERT. A former rural community in Atoka County, 9 miles northeast of Atoka. Named for Lucy Hebert, long-time local resident.

HECTOR. In northern Okmulgee County, 12 miles east of Haskell. A post office from July 26, 1909, to December 31, 1910. No longer in existence, it was named for James Hector, first postmaster.

HEFNER. In western Washita County, 6 miles south of Canute. A post office from March 11, 1900, to April 29, 1905. No longer in existence, it was named for William E. Hefner, first postmaster.

HELEN. Original name for Kingston, Marshall County. Named for Helen Willis, daughter of J. H. Willis, prominent early-day resident.

HELENA. In southern Alfalfa County. Post office established June 15, 1894. Named for Helen S. Monroe, first postmaster.

HELISWA. In western Seminole County, 5 miles northwest of Seminole. A post office from January 10, 1891, to November 27, 1895. The name is from the Creek word *heleswv*, meaning "medicine."

HEMAN. In northwestern Major County, 5 miles southwest of Waynoka. A post office from April 29, 1901, to February 15, 1922. Named for F. A. Heman, Santa Fe Railway conductor.

HEMMER. In Lincoln County, 6 miles north of Stroud. A post office from January 24, 1894, to April 16, 1894. No longer in existence, it was named for Jacob R. Hemmer, first postmaster.

HENDRIX. In southern Bryan County, 15 miles south of Durant. Post office established June 13, 1909. Named for James A. Hendrix, first postmaster.

HENNEPIN. In southern Garvin County, 14 miles west of Davis. Post office established February 16, 1885. Named for Father Louis Hennepin, a member of the La Salle expedition.

HENNESSEY. In northern Kingfisher County. Post office established July 20, 1889. Until October 7, 1889, the official post office spelling was Hennesy. Named for Pat Hennessey, freighter, killed in Indian massacre, July 4, 1874.

HENQUENET. A townsite in Blaine County, 9 miles north of Watonga. Developed about 1906, and named for Augustus Henquenet, townsite owner. No longer in existence.

HENRY. In Osage County, 15 miles west of Tulsa. A post office from September 17, 1896, to March 31, 1905. Named for Henry Anderson, husband of the first postmaster.

HENRY. In western Le Flore County near Walls. A post office from June 4, 1915, to December 15, 1919. Named for Henry Anderson, long-time local resident.

HENRYETTA. Formerly Furrs. In southern Okmulgee County. Post office name changed to Henryetta, August 28, 1900. Named for Henry G. Beard and his wife, Etta Ray Beard.

HERBERT. Present Wardville, in northwestern Atoka County. Post office established February 6, 1902, and name changed to Wardville, July 18, 1907. Named for Herbert Ward, son of H. P. Ward, territorial jurist.

HERBERT. Present Cleveland, in Pawnee County. Post office established October 28, 1893, and name changed to Cleveland, April 14, 1894. Named for Willis H. Herbert, townsite owner.

HERD. In northern Osage County, 13 miles northeast of Pawhuska. A post office from April 29, 1915, to March 31, 1945. Named for Joe Herrod, local rancher and cattleman.

HEREFORD. Present Warner, in southern Muskogee County. Post office established April 1, 1903, and name changed to Warner, April 22, 1905. Took its name from well-known Hereford cattle sales conducted locally by Campbell Russell, prominent rancher and cattleman.

HERON. In northern Pittsburg County, adjoining the Canadian River. A post office from January 15, 1910, to September 30, 1910. No longer in existence. Took its name from the heron species of bird, a long-necked wading fowl.

HERRING. In eastern Roger Mills County, 9 miles east of Cheyenne. A post office from May 31, 1913, to July 31, 1944. Named for F. E. Herring, local merchant and member of the Constitutional Convention.

HERRON. In northeastern Canadian County, 2 miles northeast of Piedmont. A post office from March 2, 1891, to July 31, 1900. No longer in existence, it was named for Francis C. Herron, first postmaster.

HESS. In southeastern Jackson County, 12 miles southwest of Tipton. A post office from May 18, 1889, to March 15, 1920. Named for Elvira P. Hess, first postmaster.

HESTER. In southeastern Greer County, 8 miles southeast of Mangum. A post office from July 21, 1910, to December 31, 1923. Named for Hester Rude, daughter of Samuel Rude, early-day rancher and cattleman.

HEWITT. In southwestern Carter County. A post office from November 29, 1889, to August 31, 1923. Named for Charles A. Hewitt, sawmill and gin operator.

HEXT. In central Beckham County, 6 miles southwest of Sayre. A post office from June 4, 1901, to November 29, 1902. Named for William Hext, prominent local resident.

HEYBURN. In Creek County, 8 miles northeast of Bristow. A post office from December 14, 1911, to October 14, 1922. Named for James Heyburn, Monett, Mo., Frisco Railroad official.

HEYWOOD. In southeastern Wagoner County. A post office from January 30, 1882, to April 14, 1884. Named for Daniel M. Heywood, first postmaster.

HIBBS. In Beaver County, 8 miles northwest of Beaver. A post office from May 9, 1903, to May 31, 1909. Named for Marshall E. Hibbs, sheriff of Beaver County, Oklahoma Territory.

HIBSAW. A switch and loading point on the Frisco in Lincoln County 5 miles west of Wellston. Named for John Hibbinger and Joel S. Sawyer, both railroad conductors.

HICKMAN. In northeastern Haskell County near Cowlington. A post office from October 3, 1894, to July 6, 1898. No longer in existence, it was named for W. P. Hickman, prominent Choctaw.

HICKMAN. In eastern Kay County, 4 miles northeast of Kaw City. Townsite plat filed January 26, 1923. No longer in existence, it was named for Lemon D. Hickman, townsite owner.

HICKMAN. In western Pittsburg County, 6 miles northeast of Stuart. A post office from May 22, 1914, to November 30, 1914. No longer in existence, it was named for Eugene A. Hickman, first postmaster.

HICKORY. In northeastern Murray County, 6 miles northeast of Sulphur. A post office from November 15, 1893, to March 31, 1964. Took its name from a stand of hickory timber growing along nearby Mill Creek.

HICKORY. In northern Nowata County, 3 miles north of Lenapah. A post office from November 19, 1884, to July 13, 1885. No longer in existence, it took its name from nearby Hickory Creek, a tributary of the Verdigris River.

HIDALGO. In eastern Cimarron County, 8 miles northeast of Willowbar. A post office from October 10, 1907, to October 14, 1916. Its name comes from a county in south Texas.

HIGBEE. In southeastern Cleveland County, 7 miles southeast of Lexington. Post office established August 23, 1901, and name changed to Corbett, February 19, 1902. Named for Joseph B. Higbee, local Pottawatomie Indian.

HIGGINS. Formerly Caminet. In western Latimer County, 6 miles southeast of Hartshorne. Post office name changed to Higgins, May 28, 1903, and discontinued December 31, 1913. Named for R. W. Higgins, territorial jurist.

HIGHLAND. In northeastern Garfield County, 7 miles north of Garber. A post office from January 12, 1894, to April 2, 1906.

HIGHT. In southwestern Greer County, 7 miles southwest of Mangum. A post office from March 2, 1904, to August 31, 1906. No longer in existence, it was named for Thomas H. Hight, first postmaster.

HIGLEY. In southwestern Woodward County, 8 miles northwest of Vici. A post office from April 24, 1901, to July 31, 1913. No longer in existence, it was named for Hubert T. Higley, first postmaster.

HILDERBRAND. In southern Delaware County, 7 miles east of Kansas. A post office from August 3, 1886, to June 25, 1889. On May 24, 1895, a post office named Beckwith was established at this same location. It took its name from nearby Hilderbrand's Mill.

HILDERBRAND'S MILL. Site near Flint, in Delaware County. An important flour mill established about 1852 by the family founded

115

by Peter Hilderbrand, a German immigrant. The mill was operated successively by Union and Confederate troops throughout the Civil War, and was a most important source of commissary supplies. The name is often spelled Hildebrand.

HILL. In northeastern Delaware County, 5 miles east of Grove. Post office established April 27, 1896, and name changed to Dodge, November 20, 1901. On June 4, 1895, a post office named Olympus had been discontinued at this same site.

HILL. In eastern Le Flore County, 9 miles northeast of Poteau. A post office from April 7, 1909, to December 14, 1929. Named for Elmer E. Hill, first postmaster.

HILLABEE. In McIntosh County, near present Stidham. A post office from October 9, 1882, to October 21, 1884. Took its name from a Creek town in Alabama.

HILLSBORO. The post office name for Laverty in western Grady County from January 4, 1904, to January 15, 1908.

HILLSDALE. In northwestern Garfield County. Post office established March 2, 1900. From July 8, 1905, to September 11, 1906, the post office name was Coldwater; another post office named Coldwater had been discontinued on May 15, 1905, 5 miles west.

HILLSIDE. On the line between Washington and Tulsa counties, 3 miles north of Skiatook. A post office from August 12, 1898, to August 31, 1913. Took its name from nearby Hillside Mission, established in 1882 by the Society of Friends.

HILLTOP. In southern Hughes County, 5 miles southeast of Calvin. A post office from January 24, 1910, to December 30, 1916. In 1903 a post office named Tandy had been discontinued at this same site. The name came from the circumstance that the location of the post office was on the top of the divide between Shawnee Creek and Coal Creek.

HILTON. In eastern Creek County, 3 miles east of Sapulpa. A post office from June 28, 1910, to April 30, 1913. Named for William Hilton, prominent local resident.

HILTON. In southwestern Lincoln County, 6 miles northeast of Harrah. A post office from February 15, 1896, to December 31, 1904. No longer in existence, it was named for Huldah E. Hill, first postmaster.

HIMMONAH. In Garvin County, several miles northeast of Pauls Valley. A post office from November 13, 1871, to February 6, 1872. Its name is Chickasaw for "new place."

HINTON. Formerly Crosby. In northern Caddo County. Post office name changed to Hinton, July 5, 1902. Named by Ivan G. Conkin, townsite developer, for his wife's family.

HIRD. In Pontotoc County, 3 miles northeast of Ada. A post office from January 4, 1894, to September 30, 1902. Named for Nicholas Hird, local resident.

HISAW. In extreme northern tip of Haskell County. A post office from August 16, 1905, to October 14, 1916.

HITCHCOCK. In Blaine County, 10 miles north of Watonga. Post office established October 9, 1901. Named for Ethan A. Hitchcock, secretary of the interior.

HITCHITA. In northwestern McIntosh County. Post office established April 23, 1901. Named for a small Indian band of Muskhogean stock living in Georgia and absorbed into the Creek tribe.

HITCHLAND. In southern Texas County, 10 miles southwest of Hardesty. Townsite plat filed October 16, 1929. Named for Henry C. Hitch, prominent rancher and cattleman.

HIX. In eastern Le Flore County, 8 miles southeast of Heavener. A post office from May 1, 1915, to March 31, 1920.

HOARDSVILLE. Formerly Senora. In southern Okmulgee County, 3 miles south of Dewar. Post office name changed to Hoardsville, February 8, 1909, and discontinued July 14, 1917. Named for John H. Hoard, first postmaster.

HOBART. County seat of Kiowa County. Formerly Speed. Post office name changed to Hobart, July 9, 1909. Named for Garrett A. Ho-

bart of New Jersey, vice president of the United States.

HOBSON. In Custer County, 5 miles west of Arapaho. A post office from December 15, 1898, to March 31, 1904. No longer in existence, it was named for Richmond P. Hobson, hero of the battle of Santiago, Cuba.

HOCHATOWN. In McCurtain County, 14 miles northeast of Broken Bow. A post office from September 5, 1894, to December 28, 1963. The name was coined from the Choctaw word *hvcha,* meaning "river" and the English word town, i.e., "river town." Site now inundated by Broken Bow Reservoir.

HOCHUBBEE. In Le Flore County, probably in the vicinity of Poteau. A post office from January 12, 1858, to January 6, 1860. No longer in existence. The name is from the Choctaw *hochukbi,* meaning "cave" or "cavern," which had reference to nearby site named Cavanal, a French word with a similar meaning.

HOCKER. In eastern Beckham County, 5 miles southwest of Elk City. A railroad switch and loading point. Named for Walter E. Hocker, Elk City banker and former United States marshal.

HOCKERVILLE. In northern Ottawa County, adjoining Baxter Springs, Kansas. A post office from January 18, 1918, to September 13, 1963. Named for Leslie C. Hocker, early-day resident.

HODGEN. Formerly Houston. In

Le Flore County, 4 miles south of Heavener. Post office name changed to Hodgen, April 25, 1910. Named for J. W. Hodgens, timber buyer for the Kansas City Southern Railway. Often spelled Hodgens.

HOFFMAN. In Okmulgee County, 9 miles northeast of Henryetta. Post office established December 18, 1905. Named for Roy Hoffman, Oklahoma City attorney.

HOLDENVILLE. County seat of Hughes County. Formerly Fentress. Post office name changed to Holdenville, November 15, 1895. Named for J. F. Holden, general manager of the Choctaw, Oklahoma and Gulf Railroad.

HOLDER. In Love County, 4 miles west of Lebanon. A post office from June 15, 1891, to March 30, 1897. No longer in existence, it was named for Lottie Holder, local rancher.

HOLLAND. In southeastern Beaver County, 5 miles west of Speermore. A post office from April 26, 1904, to April 15, 1913. No longer in existence, it was named for H. W. Holland, first postmaster.

HOLLIDAY. In southwestern Comanche County, 4 miles northeast of Faxon. A post office from January 23, 1908, to August 15, 1933. Named for Arthur O. Holliday, first postmaster.

HOLLIS. County seat of Harmon County. Post office established October 31, 1901. Named for George W. Hollis, townsite owner.

HOLLISTER. In Tillman County, 10 miles southeast of Frederick. Post office established February 1, 1909. Named for Harry L. Hollister, station agent at Frederick for the Katy Railroad.

HOLLOW. In Craig County, 9 miles west of Welch. A post office from June 20, 1904, to April 30, 1938.

HOLLOWAY'S STATION. Site in Latimer County, 7 miles northeast of Red Oak. A stage stop on the Butterfield Overland Mail route to California, which crossed southeastern Oklahoma, 1858–61. Named for William Holloway, stage agent.

HOLLY CREEK. In McCurtain County, 6 miles north of Idabel. A post office from June 7, 1915, to March 15, 1922. No longer in existence. Took its name from nearby Holly Creek, a tributary of Little River.

HOLSTEIN. In Ellis County, 12 miles west of Arnett. Townsite plat filed September 9, 1907, and now known as Goodwin.

HOMESTEAD. In northern Blaine County, 4 miles northwest of Okeene. Post office established January 26, 1893.

HOMINY. In southern Osage County, 16 miles south of Pawhuska. Post office established February 10, 1891. Although there are several versions of the origin of the name, the word is probably a corruption of Harmony, referring to the Harmony Mission in Missouri.

HONEY SPRINGS. In McIntosh County, 1 mile north of Rentiesville. On July 17, 1863, it was the site of the most important Civil War battle fought in Indian Territory, resulting in a northern victory.

HONEYVILLE. In Grant County, 10 miles northwest of Medford. A post office from February 4, 1895, to August 15, 1900. No longer in existence, it was named for Honey Salmon, daughter of James Salmon, first postmaster.

HONOBIA. In western Le Flore County, 15 miles southeast of Talihina. Post office established August 30, 1919. Located on the county line, the post office has at times operated in Pushmataha County. Named for O-no-bi-a, Choctaw allotee.

HOOD. Formerly Mamie. In Sequoyah County near Sallisaw. Post office name changed to Hood, September 11, 1911, and discontinued April 15, 1919. Named for Dennis Hood, long-time local resident.

HOOKER. In northern Texas County. Post office established October 13, 1902. Named for Joseph Hooker, local rancher and cattleman.

HOOPVILLE. Formerly Estelle. In western Major County, 10 miles northwest of Phroso. Post office name changed to Hoopville, January 7, 1908, and changed to Sherman, January 29, 1913.

HOOVER. In southern Garvin County, 7 miles west of Davis, and located at the site of old Fort Arbuckle. A post office from May 31, 1913, to December 15, 1924. Named for Dr. Daniel H. Hoover, early-day local physician.

HOOVER. In eastern Pottawatomie County, 3 miles northwest of Maud. Townsite plat filed January 16, 1929. Named for President Herbert Hoover.

HOPE. In Stephens County, 7 miles northeast of Duncan. A post office from November 25, 1890, to December 31, 1913. The name was selected at a town meeting as expressive of local optimism for the future.

HOPETON. In Woods County, 7 miles south of Alva. Original site was 3 miles south of present Hopeton. Post office established May 31, 1894.

HOPKINS. In Blaine County, 5 miles southeast of Canton. Post office established February 20, 1900, and name changed to Carlton, December 1, 1902. Named for Grace J. Hopkins, first postmaster.

HORACE. In Lincoln County, 8 miles northeast of Wellston. A post office from March 23, 1892, to January 7, 1895. No longer in existence, it was named for Horace Caldwell, son of John W. Caldwell, first postmaster.

HORSE CREEK. In northern Delaware County, 8 miles northwest of Grove. Post office name changed to Horse Creek, February 12, 1879, and discontinued September 4, 1879. Another post office of the same name operated at approximately the same site from May 2, 1908, to December 31, 1912. Took its name from nearby Horse Creek, a tributary of Grand River, now inundated by Grand Lake o' the Cherokees.

HORSESHOE RANCH. In southwestern Pontotoc County, 5 miles east of Hickory. A post office from July 13, 1916, to January 14, 1922. Took its name from nearby Horseshoe Ranch.

HOTUBBEE. A proposed district of the Choctaw Nation. Established in 1860, but never formally organized, it would have embraced all Choctaw lands between the 98th and the 100th meridians, the area usually known as the "Leased District." The name is from the Choctaw word *hot-abi*, which may be rendered "win it."

HOTULKEE. In Pottawatomie County, 3 miles southwest of Earlsboro. Townsite plat filed May 17, 1905. Named for Hotulkee Martha, prominent local Creek Indian.

HOUGH. In Texas County, 14 miles northwest of Guymon. Townsite plat filed July 20, 1928. Named for A. C. Hough, Oklahoma City attorney.

HOUSTON. Present Hodgen in Le Flore County. Post office established August 14, 1896, and name changed to Hodgen, April 25, 1910. Named for General Sam Houston, Texas patriot.

HOWARD. In eastern Harper County, adjoining Salt Springs. A post office from March 5, 1903, to August 14, 1909. On May 28, 1907, a townsite plat was filed 5 miles east in Woodward County, and the post office was moved to the new location. Named for C. F. Howard, first postmaster.

HOWARD. In eastern Le Flore County, 6 miles east of Page. Post office established March 11, 1911, and name changed to Fogel, February 25, 1914.

HOWE. In Le Flore County, 5 miles north of Heavener. First known locally as Klondike. Post office established May 5, 1898. Named for Dr. Herbert M. Howe of Philadelphia, director of the Kansas City, Pittsburg and Gulf Railway, now the Kansas City Southern.

HOXBAR. In Carter County, 7 miles southeast of Ardmore. A post office from October 4, 1895, to November 30, 1926. Took its name from $\overline{HOX}$, the cattle brand of John Washington, local rancher.

HOYLE. Present Ames, in Major County. Post office established January 31, 1894, and name changed to Ames, January 4, 1902. Took its name from nearby Hoyle Creek, a tributary of the Cimarron River.

HOYT. In northwestern Haskell County. Post office established August 19, 1890. Named for Babe Hoyt, early-day ferry operator.

HOYUBY. Present Stuart, in southeastern Hughes County. Post

120

office established June 23, 1892, and name changed to Stuart, April 14, 1896. Named for Ho-yw-bbee, full blood Choctaw allotee.

HUDSON. In northwestern Craig County, 13 miles west of Welch. A post office from November 13, 1886, to March 15, 1911. No longer in existence. Chosen to honor Louis G. Huddleston, local merchant, the name was modified arbitrarily by the Post Office Department.

HUGHART. In Haskell County, 10 miles southwest of Stigler. A post office from June 26, 1906, to June 30, 1915. Named for Richard J. Hughart, early-day resident.

HUGHES. In Latimer County, 5 miles east of Red Oak. A post office from May 17, 1900, to July 15, 1931. Named for Joe Hughes, coal operator.

HUGHES COUNTY. A county in southeastern Oklahoma, created at statehood. Named for W. C. Hughes, member of the Oklahoma Constitutional Convention.

HUGO. County seat of Choctaw County. Post office established November 1, 1901. Named by Mrs. W. H. Darrough, wife of townsite developer, for Victor Hugo, French novelist.

HULAH. In northeastern Osage County, 10 miles north of Bartlesville. Townsite plat filed March 4, 1918. The name is the Osage word *hluah*, meaning "eagle."

HULBERT. In western Cherokee County. Post office established May 4, 1903. Named for Ben H. Hulbert, prominent Cherokee.

HULEN. In northeastern Cotton County, 9 miles northeast of Walters. A post office from December 21, 1901, to October 14, 1933. Named for H. Hulen, early-day resident.

HUMPHREYS. In Jackson County, 8 miles southeast of Altus. Townsite plat filed September, 1909. Named for James Humphrey, local rancher and cattleman.

HUNT. In Pawnee County, 3 miles northeast of Hallett. A post office from June 4, 1904, to December 31, 1908. Named for John L. Hunt, townsite owner.

HUNTER. In northern Garfield County. Post office established January 10, 1901. Named for Charles Hunter, townsite owner.

HUNTON. In southwestern Coal County, 7 miles north of Wapanucka. Post office established October 19, 1896, and name changed to Kite, January 24, 1910.

HUNTVILLE. In Kingfisher County, 10 miles southwest of Kingfisher. A post office from November 1, 1892, to September 30, 1903. No longer in existence, it was named for John M. Hunt, first postmaster.

HURLEY. In Cimarron County, 5 miles northeast of Boise City. A post office from October 2, 1907, to July 10, 1925.

HURST. In southwestern Tillman County, 10 miles southwest of Frederick. A post office from July 14, 1903, to July 30, 1904. No longer in existence.

HUSKEY. A rural community in Choctaw County 3 miles south of Fort Towson. Named for John Huskey, early-day County Commissioner of Choctaw County.

HUTTONVILLE. In McIntosh County, 5 miles northwest of Eufaula. Post office established October 19, 1896, and name changed to Nerotown, February 28, 1911. Named for A. J. Hutton, first postmaster.

HYDRO. In northwestern Caddo County. Post office established September 23, 1901. Took its name from the abundance of good well water.

I

I COUNTY. Original name for Caddo County, Oklahoma Territory. Name changed to Caddo County, November 8, 1902.

ICONIUM. In Logan County, 3 miles northeast of Meridian. Took its name from Iconium, Appanoose County, Iowa, home town of the townsite owner. The name comes from the city of Iconium, now Konya in Asia Minor, mentioned in the book of Acts, and a city visited by Paul.

IDA. In Lincoln County, 5 miles northwest of Chandler. A post office from March 25, 1895, to March 15, 1904. Named for Ida Hall, wife of I. N. Hall, early-day settler.

IDA. In western McCurtain County, 6 miles northwest of Bethel. Post office established June 5, 1909, and name changed to Battiest, November 1, 1928. Named for Ida Griffin, daughter of Dan Griffin, early-day resident.

IDABEL. County seat of McCurtain County. Post office established February 3, 1904. Named for Ida and Belle Purnell, daughters of an official of the Choctaw and Arkansas Railroad.

ILLINOIS. A district of the Cherokee Nation. Took its name from the Illinois River. The river was named for the Illinois, at one time an extensive Algonquin tribe. The name was undoubtedly introduced to the region by the Osages, traditional allies of the Illinois tribe.

IMO. In Garfield County, originally 2 miles northeast of Drummond and now 5 miles southwest of Enid. The second site was first known locally as Fritz. A post office from March 18, 1895, to June 30, 1922. Named for Imogene Allen, daughter of Samuel T. Allen, long-time local resident.

INDEPENDENCE. In northern Custer County, 11 miles west of Thomas. A post office from October 5, 1892, to July 15, 1922.

INDIAHOMA. In western Comanche County, 12 miles east of Snyder. Post office established April 23, 1902. The name was coined from the words Indian and Oklahoma.

INDIANAPOLIS. In southern Custer County, 5 miles east of Clinton. First known locally as Bear Siding. A post office from February 7, 1902, to August 15, 1949. Its name comes from Indianapolis, Indiana.

INDIANOLA. In northern Pittsburg County, 7 miles west of Canadian. Post office established January 16, 1891. The name was coined from the word Indian and the Choctaw word *olah*, meaning "this side of."

INEZ. In Pottawatomie County, 5 miles southwest of Maud. A post office from August 9, 1898, to September 3, 1901. Named for Inez Hazelwood, local resident.

INGALLS. In Payne County, 9 miles east of Stillwater. A post office from January 22, 1890, to October 31, 1907, it was the site of a famous outlaw battle, September 1, 1893, when three deputy U.S. marshals were killed. Named for Senator John J. Ingalls of Kansas.

INGERSOLL. In Alfalfa County, 4 miles northwest of Cherokee. A post office from September 13, 1901, to December 31, 1942, it was named for C. E. Ingersoll, Philadelphia railroad official.

INGLETON. In northern Dewey County, 4 miles west of Seiling. A post office from January 13, 1899, to July 31, 1905. No longer in existence, it was named for Vesta A. Ingle, first postmaster.

INGRAM. In western Lincoln County, 1 mile northwest of Wellston. A post office from April 2, 1892, to December 16, 1898. No longer in existence, it was named for Nancy I. Ingram, first postmaster.

INGRAM. In southwestern Pontotoc County near Roff. A post office from December 9, 1899, to November 30, 1900. No longer in existence, it was named for Theodocia L. Ingram, first postmaster.

INOLA. In southern Rogers County. Post office established March 1, 1890. The name is a Cherokee word meaning "black fox."

IOLAND. In southeastern Ellis County, 11 miles northwest of Leedey. County seat of E County, Oklahoma Territory, and until March 8, 1895, of Day County, Oklahoma Territory. A post office from March 29, 1892, to February 28, 1918. The name was coined from the word Iowa.

IONA. In Murray County, 8 miles north of Sulphur. A post office from April 17, 1894, to July 15, 1929.

IOWA CITY. Original townsite name for Coyle in Logan County.

IRBY. In central McIntosh County, 8 miles north of Eufaula. Sometimes known as Bond. Post office established January 4, 1907, and name changed to Onapa, February 5, 1909.

IRENE. In northeastern Seminole County, 6 miles south of Boley. A post office from October 31, 1903, to November 28, 1907. Named for

Irene Davis, the late Mrs. W. S. Key of Oklahoma City, daughter of Chief Alice Brown Davis, Seminole leader. On December 19, 1907, a post office named Schoolton was established at approximately this same site.

IRETON. In Grady County, 3 miles northeast of Alex. A post office from June 1, 1898, to September 30, 1919. No longer in existence. Named for John Ireton, local Choctaw allotee and head of a large family of that name.

IRONBRIDGE. In eastern Haskell County, 3 miles southwest of Keota. Site of Civil War engagement June 19, 1864. Post office established June 25, 1891, and name changed to Kanima, August 24, 1910. Took its name from a nearby iron bridge, built prior to the Civil War over the San Bois Creek on the Beale Wagon Road.

IRONTON. In southern Noble County, 7 miles southeast of Perry. Townsite plat filed April 19, 1893. No longer in existence.

IRVING. In Lincoln County, 9 miles north of Chandler. A post office from June 11, 1892, to April 25, 1894. Named for Washington Irving, American author, who passed about 20 miles north of this site on October 20, 1832.

IRVING'S CASTLE. In Payne County, 5 miles south of Ingalls. An unusual and well-known land feature named for Washington Irving by the members of the expedition, made famous by *A Tour on the Prairies*, when they discovered the site on October 20, 1832.

ISABELLA. In Major County, 8 miles southeast of Fairview. Post office established July 25, 1894. The name was coined from the name of Belle Isbell, wife of a local landowner.

ISABELLA. In Pottawatomie County, 5 miles west of Asher. Post office established February 15, 1875, and name changed to Clardyville, February 25, 1875. Named for Isabella A. Clardy, first postmaster.

ISADORE. In Tillman County, 3 miles northeast of Hollister. A post office from October 25, 1907, to December 15, 1912. Named for Father Isadore Ricklin, Catholic missionary to Anadarko.

ISLAND BAYOU. Small stream flowing into Red River, 25 miles below mouth of Washita River. Boundary between Choctaw and Chickasaw nations.

ISOM SPRINGS. In Marshall County, 6 miles south of Kingston. A post office from February 6, 1902, to November 15, 1924. Named for Isom O'ky-um-ba, local Chickasaw.

ISON. Present Gracemont, in Caddo County. Post office established January 11, 1902, and name changed to Gracemont, January 30, 1903.

ITTITALAH. Located probably in Johnston County. A post office from August 1, 1881, to May 29, 1883. The name is a Choctaw word for wooden pin or stake.

IVA. In northwestern Beaver County, 10 miles west of Forgan. A post office from February 25, 1905, to October 31, 1907. Named for Iva LeCrone, local resident.

IVANHOE. In southeastern Beaver County, 4 miles west of Slapout. A post office from March 20, 1892, to May 31, 1920. Took its name from the novel by Sir Walter Scott.

IVANHOE. Present Custer, in Custer County. Post office established August 26, 1887, and name changed to Custer, October 28, 1891. Took its name from the novel by Sir Walter Scott.

IVY. In southern Pottawatomie County, 7 miles west of Asher. A post office from May 14, 1892, to August 25, 1893. No longer in existence, it was named for Ivy Lewis, first postmaster.

J

JACKS. In southeastern corner of Dewey County. A post office from March 7, 1895, to January 31, 1906. No longer in existence, it was named for Andrew Jackson Abercrombie, first postmaster.

JACK'S FORK. A county of Pushmataha District, Choctaw Nation.

JACKSON. In southeastern Bryan County, 6 miles southeast of Bennington. A post office from March 17, 1894, to October 30, 1920. Named for President Andrew Jackson.

JACKSON. In southern Logan County, 4 miles north of Luther. Post office established March 25, 1890, and name changed to Tohee, November 13, 1890. Named for President Andrew Jackson.

JACKSON. A county in Pushmataha District, Choctaw Nation. Organized in 1886 and named for Jacob Jackson, prominent Choctaw.

JACKSON. In Stephens County near Velma. A post office from May 21, 1886, to December 29, 1886. No longer in existence, it was named for David W. Jackson, first postmaster.

JACKSON COUNTY. A county in southwestern Oklahoma, organized at statehood from a portion of Greer County, Oklahoma Territory. Named for Major General Thomas J. "Stonewall" Jackson, Confederate hero.

JAMES. In western Texas County, 20 miles west of Guymon. A post office from May 19, 1906, to June 30, 1910. No longer in existence, it was named for O. N. James, first postmaster.

JAMESVILLE. A rural community in Muskogee County, 13 miles west of Muskogee. On October 15, 1908, a post office named Ridge had been discontinued at approximately this location. Named for Warren James, Haskell resident.

JANIS. In southeastern McCurtain County, 2 miles east of Tom. A post office from December 29, 1894, to July 31, 1915. Named for Janis

Garland, daughter of Samuel Garland, principal chief of the Choctaw Nation.

JARRELL. In Tillman County, 8 miles northeast of Frederick. A post office from May 22, 1903, to May 14, 1906. No longer in existence, it was named for Joseph Jarrell, first postmaster.

JAUNITA. Present Bromide, in northeastern Johnston County. Post office established October 20, 1905, and name changed to Zenobia, April 27, 1906. Named for Juanita Jackson, daughter of William H. Jackson, territorial jurist.

JAY. Designated county seat of Delaware County, January 3, 1912, by proclamation of the governor. Post office established May 19, 1909. Named for Jay Washbourne, grandson of an early-day Cherokee missionary. Although his name was actually Claude L. Washbourne, he always used the name given him when as a youth he wore a shirt bearing the name J. Struthers Milling Co. His grave in Polson cemetery is marked simply Jay Washbourne.

JAY. In Oklahoma County near Harrah. Post office established June 23, 1892, and name changed to Rossville, February 21, 1895.

JEFFERSON. In central Grant County. Jefferson is at the original site of Pond Creek; a post office named Pond was discontinued at this location on April 14, 1887. Named by William J. Hicks, first postmaster, for Jefferson, Texas, his home town.

JEFFERSON. In Pottawatomie County, 4 miles northwest of Asher. The post office name was Adell. The townsite, by plat filed August 19, 1898, was Jefferson City. Named for W. Jefferson McColgan, townsite developer.

JEFFERSON COUNTY. A county in southern Oklahoma, created at statehood from a portion of Comanche County, Oklahoma Territory, and the southwestern corner of the Chickasaw Nation. Named for President Thomas Jefferson.

JEFFS. Although originally in another site, present Tupelo in Coal County. Post office established June 28, 1894, moved to present site of Tupelo, October 25, 1900, and name changed to Tupelo, January 13, 1904. Named for Jefferson D. Perry, first postmaster.

JENKINS. In eastern Woods County, 3 miles west of Dacoma. A post office from April 28, 1898, to June 15, 1905. Named for William M. Jenkins, territorial secretary of state and later governor of Oklahoma Territory.

JENKS. In Tulsa County, 10 miles south of Tulsa. Post office established January 31, 1905. Named for Elmer E. Jenks, long-time local resident.

JENNESS. In Okmulgee County, 8 miles southwest of Okmulgee. A post office from May 12, 1910, to January 31, 1912. No longer in existence, it was named for J. E. Jenness, merchant and prominent early-day resident.

JENNIE. In Garfield County, 3 miles east of Breckenridge. Post office established September 27, 1894, and name changed to Cropper, January 12, 1900. Named for Jennie Jones, wife of Thomas J. Jones, first postmaster.

JENNINGS. In southern Pawnee County. Post office established November 14, 1893. Named for George Jennings, townsite developer.

JESSIE. In southeastern Pontotoc County, 6 miles south of Stonewall. A post office from July 13, 1898, to November 15, 1917. Named for Jesse Ayakatubby, local young Chickasaw lad.

JESTER. In Greer County, 15 miles northwest of Mangum. A post office from November 18, 1890, to January 31, 1938. Named for David C. Jester, first postmaster.

JET. In eastern Alfalfa County. Post office established June 28, 1894. Named for W. M. Jett, miller and first postmaster.

JETMORE. In northwestern Garfield County. A post office from November 27, 1896, to June 30, 1900. No longer in existence, it was named for Frank Jett, local resident.

JEWEL. In Caddo County, 4 miles southwest of Binger. A post office from March 27, 1902, to September 14, 1905. Named for Jewel

Browning, daughter of Robert Browning, first postmaster.

JIMTOWN. In southern Love County, 5 miles southwest of Burneyville. A post office from May 19, 1884, to October 14, 1916. Named for four prominent local residents, each with the first name of Jim, their last names being Little, Patton, Rector, and Ryan.

JOBURN. In Atoka County, 4 miles south of Lehigh. A post office from April 13, 1922, to December 15, 1925. No longer in existence. The name is an anagram of Joseph S. Hilburn, first postmaster.

JOHNS. In Pushmataha County, 6 miles north of Antlers. A post office from September 28, 1912, to May 15, 1915. Took its name from nearby Johns Valley, which had been named for Henry A. Johns, Choctaw allotee.

JOHNSON. In McClain County, 2 miles northwest of Byars. Site of old Camp Arbuckle; often known as Beaversville. A post office from October 5, 1876, to March 15, 1910. No longer in existence, it was named for Montford Johnson, prominent Chickasaw rancher.

JOHNSTON COUNTY. A county in south-central Oklahoma, created at statehood. Named for Douglas H. Johnston, governor of the Chickasaw Nation.

JOINER. Formerly Eolian. In western Carter County near Wilson. Post office name changed to Joiner, May 17, 1909, and discontinued

April 15, 1918. Named for C. M. Joiner, local oil producer.

JONES. Formerly Glaze. In northeastern Oklahoma County. Post office name changed to Jones, June 1, 1898. Named for C. G. Jones, Oklahoma City industrialist and railroad promoter.

JONES ACADEMY. Site in Pittsburg County, 3 miles northeast of Hartshorne. An Indian boys school established in 1891 by the Choctaw Nation. The post office at Jones Academy was named Dwight. Named for Wilson N. Jones, principal chief of the Choctaw Nation.

JOY. A rural community in northwestern Murray County, 3 miles south of Wynnewood. Took its name from nearby Joy School, which had been selected as the winner in a student contest for the name of the new school when the districts of Carr Flats and Wheeler consolidated.

JUANITA. In Choctaw County, 8 miles southeast of Boswell. Post office established March 21, 1902, and name changed to Crowder, June 4, 1904. Named for Juanita Harlan Crowder, wife of Dr. W. E. Crowder, early-day physician.

JUDSON. In Blaine County, 3 miles northwest of Geary. A post office from August 9, 1892, to October 31, 1908. No longer in existence.

JULY. In McCurtain County, 10 miles south of Idabel. A post office from July 27, 1918, to January 15, 1921. No longer in existence. Named from the circumstance that the post office was established during the month of July.

JUMBO. In western Pushmataha County, 10 miles north of Miller. Post office established November 8, 1906. Took its name from Jumbo Asphalt Company.

JUMPER. In southwestern Pottawatomie County. A post office from December 6, 1893, to December 11, 1894. No longer in existence, it was named for John Jumper, Seminole chief.

JUNCTION. In southern Comanche County, 2 miles south of Geronimo. A post office from February 20, 1902, to January 31, 1919. No longer in existence.

JUNOD. In eastern Harper County, 6 miles south of Salt Springs. A post office from January 10, 1911, to December 14, 1912. No longer in existence, it was named for Louis Junod, first postmaster.

JURGENSEN. In Cimarron County, 7 miles southeast of Boise City. Post office established August 4, 1906, and name changed to Garlington, February 14, 1908. Named for David Jurgensen, local resident.

K

K COUNTY. The original designation for Kay County, Oklahoma Territory.

KANIMA. Formerly Ironbridge. In eastern Haskell County, 3 miles southwest of Keota. Post office name changed to Kanima, August 24, 1910, and discontinued December 31, 1940. The name is a Choctaw word meaning "somewhere" or "someplace."

KANSAS. In southern Delaware County. Post office established January 5, 1895. Its name comes from the state of Kansas.

KARMA. Present Yuba, in Bryan County, 12 miles east of Achille. Post office established February 7, 1929, and name changed to Yuba, October 1, 1950. The name was arbitrarily assigned by the Post Office Department in lieu of Eagle Lake, the name requested by local residents.

KAROMA. Present Goltry, in Alfalfa County. Post office established May 26, 1894, and name changed to Goltry, January 27, 1904. The original site was one mile southeast of present Goltry.

KATIE. In Garvin County, 6 miles southeast of Elmore City. A post office from March 13, 1895, to August 31, 1929. Named for Katie Griffiths, daughter of G. T. Griffiths, first postmaster.

KAVANAUGH. In Le Flore County, 5 miles north of Wister. Post office established November 11, 1885, and name changed to Kennady, May 16, 1889. Took its name from nearby Mount Cavanal.

KAW. In eastern Kay County. Post office established September 12, 1902. Took its name from the Kaw, or Kansa, tribe of Indians. Known locally as Kaw City.

KAW AGENCY. In Kay County at the site of present Washunga. A post office from June 28, 1880, to October 15, 1892. Site of the agency for the Kaw, or Kansa, tribe.

KAY CENTER. In Kay County, a few miles south of Newkirk. A post office from October 9, 1897, to June 1, 1898. No longer in existence. Its name comes from the circumstance that the site was in the center of Kay County.

KAY COUNTY. A county in northern Oklahoma, and somewhat similar in area to K County, Oklahoma Territory. Flynn, for Dennis T. Flynn, had also been considered as a name for this county. Took its name from the original "K" designation of the county.

KEBOLTE. In Lincoln County, 3 miles north of Wellston. A post office from December 17, 1891, to November 15, 1892. Named for Charles Kebolte, local resident.

KECHI. In southwestern Grady County, 9 miles east of Cyril. A post office from March 25, 1902, to June 15, 1906. No longer in existence, it took its name from Kichai Indians, a Caddoan tribe, now living in Caddo County.

KEDRON. In Sequoyah County, 8 miles north of Sallisaw. Post office established May 26, 1886, and name changed to Marble, January 16, 1895. On January 22, 1869, a post office named Kidron had been discontinued at this same location. Its name comes from the Bible, and is that of the stream referred to in II Samuel 15:23 and John 18:1.

KEEFE. A rural community in Osage County, 3 miles east of Fairfax. Named for J. H. Keefe, vice president of the Santa Fe Railway.

KEEFETON. In Muskogee County, 10 miles south of Muskogee. A post office from March 31, 1905, to October 18, 1957. Named for J. H. Keefe, vice president of the Santa Fe Railway.

KEENAN. Formerly Doris. In western Woodward County, 10 miles southeast of Fargo. Post office name changed to Keenan, February 18, 1910, and discontinued July 15, 1935. Named for Julia A. Keenan, first postmaster.

KEE-TOO-WAH. In Cherokee County. A post office from August 8, 1882, to February 7, 1884. No longer in existence, it took its name from a political society organized in 1859 by Northern sympathizers among the Cherokees.

KEIRSEY. In Bryan County, 6 miles west of Durant. Often known as Mead Junction. A post office from June 16, 1904, to November 30, 1920. Named for William D. Keirsey, local rancher.

KEITH. In Alfalfa County, 7 miles northwest of Ingersoll. A post office from May 4, 1894, to October 15, 1904. No longer in existence, it was named for Charles G. Keith, first postmaster.

KEITH. In northern Jefferson County, 3 miles northwest of Addington. A post office from August 5, 1890, to December 7, 1892. No longer in existence, it was named for Jones Keith, early-day rancher and cattleman.

KELLER. In western Carter County. Post office established August 6, 1894; date of discontinuance unavailable. Named for William Keller, local merchant.

KELLY. In Harmon County, 6 miles east of Hollis. A post office from June 12, 1900, to June 15, 1910. No longer in existence.

KELLYVILLE. In central Creek County. Post office established November 27, 1893. Named for James E. Kelly, long-time local merchant.

KELSO. In Craig County, 6 miles northeast of Vinita. A post office from July 8, 1898, to October 30, 1920. Named for William C. Kelso, rodeo rider.

KELTNER. In Love County, 4 miles northeast of Courtney. A post office from June 1, 1892, to September 15, 1900. No longer in existence, it was named for William C. Keltner, first postmaster.

KELTNER. In Texas County, 25 miles northwest of Guymon. A post office from April 4, 1906, to June 30, 1910. Named for Claud Keltner, first postmaster.

KEMA. In northern Ottawa County, south of Baxter Springs. A post office from August 25, 1882, to January 3, 1884. No longer in exis-

130

tence. The name is the Peoria word *ke-mah*, meaning "chief."

KEMP. In southern Bryan County, 15 miles south of Durant. Post office established October 20, 1890. Named for Jackson C. Kemp, prominent Chickasaw.

KEMPTON. In Beckham County, 2 miles north of Carter. A post office from May 10, 1910, to January 14, 1911. Named for J. A. Kemp, president of the townsite company.

KENDRICK. Formerly Avondale. In northeastern Lincoln County. Post office name changed to Kendrick, January 21, 1903. Named for J. W. Kendrick, vice president of the Santa Fe Railway.

KENEFIC. Formerly Nail. In northern Bryan County. Post office name changed to Kenefic May 23, 1910. Named for William Kenefic, of Kansas City, president of the Kansas, Oklahoma and Gulf Railroad.

KENNADY. Formerly Kavanaugh. In Le Flore County, 5 miles north of Wister. Post office name changed to Kennady, May 16, 1889, and discontinued July 20, 1915. Named for James F. Kennady, first postmaster.

KENT. In Choctaw County, 7 miles northeast of Soper. A post office from February 9, 1905, to November 15, 1915. In 1920 a post office named Rooster was established at approximately this same location.

KENTON. Formerly Florence. In northwestern Cimarron County. Post office name changed to Kenton, May 12, 1891. County seat of Cimarron County from statehood until September 5, 1908. The name is a variant of Canton, Ohio.

KENWOOD. In western Delaware County. Post office established May 25, 1922. The name was coined from the names William Kennedy and National Hardwood Company.

KEOKUK FALLS. In northeastern Pottawatomie County, 7 miles southeast of Prague. A post office from January 13, 1892, to February 15, 1918. Named for Moses Keokuk, prominent Sac and Fox chief.

KEOTA. In northwestern Cimarron County, 10 miles northeast of Kenton. Post office established July 18, 1904, and name changed to Benola, February 7, 1906. Took its name from Keota, Iowa.

KEOTA. In eastern Haskell County. Post office established January 27, 1905. The name is a Choctaw word which may be translated "fire gone out" and is related to the circumstance that 175 newly arrived Choctaws had died from pneumonia, and the entire clan became extinct.

KERFOOT. In Canadian County, adjoining El Reno. A post office from April 13, 1911, to June 30, 1917. Named for John A. Kerfoot, El Reno business man.

KETCHUM. In southeastern Craig County. Post office established September 15, 1899. Named for James Ketchum, long-time local resident.

KEYES. Formerly Willowbar. In northeastern Cimarron County. Post office name changed to Keyes, October 15, 1926. Named for Henry Keyes, president of the Santa Fe Railway.

KEYS. In southeastern Craig County. Post office from December 3, 1890, to December 24, 1894. No longer in existence, it was named for Lucy S. Keys, first postmaster.

KEYSTONE. In southeastern Pawnee County. Site inundated by the waters of the Keystone Dam. A post office from May 26, 1900, to October 12, 1962. The name is from the circumstance that the site is in a key position at the junction of the Cimarron and Arkansas rivers.

KEYSTONE. Present Waynoka, in Woods County. Post office established February 23, 1888, and name changed to Waynoka, April 10, 1889.

KEYWEST. In Lincoln County, 3 miles southeast of Stroud. A post office from April 20, 1908, to July 31, 1909. An unsuccessful effort was made in December, 1924, to reestablish this post office. Its name comes from Key West, Florida.

KIAMICHI. In northern Pushmataha County, 6 miles east of Tuskahoma. A post office from September 27, 1887, to September 14, 1962. Took its name from nearby Kiamichi River.

KIAMICHI. A county in Pushmataha District, Choctaw Nation. Took its name from the Kiamichi River.

KIAMICHI. Name of a river and a mountain range in southeastern Oklahoma. The name is a French word, *kamichi*, meaning "horned screamer," a species of bird.

KIBBY. In Harper County, 8 miles southeast of Buffalo. A post office from October 31, 1901, to April 15, 1920. Named for Leonard D. Kibby, pioneer resident.

KICKAPOO. In northeastern Oklahoma County. A post office from July 30, 1897, to August 15, 1900. No longer in existence, its name comes from the Kickapoo Indians.

KICKAPOO STATION. In Pottawatomie County, 3 miles northwest of Shawnee. A post office from January 6, 1876, to September 4, 1879. Took its name from a nearby, and still existing, settlement of Kickapoo Indians.

KIDDER. In northern Caddo County, 7 miles west of Hinton. A post office from February 24, 1902, to December 14, 1905. No longer in existence, its name comes from Kidder, Missouri.

KIDRON. In northern Sequoyah County, 8 miles north of Sallisaw. Post office established September 17, 1835; it was moved and its name changed to Marble Salt Works, September 8, 1858. Thereafter, on October 27, 1859, another post office was established at the original site, continuing the name Kidron, but was, in turn, discontinued January 22, 1869. On May 26, 1886, a post office known as Kedron was established at this same location. The name is a Biblical word, referring to the stream mentioned in II Samuel 15:23 and John 18:1.

KIEFER. Formerly Praper. In eastern Creek County. Post office name changed to Kiefer, December 12, 1906. Named for Smith Kiefer, long-time local resident.

KIEL. Present Loyal, in Kingfisher County. Post office established June 15, 1894, and name changed to Loyal, October 1, 1918. Its name came from Kiel, Germany.

KILDARE. In central Kay County. Post office established October 14, 1893. Its name comes from a town and county in Ireland.

KILLGORE. In extreme southeastern Grady County. A post office from June 22, 1907, to December 31, 1913. No longer in existence, it was named for William C. Killgore, first postmaster.

KING. Present Dale, in Pottawatomie County. Post office established April 25, 1891, and name changed to Dale, October 26, 1893. Named for John King, townsite owner.

KINGFISHER. County seat of Kingfisher County. Formerly Lisbon. Post office name changed to Kingfisher, July 18, 1889. Originally, Lisbon and Kingfisher were adjoining townsites. Took its name from nearby Kingfisher Creek, which, in turn, had been named for King Fisher, operator of an early-day stage station.

KINGFISHER COUNTY. A county in west-central Oklahoma, similar in size to Kingfisher County, Oklahoma Territory. Named for King Fisher.

KINGMAN. In Woods County, 15 miles northeast of Freedom. A post office from January 13, 1906, to October 13, 1912. No longer in existence.

KINGSTON. In central Marshall County. Post office established April 4, 1894. First known locally as Helen. Named for Jeff King, long-time local resident.

KINLOCK. In Marshall County, 7 miles southeast of Madill. A post office from February 7, 1905, to November 30, 1927. No longer in existence.

KINNEY. In southern Kiowa County, 4 miles southeast of Snyder. A post office from March 12, 1902, to March 15, 1905. No longer in existence, it was named for Rebecca Kinney, first postmaster.

KINNICK. In Tillman County, 5 miles northwest of Frederick. A post office from December 2, 1902, to May 14, 1906. No longer in existence, it was named for E. B. Kinnick, first postmaster.

KINNISON. In Craig County, 6 miles northwest of Welch. A post office from September 13, 1886, to February 28, 1922. Named for Presly Kinnison, first postmaster.

KINSEY. In central Mayes County. A post office from August 22, 1913, to June 15, 1916. No longer in existence, it was named for Ernest V. Kinsey, first postmaster.

KINTA. In southern Haskell County. Post office established September 26, 1902. The name is an Indian word for beaver.

KIOGRE. In southwestern Kiowa County, 3 miles northeast of Headrick. A post office from May 3, 1902, to March 15, 1904. No longer in existence. The name was coined from the names of two counties, Kiowa and Greer.

KIOWA. In southern Pittsburg County. Post office established May 6, 1881. Took its name from nearby Kiowa Hill.

KIOWA COUNTY. A county in southwestern Oklahoma, similar in area to Kiowa County, Oklahoma Territory. Named for the Kiowa tribe of Indians.

KISER. In Garvin County, 4 miles east of Pauls Valley. A post office from June 26, 1901, to December 31, 1907. Named for George Kiser, local merchant.

KITE. Formerly Hunton. In southwestern Coal County, 7 miles northwest of Wapanucka. Post office name changed to Kite, January 24, 1910, and discontinued August 15, 1912. Named for C. H. Kite, early-day resident.

KITTIE. Present Clarita, in Coal County. Post office established January 3, 1902, and name changed to Clarita, January 19, 1910. Named for Kittie Toler, daughter of E. B. Toler, first postmaster.

KLAUS. In Delaware County, 6 miles northeast of Ketchum. Post office established April 13, 1896, and name changed to Cleora, November 28, 1900. Named for Robert H. Klaus, ferry operator.

KLONDIKE. In Garvin County, 6 miles southwest of Pauls Valley. A post office from April 23, 1901, to July 15, 1907. Its name comes from the Klondike River, a tributary of the Yukon River in Alaska.

KNICKERBOCKER. In northern Texas County. A post office from July 22, 1905, to February 15, 1907. No longer in existence. The name is a coined word made popular by Washington Irving and now means an early Dutch settler of New York.

KNOWLES. In northeastern Beaver County. Post office established March 16, 1907. Original townsite name was Sands. Named for F. E. Knowles, long-time local schoolteacher.

KNOWLTON. In Alfalfa County, 8 miles southeast of Cherokee. A post office from July 20, 1901, to January 14, 1904. No longer in existence, it was named for George W. Knowlton, first postmaster.

KOKOMO. In Beaver County, 7 miles southwest of Beaver. A post office from March 20, 1888, to October 6, 1891. No longer in existence. Its name comes from Kokomo, Indiana.

KOLB. In Le Flore County, 8 miles south of Wister. Post office established February 5, 1892, and name changed to Reichert, May 7, 1892. Named for Philip Kolb, first postmaster.

KOMALTY. In Kiowa County, 5 miles northeast of Hobart. A post office from December 6, 1901, to March 31, 1938. Named for Komal-te, chief of a minor Kiowa band.

KONAWA. In southwestern Seminole County. Post office established July 15, 1904. The word is a Seminole one meaning "string of beads."

KOONKAZACHEY. In Kiowa County, 6 miles east of Lugert. Townsite plat filed April 30, 1907. Named for a leading Kiowa-Apache chief whose enrolled name was Gon-kon, but was known always as "Apache John."

KORN. In northeastern Washita County. Post office established April 27, 1896, and name changed to Corn, September 26, 1918. Took its name from the cornfield of Henry Kendall which became the site of the post office.

KOSOMA. In Pushmataha County, 9 miles north of Antlers. A post office from November 28, 1888, to October 31, 1954. The name is a Choctaw word meaning "stink" and was selected because of the smell of a nearby swamp.

KREBS. In Pittsburg County, 3 miles east of McAlester. Post office established February 10, 1886. Named for Judge Edmond F. Krebs, prominent Choctaw.

KREMLIN. In northern Garfield County. Post office established November 7, 1893. Its name comes from the Kremlin, in Moscow, Russia.

KULI-CHUK-CHU. Present Shawneetown, in McCurtain County. Post office established January 18, 1882, and name changed to Kuli Inla, August 7, 1882. Site of Miller Court House, Arkansas Territory. The name is a Choctaw word meaning "maple tree spring."

KULI INLA. Present Shawneetown, in McCurtain County. Formerly Kuli-Chuk-Chu. Post office name changed to Kuli Inla, August 7, 1882, and changed to Shawneetown August 16, 1892. On March 4, 1886, the Post Office Department changed the spelling of this post office to Kulli Inla. The name is a Choctaw word meaning "new spring."

KULLITUKLO. In southern McCurtain County, 7 miles southeast of Idabel. A post office from October 22, 1895, to November 30, 1932. The name is a Choctaw word meaning "two springs."

KULLY CHAHA. In Le Flore County, 3 miles south of Cameron. A post office from February 15, 1881, to November 15, 1913. The name is the Choctaw word meaning "high spring" and has reference to a spring high on Sugar Loaf Mountain.

KUSA. In southern Okmulgee County, 2 miles northeast of Dewar. A post office from April 1, 1916, to

May 30, 1936. Its name comes from Coosa, a Creek town in Alabama.

L

L COUNTY. Original designation for Grant County, Oklahoma Territory. Name changed to Grant County, November 6, 1894.

LACEY. In Kingfisher County, 10 miles west of Hennessey. A post office from April 16, 1890, to April 30, 1909. Named for John F. Lacey of Iowa, member of Congress and prominent in public land matters.

LACROSSE. In Caddo County, 6 miles northeast of Gracemont. A post office from March 18, 1902, to December 31, 1908. Took its name from the Indian ball game.

LADESSA. In Greer County, 5 miles southwest of Mangum. A post office from March 4, 1902, to December 10, 1908. Named for Ladessa Wright, daughter of R. P. Wright, long-time local resident.

LADYSMITH. Local name for present-day Hayward in Garfield County. Its name comes from Ladysmith, Natal, besieged in 1899–1900 during the Boer War.

LAFAYETTE. In central Haskell County, 7 miles south of Stigler. A post office from June 21, 1907, to August 15, 1914. No longer in existence. Its name comes from Lafayette, Indiana.

LAHOMA. In western Garfield County. Post office established January 22, 1894. The word is a diminutive of the name Oklahoma.

LAKE. In Beaver County, 15 miles southeast of Beaver. Post office established December 24, 1887, and name changed to Clear Lake, February 11, 1888.

LAKE. In eastern Woods County, 6 miles west of Aline. A post office from March 7, 1895, to August 14, 1905. Took its name from a nearby lake that had been built by stockmen prior to the land opening.

LAKE ALUMA. In Oklahoma County. A separate municipality adjoining Oklahoma City on the northeast. Originally a game preserve, the corporate name is Aluma Chulosa, a Choctaw phrase meaning "peaceful retreat."

LAKEMP. Formerly Conroy. In Beaver County, 6 miles south of Elmwood. Post office name changed to Lakemp, July 26, 1909, and on September 4, 1919, the post office was moved and its name was changed to Booker, Texas. Named for D. L. Kemp, townsite owner.

LAKE THUNDERBIRD. A large central Oklahoma reservoir, sponsored jointly by Midwest City, Del City, and Norman with the United States. Name selected by Frankie McKenzie, as a tribute to the 45th Division.

LAKE VALLEY. A rural community in Washita County, 10 miles southeast of Cordell. The name first came into use about

1910, after the consolidation of four school districts resulted in the selection of Lake Valley as the new name.

LAKEVIEW. In western Logan County, 3 miles west of Crescent. Post office from April 25, 1891, to October 25, 1894. No longer in existence, it took its name from nearby Twin Lakes, two small natural lakes.

LAKEVIEW. In southwestern Pottawatomie County, 5 miles west of Wanette. A post office from December 29, 1896, to July 31, 1905. No longer in existence.

LAMAR. In central Hughes County. Post office established July 23, 1907.

LAMBDIN. In southeastern Lincoln County, 2 miles east of Prague. A post office from December 21, 1896, to July 15, 1904.

LAMBERT. In Alfalfa County, 8 miles southwest of Cherokee. A post office from November 21, 1901, to April 30, 1952. Named for Ambrose Lambert, townsite owner.

LAMEREUX. Original name for Newkirk, Kay County. Named for S. W. Lamereux, commissioner of the General Land Office.

LAMONT. In southeastern Grant County. Post office established December 15, 1893. Named for Daniel S. Lamont, secretary of war under President Cleveland.

LAND. In western Osage County, adjoining Ponca City. A post office

from July 6, 1894, to March 19, 1895. No longer in existence, it was named for James T. Land, first postmaster.

LANE. In southeastern Atoka County. Post office established October 6, 1902. Took its name from the circumstance that the first post office was located in a store situated at the end of a lane bounded by rail fencing.

LANGLEY. In eastern Mayes County. Post office established January 20, 1939. Named for J. Howard Langley of Pryor, chairman of the Grand River Dam Authority.

LANGSTON. In northeastern Logan County. Post office established June 25, 1891. Named for John M. Langston of Virginia, well-known Negro educator and member of Congress.

LARK. In southern Marshall County, 9 miles south of Kingston. A post office from January 14, 1889, to April 14, 1934.

LARNED. In eastern Roger Mills County, 6 miles south of Hammon. A post office from July 16, 1902, to October 31, 1906. No longer in existence. Its name comes from Fort Larned, Kansas.

LATHAM. In Le Flore County, 10 miles west of Shady Point. A post office from May 10, 1901, to February 15, 1918. Site of Trahern's Station on the Butterfield Overland Mail route. In 1882 a post office named Opossum had been discontinued at this same site. Named for

Thomas B. Latham, United States commissioner.

LATIMER COUNTY. A county in southeastern Oklahoma, created at statehood. Named for James S. Latimer, a member of the Oklahoma Constitutional Convention.

LAURA. In southern Latimer County, 12 miles west of Talihina. A post office from June 3, 1910, to May 1, 1924.

LAVERNE. In western Harper County. Post office established March 30, 1898. Named for Laverne Smith, local resident.

LAVERTY. In western Grady County, 5 miles northeast of Cement. A post office from November 19, 1901, to November 30, 1933. From January 4, 1904, to December 15, 1908, the name of this post office was Hillsboro. Named for Lealis F. Laverty, townsite developer.

LAVROCK. In southeastern Texas County near Hardesty. A post office from January 8, 1889, to April 30, 1892. No longer in existence. The name was coined from the phrase lava rock.

LAW. In northeastern Lincoln County, 4 miles southeast of Avery. A post office from September 7, 1892, to May 31, 1900. Named for Jay Law, first postmaster.

LAWRENCE. In Kiowa County, 5 miles northeast of Hobart. A post office from October 24, 1902, to March 31, 1904. Named for Law-

rence Standeven, son of Susan L. Standeven, first postmaster.

LAWRENCE. Formerly Oolite. In Pontotoc County, 3 miles northeast of Fitzhugh. Post office name changed to Lawrence, June 27, 1907, and discontinued March 15, 1935. Named for Joseph Lawrence, early-day local resident.

LAWRIE. In Logan County, 6 miles north of Guthrie. A post office from August 22, 1890, to October 15, 1900. No longer in existence, it was named for Lawrie Tatum, Quaker Indian agent.

LAWSON. In southern Pawnee County, 6 miles west of Jennings. Post office established January 17, 1894, and name changed to Quay, February 24, 1903. Named for Stonewall J. Lawson, townsite owner.

LAWTER. In southeastern Custer County. A post office from February 2, 1897, to July 6, 1899. No longer in existence, it was named for Henry A. Lawter, first postmaster.

LAWTON. County seat of Comanche County. Post office established July 15, 1901. Named for Major General Henry W. Lawton, killed during the Philippine insurrection.

LAWTON. Present Copan, in Washington County. Post office established January 6, 1900, and name changed to Weldon, July 10, 1901.

LAYTON. In southwestern Garvin County. A post office from December 21, 1911, to September 31, 1913. No longer in existence, it was named for Lee Layton, first postmaster.

LEACH. Formerly Ulm. In southwestern Delaware County. Post office name changed to Leach, February 20, 1897. Named for John R Leach, first postmaster.

LEADER. In Hughes County, 5 miles northeast of Allen. A post office from September 18, 1889, to July 15, 1902. Named for Edward Leadree, local Chickasaw allotee.

LEAL. In northeastern Caddo County, 6 miles west of Minco. A post office from February 10, 1902, to April 30, 1910. Named for Noah Lael, prominent rancher and son-in-law of Cyrus Harris.

LEBANON. In southwestern Marshall County. Post office established February 17, 1882. Its name comes from Lebanon, Tennessee, because the Cumberland Presbyterian Church had its headquarters there.

LEE. Formerly Wellington. In western Muskogee County, 3 miles northwest of Boynton. Post office name changed to Lee, July 22, 1892, and discontinued November 30, 1911. Named for David A. Lee, first postmaster.

LEEDEY. In southwestern Dewey County. Post office established January 6, 1900. Named for Amos Leedey, first postmaster.

LEEPER. In McClain County, 16 miles northwest of Purcell. A post office from July 2, 1888, to July 21, 1892. No longer in existence, it was named for William P. Leeper, rancher and prominent Chickasaw.

LEE'S CREEK. A district of the Cherokee Nation, organized prior to 1831 and abolished November 6, 1840. Named for a trapper with the Nuttall expedition.

LeFLORE. A post office in western Le Flore County, established August 26, 1887. Named for the LeFlore family.

LE FLORE COUNTY. A county in eastern Oklahoma, created at statehood. Named for the well-known Choctaw family of French descent, whose most prominent member was Greenwood LeFlore.

LEFT HAND SPRING. In Blaine County, 4 miles east of Greenfield. A well-known spring on the Chisholm Trail and near the location of the grave of Jesse Chisholm. Named for Left Hand, an Arapaho chief.

LEGAL. In extreme northeastern Coal County. A post office from June 1, 1896, to April 15, 1918. No longer in existence.

LEGATE. In extreme northeastern Love County. A post office from September 25, 1905, to September 15, 1921. No longer in existence.

LEGER. The post office name for Altus, Kiowa County, from July 10, 1901, to May 14, 1904. Named for the father-in-law of a railroad official.

LEHIGH. In southeastern Coal County. County seat of Coal County from statehood until June 13, 1908. Post office established April 4, 1882. Its name comes from Lehigh, Pennsylvania.

LELA. On the line between Pawnee and Noble counties, 5 miles west of Pawnee. A post office from February 17, 1894, to October 31, 1954. From October 3, 1904, to March 18, 1905, the post office name was Valeria. Named for Lela McClellan, daughter of Charles McClellan, early-day rancher.

LEMON. In western Caddo County near Eakly. A post office for a short time in 1903. Named for Robert M. Lemons, first postmaster.

LENAPAH. In northern Nowata County. Post office established April 9, 1890. The word is a variant of Lenápe, original name of the Delaware tribe of Indians.

LENNA. In McIntosh County, 13 miles northwest of Eufaula. Post office established January 4, 1902. Named for Lenna Moore, local Creek Indian.

LENORA. In Dewey County, 6 miles west of Taloga. A post office from March 24, 1896, to June 30, 1955. The name was coined from the name of two early settlers, Lee Moore and Nora Stovall.

LENOX. In Le Flore County, 9 miles east of Whitesboro. A post office from October 2, 1896, to April 15, 1913. Its name comes from nearby Lenox Mission, established in

1852 by the American Board of Foreign Missions. The name is from Lenox, Kentucky.

LENTON. In Choctaw County, 6 miles southwest of Hugo. Post office established October 22, 1901, and name changed to Gay, April 28, 1908.

LEON. In southwestern Love County. Post office established June 28, 1883. The name is a Spanish word meaning "lion."

LEONARD. In southeastern Tulsa County. Post office established August 22, 1908. Named for Oliver H. Leonard, Tulsa banker.

LEONEL. In Dewey County, 5 miles northeast of Oakwood. A post office from September 13, 1915, to June 30, 1919. Named for Leonel Boucher, son of townsite owner.

LEOTA. In northeastern Custer County, 5 miles northwest of Thomas. A post office from December 15, 1898, to June 15, 1905. Named for Leota Noble, daughter of George H. Noble, first postmaster.

LEQUIRE. In southern Haskell County. Post office established December 12, 1906. Named for P. H. Lequire, local sawmill operator.

LEROY. In eastern Pawnee County, 3 miles north of Keystone. A post office from May 31, 1894, to January 15, 1906. Named for Lee Jordan and Roy LeMaster, local residents.

LESTER. In northwestern Johnston County, 4 miles south of Mill

Creek. A post office from September 15, 1899, to August 31, 1910. No longer in existence.

LETITIA. Formerly Rucker. In Comanche County, 7 miles east of Lawton. Post office name changed to Letitia, November 28, 1903, and discontinued April 30, 1917. Named for Letitia Haggard, early-day resident.

LEWIS. Present Tushka, in Atoka County. Formerly Peck. Post office name changed to Lewis, April 13, 1905, and name changed to Dayton, January 21, 1909. Named for Charles S. Lewis, local resident.

LEWISTON. In southwestern Lincoln County, 6 miles north of McLoud. A post office from October 27, 1895, to December 31, 1904. No longer in existence, it was named for Mattie C. Lewis, first postmaster.

LEWISVILLE. In southwestern Haskell County, 5 miles east of Quinton. A post office from August 26, 1909, to November 30, 1915. No longer in existence, it was named for Calvin H. Lewis, first postmaster.

LEXINGTON. In southern Cleveland County. Post office established February 21, 1890. Its name comes from Lexington, Kentucky.

LIBBIE. In northwestern Caddo County, 6 miles south of Hydro. A post office from May 10, 1902, to June 15, 1905. No longer in existence, it was named for Libbie Hammer, first postmaster.

LIBERTY. In Canadian County, 3 miles north of Union City. A post office from June 14, 1890, to January 14, 1904.

LIBERTY. In Noble County, 3 miles north of Perry. The townsite was developed in 1893 by E. P. McCade, prominent Territorial black, formerly auditor of the State of Kansas, as a Negro town. Notwithstanding extensive efforts, especially by the African Methodist Church, to secure settlers, the project did not survive. The Santa Fe later established a switch and loading point near the townsite known as Arnettville.

LIBERTY. In eastern Sequoyah County, 7 miles northeast of Muldrow. A post office from August 24, 1914, to August 15, 1927.

LIDDLE. Present Coalgate, in Coal County. Post office established September 18, 1889, and name changed to Coalgate, January 23, 1890. Named for William Liddle, coal mining superintendent.

LIGHTNING CREEK. In western Craig County, 9 miles north of Chelsea. A post office from December 14, 1911, to November 30, 1913, and located about 8 miles northeast of the former post office of the same name. Took its name from Lightning Creek, a tributary of the Verdigris River.

LIGHTNING CREEK. In southeastern Nowata County, 8 miles southeast of Nowata. Post office established October 23, 1872, and name changed to Alluwe, June 27,

1883. Took its name from nearby Lightning Creek, a tributary of the Verdigris River.

LILLIVALE. In northern Kay County, 4 miles northeast of Braman. A post office from May 3, 1894, to April 30, 1903. No longer in existence, it was named for James E. Lilly, first postmaster.

LILLY. In eastern Lincoln County. A post office from June 23, 1892, to December 16, 1898. No longer in existence, it was named for Joel F. Lilly, first postmaster.

LIMA. In Logan County, 6 miles east of Crescent. A post office from March 3, 1892, to July 15, 1901. No longer in existence.

LIMA. In Seminole County, 6 miles southeast of Seminole. A post office from July 17, 1907, to August 23, 1957.

LIMESTONE GAP. In northern Atoka County, 9 miles south of Kiowa. A post office from March 29, 1875, to February 28, 1922. From September 22, 1897, to July 15, 1901, the name of the post office was Limestone. The locality is now known as Gap.

LINCOLN. In western Jackson County, 12 miles south of Gould. A post office from May 18, 1899, to February 28, 1906. It was named for President Abraham Lincoln.

LINCOLN. In eastern Kingfisher County, 6 miles southwest of Crescent. A post office from December 14, 1889, to September 22, 1894. No longer in existence, it was named for President Abraham Lincoln.

LINCOLN COUNTY. A county in central Oklahoma, similar in area to Lincoln County, Oklahoma Territory. Named for President Abraham Lincoln.

LINDEN. In northeastern Cleveland County, 7 miles south of Newalla. A post office from October 17, 1893, to February 14, 1906. No longer in existence. Took its name from the basswood or lime tree.

LINDSAY. In northwestern Garvin County. Post office established March 28, 1902. Named for Lewis Lindsay, townsite owner.

LINK. In Nowata County, 8 miles southwest of Nowata. A post office from July 31, 1914, to January 31, 1916. Took its name from the Link Oil Company of Marietta, Ohio.

LINN. In eastern Marshall County, 9 miles east of Madill. A post office from May 14, 1890, to July 31, 1915. Named for the three Linn brothers, Simon, George, and Matthew, ranchers.

LINWOOD. In Jefferson County, 6 miles southeast of Waurika. A post office from January 19, 1895, to January 2, 1907. No longer in existence.

LISBON. Present Kingfisher, in Kingfisher County. Post office established April 20, 1889, and name changed to Kingfisher, July 18, 1889. Its name comes from Lisbon, Ohio.

LITTLE. In northern Seminole County, 8 miles north of Seminole. A post office from August 14, 1902, to November 30, 1916. It was named for Thomas Little, prominent Seminole and second chief of the tribe.

LITTLE CHIEF. A rural community in western Osage County, 5 miles southeast of Burbank. Took its name from nearby Little Chief Creek.

LITTLE CITY. In Marshall County, 9 miles east of Madill. Original townsite name was Pure City. Named for Ruel W. Little, Madill attorney.

LITTLEROBE. In southwestern Ellis County, 14 miles southwest of Arnett. A post office from March 24, 1902, to September 30, 1909. No longer in existence, it was named for Little Robe, Cheyenne chief.

LOAF. In northern Mayes County near Adair. A post office from December 21, 1915, to May 15, 1929. The name was assigned by the Post Office Department after local residents had requested Sugar Loaf as the name for the proposed post office.

LOAM. In southern Carter County, 9 miles southwest of Ardmore. A post office from May 14, 1913, to March 15, 1918. No longer in existence. Took its name from the character of the surrounding soil.

LOCK. In Jackson County, 6 miles east of Olustee. A post office from May 25, 1891, to January 15, 1906. No longer in existence, it was named for James Lock, long-time local resident.

LOCKHART. In Oklahoma County, 5 miles northwest of Britton. A post office from March 21, 1894, to August 15, 1903. No longer in existence, it was named for George D. Lockhart, first postmaster.

LOCKRIDGE. In extreme southwestern corner of Logan County. A post office from November 7, 1903, to November 30, 1928. The name is a coined word, referring to a ridge at the corner of the four counties, Logan, Oklahoma, Canadian, and Kingfisher.

LOCKWOOD. In southeastern Beaver County, 5 miles southwest of Logan. A post office from March 10, 1887, to June 30, 1917.

LOCO. In southeastern Stephens County. Post office established June 3, 1890. Took its name from the locoweed, an herb of the pea family, usually poisonous to livestock.

LOCUST GROVE. In southeastern Mayes County. Post office established March 26, 1873. Site of a Civil War engagement, July 3, 1862, it took its name from a well-known grove of locust trees.

LODI. In Latimer County, 6 miles northeast of Red Oak. A post office from March 23, 1894, to April 15, 1955. Named for Lodi Latimer, daughter of prominent early-day resident.

LOEWEN. In Ellis County, 6 miles west of Arnett. A post office from May 6, 1904, to October 14, 1905.

No longer in existence, it was named for Jacob J. Loewen, first postmaster.

LOFTUS. Present Earlsboro, in Pottawatomie County. Post office established May 26, 1894, and name changed to Earlsboro, June 12, 1895.

LOGAN. In southeastern Beaver County. Post office established December 10, 1888. Named for Senator John A. Logan of Illinois.

LOGAN COUNTY. A county in north-central Oklahoma, similar in area to Logan County, Oklahoma Territory. Named for Senator John A. Logan of Illinois.

LOMETA. In Wagoner County, 10 miles northeast of Wagoner. A post office from November 5, 1904, to January 15, 1910. Took its name from nearby Lometa Ranch.

LONA. In western Haskell County, 6 miles northeast of Quinton. A post office from September 6, 1895, to March 31, 1913. No longer in existence.

LONDON. In extreme southeastern Beckham County. A post office from July 21, 1904, to December 14, 1905. No longer in existence. Its name comes from London, England.

LONEBELL. In southern Ellis County, 7 miles south of Peek. A post office from May 15, 1903, to June 30, 1910.

LONE GROVE. In Carter County, 7 miles west of Ardmore. Post office established February 4, 1885.

LONELM. In Marshall County, 6 miles west of Kingston. A post office from February 25, 1903, to October 15, 1913.

LONESTAR. In Custer County, 6 miles west of Clinton. A post office from July 10, 1895, to June 30, 1904. No longer in existence. Its name refers to the state of Texas.

LONETREE. In northeastern Alfalfa County, 4 miles northeast of Amorita. A post office from October 7, 1895, to February 28, 1902. No longer in existence, it took its name from a nearby lone cottonwood tree "prized by all."

LONE WOLF. In western Kiowa County. Post office established January 29, 1901. Named for Mam-a-day-te, or Lone Wolf, Kiowa chief.

LONG. In Sequoyah County, 6 miles north of Muldrow. A post office from August 22, 1894, to April 15, 1937. Named for Peter Long, Cherokee leader.

LONGDALE. Formerly Cainville. In northwestern Blaine County. Post office name changed to Longdale, November 28, 1903. Named for W. H. Long, townsite owner.

LOOKEBA. In northern Caddo County. Post office established June 28, 1902. The name was coined from those of Lowe, Kelly, and Baker, the three townsite developers.

LOOKOUT. In northwestern Woods County. Post office established October 16, 1901.

LOONEY. In Harmon County, 10 miles southeast of Gould. A post office from June 1, 1892, to October 15, 1912. Named for Tourney Looney, first postmaster.

LORENA. Present Turpin, in northwestern Beaver County. Post office established January 13, 1904, and name changed to Turpin, April 8, 1925. Named for Lorena M. Stone, first postmaster.

LORETTA. Present Texhoma, in southwestern Texas County. Post office established May 7, 1898, and name changed to Texhoma, March 18, 1902. Named for Loretta McCain, first postmaster.

LOU. Present Gene Autry, in Carter County. Post office established July 11, 1883, and name changed to Dresden, November 22, 1883. Named for Lou Henderson, wife of C. C. Henderson, local merchant.

LOUIS. In southeastern Harmon County, 8 miles southeast of Hollis. A post office from April 25, 1891, to April 30, 1925. Named for Louis Goemann, first postmaster.

LOVE COUNTY. A county in southern Oklahoma, created at statehood. Named for a prominent Chickasaw family, whose best-known members were Robert H. Love and Overton Love.

LOVEDALE. A railroad switch and loading point in eastern Harper County, 5 miles west of Salt Springs. Named for Claude L. Love, land owner.

LOVEL. In western Payne County, 6 miles east of Orlando. A post office from December 8, 1893, to March 31, 1902. No longer in existence, it was named for Lovel P. Fortner, first postmaster.

LOVELAND. In southeastern Tillman County. Post office established October 23, 1908. The name was coined by E. T. Duncan, local merchant.

LOVELL. Formerly Perth. In Logan County, 7 miles north of Crescent. Post office name changed to Lovell, February 12, 1906, and discontinued March 8, 1957. Named for James W. Lovell, townsite owner.

LOVELY COUNTY. A county established October 13, 1827, by the Arkansas legislature which was intended to comprise all land west of Arkansas, south and east of a point 40 miles west of the northwest corner of Arkansas and north of the Arkansas River. Nicksville was designated as the county seat. County abolished October 17, 1828. Named for Major William Lovely of Virginia, Cherokee agent.

LOVING. In Le Flore County, 10 miles east of Heavener. A post office from December 2, 1908, to June 15, 1922. Named for John Loving, local Choctaw.

LOWE. Formerly Speer. In Lincoln County, 6 miles north of Chandler. Post office name changed to Lowe, December 15, 1903, and discontinued June 30, 1904. Named for Thomas J. Lowe, territorial secretary of state.

145

LOWREY. In Cherokee County, 10 miles northeast of Tahlequah. A post office from July 20, 1903, to December 31, 1929. Named for George Lowrey, Cherokee chief.

LOYAL. Formerly Kiel. In northwestern Kingfisher County. Post office name changed to Loyal, October 1, 1918. The German name was changed during World War I to show loyalty to the United States.

LUCAS. Present Centralia, in northwestern Craig County. Post office established November 1, 1892, and name changed to Centralia, April 11, 1899.

LUCERNE. In southwestern Woods County, 8 miles west of Sharon. A post office from May 29, 1903, to November 15, 1907. No longer in existence. Its name comes from Lucerne, Switzerland.

LUCIEN. In southwestern Noble County. Post office established June 27, 1903. Named for Lucien Emerson, mother of a long-time local merchant.

LUCILE. In Grady County, 6 miles southeast of Chickasha. A post office from July 8, 1905, to October 31, 1912. No longer in existence. Named for Lucile Hill, daughter of David D. Hill, rancher and townsite owner.

LUCKEY. In northwestern Cherokee County, 3 miles northeast of Peggs. A post office from October 11, 1913, to November 15, 1922. Named for Dan Luckey, local sawmill proprietor.

LUCY. In Harper County, 11 miles south of Buffalo. A post office from December 19, 1907, to September 20, 1909. Named for Lucy Twogood, local resident.

LUDLOW. In extreme southwestern Le Flore County. A post office from April 22, 1901, to November 15, 1954. Named for Edwin N. Ludlow of New York, mining engineer.

LUELLA. In Garfield County, 2 miles east of Fairmont. Post office established June 6, 1894; name changed and post office moved to Fairmont, December 24, 1902. Named for Luella Riley, wife of John W. Riley, first postmaster.

LUGERT. In western Kiowa County, 7 miles south of Lone Wolf. A post office from April 18, 1902, to September 30, 1950. Named for Frank Lugert, first postmaster.

LUK-FAH-TAH. In McCurtain County, 3 miles west of present-day Broken Bow. A post office from February 14, 1853, to July 9, 1866, and a well-known early-day settlement. On January 21, 1873, the post office was re-established under the name Lukfata. The name is a Choctaw word meaning "white clay," and has reference to the name of a Choctaw village.

LUKFATA. In McCurtain County, 3 miles west of Broken Bow. A post office from January 21, 1873, to March 31, 1917. Took its name from an earlier post office, Luk-fah-tah, which had been discontinued July 9, 1866, at the same site.

LULA. In eastern Pontotoc County, 6 miles northeast of Stonewall. A post office from December 12, 1902, to November 30, 1955. Named for Lula Scott, daughter of John Scott, early resident.

LUMKEE. In Hughes County, 5 miles southeast of Holdenville. A post office from May 14, 1892, to November 2, 1895. The name is adopted from the Creek word *lu mehe,* meaning Eagle.

LUTHER. In northeastern Oklahoma County. Post office established July 26, 1898. Named for Luther Jones, Oklahoma City businessman and son of C. G. Jones.

LUTIE. Formerly Ola. In Latimer County, 3 miles east of Wilburton. Post office name changed to Lutie, October 4, 1901, and discontinued January 31, 1942. Named for Lutie Hailey Walcott, daughter of Dr. D. M. Hailey, prominent territorial leader.

LYCEUM. In northern Pushmataha County, 2 miles west of Tuskahoma. A post office from March 23, 1896, to July 30, 1900. Name chosen because the post office was located at the Choctaw Female Academy.

LYDIA. In Lincoln County, 3 miles southeast of Sparks. A post office from May 28, 1892, to August 13, 1904. No longer in existence, it was named for Lydia Amberg, wife of Jacob Amberg, first postmaster.

LYLE. In northern Grant County, 7 miles northwest of Renfrow. A post office from October 1, 1896, to March 30, 1907. No longer in existence.

LYLE. In central Grady County near Ninnekah. A post office from July 27, 1923, to October 15, 1925. No longer in existence, it was named for Robert A. Lyle, first postmaster.

LYMAN. In northwestern Osage County, 6 miles northwest of Shidler. A post office from March 22, 1924, to February 15, 1956. Named for A. J. Lyman, townsite owner.

LYNCH. In Mayes County, 5 miles northwest of Spavinaw. Post office established October 30, 1905, and name changed to Strang, March 18, 1913. On March 31, 1905, a post office named Walnut, a short distance to the west, had been discontinued. Took its name from nearby Lynch's Prairie, well-known land feature.

LYNCH'S PRAIRIE. In Mayes County, 4 miles west of Spavinaw. Post office established May 9, 1878, and name changed to Spavina Mills, October 10, 1878. Named for Joseph M. Lynch, mill operator and proprietor of a salt works.

LYNN. In Major County, 3 miles west of Ames. A post office from March 12, 1895, to January 30, 1904. No longer in existence.

LYNN LANE. A rural community in Tulsa County, now in the Tulsa city limits. Named by Mrs. Lela W. Hodges, local resident, after reading *East Lynne.*

147

LYONS. In Adair County, 5 miles southwest of Stilwell. A post office from January 29, 1909, to November 30, 1923.

LYONS. In Major County, 4 miles south of Ames. A post office from March 21, 1894, to August 31, 1905. No longer in existence.

M

M COUNTY. Original designation for Woods County, Oklahoma Territory. Name changed to Woods County, November 6, 1894.

MABELLE. Formerly Santown. In western Sequoyah County, 5 miles south of Vian. Post office name changed to Mabelle, July 3, 1907, and discontinued April 20, 1915. Named for Mabelle Mitchell, daughter of Ed Mitchell, well-known local Negro resident.

McALESTER. Record Town for Recording District No. 15, Indian Territory. This townsite was 2 miles north of present McAlester. Post office established March 31, 1873, and name changed to North McAlester, May 11, 1907. Until November 12, 1885, the official spelling for the post office was McAlister. Named for John J. McAlester, prominent merchant and coal producer, member of the first Corporation Commission and second lieutenant governor of Oklahoma.

McALESTER. County seat of Pittsburg County. Formerly South McAlester. On February 5, 1890, a post office named South McAlester was established about 2 miles south of the original McAlester townsite and on May 10, 1907, its name was changed to McAlester, as a continuation of that given the earlier townsite.

MacARTHUR. In Roger Mills County, 6 miles west of Hammon. A post office from October 14, 1901, to January 31, 1907. No longer in existence, it was named for Major General Arthur MacArthur, hero of the Philippine insurrection and father of General Douglas MacArthur.

McBRIDE. In western Cherokee County, 6 miles north of Fort Gibson. A post office from October 11, 1911, to April 30, 1936. Named for Dr. George A. McBride, a long-time resident.

McCARDIE. Present Garber, in Garfield County. Post office established March 13, 1894, and name changed to Garber, April 20, 1894.

McCARTY. In Garvin County, 7 miles southwest of Pauls Valley. A post office from April 15, 1905, to May 31, 1919. Named for John W. McCarty, local resident.

McCLAIN COUNTY. A county in south-central Oklahoma, created at statehood. Named for Charles M. McClain, member of the Oklahoma Constitutional Convention.

McCLURE. In western Custer County, 3 miles east of Hammon. Named for Guy V. McClure, chief engineer for the Clinton and Oklahoma Western Railroad.

McCOMB. In central Pottawatomie County. Post office established May 29, 1903, and name changed to Macomb, July 16, 1915. Named for J. deN. Macomb, Santa Fe Railway engineer.

McCURTAIN. Formerly Panther. In southeastern Haskell County. Post office name changed to McCurtain, April 5, 1902. Named for Green McCurtain, Choctaw chief.

McCURTAIN COUNTY. A county in extreme southeastern Oklahoma, created at statehood. Named for a well-known Choctaw family, of which the father and his three sons had each served as chief of the Choctaw Nation.

McDERMOTT. Formerly Springfield. In Okfuskee County, 3 miles southeast of Okemah. Post office name changed to McDermott, March 10, 1894, and discontinued July 15, 1903. Named for Louis H. McDermott, first postmaster.

McFALL. Present Vera, in Washington County. Post office established November 4, 1892, and name changed to Vera, December 15, 1899. Named for John McFall, local merchant.

McGEE. In northeastern Garvin County, 2 miles north of Stratford. A post office from April 15, 1891, to March 30, 1907. Named for William W. McGee, local blacksmith.

McINNIS. A switch and loading point on the Santa Fe Railway in Osage County, 8 miles west of Pawhuska. Named for E. E. McInnis, Santa Fe Railway attorney.

McINTOSH COUNTY. A county in east-central Oklahoma, created at statehood. Named for the well-known Creek family, a number of whose members were prominent tribal chiefs.

McKENNEY. In northwestern Pontotoc County, 3 miles east of Stratford. A post office from June 22, 1892, to November 15, 1893. No longer in existence, it was named for James E. McKenney, first postmaster.

McKEY. In Sequoyah County, 6 miles west of Sallisaw. A post office from March 13, 1891, to July 14, 1928. Named for Lugie Mackey, local resident.

McKIM. Formerly Wyatt. In northwestern Harper County, 10 miles north of Rosston. Post office name changed to McKim, July 18, 1907, and discontinued February 27, 1909. Named for J. S. McKim, local resident.

McKINLEY. In eastern Logan County, 3 miles east of Meridian. A post office from December 12, 1891, to February 15, 1904. No longer in existence, it was named for William McKinley of Ohio, member of Congress and later President of the United States.

McKINLEY. A rural community in Woods County, 3 miles northwest of Waynoka. Townsite plat filed October 19, 1918. Took its name from McKinley Township, which in turn, had been named for President William McKinley.

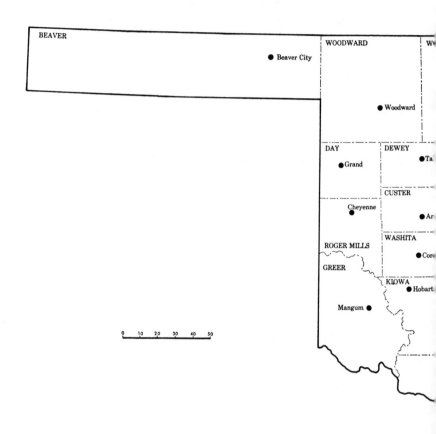

BEAVER

● Beaver City

WOODWARD

W

● Woodward

DAY

● Grand

DEWEY

●Ta

CUSTER

Cheyenne
●

●Ar

WASHITA

ROGER MILLS

●Cor

GREER

KIOWA

● Hobart

Mangum ●

0 10 20 30 40 50

Counties of Oklahoma Territory and Recording Districts of Indian Territory, 1906

Reproduced from *Historical Atlas of Oklahoma*, by John W. Morris and Edwin C. McReynolds. Copyright 1965 by the University of Oklahoma Press.

McKINNEY. In Noble County, 7 miles west of Red Rock. Post office established December 15, 1893, and name changed to Ceres, February 6, 1897. Named for George R. McKinney, first postmaster.

McKNIGHT. In Harmon County, 3 miles north of Hollis. A post office from June 27, 1901, to August 15, 1911. Named for Edward McKnight, pioneer resident.

McLAIN. In Muskogee County, 5 miles north of Warner. A post office from September 18, 1894, to June 30, 1915. Named for William McLain, long-time Cherokee jurist.

McLEMORE. In Oklahoma County, southwest of Oklahoma City and now within its city limits. Incorporated August 1, 1951, and dissolved 1963. Named for J. D. McLemore, townsite developer.

McLOUD. In extreme northwestern Pottawatomie County. Post office established June 21, 1895. Until October 24, 1895, the official spelling of this post office was McCloud. Named for John W. McLoud, attorney for the Choctaw, Oklahoma and Gulf Railroad.

McMAHON. A switch and loading point on the Santa Fe in Noble County, 3 miles north of Perry. Named for J. E. McMahon, Santa Fe official. An earlier name for the stop had been Arnettville.

McMAN. In western Carter County, 4 miles west of Healdton. A post office from November 17, 1916, to March 11, 1966. Took its name from McMan Oil Company, now a part of Magnolia Petroleum Company. The name was coined from the names of R. M. McFarlin and P. A. Chapman, organizers of the company. The community was often referred to as Dundee.

McMILLAN. In Marshall County, 9 miles west of Madill. Post office established March 28, 1892. Named for Joseph E. A. McMillan, first postmaster.

McNEAL. In southeastern Woodward County, 3 miles east of Mutual. A post office from April 6, 1899, to January 14, 1904. No longer in existence, it was named for J. W. McNeal, Guthrie businessman.

MACOMB. Formerly McComb. In central Pottawatomie County. Post office name changed to Macomb, July 16, 1916. Named for J. deN. Macomb, engineer for the Santa Fe Railway.

McQUEEN. In Harmon County, 3 miles east of Gould. A post office from August 29, 1910, to September 30, 1955. Named for Edward B. McQueen, townsite owner.

McWILLIE. In Alfalfa County, 6 miles west of Helena. A post office from February 8, 1910, to August 31, 1934.

MADDEN. In southeastern Jackson County, 15 miles south of Altus. A post office from June 17, 1901, to August 20, 1902. No longer in existence, it was named for W. Z. Madden, early-day resident.

MADGE. In northwestern Har-

152

mon County, 14 miles north of Hollis. A post office from March 13, 1895, to December 31, 1913. Named for Madge Lumpkin, daughter of a pioneer resident.

MADILL. County seat of Marshall County. Post office established April 29, 1901. Named for George A. Madill of St. Louis, attorney for the Frisco Railroad.

MADISON. Formerly Custer. In southeastern Beaver County, 2 miles north of Slapout. Post office name changed to Madison, June 17, 1904, and discontinued October 15, 1925. Named for Frank Madison, son-in-law of F. J. Birdsall, first postmaster.

MAGNOLIA. Present Red Rock, in Noble County. Post office established March 28, 1890, and name changed to Red Rock, June 9, 1892.

MAGUIRE. In Cleveland County, 4 miles east of Noble. A post office from May 29, 1900, to January 2, 1907. Named for James D. Maguire, Norman hardware dealer.

MAHARG. In northwestern Washita County near Foss. A post office from June 17, 1898, to June 15, 1901. No longer in existence. The name is an anagram of the last name of John R. Graham, first postmaster.

MAIN. Original name for Iconium in Logan County. Named for George W. Main, townsite developer.

MAIN. Local name for Stanton in Payne County. On March 3, 1903,

a post office named Vinco was established at the townsite, and the earlier name soon fell into disuse. Named for George W. Main, townsite developer.

MAJOR COUNTY. A county in northwestern Oklahoma, created at statehood from the southern portion of Woods County, Oklahoma Territory. Named for John C. Major, member of the Oklahoma Constitutional Convention.

MALLON. In northeastern Lincoln County, 7 miles north of Stroud. A post office from November 29, 1899, to May 31, 1905. No longer in existence.

MALLORY. In southwestern Beaver County. A post office from July 15, 1905, to December 31, 1907. No longer in existence, it was named for F. C. Mallory, first postmaster.

MALVERN. In McClain County, 6 miles west of Purcell. A post office from November 3, 1903, to December 31, 1905. No longer in existence, it was named for Malvern Hill, site of a Civil War battle in Virginia.

MAMIE. In central Sequoyah County. Post office established February 14, 1911, and name changed to Hood, September 11, 1911.

MANARD. In Cherokee County, 7 miles east of Fort Gibson. A post office from August 23, 1883, to September 30, 1913. Took its name from nearby Bayou Manard, which, in turn, had been named for Pierre Menard, missionary.

MANCHESTER. In northwestern Grant County. Post office established January 25, 1897. Its name comes from Manchester, England.

MANESE. In Blaine County, 7 miles southwest of Watonga. A post office from October 17, 1893, to October 31, 1906. No longer in existence, it was named for Thomas J. Manese, first postmaster.

MANESS. In southeastern Grady County, 3 miles south of Bradley. A post office from May 13, 1911, to October 31, 1911. No longer in existence, it was named for Thomas B. Maness, first postmaster.

MANGUM. County seat of Greer County. Post office established April 15, 1886. Named for A. S. Mangum, townsite owner.

MANILA. In eastern Lincoln County, 4 miles southeast of Sparks. A post office from December 24, 1898, to December 31, 1902. No longer in existence. Its name comes from the Battle of Manila Bay, May 1, 1898.

MANITOU. In northern Tillman County. Post office established January 29, 1902. The name is an Algonquian word for God or guardian spirit.

MANKO. In Pottawatomie County, 5 miles southeast of Asher. A post office from May 28, 1896, to September 30, 1902. No longer in existence. Named for Me-an-ko, Pottawatomie allotee.

MANNFORD. In northern Creek County. The town has been recent-ly relocated to avoid the waters of the Keystone Dam. Post office established April 11, 1903. Took its name from Mann's Ford across the Cimarron River, adjoining the townsite. The ford, in turn, had been named for Hazel and Tom Mann, allotees.

MANNSVILLE. In southwestern Johnston County. Post office established August 28, 1888. Named for Wallace A. Mann, first postmaster.

MANTEE. In northern Hughes County, 6 miles northwest of Wetumka. A post office from January 6, 1905, to November 15, 1912.

MAPLE. In Sequoyah County, 5 miles north of Muldrow. A post office from February 3, 1899, to January 14, 1921. Took its name from nearby Maple Springs.

MARAMEC. Formerly Crystal. In southern Pawnee County. Post office name changed to Maramec, April 8, 1903. It was named for the *Merrimac*, renowned Confederate ship. The name is an Algonquian word *marameck*, meaning "fish."

MARBLE. Formerly Kedron. In northern Sequoyah County. Post office name changed to Marble, January 16, 1895, and name changed to Marble City, April 2, 1906. Took its name from surrounding rock formations.

MARBLE CITY. In northern Sequoyah County. Post office name changed from Marble to Marble City, April 2, 1906.

MARBLE SALT WORKS. For-

154

merly Kidron. In Sequoyah County, 8 miles north of Sallisaw. Post office name changed to Marble Salt Works, September 8, 1858, and discontinued October 23, 1871. Here was the site of Nicksville, county seat of Lovely County, and of Dwight Mission, well-known Indian school established in 1829.

MARDOCK. In eastern Cleveland County, 14 miles east of Norman. A post office from January 31, 1900, to January 2, 1907. No longer in existence.

MARELLA. In southeastern Cimarron County, 18 miles southeast of Boise City. A post office from May 12, 1906, to September 30, 1915. No longer in existence.

MARENA. In western Payne County, 10 miles east of Mulhall. A post office from January 5, 1892, to February 15, 1907. No longer in existence.

MARENGO. In southeastern Beaver County, 10 miles southwest of Slapout. A post office from October 18, 1904, to May 15, 1908. No longer in existence. Its name comes from Marengo County, Alabama.

MARIE. In Greer County, 7 miles northwest of Mangum. A post office from October 26, 1899, to November 15, 1911. Named for Marie Warlick, daughter of H. E. Warlick, local pioneer resident.

MARIETTA. County seat of Love County. Post office established December 20, 1887. Its name comes from Marietta, Pennsylvania.

MARION. In Alfalfa County near Ingersoll. A post office from January 26, 1897, to December 31, 1901. No longer in existence.

MARION. A station and loading point on the Oklahoma City, Ada & Atoka Railroad (now part of the Santa Fe system) adjoining Oklahoma City on the southeast. Named for Marion Cunningham, landowner.

MARK. In Mayes County, 5 miles southwest of Locust Grove. A post office from August 6, 1904, to November 30, 1912. Named for Carter C. Markham, longtime local resident.

MARKHAM. In northwestern Creek County, 2 miles southwest of Oilton. A post office from February 26, 1915, to July 31, 1930. First known locally as Dropright. Named for John H. Markham, oil producer.

MARKHAM. In Mayes County, 6 miles southeast of Pryor. Site of a ferry over Grand River. A post office from March 21, 1895, to February 25, 1911. Named for Carter C. Markham, first postmaster.

MARLAND. Formerly Bliss. In northeastern Noble County. Post office name changed to Marland, April 8, 1922. Named for E. W. Marland of Ponca City, later governor of Oklahoma.

MARLOW. In northwestern Stephens County. Post office established March 13, 1891. Took its name from nearby Marlow Brothers Ranch. The five brothers were named Boone, Alfred, Epp, George, and Charles.

MARSDEN. In northern Love County, 5 miles west of Overbrook. A post office from February 7, 1895, to June 30, 1922.

MARSHALL. In northwestern Logan County. Post office established March 1, 1890. It was named by its founder, Sylvan T. Rice, for his home town of Marshaltown, Iowa.

MARSHALL COUNTY. A county in south-central Oklahoma, created at statehood. Given his mother's maiden name in her honor by George A. Henshaw of Madill, member of the Oklahoma Constitutional Convention.

MARTHA. In Jackson County, 6 miles northwest of Altus. Post office established May 18, 1889. Named for Martha Medlin, daughter of an early-day Baptist minister.

MARTIN. In Harmon County, 6 miles southeast of Hollis. A post office from September 16, 1892, to April 15, 1912. No longer in existence, it was named for Levi F. Martin, first postmaster.

MARTIN. Formerly Elm. In northeastern Logan County, 2 miles west of Langston. Post office name changed to Martin, October 27, 1890, and discontinued October 26, 1891. Named for Birdie Martin, first postmaster.

MARTIN. A rural community in Muskogee County, 6 miles north of Warner. Named for John A. Martin, local resident.

MARVEL. In southwestern Canadian County, 10 miles southeast of Hinton. A post office from March 4, 1902, to April 25, 1911.

MARY. In western Rogers County, 3 miles east of Collinsville. A post office from February 13, 1914, to March 31, 1915. No longer in existence. Named for Mary Stuart, daughter of Joseph F. Stuart, first postmaster.

MASHAM. In Pawnee County, 8 miles northwest of Pawnee. A post office from February 3, 1899, to August 14, 1909.

MASON. In Okfuskee County, 8 miles north of Castle. Post office established October 17, 1910. Named for Daniel S. Mason, first postmaster.

MASSEY. In Pittsburg County, 6 miles southeast of Crowder. A post office from August 17, 1900, to May 31, 1918. Named for W. W. Massey, prominent Choctaw.

MATEER. Present Lucien, in southwestern Noble County. Post office established December 23, 1899, and name changed to Lucien, June 27, 1903. Named for John K. Mateer, first postmaster.

MATEER. In western Roger Mills County, 15 miles southwest of Cheyenne. A post office from October 24, 1904, to November 30, 1907. No longer in existence, it was named for Edward C. Mateer, first postmaster.

156

MATHEWSON. In northeastern Canadian County, 2 miles northwest of Piedmont. A post office from March 25, 1890, to February 29, 1904. No longer in existence.

MATOY. In northeastern Bryan County, 10 miles north of Bennington. A post office from January 23, 1901, to October 15, 1921. Named for Mary Matoy, early-day schoolteacher.

MAUD. In western Seminole County. Post office established April 16, 1896. Named for Maud Stearns, later Maud Tinkle, local resident.

MAX. In Ottawa County, 9 miles east of Miami. A post office from March 19, 1891, to May 4, 1894. A variant of Mac's, Max was the name used by John P. McNaughton, prominent local rancher.

MAXEY. In Le Flore County, 3 miles west of Wister. Post office established June 4, 1884, and name changed to Caston, November 5, 1887. Named for N. B. Maxey, later a Muskogee attorney.

MAXWELL. In eastern Garfield County, 5 miles northeast of Covington. A post office from February 2, 1894, to July 12, 1895. No longer in existence, it was named for Robert A. Maxwell, fourth assistant postmaster general.

MAXWELL. In northwestern Pontotoc County, 7 miles southeast of Asher. A post office from February 14, 1896, to October 15, 1929.

MAY. In Harper County, 11 miles northwest of Fort Supply. Post office established July 25, 1896. Named for May Innis, daughter of J. A. Innis, townsite developer.

MAYES. The post office name for Oo-wa-la from September 19, 1887, to June 14, 1888. In Rogers County, adjoining present-day Sageeyah. Named for Samuel H. Mayes, Cherokee chief.

MAYES COUNTY. A county in northeastern Oklahoma, created at statehood. Named for Samuel H. Mayes, Cherokee chief.

MAYFIELD. In Beckham County, 15 miles northwest of Sayre. Post office established December 23, 1902. Named for Alfred S. Mayfield, first postmaster.

MAYHEW. Two miles north of present-day Boswell, in Choctaw County. Post office established February 5, 1845; name changed to Boswell and moved to new site September 30, 1902. Its name comes from the Mayhew Presbyterian Mission in Mississippi.

MAYO. A rural community in western Kiowa County near Lugert. Townsite plat filed September 30, 1942. Named for C. E. Mayo, Hobart businessman.

MAYS. Formerly Sallisaw. In Adair County, 10 miles southwest of Stilwell. Post office name changed to Mays, June 7, 1888, and discontinued September 19, 1896. Named for Samuel H. Mayes, Cherokee chief.

MAYSVILLE. In northwestern

Garvin County. Original post office operated from March 19, 1878, to May 29, 1878. Thereafter, on June 17, 1878, a post office named Beef Creek was established at this same site, and its name was changed to Maysville, September 19, 1902. Named for David and John Mayes, ranchers.

MAZIE. In southwestern Mayes County, 6 miles south of Chouteau. Post office established July 11, 1905. Named for Mazie Fishback of Fort Smith, friend of townsite developer.

MEAD. In western Bryan County. Post office established April 10, 1894. Named for Minor Mead, Chickasaw allotee.

MEANS. In Pontotoc County, 5 miles southwest of Ada. A post office from May 17, 1902, to December 31, 1902. No longer in existence, it was named for Eliza B. Means, first postmaster.

MEDFORD. Designated county seat of Grant County by proclamation of the governor, June 9, 1908. Post office established October 31, 1893. Its name comes from Medford, Massachusetts.

MEDIA. In northwestern Major County, 15 miles southeast of Quinlan. A post office from June 17, 1905, to February 28, 1915.

MEDICINE PARK. In Comanche County, northwest of Fort Sill. Post office established October 13, 1908. Took its name from nearby Medicine Creek.

MEEKER. Formerly Clifton. In southern Lincoln County. Post office name changed to Meeker, May 29, 1903. Named for Julian L. Meeker, townsite owner.

MEERS. In northwestern Comanche County. Post office established March 12, 1902. Named for Andrew J. Meers, early-day mine operator.

MEHAN. In Payne County, 10 miles southeast of Stillwater. A post office from February 8, 1900, to June 30, 1943. Named for John Mehan, townsite developer.

MEKASUKEY. In Seminole County, 3 miles southwest of Seminole. A post office from October 17, 1894, to February 28, 1915. Site of Mekasukey Academy, established in 1891 as a Seminole school for boys. The name is the Creek word *mekko-tku-cuko*, originally meaning "where the chiefs meet," but which later developed the meaning "place where Christianity is taught."

MELLETTE. In southern McIntosh County, 10 miles southwest of Eufaula. A post office from May 1, 1901, to July 14, 1934. Named for William Mellette of Muskogee, United States district attorney.

MELVIN. In Cherokee County, 11 miles west of Tahlequah. A post office from March 2, 1894, to October 31, 1919.

MENDON. In northeastern Alfalfa County, 3 miles east of Byron. A post office from February 19, 1897, to December 15, 1910. No longer in existence.

MENO. In northeastern Major County, 15 miles west of Enid. Post office established October 19, 1899. Named for Menno Simons, 1492–1559, early Mennonite leader.

MERIDIAN. In central Logan County. Post office established March 10, 1894. Named from the circumstance that the site is on the Indian Meridian.

MERRICK. In western Lincoln County, 9 miles west of Tryon. A post office from August 28, 1903, to October 31, 1935. Named for James J. Merrick, townsite owner.

MERRITT. In Beckham County, 6 miles southwest of Elk City. A post office from August 9, 1901, to July 15, 1908. No longer in existence, it was named for Lafe Merritt, publisher of the *El Reno Globe*.

MESQUITE. In southwestern Jackson County, 4 miles southwest of Eldorado. A post office from January 14, 1901, to July 14, 1905. No longer in existence. Took its name from the surrounding mesquite brush, a deep-rooted shrub of pea family.

MESSER. In Choctaw County, 6 miles northeast of Hugo. A post office from January 4, 1907, to February 29, 1916. Named for Columbus G. Messer, first postmaster.

METCALF. In northern Cimarron County, 14 miles north of Boise City. A post office from May 23, 1894, to September 15, 1900. No

longer in existence, it was named for John J. Metcalf, first postmaster.

METCALF. In Harmon County, 9 miles northeast of Hollis. A post office from February 20, 1905, to August 31, 1911. Named for Hugh Metcalf, first postmaster.

METORY. In Cherokee County, 5 miles southwest of Tahlequah. A post office from February 13, 1906, to June 15, 1914. The name was coined from the initial letter of the last names of six local families.

METZ. Present Nowata, in Nowata County. First known locally as California Station. Post office established November 1, 1887, and name changed to Nowata, November 8, 1889. Named for Fred Metzner, first postmaster.

MIAH. Present Sawyer, in Choctaw County. Post office established June 27, 1902, and name changed to Sawyer, April 1, 1903. Named for Miah Cravens, son of William E. Cravens, first postmaster.

MIAMI. County seat of Ottawa County. Record Town for Recording District No. 1, Indian Territory. Post office established April 13, 1891. Took name from the Miami Indian tribe whose reservation was nearby as part of the confederated Peoria. The name was chosen to honor Thomas Richardville, Miami chief, who had been instrumental in securing the legislation necessary to acquire the townsite.

MICAWBER. In northwestern Okfuskee County, 9 miles northwest of Boley. A post office from May

10, 1904, to March 15, 1955. It was named for a character created by Charles Dickens.

MICCO. In McIntosh County, 2 miles east of Eufaula. An important settlement prior to the Civil War, usually known as North Fork Town. A post office from August 4, 1853, to March 30, 1886. The name is the Creek word for chief.

MIDDLEBURG. In Grady County, 10 miles northeast of Chickasha. A post office from November 2, 1908, to March 31, 1932. The name comes from its location, halfway between Chickasha and Blanchard.

MIDDLETON. Formerly Gray. In Kay County, 6 miles northwest of Newkirk. Post office name changed to Middleton, July 30, 1900, and discontinued January 31, 1908. The name comes from the circumstance that the site was halfway between Beaumont, Kansas, and Enid, division points on the Frisco Railroad.

MIDLOTHIAN. In Lincoln County, 4 miles southwest of Chandler. First post office in operation from June 8, 1902, to September 15, 1902. On September 23, 1904, the post office several miles to the west named Ellis was changed to Midlothian and continued as a post office until November 15, 1919. Its name comes from a county in southeastern Scotland in which Edinburgh is located.

MIDWAY. In Coal County, 3 miles south of Lehigh. A post office from January 16, 1902, to March 15, 1911. The name comes from its location, midway between Lehigh and Atoka.

MIDWAY. In northwestern Roger Mills County, 16 miles northwest of Cheyenne. A post office from June 10, 1924, to June 15, 1930. Named because its location was halfway between Durham and Rankin.

MIDWAY VILLAGE. In Oklahoma County, adjoining Midwest City. Townsite developed 1951 and municipality consolidated with Del City, July 8, 1963.

MIDWELL. In eastern Cimarron County, 24 miles east of Boise City. A post office from January 22, 1908, to May 31, 1935. Took its name from a well-known and widely used water well.

MIDWEST CITY. A separate municipality adjoining Oklahoma City on the southeast. Incorporated March 11, 1943. Took its name from adjoining Midwest Air Depot, now Tinker Air Force Base.

MILAN. In eastern Alfalfa County, 5 miles northeast of Helena. A post office from January 28, 1895, to October 31, 1902. No longer in existence.

MILAN. In southern Ellis County, 12 miles south of Arnett. A post office from September 19, 1905, to November 15, 1906. No longer in existence. Its name comes from Milan, Sumner County, Kansas.

MILBURN. Formerly Ellen. In

southeastern Johnston County. Post office name changed to Milburn, August 17, 1901. Named for W. J. Milburn, prominent early-day resident.

MILES. In Craig County, 11 miles northwest of Vinita. A post office from March 29, 1892, to September 30, 1935. Named for J. B. Miles, prominent early-day resident.

MILFAY. In southwestern Creek County, 4 miles southwest of Depew. Post office established December 14, 1911. The name was coined from the last names of two railroad officials, Charles Mills and Edward Fay.

MILL CREEK. In northwestern Johnston County. Post office established June 11, 1879. Took its name from nearby Mill Creek, a tributary of the Washita River, which had been named for a mill operated by Governor Cyrus Harris.

MILLER. In western Oklahoma County, 6 miles west of Britton. A post office from February 21, 1890, to March 15, 1904. Named for Samuel H. Miller, first postmaster.

MILLER. In southwestern Pushmataha County, 10 miles northwest of Antlers. A post office from June 22, 1905, to October 31, 1954. Named for Dr. J. H. Miller, Antlers rancher.

MILLER COUNTY. A county established by the Arkansas legislature, April 1, 1820, comprising the eastern portion of present-day Oklahoma south of the Arkansas River. Named for Governor James Miller of Arkansas.

MILLER COURT HOUSE. In present McCurtain County near Shawneetown. The first post office in what is now Oklahoma. A post office from September 5, 1824, to December 28, 1838. The county seat of Miller County.

MILLERTON. Formerly Parsons. In southwestern McCurtain County. Post office name changed to Millerton, March 5, 1908. Named for Benedict Miller, townsite owner.

MILLS. In Lincoln County, 6 miles north of Meeker. A post office from May 5, 1899, to October 31, 1904. First known locally as Wheelersburg. Named for Millicent Easter, wife of Ed H. Easter, first postmaster.

MILLSVILLE. In eastern Roger Mills County, 7 miles northwest of Hammon. A post office from March 12, 1901, to January 31, 1906. No longer in existence, it was named for Jennie Mills, first postmaster.

MILO. In Carter County, 15 miles northwest of Ardmore. Post office established October 28, 1899. The name was coined from the initials of the names of the four daughters of J. W. Johnson, local resident.

MILTON. In northwestern Le Flore County, 5 miles east of McCurtain. A post office from June 20, 1890, to November 10, 1942. Named for John Milton, English man of letters.

MINCO. In western Grady County. Post office established June 20, 1890. The name is an Indian word meaning "chief."

MINERAL CITY. In western Cimarron County, 6 miles southeast of Kenton. Post office established February 6, 1888; name changed to Mineral, March 29, 1895; and discontinued February 15, 1911. Took its name from nearby deposits of lignite.

MINERAL HILL. In extreme eastern McCurtain County. Post office established August 12, 1852, and site and name changed to Harris Mill, April 5, 1859.

MINERAL WELLS. In Washita County, 5 miles northeast of Cordell. Townsite developed in 1908. No longer in existence.

MINNETONKA. In Cimarron County, 6 miles south of Keyes. A post office from January 4, 1907, to April 15, 1910. No longer in existence. Its name comes from Lake Minnetonka, adjoining Minneapolis, Minnesota.

MIRABILE. In northeastern Woods County, 10 miles northeast of Alva. A post office from May 11, 1895, to April 18, 1896. No longer in existence. The name is from the Latin word meaning "remarkable."

MIRAGE. In southwestern Tillman County, 3 miles south of Tipton. A post office from December 2, 1902, to September 30, 1905. No longer in existence.

MISHAK. In Oklahoma County, south of present Midwest City. A post office from March 29, 1900, to June 30, 1904. No longer in existence, it was named for Frank Mishak, first postmaster.

MISSION. Present Fallis in Lincoln County. Post office established December 28, 1892, and name changed to Fallis, July 13, 1894. Took its name from the nearby Iowa Mission.

MITCH. In southwestern Sequoyah County, 6 miles south of Vian. A post office from August 13, 1920, to September 30, 1933. Named for Edward D. Mitchell, first postmaster.

MITCHELL. In northwestern Lincoln County, 5 miles north of Fallis. A post office from April 5, 1895, to February 15, 1905. No longer in existence. Named for R. B. Mitchell, local resident.

MITCHELL. In southeastern Texas County, 8 miles southeast of Hardesty. A post office from August 28, 1888, to September 24, 1890. No longer in existence, it was named for James W. Mitchell, first postmaster.

MITSCHER. In northern Osage County, 6 miles northeast of Foraker. A post office from October 3, 1901, to June 14, 1902. Named for O. A. Mitscher of Pawhuska, later mayor of Oklahoma City and father of Admiral Marc Mitscher.

MOCANE. In Beaver County, 10 miles northeast of Beaver. A post office from March 18, 1909, to

April 30, 1948. Took its name from Mokane, Calloway County, Missouri.

MOFFETT. In eastern Sequoyah County, adjoining Fort Smith. Post office established January 8, 1908. Named for Martha Jane Moffett Payne, wife of Dr. Samuel H. Payne, local planter.

MOHAWK. In Tulsa County, 4 miles northwest of Tulsa. A post office from May 18, 1906, to July 10, 1915. Took its name from the Mohawk Indians, one of the Six Nations of the Iroquois Confederacy.

MONDAMIN. Five miles south of Roosevelt, in Kiowa County. Post office established July 24, 1903, and name changed to Cold Springs, January 27, 1913. The name is a word meaning corn, adopted from *Hiawatha*.

MONEKA. Formerly Peery. In Jefferson County at site of Waurika. Post office name changed to Moneka, April 18, 1895, and discontinued May 15, 1898.

MONK. In northwestern Carter County, adjoining Ratliff City. A post office from February 25, 1896, to December 31, 1905. No longer in existence.

MONROE. In Le Flore County, 10 miles northeast of Heavener. Post office established February 25, 1881. Named for Simon Monroe Griffith, first postmaster.

MONUMENT HILL. Prominent land feature in Jefferson County near Waurika. Named for a pile of rocks on the site, used as a landmark on the Chisholm Trail.

MOODYS. In Cherokee County, 7 miles north of Tahlequah. Post office established March 21, 1896. Took its name from nearby Moody's Springs, which had been named for William Moody, pioneer settler.

MOONAN. In Washita County, 7 miles northwest of Sentinel. A post office from March 14, 1901, to April 29, 1905.

MOORE. In northern Cleveland County. Post office established May 27, 1889, and discontinued January 7, 1972, to become a branch of the Oklahoma City office. Named for Al Moore, Santa Fe Railway conductor. Original railroad name was Verbeck.

MOORELAND. In Woodward County, 11 miles east of Woodward. Post office established February 5, 1902. Original townsite name was Dail City. The name was coined to refer to the nature of the surrounding terrain, suggestive of moors, and through error the Post Office Department did not adopt the spelling intended, Moorland.

MOOREWOOD. In northeastern Custer County, 7 miles north of Hammon. In 1905 a post office named Quartermaster had been discontinued at this approximate site. A post office from June 12, 1912, to October 26, 1962. Named for Solomon J. Moore and R. R. Wood, townsite owners.

MORAL. In Pottawatomie County, 2 miles north of Trousdale. A post office from May 28, 1892, to December 15, 1908. Name selected by Brooks Walker because he had been successful in preventing saloons at the townsite.

MORAN. In western Grant County, 3 miles northeast of Nash. A post office from March 13, 1894, to May 18, 1904. No longer in existence, it was named for Clara Moran, popular local schoolteacher.

MORAVIA. In southern Beckham County, 7 miles south of Carter. A post office from December 22, 1913, to February 28, 1915. On June 13, 1916, a post office named Ocina was established at this approximate site. Its name comes from a region in central Czechoslovakia.

MORETZ. In western Stephens County, 8 miles west of Marlow. A post office from September 6, 1902, to April 30, 1904. No longer in existence, it was named for William L. Moretz, first postmaster.

MORGAN. Formerly Berry. In northern Cleveland County, 6 miles east of Moore. Post office name changed to Morgan, April 24, 1901, and discontinued July 31, 1906. Named for M. G. Morgan, first postmaster.

MORGAN. A former switch and loading point in Pottawatomie County, 5 miles north of Asher. Named for George W. Morgan, Rock Island Railroad agent at Shawnee.

MORRIS. In central Okmulgee County. Post office established March 26, 1903. Named for H. E. Morris of Joplin, Mo., railroad official.

MORRISON. Formerly Autry. In southeastern Noble County. Post office name changed to Morrison, February 27, 1894. Named for James H. Morrison, townsite owner.

MORROW. In southwestern Grady County, adjoining Rush Springs. Post office established April 8, 1887, and name changed to Petuna, March 6, 1888. Named for Thomas T. Morrow, first postmaster.

MORSE. In Okfuskee County, 7 miles north of Okemah. A post office from June 28, 1897, to January 30, 1926.

MORVIN. In Pottawatomie County, 3 miles north of Macomb. Post office established April 13, 1898; date of discontinuance unavailable. Named for the favorite horse of R. C. Hurst, prominent early-day settler.

MOSCOW. In Woodward County, 7 miles north of Mutual. A post office from May 3, 1894, to November 15, 1906. Its name comes from Moscow, Russia.

MOSELEY. In southeastern Delaware County, 6 miles east of Flint. A post office from February 16, 1910, to May 31, 1923. Took its name from nearby Moseley Prairie.

MOSHULATUBBEE. One of the

three districts of the Choctaw Nation. Presided over by a district chief. Named for a well-known tribal chief.

MOUND CITY. Original townsite name for Avery, in Lincoln County, by townsite plat filed August 5, 1902.

MOUNDS. Formerly Posey. In southeastern Creek County. Present site is 5 miles southwest of original post office location. Name changed to Mounds, April 19, 1898. Took its name from prominent twin mound feature northeast of the present townsite.

MOUNTAIN. In Latimer County, 6 miles southwest of Wilburton. A post office from October 10, 1873, to May 6, 1886. No longer in existence. Took its name from Mountain Station atop Blue Mountain, a stage stand on the overland mail route.

MOUNTAIN. In northern Le Flore County, 6 miles northeast of Spiro. A post office from December 21, 1896, to December 31, 1907. No longer in existence. Took its name from nearby Mount Cavanal.

MOUNTAIN PARK. Formerly Burford. In southern Kiowa County, 5 miles north of Snyder. Post office name changed to Mountain Park, February 28, 1902. County seat of proposed Swanson County. Took its name from the surrounding Wichita Mountains.

MOUNTAIN VIEW. Formerly Oakdale. In northeastern Kiowa County. Post office name changed to Mountain View, October 9, 1900. Named because of an excellent view of the nearby Wichita Mountains.

MOUNT CLARIMIER. In present Rogers County, northwest of Claremore. A post office from May 30, 1860, to February 11, 1867. Took its name from nearby Claremore Mound.

MOUNT SCOTT. A prominent land feature at the eastern end of the Wichita Mountains. Elevation 2,464 feet. Named for Lieutenant General Winfield Scott.

MOUNT SCOTT. In Comanche County, 2 miles northeast of Mount Scott. A post office from November 13, 1901, to March 15, 1914. No longer in existence. Took its name from nearby Mount Scott.

MOUNTVIEW. In eastern Washita County, 3 miles south of Colony. A post office from June 14, 1894, to March 15, 1900. No longer in existence.

MOUNT WEBSTER. A prominent land feature southwest of Hobart, in Kiowa County. Now known as Tepee Mountain. Named for Daniel Webster.

MOUSER. A rural community in Texas County, 14 miles northeast of Guymon. Townsite plat filed July 2, 1928. Named for Alfred C. Mouser, townsite owner.

MOYERS. In Pushmataha County, 6 miles north of Antlers. Post office established November 27, 1908.

Named for Roy A. Moyer, long-time local resident.

MUDSAND. In Choctaw County, adjoining Soper. A post office from June 9, 1923, to April 30, 1935. No longer in existence.

MULDROW. In southeastern Sequoyah County. Post office established November 19, 1887. Named for Henry L. Muldrow of Mississippi, member of Congress and assistant secretary of the interior.

MULHALL. In northern Logan County. Post office established June 6, 1890. Named for Colonel Zack Mulhall, rancher and showman.

MULKEY. In Carter County, 5 miles northeast of Ardmore. A post office from February 24, 1905, to October 31, 1919. Named for John C. Mulkey, first postmaster.

MULKIN. In southern Blaine County, 5 miles west of Bridgeport. A post office from January 16, 1902, to October 31, 1902. No longer in existence, it was named for Lida Mulkin, first postmaster.

MULLINS. In southern Kiowa County, 6 miles west of Mountain Park. A post office from November 11, 1903, to August 13, 1904. No longer in existence, it was named for A. E. Mullins, first postmaster.

MUNCIE. In Dewey County, 7 miles northeast of Taloga. A post office from August 3, 1901, to October 31, 1908. No longer in existence. Its name comes from Muncie, Indiana.

MUNDEN. In central Beaver County, 5 miles southeast of Beaver. A post office from May 17, 1907, to May 15, 1909. No longer in existence, it was named for H. W. Munden, first postmaster.

MUNGER. Present Spencer, in northeastern Oklahoma County. Post office established January 16, 1899, and name changed to Spencer, February 25, 1903. Named for G. W. Munger, townsite owner.

MURPHY. A rural community established about 1912, in Mayes County, 5 miles southwest of Locust Grove. Named for Blue Murphy, local Cherokee.

MURRAY. In western Harper County, adjoining Rosston. A post office from November 11, 1902, to December 31, 1914. Named for Walter T. Murray, townsite owner.

MURRAY COUNTY. A county in south-central Oklahoma, created at statehood. Named for William H. Murray, president of the Oklahoma Constitutional Convention and later governor.

MUSE. In Le Flore County, 6 miles west of Big Cedar. First post office established October 1, 1896, and name changed to Pine Valley on December 16, 1926. On May 11, 1927, another post office named Muse was established at a slightly different location. Named for Reverend Joseph Muse, Baptist minister.

MUSKOGEE. County seat of Muskogee County. Record Town for Recording District No. 10, Indian Territory. Post office established January 18, 1872. Until July 19, 1900, the official spelling of the post office was Muscogee. Took its name from the Creek Indians who were sometimes called Muskogee from the Muskogean language which they spoke.

MUSKOGEE COUNTY. A county in eastern Oklahoma, created at statehood. Named for the Muskogee, or Creek, Indians.

MUSTANG. In southeastern Canadian County. Post office established February 4, 1895. Took its name from nearby Mustang Creek.

MUTUAL. In southern Woodward County. Post office established June 4, 1895. The name was selected by the Post Office Department instead of Trenton, the name requested by the local residents.

MYRTLE. In Kingfisher County, 6 miles southeast of Hennessey. A post office from September 24, 1890, to August 13, 1904. No longer in existence.

N

N COUNTY. Original designation for Woodward County, Oklahoma Territory. Name changed to Woodward County, November 6, 1894.

NABISCO. In Texas County, 12 miles east of Hooker. A post office from January 13, 1904, to September 29, 1906. No longer in existence. Presumedly named for the National Biscuit Company.

NAGLE. Formerly Snyder. In southeastern Kingfisher County, 9 miles southwest of Cashion. Post office name changed to Nagle, March 18, 1896, and discontinued August 31, 1903. Named for Patrick S. Nagle, early-day United States marshal.

NAIL. Present Kenefic, in northwestern Bryan County. Post office established October 13, 1888, and name changed to Kenefic, May 23, 1910. Took its name from nearby Nail's Crossing, a well-known ford over Blue River, which had been named for Joel H. Nail.

NAIL'S STATION. Site in northern Bryan County, 3 miles southwest of Kenefic. A stage stop on the Butterfield Overland Mail route to California which crossed southeastern Oklahoma, 1858–61. Named for Joel H. Nail, local merchant and stage stand operator.

NAPLES. In Grady County, 6 miles north of Alex. A post office from May 5, 1890, to April 30, 1932.

NARCISSA. In Ottawa County, 5 miles southwest of Miami. A post office from January 15, 1902, to November 15, 1916. Named for Narcissa Walker, early-day resident.

NARDIN. Formerly Vilott. In western Kay County. Post office name changed to Nardin, April 12,

1898. Named for George F. Nardin, long-time resident.

NASH. Formerly Nashville. In southwestern Grant County. Post office name changed to Nash, March 23, 1911. Named for Clark L. Nash, first postmaster of Nashville.

NASHOBA. A county in Apukshunnubbee District, Choctaw Nation. The name is a Choctaw word meaning "wolf," and the county was often referred to as Wolf County.

NASHOBA. In Pushmataha County, 11 miles southeast of Tuskahoma. Post office established September 13, 1886. Took its name from Nashoba County, Choctaw Nation.

NASHVILLE. Present Nash, in southwestern Grant County. Post office established February 14, 1894, and name changed to Nash, March 23, 1911. Named for Clark L. Nash, first postmaster.

NATURA. In Okmulgee County, 9 miles east of Beggs. A post office from January 3, 1905, to December 15, 1910. The name is the Latin word for nature.

NAUDACK. In Okmulgee County, 5 miles south of Morris. A post office from July 20, 1903, to February 14, 1906. No longer in existence, it was named for Rufus B. Naudack, first postmaster.

NAVAJOE. In eastern Jackson County, 3 miles northwest of Headrick. A post office from September 1, 1887, to May 15, 1905. Took its name from nearby Navajoe Mountain, which had been named for the Navaho Indian tribe because of a tradition among the Comanches that a battle had been fought at the mountain with the Navaho tribe.

NAVINA. In southwestern Logan County, 5 miles west of Seward. A post office from October 2, 1900, to October 15, 1935. Original townsite name was Berg. Named for Lavina Berg, daughter of John Berg, townsite owner.

NEAL. In Pottawatomie County, 5 miles east of Shawnee. A post office from June 2, 1894, to May 15, 1907. Named for Isaac N. Neal, early-day resident.

NEBO. In southern Murray County, 5 miles southeast of Dougherty. A post office from August 22, 1890, to February 15, 1922. Its name comes from Mount Nebo, of Biblical reference.

NEEDMORE. In northwestern Delaware County, 6 miles south of Afton. Post office established December 14, 1894, and name changed to Bernice, February 12, 1913. Its name comes from the impecunious condition of the local residents.

NEEDS. In northeastern Alfalfa County near Byron. A post office from January 28, 1896, to January 31, 1900. No longer in existence.

NEFF. In Texas County, 9 miles southeast of Hooker. A post office from August 8, 1904, to May 15, 1909. Named for Boss S. Neff, prominent rancher.

NELAGONEY. In Osage County, 7 miles southeast of Pawhuska. A post office from December 1, 1906, to February 28, 1959. The name is an Osage word meaning "good water" or "spring."

NELLDA. In Carter County, 6 miles southeast of Ardmore. A post office from April 28, 1914, to May 31, 1921.

NELLIE. In northwestern Stephens County, 10 miles northwest of Duncan. A post office from June 5, 1902, to January 31, 1912. Named for Nellie Sharp, local resident.

NELMS. In northeastern Tillman County, 6 miles northwest of Chattanooga. A post office from November 7, 1901, to October 15, 1908. No longer in existence, it was named for Clark C. Nelms, first postmaster.

NELSON. In Choctaw County, 6 miles north of Soper. Spencer Academy was moved here from Spencerville. A post office from March 10, 1881, to November 30, 1954. Until September 15, 1881, the official name of this post office was Nelsons. Named for Cole Nelson, prominent Choctaw.

NEODESHA. In Wagoner County, 6 miles north of Wagoner. A post office from August 1, 1905, to July 15, 1937. Railroad name was Ross. Its name comes from Neodesha, Kansas.

NEOLA. In western Caddo County, 9 miles southeast of Carnegie. A post office from February 17, 1902, to September 30, 1910. Took its name from Neola, Iowa.

NEOSHO. A district of the Cherokee Nation. Established prior to 1831 and abolished November 4, 1840. Took its name from the Neosho River.

NEOSHO RIVER. An important drainage system in northeastern Oklahoma. Also known as Grand River, it empties into the Arkansas River at the Three Forks, near Fort Gibson. The name is an Osage word meaning "clear water."

NEROTOWN. Formerly Huttonville. In McIntosh County, 5 miles northwest of Eufaula. Post office name changed to Nerotown, February 28, 1911, and discontinued July 20, 1915. Named for Governor Nero, Creek allotee.

NEWALLA. Formerly Halifax. In southeastern Oklahoma County. Post office name changed to Newalla, June 22, 1904. The name is an adaptation of the Osage word for the Canadian River.

NEW BOGGY DEPOT. The post office name for Boggy Depot in Atoka County, from March 22, 1872, to December 26, 1883.

NEWBURG. Present Atwood, in Hughes County. Post office established January 23, 1897, and name changed to Atwood, December 3, 1909.

NEWBY. In Creek County, 10 miles south of Bristow. A post office from October 17, 1902, to November 30, 1955.

NEWCASTLE. In northern Mc-Clain County, 7 miles northwest of Norman. Post office established March 26, 1894. Its name comes from Newcastle, Texas.

NEW DURWOOD. Name of a second Durwood townsite, established in Marshall County a few miles east of first Durwood. Post office name was New Durwood from April 8, 1913, to October 11, 1913.

NEW GOODWIN. In Ellis County, 12 miles west of Arnett. A post office from August 31, 1909, to August 15, 1913. Named for George L. Goodwin, assistant treasurer of the Santa Fe Railway.

NEW HOME. In Le Flore County, 5 miles east of Big Cedar. A post office from January 12, 1924, to February 28, 1934.

NEWHOPE. In northwestern Grant County, 9 miles west of Wakita. A post office from August 4, 1903, to August 14, 1904. No longer in existence.

NEWKIRK. County seat of Kay County. Former post office name was Santa Fe, and original townsite name was Lamereux. Post office name changed to Newkirk, January 18, 1894. The name was chosen to distinguish the site from a former stop on the Santa Fe Railway 2 miles north known as Kirk.

NEW LIMA. In Seminole County, 5 miles west of Wewoka. Post office established October 5, 1929.

NEWMAN. Present Stigler, in Haskell County. Post office established April 30, 1892, and name changed to Stigler, May 3, 1893. Named for Dr. Martin W. Newman, pioneer territorial physician.

NEW PONCA. Present Ponca City, in Kay County. Post office established January 12, 1894. Name changed to Ponca, July 7, 1898, and to Ponca City, October 23, 1913. The name was adopted to distinguish this townsite from an earlier Ponca a few miles to the south. Took its name from the Ponca tribe of Indians.

NEWPORT. In Carter County, 8 miles northwest of Ardmore. A post office from May 17, 1892, to May 26, 1961.

NEW PRUE. In Osage County north of the former Prue townsite. Relocated because of the Keystone Reservoir.

NEWTON. In northern Pontotoc County, 7 miles northeast of Ada. Post office established April 17, 1894, and name changed to Francis, June 5, 1902.

NEW WILSON. Present Wilson, in western Carter County. Post office established January 7, 1914, and name changed to Wilson, January 28, 1920. Named to distinguish the site from a former Wilson, 7 miles southeast of Ardmore.

NEW WOODVILLE. In Marshall County northwest of the former Woodville townsite. Relocated because of Lake Texoma.

NICHOLS HILLS. Municipality located north of and adjacent to Oklahoma City. Incorporated 1929; named for G. A. Nichols, Oklahoma City developer and civic leader.

NICHOLSON. In Muskogee County, 6 miles east of Muskogee. A post office from July 6, 1907, to October 15, 1913.

NICKSVILLE. County seat of former Lovely County. In Sequoyah County, 8 miles north of Sallisaw. A post office from April 25, 1828, to October 2, 1829. At later dates post offices named Kidron and Marble Salt Works were located at this same site. Named for General John Nicks, War of 1812 hero.

NICOMA PARK. In eastern Oklahoma County. Post office established February 7, 1929. The name was coined from the names Dr. G. A. Nichols, townsite developer, and Oklahoma.

NICUT. Formerly Vrona. In northeastern Sequoyah County, 12 miles north of Muldrow. Post office name changed to Nicut, December 16, 1925, and discontinued November 30, 1954. The name is an adaptation of "nigh cut," referring to a short cut on the road to Muldrow.

NIDA. In southeastern Johnston County, 7 miles west of Kenefic. A post office from October 26, 1895, to October 30, 1915. Named for Nida French, wife of R. F. French, first postmaster.

NILES. In southwestern Canadian County, 7 miles east of Hinton. A post office from August 25, 1902, to July 31, 1929. Named for William E. Niles, first postmaster.

NINEMILE. In western Blaine County, 3 miles east of Eagle City. A post office from March 6, 1899, to September 30, 1899. No longer in existence. It took its name from nearby Ninemile Crossing on the North Canadian River, on the military road from Cantonment to Fort Reno.

NINNEKAH. In central Grady County. Post office established July 28, 1892. The name is from the Choctaw root word *ninek*, referring to night or darkness.

NIRA. Formerly Funston. In Woods County, 4 miles southwest of Avard. Post office name changed to Nira, May 18, 1903, and discontinued October 31, 1904.

NIXON. In Coal County, 6 miles southwest of Coalgate. A post office from May 2, 1896, to November 30, 1911.

NOAH. In northwestern McCurtain County, 6 miles northwest of Bethel. A post office from October 2, 1903, to January 31, 1912. Named for Simian Noah, local Choctaw allotee.

NOBLE. In Cleveland County, 7 miles southeast of Norman. Post office established June 18, 1889. Named for John W. Noble, secretary of the interior under President Benjamin Harrison.

NOBLE COUNTY. A county in north-central Oklahoma, comprising approximately the same area as Noble County, Oklahoma Territory. Named for John W. Noble.

NOBSCOT. Formerly South Canadian. In southeastern Dewey County, 6 miles northwest of Fay. Post office name changed to Nobscot, October 26, 1915, and discontinued June 15, 1918.

NOLIA. In eastern Pushmataha County, 5 miles east of Nashoba. A post office from October 26, 1912, to December 15, 1920. Named for Nolia Johnson, wife of Ben F. Johnson, first postmaster.

NON. In southern Hughes County, 12 miles south of Calvin. A post office from October 22, 1901, to October 31, 1954. The name is the last syllable in the name of the first postmaster, John W. Cannon.

NORDEN. In Grady County, 4 miles southwest of Chickasha. Post office established January 27, 1908, and name changed to Norge, March 21, 1908.

NORGE. Formerly Norden. In Grady County, 4 miles southwest of Chickasha. Post office name changed to Norge, March 21, 1908, and discontinued September 30, 1954. Named in honor of the homeland of a local group of Norwegian settlers.

NORMAN. County seat of Cleveland County. Post office established May 27, 1889. Took its name from Norman Switch, established by the Santa Fe Railway at the site of Camp Norman, named for Aubrey Norman, surveyor.

NORTH ENID. In Garfield County, 2 miles north of Enid, and at the townsite intended by the Rock Island Railroad as the county seat of Garfield County. A post office from January 19, 1894, to August 31, 1923.

NORTH FORK. In southeastern Okfuskee County, 6 miles northeast of Weleetka. A post office from October 9, 1908, to March 31, 1916. Took its name from nearby North Canadian River.

NORTH FORK TOWN. An important Creek settlement prior to the Civil War. Often known as Micco. Site two miles east of Eufaula, in McIntosh County.

NORTH McALESTER. At original site of McAlester. The name was changed to North McAlester on May 11, 1907, to distinguish it from the new townsite, then known as South McAlester, which had developed at the railroad junction 2 miles to the south. North McAlester post office was discontinued June 30, 1909.

NORTH MIAMI. Present Commerce, in Ottawa County. Post office established June 31, 1913, and name changed to Commerce, June 1, 1914. Another community by this name developed two miles south, the post office for which was established June 1, 1915.

NORTH MUSKOGEE. Formerly Rex. Present Okay, in southeastern

172

Wagoner County. In 1893 a post office named Coretta had been discontinued at approximately this same site. Post office name changed to North Muskogee, May 1, 1911, and changed to Okay October 18, 1919.

NORTHVILLE. In western Canadian County, adjoining Geary. A post office from January 24, 1894, to October 27, 1898. No longer in existence, it was named for James C. North, first postmaster.

NORTON. In southwestern Johnston County, 5 miles north of Mannsville. A post office from May 22, 1894, to December 15, 1912. No longer in existence, it was named for Sealy Norton, rancher and cattleman.

NORWOOD. Present Haworth in southeastern McCurtain County. Post office established March 28, 1902, and name changed to Haworth, November 17, 1906. Took its name from nearby Norwood Creek, which had been named for Elijah Norwood, early day landowner.

NOWATA. Formerly Metz. County seat of Nowata County. Record Town for Recording District No. 3, Indian Territory. Post office name changed to Nowata, November 8, 1889. The name is from the Delaware word *no-we-ata*, meaning "welcome."

NOWATA COUNTY. A county in northeastern Oklahoma, created at statehood. Took its name from the town designated as its county seat, Nowata.

NOWERS. Former station on the Santa Fe located at present Northwest 36th Street in Oklahoma City. Named for J. W. Nowers, Santa Fe official.

NUMA. In Grant County, 6 miles east of Medford. A post office from April 20, 1898, to August 31, 1943. Its name comes from Numa, a village in Ireland.

NUNNA. In southeastern McCurtain County near Tom. A post office from October 7, 1870, to March 6, 1872. No longer in existence. The name is the Choctaw word for cooked and probably had reference to a location where cooked meals could be obtained.

NUYAKA. Formerly Hance. In Okmulgee County, 9 miles west of Okmulgee. Site of Nuyaka Mission, established in 1882 by Alice Robertson. Post office name changed to Nuyaka, October 14, 1912, and discontinued August 15, 1954. The name is a Creek corruption of "New Yorker Town," a Creek town in Alabama.

NYE. In northern Beaver County. Post office established November 15, 1893, and moved into Meade County, Kansas, December 8, 1919. Named for William Nye, popular humorist of the period.

O

O COUNTY. Original designation for Garfield County, Oklahoma

Territory. Name changed to Garfield County, November 6, 1894.

OAKDALE. Present Mountain View, in northeastern Kiowa County. Post office established October 14, 1893, and name changed to Mountain View, October 9, 1900.

OAK GROVE. In Adair County, 6 miles east of Stilwell. A post office from March 28, 1892, to January 15, 1916.

OAK HILL. In McCurtain County, 6 miles west of Broken Bow. A post office from May 15, 1914, to October 12, 1948.

OAKHURST. In Tulsa County, 4 miles southwest of Tulsa. Post office established December 12, 1918.

OAKLAND. In Marshall County, 2 miles northwest of Madill. Post office established July 20, 1881. Took its name from a surrounding grove of oak timber.

OAKLEY. In Dewey County, 8 miles southeast of Taloga. A post office from October 9, 1899, to October 15, 1913.

OAK LODGE. At Skullyville, 2 miles northeast of Spiro in Le Flore County. A post office from December 22, 1871, to March 31, 1917. On October 10, 1871, a post office named Choctaw Agency had been discontinued at this same site.

OAKMAN. In Pontotoc County, 5 miles northeast of Ada. Railroad name was Rainey. A post office from December 24, 1896, to June 30, 1929. Named by Silas Heflin, first postmaster, for his home town of Oakman, Alabama.

OAKS. In southern Delaware County, 5 miles southwest of Kansas. Post office established July 18, 1881. Site of New Spring Place, established 1842 as a mission by the Moravian church.

OAKWOOD. In eastern Dewey County. Post office established June 15, 1899.

OBERLIN. In southeastern Bryan County, 10 miles south of Boswell. A post office from October 6, 1897, to July 31, 1937. Its name comes from Oberlin College in Oberlin, Ohio.

OBERLIN. Formerly Clardyville. In Pottawatomie County, 5 miles west of Asher. Post office name changed to Oberlin, April 25, 1876, and changed to Wagoza, July 18, 1888. Its name comes from Oberlin College in Oberlin, Ohio.

OBI. In northeastern Sequoyah County, 10 miles east of Marble City. A post office from December 9, 1910, to September 30, 1921. Named for Obi Binge, early-day resident.

OCATE. In southern Harper County, 6 miles west of May. A post office from January 31, 1899, to November 15, 1906. No longer in existence.

OCHELATA. In Washington County, 10 miles south of Bartlesville. Post office established March 23, 1900. Named for Charles

Thompson, Cherokee principal chief, 1875–79, whose Indian name was Ochelata.

OCINA. In northern Greer County, 5 miles north of Willow. A post office from June 13, 1916, to October 31, 1935. On February 20, 1915, a post office named Moravia had been discontinued at this approximate location. The name was coined upon the consolidation of three school districts, Ozona, Arbana, and Moravia.

OCONEE. In Coal County, 7 miles southwest of Coalgate. A post office from October 6, 1897, to July 31, 1907. Took its name from a Creek town on the Chattahoochee River. The word is from *okoni eknoni,* meaning "great big water."

OCTAVIA. In southern Le Flore County, 5 miles northwest of Smithville. A post office from October 29, 1898, to September 30, 1953. Named for Octavia Lewis, first postmaster.

ODELL. In McCurtain County, 5 miles north of Haworth. A post office from February 28, 1903, to June 30, 1925. Named for Elsie Odell Hughes, local resident.

ODEMA. In Jackson County, 5 miles southeast of Eldorado. A post office from June 18, 1901, to May 14, 1906. No longer in existence.

ODESSA. In southeastern Washita County near Mountain View. A post office from August 15, 1894, to December 31, 1901. No longer in existence. Named by J. C. Broughton, townsite owner, for his hometown of Odessa, Texas.

ODETTA. In southeastern Kiowa County, 5 miles east of Snyder. A post office from July 13, 1903, to November 15, 1924. Named for Odetta Dunn, daughter of W. L. Dunn, first postmaster.

OGEECHEE. In Ottawa County, 7 miles southeast of Miami. A post office from January 4, 1895, to June 15, 1907. The name is from the Cherokee word *a-git-si,* meaning "my mother" and comes from a Cherokee tradition that a Shawnee captive lost her life protecting her captors from a great serpent and henceforth was known as their "mother."

OGLESBY. In Washington County, 7 miles northeast of Ramona. A post office from November 13, 1900, to August 15, 1933. Named for Tom Oglesby, local rancher.

OIL CITY. Formerly Wheeler. In western Carter County, 7 miles north of Wilson. Post office name changed to Oil City, October 15, 1909, and discontinued January 5, 1930.

OILTON. In northwestern Creek County. Post office established May 5, 1915. Named as an oil boom town during the development of the great Cushing field in 1915.

OKARCHE. Situated on the line between Canadian and Kingfisher counties. Post office established June 28, 1890. The name was coined by Charles Hunter from

OK(lahoma), AR(apaho), and CHE(yenne).

OKAY. Formerly North Muskogee. In southeastern Wagoner County. Post office name changed to Okay, October 18, 1919. Took its name from The OK Truck Manufacturing Company, a local industry.

OKEENE. In northeastern Blaine County. Post office established January 27, 1893. The name was coined by Elmer Bordrick from the words Oklahoma, Cherokee, and Cheyenne.

OKEMAH. County seat of Okfuskee County. Post office established May 16, 1902. Name selected by H. B. Dexter, town developer, for Okemah, a Creek chief. The word is Creek and may be rendered "big chief."

OKESA. In Osage County, 11 miles west of Bartlesville. A post office from January 17, 1906, to December 31, 1940. The name is an Osage word meaning "halfway," the site being halfway between Pawhuska and the Cherokee Nation boundary.

OKFUSKEE. In northern Okfuskee County, 12 miles north of Okemah. A post office from July 18, 1896, to March 15, 1955. Chosen for a Creek town in Cleburne County, Alabama, the name referred to the origin of a clan of the Muskogee, or Creek, Indians.

OKFUSKEE COUNTY. A county in east-central Oklahoma, created at statehood. Named for a Creek town in Cleburne County, Alabama.

OKLAHOMA. Present Whitefield, in Haskell County. Post office established December 21, 1881, and name changed to Whitefield, November 27, 1888, at the request of the Post Office Department to avoid confusion with Oklahoma Station, established as a post office December 30, 1887. The designation of this post office name on December 21, 1881, was the first official use of the word destined to become the name of a state in the Union.

OKLAHOMA CITY. County seat of Oklahoma County and the capital of Oklahoma since June 11, 1910. Post office established December 30, 1887, as Oklahoma Station. Name changed to Oklahoma, December 18, 1888, and to Oklahoma City, July 1, 1923. Although known since the opening of the Unassigned Lands as Oklahoma City, the post office did not adopt the name Oklahoma City until July 1, 1923.

OKLAHOMA COUNTY. A county in central Oklahoma, identical to Oklahoma County, Oklahoma Territory. The county name is a logical projection of the name of the principal community and city of the county, first known as Oklahoma Station, a stop on the Santa Fe Railway, and now Oklahoma City.

OKLAHOMA STATION. The original designation of the stop on the Santa Fe Railway that later became Oklahoma City. Post office established December 30, 1887, and name changed to Oklahoma, December 18, 1888.

OKMULGEE. County seat of Okmulgee County. Record Town for Recording District No. 9, Indian Territory. Capital of the Creek Nation. Post office established April 29, 1869. Until November 15, 1883, the official spelling for the post office was Okmulkee. The name comes from a Creek town in Russell County, Alabama, and is a Creek word *oki mulgi,* meaning "boiling waters."

OKMULGEE COUNTY. A county in east-central Oklahoma, created at statehood. Its name comes from a Creek town in Russell County, Alabama.

OKOEE. In Craig County, 3 miles north of Ketchum. A post office from October 22, 1901, to July 31, 1913. Its name comes from a settlement on the Ocoee River, Polk County, Tennessee. The name is from the Cherokee word *uwagahi,* meaning "passion flower vine."

OKOLONA. In McCurtain County, 7 miles southeast of Broken Bow. A post office from June 25, 1890, to July 25, 1894. The name is from the Choctaw word *oka lobali,* meaning "a place caved in or washed out by water."

OKRA. In McClain County near Rosedale. A post office from July 26, 1898, to August 31, 1908. No

longer in existence, it took its name from the garden vegetable.

OKTAHA. In central Muskogee County. Post office established August 6, 1900. Named for Oktahasars Harjo, or Sands, well-known Creek chief of the Civil War period who pursued a neutral or pro-Northern tribal policy.

OLA. In Latimer County, 3 miles east of Wilburton. A post office established May 1, 1886, and name changed to Lutie, October 4, 1901. Named for Ola Woods, daughter of Oscar Woods, mineowner.

OLDS. Present Davidson, in southwestern Tillman County. Post office established May 21, 1902, and name changed to Davidson, June 20, 1903.

OLETA. Formerly Whitehead. In northeastern Ellis County, 13 miles southwest of Woodward. Post office name changed to Oleta, August 24, 1901, and changed to Fargo, February 17, 1905. Named for Oleta Ooley, daughter of David Ooley, early settler.

OLETA. In southern Pushmataha County, 15 miles east of Antlers. Post office established October 10, 1935. Named for Oleta Morris, wife of Alvin J. Morris, first postmaster.

OLIVE. In Creek County, 6 miles northeast of Drumright. A post office from November 20, 1896, to September 30, 1938. Townsite originally platted as Mount Olive, the name having been taken from the Bible.

177

OLNEY. In Coal County, 7 miles west of Lehigh. A post office from July 12, 1902, to June 15, 1955. Named for Richard Olney, railroad surveyor.

OLUSTEE. In Jackson County, 6 miles southwest of Altus. Post office established February 27, 1895. Its name comes from the Battle of Olustee in the Florida-Seminole War. The name is a Seminole word meaning "pond."

OLYMPUS. In northeastern Delaware County, 5 miles east of Grove. A post office from December 30, 1885, to June 4, 1895. On April 27, 1896, a post office named Hill was established at this same site. Its name comes from a mountain in Thessaly, Greece, regarded in antiquity as the home of the gods.

OMEGA. In Kingfisher County, 11 miles east of Watonga. Post office established August 9, 1892. Took its name from the last letter in the Greek alphabet; a post office named Alpha was located 5 miles east.

ONA. In Texas County, 27 miles northwest of Guymon. A post office from April 22, 1907, to July 15, 1919. Named for Ona Schmoyer, daughter of Ida V. Schmoyer, first postmaster.

ONAPA. Formerly Irby. In McIntosh County, 8 miles north of Eufaula. Post office name changed to Onapa, February 5, 1909, and discontinued June 30, 1914. The name is a Creek word meaning "above."

ONASCO. In southwestern Caddo County, 7 miles northwest of Apache. A post office from March 18, 1902, to March 30, 1907. No longer in existence. The name was assigned arbitrarily by the Post Office Department after rejecting all locally suggested names.

ONEIDA. In western Kingfisher County near Loyal. A post office from June 23, 1892, to February 14, 1901. No longer in existence. The name is that of an Indian tribe of Iroquoian stock; the word means "standing stone."

ONEIL. In western Major County, 7 miles southeast of Quinlan. A post office from August 13, 1907, to December 31, 1908. The post office is the same as O'Neil, discontinued July 30, 1904, across the county line in Woodward County, Oklahoma Territory.

O'NEIL. In eastern Woodward County, 7 miles southeast of Quinlan. A post office from January 23, 1901, to July 30, 1904.

ONETA. In western Wagoner County, 5 miles southeast of Broken Arrow. A post office from July 7, 1905, to November 30, 1922.

ONEY. At the site of Albert in Caddo County. A post office from March 12, 1902, to April 14, 1906. Named for Richard Oney, early-day resident.

ONYX. Present Douglas, in southeastern Garfield County. Post office established May 23, 1894, and name changed to Douglas, February 25, 1903. Took its name from a type of quartz rock found nearby.

OOLITE. In Pontotoc County, 3 miles northeast of Fitzhugh. Post office established May 1, 1906, and name changed to Lawrence, June 27, 1907. Took its name from the Oklahoma Oolite Stone Company, organized to mine a variety of limestone found nearby.

OOLOGAH. In Rogers County, 12 miles northwest of Claremore. Post office established May 25, 1891. Named for Oologah, or Dark Cloud, a Cherokee chief.

OO-WA-LA. In Rogers County, adjoining Sageeyah. A post office from March 18, 1881, to December 4, 1889. From September 19, 1887, to June 14, 1888, the post office name was Mayes. The word is the Cherokee name of the Lipe family, prominent Cherokees.

OPAH. In McCurtain County, 10 miles northwest of Broken Bow. A post office from August 20, 1913, to December 31, 1915. No longer in existence. The name is the Choctaw word for owl.

OPAL. In Woodward County, 10 miles southwest of Woodward. A post office from October 2, 1900, to January 30, 1904. Named for Opal Thomas, daughter of L. S. Thomas, early-day resident.

OPIE. In Jefferson County, 7 miles east of Ryan. A post office from August 3, 1894, to November 30, 1901. No longer in existence. The name was a coined word based on a re-versal of P.O., the abbreviation for post office.

OPPOSUM. In western Le Flore County, 10 miles west of Shady Point. A post office from June 23, 1881, to February 20, 1882. In 1901 a post office named Latham was established at this approximate site. Took its name from nearby Opossum Creek, a tributary of Brazil Creek, but postal records made it "Opposum."

OPTIMA. In Texas County, 9 miles northeast of Guymon. Post office established September 13, 1886. The name is a Latin word, being the plural of optimum, meaning "best possible result."

ORA. In northwestern Stephens County, 6 miles west of Marlow. Post office established June 25, 1902, and name changed to Tallaville, June 24, 1905. Named for Ora L. Kirke, first postmaster.

ORCUTT. In Okmulgee County, 5 miles north of Beggs. A post office from February 21, 1894, to January 4, 1898. Named for A. D. Orcutt, prominent local rancher.

ORD. In Choctaw County, 6 miles south of Hugo. A rural community named for Ord, Nebraska.

OREANA. In northwestern Comanche County, 7 miles north of Indiahoma. A post office from September 27, 1901, to September 30, 1905. No longer in existence. A mining town, it took its name from the words ore and Anne, the given name of the wife of B. N. Turk, the first postmaster.

179

ORIE. Present Deer Creek, in Grant County. Post office established June 5, 1894, and name changed to Deer Creek, February 27, 1899.

ORIENTA. In northern Major County, 6 miles north of Fairview. Post office established March 12, 1901. Took its name from the Kansas City, Mexico and Orient Railway.

ORINNE. In Love County, 6 miles north of Marietta. Post office established June 13, 1895, and name changed to Greenville, December 4, 1902.

ORION. In western Major County, 12 miles northeast of Seiling. A post office from April 10, 1895, to June 30, 1932. The name, from Greek mythology, is also given to a constellation in the northern sky.

ORLANDO. In northeastern Logan County. Post office established July 18, 1889. Named for Orlando Hysell, relative of townsite developer.

ORR. In northwestern Love County, 9 miles southeast of Ringling. A post office from July 21, 1892, to November 29, 1957. Named for W. E. Orr, rancher and cattleman.

ORTLEY. In northwestern Kingfisher County, 13 miles west of Hennessey. A post office from June 5, 1894, to April 8, 1896. No longer in existence. Named for Henry Ortley Coleman, father of Catherine Coleman, a friend of the first postmaster.

OSAGE. In western Osage County, 1 mile east of Cleveland. Post office established November 23, 1906.

OSAGE. In eastern Pawnee County, 5 miles east of Skedee. A post office from May 23, 1894, to September 15, 1902. No longer in existence.

OSAGE COUNTY. A county in north-central Oklahoma, similar in size to Osage County, Oklahoma Territory. Named for the Osage tribe of Indians, whose reservation comprised the area of the county. The name is a corruption by the French of the tribal name *Wah-Sha-She*, the exact meaning of which appears lost.

OSBORNE. In Kay County, 11 miles southwest of Blackwell. Post office established February 6, 1894, and name changed to Eddy, January 3, 1901.

OSCAR. In southern Jefferson County, 12 miles east of Ryan. Post office established November 23, 1892. Named for Oscar W. Seay, rancher and cattleman.

OSCEOLA. In northwestern Custer County, 9 miles north of Butler. A post office from May 18, 1895, to January 31, 1909. Named for *Asi Yahola* or Osceola, prominent Seminole chief.

OSEUMA. In Ottawa County, 5 miles northeast of Afton. A post office from March 4, 1868, to May 15, 1909. The name is from the Cherokee word *a'siyu ama*, meaning "good water."

OSHUSKEY. In eastern Cimarron County, 21 miles east of Boise City. A post office from October 15, 1906, to May 31, 1913. No longer in existence, it was named for Maye Oshuskey, first postmaster.

OSIRIS. In Woodward County, 7 miles north of Mooreland. A post office from July 21, 1900, to January 31, 1909. No longer in existence. Its name comes from the Egyptian god of the underworld.

OSMIT. In southeastern Pottawatomie County, 5 miles east of Asher. A post office from February 4, 1884, to June 29, 1888. No longer in existence.

OSWALT. In northern Love County, 14 miles northwest of Marietta. A post office from July 13, 1898, to May 31, 1949. Named for William Oswalt, early-day resident.

OTEGO. In Payne County, 6 miles south of Stillwater. A post office from April 19, 1894, to September 30, 1903. Its name comes from Otego, Cowley County, Kansas.

OTEX. In southwest Texas County, adjoining Texhoma. A post office from October 15, 1906, to July 31, 1907. No longer in existence. The name was coined from the words Oklahoma and Texas.

OTEX. A rural community in Harmon County, 6 miles northwest of Arnett. The name was coined from the words Oklahoma and Texas.

OTOE. Formerly Redrock. In Noble County, 7 miles north of Perry. Post office name changed to Otoe, May 3, 1892, and discontinued July 31, 1917. Took its name from the nearby community of Oto Indians. Otoe is a Sioux word, *wat ota.*

OTTAWA. In Ottawa County, 6 miles east of Miami. A post office from June 28, 1898, to December 15, 1908.

OTTAWA COUNTY. A county in extreme northeastern Oklahoma, created at statehood. Its name comes from the Ottawa tribe of Indians. The word is an Algonquian term *adawe,* meaning "to buy and sell."

OTTER. In western Kingfisher County, 9 miles west of Kingfisher. A post office from December 24, 1892, to July 31, 1899. No longer in existence. Took its name from nearby Otter Creek, a tributary of Kingfisher Creek.

OURAY. In extreme southeastern corner of Ottawa County. A post office from June 23, 1890, to October 3, 1895. No longer in existence. Named for Ouray, well-known Ute chief. The word is generally understood to mean arrow.

OVERBROOK. In northern Love County. Post office established June 21, 1887. Its name comes from Overbrook, Pennsylvania.

OVERTON SPRINGS. A former rural community in southern Marshall County, adjoining the Red River, and now inundated by Lake Texoma. Named for Benjamin F. Overton, Chickasaw governor.

OWASSO. In Tulsa County, 8 miles northeast of Tulsa. Post office established January 24, 1900. The name is an Osage word, meaning "the end," and came into use when the site was a terminus of a branch of the Santa Fe Railway.

OWEN. A railroad junction and switching point in northern Washington County, 2 miles south of Caney, Kansas. Named for Robert L. Owen, United States Senator from Oklahoma (1907–1925) whose extensive ranch adjoined the site.

OWENS. In southwestern Kay County, 6 miles north of Billings. A post office from December 8, 1898, to August 31, 1911. Townsite name was Owen. Named for Frank Owens, early-day resident.

OWL. Formerly Byrd. In Coal County, 9 miles northwest of Coalgate. Post office name changed to Owl, July 10, 1894. On June 11, 1907, the post office was moved a few miles northeast and the name changed to Centrahoma. Took its name from nearby Owl Creek, a branch of Leader Creek, a tributary of the Clear Boggy River.

OXFORD. In southern Alfalfa County, 6 miles northeast of Cleo Springs. A post office from November 4, 1898, to December 31, 1903. No longer in existence.

OXLEY. In Blaine County, 6 miles northeast of Watonga. A post office from November 23, 1893, to October 31, 1901. No longer in existence, it was named for William T. Oxley, early-day resident.

OZARK. In Jackson County, 7 miles east of Altus. The word is from the French *aux arcs*, the designation of a trading post in present Arkansas. Took its name from the Ozark Trail, now U. S. Highway 62, on which the community is located.

P

P COUNTY. Original designation for Noble County, Oklahoma Territory. Name changed to Noble County, November 6, 1894.

PADEN. In Adair County, 6 miles south of Stilwell. A post office from May 5, 1890, to August 8, 1896. No longer in existence, it was named for Benjamin F. Paden, first postmaster.

PADEN. In western Okfuskee County. Post office established January 21, 1903. Named for Paden Tolbert, deputy United States marshal.

PAGE. In Le Flore County, 12 miles south of Heavener. Post office established April 6, 1896. Named for William C. Page, prominent Choctaw.

PAHE. In western Osage County, 8 miles southeast of Ponca City. A post office from June 26, 1908, to January 14, 1911. Named for Pretty Hair, an Osage tribal leader.

PALACE. In Harper County, 5 miles east of Buffalo. A post office from April 17, 1903, to December 15, 1908. No longer in existence.

PALADIN. In southeastern Beaver County, 6 miles west of Logan. A post office from March 5, 1903, to August 31, 1908. No longer in existence. Its name comes from one of the 12 peers of Charlemagne, and now means a legendary hero.

PALADORA. In extreme northwestern Beaver County. A post office from April 25, 1888, to January 14, 1899. No longer in existence. The name is a variant of the Spanish word *paloduro,* meaning "hard wood."

PALMER. In Murray County, 5 miles north of Sulphur. A post office from June 23, 1892, to June 15, 1915. Named for Thomas L. Palmer, townsite owner.

PANA. In northeastern Garfield County, 3 miles northwest of Hunter. A post office from October 19, 1895, to March 15, 1902. No longer in existence.

PANAMA. In Le Flore County, 9 miles north of Poteau. Post office established January 14, 1898. Its name comes from the Panama Canal.

PANHANDLE CITY. In Texas County, 7 miles north of Guymon. Incorporated October 30, 1973. The name was selected by the developers to identify the location of the municipality.

PANOLA. *See* Ponola.

PANOLA. In northern Haskell County, 7 miles northeast of Keota. Post office established April 17, 1884, and name changed to Blaine, October 1, 1884. The name is the Choctaw word for cotton.

PANOLA. In Latimer County, 7 miles east of Wilburton. Post office established March 18, 1911.

PANTHER. Present McCurtain, in southeastern Haskell County. Post office established June 11, 1890, and name changed to McCurtain, April 5, 1902. Panther was located about one-half mile west of the present site. Its name comes from a member of the cat family.

PAOLI. In northern Garvin County, 8 miles north of Pauls Valley. Post office established June 27, 1888. Its name comes from Paoli, Pennsylvania.

PAPOOSE. In extreme northern Hughes County, 6 miles northwest of Wetumka. A post office from September 14, 1925, to November 14, 1931. The name is from the Algonquian word *papoos,* meaning "child."

PARADISE. In southwestern Payne County, 4 miles north of Coyle. A post office from June 23, 1892, to January 14, 1905. Now a rural community known as Paradise Valley.

PARIS. In Kingfisher County, 6 miles northwest of Dover. A post office from June 13, 1891, to December 31, 1901. No longer in existence. Its name comes from Paris, Texas.

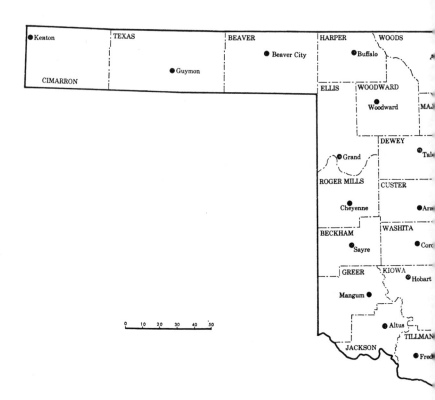

Oklahoma Counties, 1907

Reproduced from *Historical Atlas of Oklahoma*, by John W. Morris and Edwin C. McReynolds. Copyright 1965 by the University of Oklahoma Press.

PARKER. In northern Coal County, 14 miles north of Coalgate. A post office from June 11, 1913, to April 30, 1946. Named for Pharm Parker, local resident.

PARKER. In southern Custer County, 5 miles west of Clinton. A post office from April 24, 1901, to April 30, 1906. The railroad name was Parkersburg. Named for J. N. Parker, townsite owner.

PARKER. The post office name for Blackwell in Kay County from April 2, 1894, to February 4, 1895.

PARK HILL. In Cherokee County, 3 miles south of Tahlequah. Original post office established May 18, 1838; post office and name changed to Tahlequah, May 6, 1847. On April 22, 1892, another post office named Park Hill was established at the original location. Park Hill was the location of the Cherokee Female Seminary, and for many years was the center of culture among the Cherokees. Took its name from Park Hill Mission, established in 1829.

PARKLAND. In Lincoln County, 4 miles south of Agra. A post office from December 19, 1894, to June 15, 1918. No longer in existence. The name was adopted to describe the character of the townsite.

PARKMAN. In Ellis County, 13 miles east of Arnett. A post office from August 19, 1902, to December 8, 1917. No longer in existence.

PARKS. In Stephens County, 15 miles southeast of Duncan. A post

office from March 28, 1902, to September 15, 1913. No longer in existence.

PARKVILLE. In Dewey County, 7 miles southeast of Taloga. A post office from June 17, 1895, to November 30, 1900. No longer in existence, it was named for Samuel L. Park, early-day resident.

PARMICHO. In Coal County, 7 miles west of Lehigh. Post office established August 31, 1901, and name changed to Olney, July 12, 1902. The name is from the Choctaw words *pala misha*, meaning "lighted place in the distance," and has reference to a lantern hanging at the railroad station.

PARNELL. In southern Lincoln County, 5 miles north of Meeker. Post office established July 13, 1895, and name changed to Payson, August 22, 1903. Named for William C. Parnell, first postmaster.

PARO. In Hughes County, 7 miles east of Holdenville. A post office from April 17, 1903, to June 15, 1907. No longer in existence.

PARR. Present Rush Springs, in southern Grady County. Post office established July 11, 1883, and name changed to Rush Springs, May 13, 1892.

PARSONS. Present Millerton, in southwestern McCurtain County. Post office established December 15, 1902, and name changed to Millerton, March 5, 1908. On May 3, 1895, a post office named Wheelock had been discontinued at this same site. Parsons was the post office for Wheelock Academy. Named for W. S. Parsons, first postmaster.

PARTON. In Tillman County, 2 miles east of Hollister. A post office from December 28, 1908, to August 14, 1909. No longer in existence, it was named for Wiley J. Parton, townsite owner.

PARTRIDGE. In northwestern Lincoln County, 3 miles northwest of Carney. A post office from April 9, 1892, to July 31, 1908. No longer in existence, it was named for George R. Partridge, first postmaster.

PARUNA. In Harper County, 12 miles northeast of Buffalo. A post office from March 5, 1903, to May 31, 1919. No longer in existence. Presumably named for a popular patent medicine.

PARVIN. In northwestern Kingfisher County, 9 miles southeast of Okeene. A post office from November 23, 1892, to March 2, 1904. Named for Alexander M. Parvin, early-day landowner.

PATRICK. Present Braggs, in Muskogee County. Post office established May 26, 1886, and name changed to Braggs, September 10, 1888. Named for John J. Patrick, first postmaster.

PATTERSON. Formerly Thurston. In Latimer County, 6 miles northwest of Wilburton. Post office name changed to Patterson,

October 31, 1906, and discontinued October 17, 1922.

PATTON. A switch and loading point in Mayes County, 4 miles north of Adair. Named for William C. Patton, local rancher and cattleman.

PAUCAUNLA. In Bryan County, 6 miles east of Colbert. A post office from September 23, 1897, to July 15, 1910. The name is from the Chickasaw word *Pak-an-li,* meaning "blossom," the name of a woman prominent in Chickasaw history.

PAUL. In western Dewey County, 6 miles west of Camargo. A post office from July 18, 1904, to March 31, 1911. No longer in existence, it was named for Paul Jones, son of L. D. Jones, first postmaster.

PAULS VALLEY. County seat of Garvin County. Record Town for Recording District No. 17, Indian Territory. Post office established August 21, 1871. Named for Smith Paul, prominent early settler.

PAWHUSKA. County seat of Osage County. Post office established May 4, 1876. Named for the well-known Osage chief *Paw-Hiu-Skah,* whose name means white hair.

PAWNEE. County seat of Pawnee County. Post office established May 4, 1876. Until October 26, 1893, the official name of the post office was Pawnee Agency. The word is French, of somewhat uncertain meaning, and is often spelled Pana or Pani.

PAWNEE COUNTY. A county in north-central Oklahoma, slightly larger in area than Pawnee County, Oklahoma Territory. The name Platte was also considered as a name for this county. Its name comes from the Pawnee tribe of Indians.

PAW PAW. In Sequoyah County, 7 miles southeast of Muldrow. A post office from December 26, 1882, to May 31, 1915. Took its name from the Paw Paw society, a semi-secret organization of Southern sympathy during the Civil War.

PAYNE. In southwestern McClain County, 5 miles northeast of Lindsay. A post office from December 15, 1904, to October 31, 1922. Named for Jeff D. Payne, first postmaster.

PAYNE. In Payne County, 8 miles southwest of Stillwater. A post office from June 19, 1890, to February 12, 1894. Named for David L. Payne, central figure in the Boomer movement.

PAYNE COUNTY. A county in central Oklahoma, similar in area to Payne County, Oklahoma Territory. Named for David L. Payne.

PAYSON. Formerly Parnell. In southern Lincoln County, 5 miles north of Meeker. Post office name changed to Payson, August 22, 1903, and discontinued October 15, 1954. Named for Payson Ripley, nephew of the president of the Santa Fe Railway.

PEACE. In Woodward County, 6 miles north of Quinlan. A post office from December 10, 1903, to February 15, 1908. No longer in existence. Took its name from *Peacemakers*, a novel by H. E. Stannard.

PEARL. In southeastern Woodward County, 12 miles south of Quinlan. A post office from December 16, 1897, to September 30, 1911.

PEARSON. In Pottawatomie County, 10 miles south of Tecumseh. A post office from May 31, 1927, to March 31, 1965. First known locally as Wamego.

PEARSON. In Tillman County, 6 miles south of Frederick. A post office from December 5, 1901, to October 15, 1904. No longer in existence, it was named for James E. Pearson, first postmaster.

PEARSONIA. Formerly Blackland. In Osage County, 9 miles northwest of Pawhuska. Post office was moved 3 miles southeast and name changed to Pearsonia, December 14, 1917; post office discontinued December 31, 1936. Named for Joseph R. Pearson, townsite owner.

PEASTER. In extreme eastern Beckham County, 9 miles southwest of Elk City. A post office from December 3, 1900, to February 28, 1907. No longer in existence.

PECAN. In southern Cleveland County, 9 miles southeast of Lexington. A post office from January 20, 1896, to May 31, 1905. No longer in existence. Took its name from a nearby grove of pecan trees.

PECAN POINT. A very early Red River settlement in southern McCurtain County near Harris. One of the earliest white settlements in present-day Oklahoma.

PECK. Present Tushka, in Atoka County. Post office established April 17, 1903, and name changed to Lewis, April 13, 1905.

PECKHAM. In Kay County, 9 miles northeast of Blackwell. Post office established July 15, 1899. Named for Ed L. Peckham of Blackwell, railroad developer.

PEDEE. In Noble County, 6 miles southeast of Billings. A post office from July 27, 1894, to May 31, 1904. No longer in existence. Its name comes from a small Siouan tribe living originally along the Pedee River in South Carolina.

PEEK. In southern Ellis County, 14 miles southeast of Arnett. A post office from February 15, 1906, to December 15, 1954. Named for Vestal Peek, local landowner.

PEERY. Present Waurika, in Jefferson County. Post office established May 22, 1890, and name changed to Moneka, April 18, 1895.

PEGGS. In northwestern Cherokee County, 15 miles northwest of Tahlequah. Post office established December 6, 1899. Named for Thomas Pegg, acting principal chief of the Cherokee Nation in the absence of John Ross during the Civil War period.

PEMETA. In western Creek County, 3 miles north of Drumright. A

post office from August 9, 1915, to October 30, 1923.

PENNINGTON. Present Harrah, in Oklahoma County. Post office established March 13, 1894, and name changed to Sweeney, June 22, 1896.

PENO. In northeastern Le Flore County, 4 miles southwest of Fort Smith. A post office from March 27, 1916, to June 15, 1932. No longer in existence, it was named for a local resident of Mexican extraction always known as Penocho.

PENSACOLA. In Mayes County, 8 miles east of Adair. A post office from May 23, 1896, to November 30, 1955. Took its name from nearby Pensacola Ranch, property of Joseph Martin, prominent Cherokee.

PENSEE. Formerly Waco. Present Chickasha, in Grady County. Post office name changed to Pensee, September 11, 1891, and to Chickasha, June 20, 1892. *Pensée* is the French word for thought, and was adopted by Jacob Descombs, the postmaster, a French Canadian, who "thought" it would be wise to change the name of his post office from Waco.

PEORIA. In central Beaver County. A post office from March 1, 1890, to April 29, 1891. No longer in existence. Its name comes from Peoria, Illinois.

PEORIA. In northeastern Ottawa County, 13 miles east of Miami. A post office from June 13, 1891, to November 29, 1941. Named for the

Peoria tribe of Indians, because the site was on the Peoria reserve. The word is from the French *Peouarea*, which was based on a Peoria word meaning "carrying a pack on his back."

PERDUE. In Woodward County, 12 miles north of Mooreland. A post office from April 24, 1901, to July 31, 1909. No longer in existence.

PERKINS. In southern Payne County. Post office established January 31, 1890. Named for B. W. Perkins, United States senator from Kansas.

PERNELL. In southwestern Garvin County, 7 miles southwest of Elmore City. Post office established June 28, 1922. Named for Thomas Pernell, long-time local resident.

PERRIER. In Osage County, 8 miles east of Hominy. Townsite plat filed September 3, 1918. No longer in existence, it was named for James Perrier, prominent Osage.

PERRY. A county in Chickasaw District, Choctaw Nation. Later partly in Chickasaw Nation. Named for a prominent family of intermarried Choctaws.

PERRY. County seat of Noble County. Post office established August 25, 1893. Named for J. A. Perry, a member of the Cherokee Strip Commission during the administration of President Grover Cleveland.

PERRYVILLE. Site in Pittsburg County, 5 miles southwest of Mc-Alester. Important settlement in the Choctaw Nation prior to the Civil War and site of a Civil War engagement, August 26, 1863. Named for James Perry, prominent early-day settler.

PERSHING. In Osage County, 5 miles southeast of Pawhuska. A post office from May 31, 1919, to March 8, 1957. Named for General John J. Pershing.

PERSIMMON. In southern Woodward County, 2 miles west of Mutual. A post office from April 21, 1894, to March 30, 1907. No longer in existence. It took its name from a nearby grove of persimmon trees. The persimmon is a tree of the ebony family, and its name is from the Algonquian word *pasiminan*, meaning "dried fruit."

PERTH. Present Lovell, in Logan County. Post office established May 22, 1899, and name changed to Lovell, February 12, 1906. Its name comes from Perth, Kansas.

PETERSBURG. In southeastern Jefferson County, 16 miles south of Ringling. A post office from July 10, 1891, to September 15, 1919. Named for Peter Meekins, early-day resident.

PETROS. In Le Flore County, 2 miles south of Heavener. A post office from January 21, 1898, to March 30, 1901. First known locally as Petros Cut. The name is Greek for rock, and came from the circumstance that it was Greek immigrants working on the Kansas City Southern Railway who cut solid rock for the railroad right of way.

PETTIT. In Cherokee County, 10 miles south of Tahlequah. A post office from May 11, 1913, to November 30, 1933. Named for Mark and Eliza Pettit, townsite allotees.

PETUNA. Formerly Morrow. In southwestern Grady County, adjoining Rush Springs. Post office name changed to Petuna, March 6, 1888, and discontinued April 10, 1889. Took its name from a plant of the nightshade family, ever popular because of its bright flowers.

PEYTONVILLE. Formerly a rural community in Dewey County, 10 miles southwest of Taloga. Named for Peyton Mayfield, early-day resident.

PHAROAH. In southeastern Okfuskee County, 9 miles east of Okemah. Post office established June 8, 1921. Named for O. J. Pharoah, rancher and cattleman.

PHELPS. In Comanche County, 7 miles southeast of Lawton. A post office from January 11, 1902, to August 15, 1904. No longer in existence, it was named for Robert Phelps Simpson, first postmaster.

PHILIPSBURG. In Creek County near Bristow. A post office from July 16, 1894, to August 20, 1898. The site is now a rural community known as Phillipsburg.

PHILLIPS. In Coal County, 3 miles south of Coalgate. A post office from April 2, 1892, to April 2,

1927. Named for Henry L. Phillips, coal mine operator.

PHROSO. In western Major County, 8 miles northeast of Chester. A post office from September 19, 1900, to May 29, 1937. Took name from *Phroso*, a novel by Anthony Hope.

PICHER. In Ottawa County, 8 miles north of Miami. Post office established June 2, 1916. Named for W. S. Picher of the Eagle-Picher Lead Company.

PICKENS. A county in the Chickasaw Nation. Named for Edmond Pickens, prominent Chickasaw.

PICKENS. In northwestern McCurtain County, 10 miles northwest of Bethel. Post office established October 26, 1912. Named for John T. Pickens, first postmaster.

PICKENS. In southeastern Marshall County, adjoining Lebanon. A post office from February 7, 1895, to December 15, 1899. No longer in existence, it took its name from Pickens County, Chickasaw Nation.

PICKETT. In Pontotoc County, 5 miles west of Ada. A post office from January 27, 1913, to January 15, 1916. First known locally as Center Switch. Took its name from the Pickett Store, so named because of a well-cared-for picket fence.

PIEDMONT. In northeastern Canadian County, 13 miles north of Yukon. Post office established December 26, 1903. Its name comes from the Piedmont Region of the eastern United States, the area between the Appalachian Mountains and the coastal plain.

PIERCE. In McIntosh County, 11 miles west of Checotah. A post office from March 26, 1907, to November 19, 1965. Named for Homer Pierce Lee, first postmaster.

PIERCETON. In central Kay County, 4 miles northeast of Tonkawa. Post office established May 26, 1894, and name changed to Autwine, March 5, 1903. Named for Louis M. Pierce, first postmaster.

PIKE. In Love County, 13 miles northwest of Marietta. A post office from November 25, 1892, to November 30, 1933. Named for Brigadier General Albert Pike, Confederate leader.

PINE. In northern Coal County, 12 miles north of Coalgate. A post office from March 3, 1900, to December 15, 1912. Took its name from nearby Pine Creek.

PINE RIDGE. A mission established in 1835 about 2 miles north of Doaksville, Choctaw Nation.

PINE VALLEY. In Le Flore County, 5 miles west of Big Cedar. A post office from December 16, 1926, to August 15, 1942. Took its name from the Oklahoma, Rich Mountain and Pine Valley Railroad.

PINEY. In eastern Adair County, 6 miles north of Stilwell. A post office from November 24, 1913, to August 20, 1921. Named for Frank C. Piney, first sheriff of Adair County.

PINK. In western Pottawatomie County, 9 miles west of Tecumseh. A post office from March 19, 1894, to February 14, 1906.

PINKSTON. In southern Ellis County, 12 miles south of Arnett. A post office from October 31, 1904, to February 15, 1908. No longer in existence, it was named for Burr H. Pinkston, townsite owner.

PIOR. In Beckham County, 3 miles northeast of Sayre. Post office established March 3, 1900, and name changed to Doxey, December 5, 1902. Named for John B. Pior, prominent local resident.

PIRTLE. In Bryan County, 5 miles east of Durant. A post office from January 30, 1904, to July 20, 1915. Original townsite name was Hunter; name changed to Elliott; and thereafter to Pirtle. Named for Milton A. Pirtle, local resident.

PITTS. In Cherokee County, 9 miles west of Tahlequah. A post office from October 9, 1908, to July 31, 1916. Named for James W. Pitts, first postmaster.

PITTSBURG. Formerly Edwards. In Pittsburg County, 3 miles east of Kiowa. Post office name changed to Pittsburg, August 27, 1909. Took its name from Pittsburg County.

PITTSBURG COUNTY. A county in southeastern Oklahoma, created at statehood. Its name comes from Pittsburgh, Pennsylvania.

PLAINS. In northwestern Ellis County, 3 miles northwest of Catesby. A post office from March 18, 1907, to April 30, 1908. No longer in existence, it took its name from the surrounding plains.

PLAINVIEW. Formerly Ecter. In southwestern Beaver County, near Gray. Post office name changed to Plainview, November 7, 1910, and discontinued December 31, 1912.

PLAINVIEW. A rural community in Greer County, 10 miles west of Willow.

PLAINVIEW. A rural community in western Woods County, 20 miles east of Buffalo. Took its name from a remarkable view towards the south of broad plain of the valley of the Cimarron River.

PLANO. In southeastern Washita County, 3 miles north of Mountain View. A post office from July 21, 1897, to March 31, 1904. No longer in existence. The name is the Spanish word for level or smooth.

PLATT NATIONAL PARK. Located at Sulphur, in Murray County. Established in 1902, it is the only national park or monument in Oklahoma. Named for Senator Orville T. Platt of Connecticut.

PLATTER. In southern Bryan County, 3 miles northwest of Colbert. Post office established April 11, 1901. Named for A. F. Platter of Denison, Texas, merchant and business leader.

PLEASANT HILL. In southeastern McCurtain County, 6 miles south of Haworth. A post office from September 21, 1912, to November 1, 1934.

PLEASANT VALLEY. In Logan County, 5 miles northwest of Coyle. A post office from February 29, 1904, to May 31, 1947.

PLOVER. On the line between Cotton and Stephens counties, 7 miles west of Comanche. A post office from June 12, 1902, to August 31, 1904. No longer in existence. Took its name from a member of the shore bird family.

PLUMA. In southeastern Woodward County, 7 miles northeast of Mutual. A post office from February 15, 1902, to January 15, 1906. No longer in existence. The name is the Spanish word for feather.

PLUMB. In Payne County, 5 miles northwest of Cushing. A post office from March 21, 1892, to August 31, 1900. No longer in existence, it was named for Preston B. Plumb, United States senator from Kansas.

PLUNKETTVILLE. In northeastern McCurtain County, 10 miles southeast of Smithville. Post office established November 4, 1931. Named for Robert C. Plunkett, first postmaster.

PLUVER. In southwestern Jefferson County near Sugden. A post office from September 23, 1912, to January 15, 1914. No longer in existence. Its name comes from plover, the name of a shore bird.

PLYMOUTH. In southern Major County, 7 miles south of Fairview.

A post office from August 22, 1894, to September 30, 1905. No longer in existence.

POARCH. In southeastern Beckham County, 3 miles east of Carter. A post office from July 15, 1899, to December 31, 1911. No longer in existence, it was named for James H. Poarch, first postmaster.

POCAHONTAS. Formerly Braidwood. In Le Flore County, 3 miles west of Wister. Post office name changed to Pocahontas, May 11, 1895, and name changed to Caston, April 18, 1898. Pocahontas, the young daughter of Chief Powhatan, married John Rolfe in 1614. The word is usually considered to mean playful.

POCAHONTAS. In Pittsburg County, 8 miles east of McAlester. A post office from March 31, 1905, to April 24, 1916. Took its name from the Pocahontas Coal Company.

POCASSET. In Grady County, 10 miles north of Chickasha. Post office established December 13, 1902. Took its name from an Indian village of the same name in Massachusetts. The word means "where the strait widens out."

POCOLA. In northeastern Le Flore County, 9 miles east of Spiro. A post office from February 15, 1881, to February 29, 1916. The name is the Choctaw word for ten, the site being 10 miles from Fort Smith.

POE. In southwestern Jackson County, 6 miles northwest of El-

dorado. A post office from December 17, 1891, to October 12, 1895. No longer in existence, it was named for Edgar Allan Poe.

POLK. In southwestern Kay County, 6 miles north of Billings. A post office from April 4, 1894, to October 15, 1904. No longer in existence. The name was coined from the names of four counties: Pawnee, Oklahoma, Logan, and Kay.

POLLAN. In northwestern Dewey County, 5 miles south of Vici. A post office from June 8, 1901, to August 31, 1913. No longer in existence, it was named for Joseph Z. Pollan, first postmaster.

POLLARD. In southern McCurtain County, 7 miles southwest of Haworth. A post office from May 10, 1904, to April 30, 1923. Named for Tilden H. Pollard, first postmaster.

POLLOCK. In northwestern Lincoln County, 6 miles southeast of Langston. Post office established September 16, 1892, and name changed to Belton, November 20, 1893. Named for Sir Frederick Pollock, English legal scholar and man of letters.

POLO. In Noble County, 9 miles northwest of Perry. A post office from January 31, 1894, to September 15, 1904. No longer in existence.

POLSON. A townsite established in 1906 in northern Nowata County. Now South Coffeyville. Named for Martin and Earl Polson, townsite allotees.

194

POLSON CEMETERY. In Delaware County, 2 miles northwest of Southwest City, Missouri. A most important rural cemetery where are buried a number of prominent Cherokees, including Stand Watie, Major Ridge, and Major General Lee B. Washbourne. The name is from the family of Dr. W. D. Polson (1839–1893), whose wife Flora, a daughter of John Ridge, was interred there in 1876.

PONCA. Present Whiteagle in Kay County. Post office established December 4, 1879, and name changed to Whiteagle, August 21, 1896. This post office was at the Ponca Indian Agency. The name is from *pa-honga*, meaning "sacred leader."

PONCA CITY. Formerly New Ponca. In southeastern Kay County. Post office name changed to Ponca, July 7, 1898, and to Ponca City, October 23, 1913. This post office name was adopted and New Ponca discarded after the post office at the Ponca Indian Agency changed its name to Whiteagle in 1896.

POND. At site of Jefferson, in Grant County. A post office from November 13, 1879, to April 14, 1887, this was the original Pond Creek. On January 12, 1894, a post office named Jefferson was established at this site after a new townsite named Pond Creek had been established 3 miles south.

POND CREEK. County seat of Grant County from statehood to June 9, 1908. Original townsite name was Round Pond. Post office established September 29, 1893. Present Pond Creek is 3 miles south of the original townsite, now known as Jefferson.

PONOLA. A county in Chickasaw District, Choctaw Nation. Later part of Chickasaw Nation. The name is a Choctaw word meaning "cotton," and the county was often referred to as Cotton County.

PONTOTOC. A county in the Chickasaw Nation. Its name comes from a settlement of the same name in northern Mississippi. The word has a meaning "cattails growing on the prairie."

PONTOTOC. In extreme northern Johnston County, 17 miles north of Tishomingo. Post office established September 22, 1858. Took its name from Pontotoc County, Chickasaw Nation.

PONTOTOC COUNTY. A county in south-central Oklahoma, created at statehood. Took its name from Pontotoc County, Chickasaw Nation.

POOLER. In Ottawa County, 7 miles southeast of Miami. A post office from October 9, 1882, to November 28, 1892. No longer in existence, it was named for Moses Pooler, prominent Indian leader.

POOLEVILLE. Formerly Elk. In Carter County, 7 miles north of Milo. Post office name changed to Pooleville, July 20, 1907. Named for E. S. Poole, Ardmore banker.

PORT. In western Washita County, 8 miles northwest of Sentinel. A post office from February 21, 1901, to February 29, 1940. Named for Mrs. F. M. Port, local druggist.

PORTER. In southern Wagoner County, 10 miles southwest of Wagoner. A post office established June 1, 1903. Named for Pleasant Porter, Creek chief.

PORTLAND. Formerly Salem. In Washita County, 3 miles north of Sentinel. Post office name changed to Portland, May 16, 1904, and discontinued December 31, 1905.

PORUM. In southern Muskogee County, 10 miles south of Warner. Post office established March 25, 1890. Named for J. Porum Davis, usually known as Dave Porum, prominent Indian leader.

POSEY. In southern Tulsa County, 5 miles northeast of Mounds. Post office established March 18, 1895, and on April 19, 1898, it was moved 5 miles southwest and the name changed to Mounds. Named for Alexander L. Posey (1873–1908) Creek leader and poet.

POST FIELD. The airfield for Fort Sill. Named for Lieutenant Henry B. Post, Twenty-fifth Infantry, killed in 1914 at San Diego, California, while attempting an altitude record.

POSTLE. In northwest Texas County, 19 miles northwest of Guymon. A post office from July 6, 1905, to June 15, 1915. Named for George W. Postle, local rancher.

POTAPO. In Atoka County, 7 miles east of Stringtown. A post office from August 2, 1922, to February 21, 1934. Took its name from nearby Potapo Creek, which had been named for Potapo, a local Choctaw Indian.

POTEAU. County seat of Le Flore County. Record Town for Recording District No. 14, Indian Territory. Post office established October 27, 1887. Took its name from nearby Poteau River, a tributary of the Arkansas River. The word is French, meaning "post."

POTTAWATOMIE COUNTY. A county in central Oklahoma, similar in size to Pottawatomie County, Oklahoma Territory. Took its name from the Pottawatomie tribe of Indians. The name is a Chippewa term meaning "people of the place of the fire."

POTTER. In Garfield County, 11 miles southeast of Covington. A post office from February 4, 1895, to June 15, 1904. No longer in existence, it was named for Lida Potter, first postmaster.

POWELL. In southwestern Marshall County, 3 miles south of Lebanon. A post office from January 31, 1894, to April 30, 1945. Named for Lee E. Powell, local sawmill operator.

PRAGUE. In southeastern Lincoln County. Post office established August 12, 1902. Its name comes from Prague, Czechoslovakia.

PRAIRIE. In southwestern Grant County, 4 miles north of Hillsdale.

A post office from June 28, 1894, to April 30, 1901. No longer in existence, it took its name from the surrounding countryside.

PRAIRIE CITY. In Ottawa County, 4 miles northeast of Fairland. Post office established February 26, 1872. On December 1, 1876, the post office was moved 3 miles east and the name changed to Grand River. On September 12, 1879, another post office of the same name was established at the original site and continued in operation until November 4, 1893.

PRAPER. Present Kiefer, in Creek County. Post office established June 26, 1901; on December 12, 1906, the site was moved 2½ miles west and name changed to Kiefer.

PRATT. In northwestern Woods County, 3 miles northeast of Freedom. A post office from April 17, 1903, to May 14, 1906. No longer in existence. Its name comes from Pratt, Kansas.

PRENTISS. In Beckham County, 7 miles northwest of Sayre. A post office from January 26, 1903, to January 31, 1920.

PRESTON. In Okmulgee County, 7 miles north of Okmulgee. First known locally as Hamilton Switch. Post office established December 13, 1909. Named for Harry Preston, Okmulgee oil operator.

PREVO. In Harper County, adjoining May. Townsite plat filed December 2, 1902. Named for Charles Prevo, townsite owner.

PRICE. In Murray County, 4 miles west of Dougherty. A post office from August 20, 1884, to May 15, 1896. First known locally as Sorghum Flats. Named for William N. Price, prominent early-day settler.

PRICE. In northeastern Seminole County, 6 miles east of Castle. A post office from September 3, 1903, to April 29, 1916. Named for Victoria Price, first postmaster.

PRICE'S FALLS. In Murray County, 6 miles south of Davis. Situated on Price's Creek, the falls are named for William N. Price, rancher and prominent early-day settler.

PRINGEY. In Woodward County, 14 miles northwest of Quinlan. A post office from May 18, 1901, to May 31, 1914.

PROCTOR. In western Adair County, 14 miles northeast of Tahlequah. Post office established March 5, 1903. Named for Ezekiel Proctor, a Cherokee and sheriff of Flint District, Cherokee Nation.

PROCTOR. In southern McIntosh County, 12 miles southwest of Eufaula. A post office from April 2, 1892, to May 31, 1901. No longer in existence.

PROGRESS. In northeastern Roger Mills County, 11 miles northwest of Hammon. A post office from April 4, 1906, to July 31, 1907. No longer in existence.

PRONTO. In southwestern Beaver County, 6 miles west of Gray. A post office from February 23, 1904, to February 27, 1909. No longer in existence.

PROSPECT. In southeastern Harmon County, 5 miles northwest of Eldorado. A post office from June 6, 1900, to March 31, 1906. No longer in existence.

PROVENCE. In Carter County, 6 miles southwest of Ames. A post fice from January 4, 1895, to October 14, 1933. Named for George Provence, local merchant.

PROVIDENCE. In Ellis County, 2 miles south of Harmon. A post office from May 15, 1903, to February 15, 1907. No longer in existence.

PRUDENCE. In Major County, 4 miles southwest of Ames. A post office from April 30, 1895, to June 15, 1901. No longer in existence.

PRUE. In southern Osage County, 9 miles southeast of Cleveland. Post office established September 30, 1905. Named for Henry Prue, townsite owner.

PRYOR. County seat of Mayes County. Formerly Pryor Creek. Post office name changed to Pryor, January 26, 1909. The name was shortened from the former post office name Pryor Creek.

PRYOR CREEK. Formerly Coo-y-yah. Record Town for Recording District No. 5, Indian Territory. Post office name changed to Pryor Creek, April 23, 1887, and to Pryor, January 26, 1909. It took its name from the former Pryor Creek, located a few miles north.

PRYOR CREEK. In Mayes County, 3 miles north of Pryor. A post office from November 27, 1878, to October 28, 1884. Named for Nathaniel Pryor, early-day Osage Indian agent and veteran of the War of 1812.

PRYORS CREEK. Present Chouteau, in Mayes County. Post office established August 19, 1869, and name changed to Choteau, October 18, 1871.

PULARE. In southeastern Osage County, 9 miles northwest of Sand Springs. A post office from August 2, 1920, to September 29, 1928.

PULCHER. In eastern Pittsburg County near Hartshorne. A post office from August 20, 1913, to July 10, 1915. No longer in existence. The name is the Latin word for beautiful.

PULIS. In eastern Cimarron County, 8 miles southeast of Keyes. A post office from August 4, 1906, to December 14, 1907. No longer in existence, it was named for Joseph Pulis, first postmaster.

PURCELL. County seat of McClain County. Record Town for Recording District No. 18, Indian Territory. Post office established April 21, 1887. Named for E. B. Purcell, of Manhattan, Kansas, Santa Fe Railway director.

PURDY. In western Garvin County, 8 miles south of Lindsay. A post office from March 14, 1892, to November 15, 1918. Named for R. S. Purdy, first postmaster.

PURVIS. In southeastern Harmon County, 8 miles northwest of Eldorado. A post office from April 9, 1892, to February 14, 1903. No longer in existence.

PUSHMATAHA. One of the three districts of the Choctaw Nation. Named for Chief Pushmataha, a renowned Choctaw leader and friend of Andrew Jackson, who fought with the United States in the War of 1812. He died in Washington in 1824.

PUSHMATAHA COUNTY. A county in southeastern Oklahoma, created at statehood. Took its name from Pushmataha District, Choctaw Nation.

PUSLEY'S STATION. Site in southwest Latimer County near Higgins. A stage stop on the Butterfield Overland Mail route to California which crossed southeastern Oklahoma, 1858–61. Named for Silas Pusley, local trader.

PUTNAM. In southern Dewey County, 13 miles south of Taloga. Post office established June 4, 1895. Named for General Israel Putnam, Revolutionary War hero.

PUTNAM CITY. In Oklahoma County, adjoining Oklahoma City on the northwest and not a separate municipality. Townsite plat filed December 24, 1909. Named for I. M. Putnam, real estate developer and Oklahoma City business leader.

PYRAMID CORNERS. In Craig County, 11 miles north of Vinita. Located on the old Jefferson Highway, the name comes from a large pyramid-shaped directional marker located in the adjoining intersection.

Q

Q COUNTY. Original designation for Pawnee County, Oklahoma Territory.

QUALLS. In Cherokee County, 10 miles northeast of Braggs. A post office from January 20, 1909, to August 31, 1942. Named for William A. Qualls, first postmaster.

QUANAH. In Tillman County, 10 miles west of Grandfield. A post office from October 25, 1907, to July 31, 1911. Named for Quanah Parker, prominent Comanche Indian leader and son of Cynthia Ann Parker.

QUAPAW. In Ottawa County, 7 miles northeast of Miami. Post office established June 9, 1897. Took its name from the Quapaw tribe of Indians. The word is a tribal term *Ugakhpa,* meaning "downstream people."

QUARTERMASTER. In northwest Custer County, 7 miles north of Hammon. A post office from September 13, 1901, to October 14, 1905. Took its name from nearby Quartermaster Creek, which had been named for James M. Bell, quartermaster for Custer at the Battle of the Washita.

QUARTZ. In eastern Greer County, 2 miles west of Lugert. A post office from February 25, 1888, to

July 31, 1900. Took its name from the surrounding Quartz Mountains, the same land feature which has provided the name for one of the Oklahoma state parks.

QUAY. Formerly Lawson. In southern Pawnee County, 5 miles north of Yale. Post office name changed to Quay, February 24, 1903, and discontinued March 31, 1957. Named for M. S. Quay, United States senator from Pennsylvania.

QUINCY. In northwestern Cleveland County, 6 miles west of Moore. A post office from March 21, 1892, to February 29, 1904. No longer in existence. Named by Vincent E. Breese, first postmaster, for his home town of Quincy, Illinois.

QUINLAN. In eastern Woodward County. Post office established April 27, 1901. Named for the Quinlan brothers, William, Thomas, and Robert, well-known ranchers and cattlemen.

QUINTON. In northeastern Pittsburg County. Post office established March 28, 1902. Named for Martha E. Quinton, prominent local Choctaw.

R

RABBIT FORD. A well-known crossing on the Arkansas River, 5 miles east of Muskogee. Named for Rabbit, a Negro slave of William S. Coodey, early-day resident.

RABIT. In northern Delaware County, 6 miles southeast of Afton.

A post office from March 11, 1914, to April 15, 1925. Named for Rabit Copeland, relative of George W. Copeland, first postmaster.

RACINE. Formerly Clermont. In northeastern Canadian County, 7 miles southeast of Okarche. Post office name changed to Racine, June 24, 1895, and discontinued January 31, 1902. Took its name from Racine, Wisconsin.

RADIUM. In Caddo County, 5 miles northeast of Gracemont. A post office from April 23, 1904, to August 14, 1905. No longer in existence. Named in honor of the then recent discovery of radium by the Curies.

RAGSDALE. In southwestern Beaver County, 3 miles northeast of Gray. A post office from March 24, 1904, to August 31, 1907. No longer in existence. Named for George R. Ragsdale, first postmaster.

RAIFORD. In southern McIntosh County, 15 miles southwest of Eufaula. A post office from June 17, 1905, to May 15, 1926. Named for Mrs. Jeannetta Thomas Raiford, rancher and landowner.

RAINY. In southern Washita County, 6 miles east of Rocky. A post office from April 28, 1894, to May 15, 1905. Took its name from nearby Rainy Mountain Indian Church and Mission.

RALLEY. In southeastern Cimarron County, 5 miles northwest of Griggs. A post office from April

26, 1907, to March 31, 1914. No longer in existence.

RALSTON. In northern Pawnee County. Post office established June 15, 1894. Original townsite name was Riverside. Named for J. H. Ralston, townsite developer.

RAMBO. In southwestern Pawnee County, 6 miles southwest of Pawnee. A post office from December 3, 1900, to October 14, 1903. No longer in existence, it was named for C. W. Rambo, Pawnee resident.

RAMONA. Formerly Bonton. In Washington County, 13 miles south of Bartlesville. Post office name changed to Ramona, December 9, 1899. Its name comes from *Ramona*, a novel by Helen Hunt Jackson.

RAMSEY. In Cimarron County, 12 miles north of Boise City. Townsite plat filed February 21, 1927. No longer in existence, it was named for W. R. Ramsey, Oklahoma City oil developer.

RAN. In eastern Love County, 6 miles northwest of Lebanon. A post office from June 26, 1894, to April 15, 1916. No longer in existence.

RANDLETT. In Caddo County, 4 miles south of Anadarko. A post office from May 3, 1902, to October 31, 1905. No longer in existence, it was named for James F. Randlett, Kiowa-Comanche Indian agent.

RANDLETT. In southwestern Cotton County. Post office established May 3, 1907. Named for James F. Randlett, Kiowa-Comanche Indian agent.

RANDOLPH. In southern Johnston County, 5 miles southwest of Tishomingo. A post office from September 5, 1901, to June 30, 1919. Named for Thomas Randolph, Frisco Railroad official.

RANGE. In southeastern Texas County, 11 miles southeast of Hardesty. A post office from May 21, 1895, to February 15, 1934. No longer in existence. Took its name from the character of the surrounding countryside.

RANKIN. In western Roger Mills County, 2 miles south of Reydon. Post office established May 12, 1902; on October 1, 1929, the post office was moved 2 miles north and its name changed to Reydon. Named for John T. Rankin, long-time local merchant.

RASOR. In Pittsburg County, adjoining McAlester. A post office from September 23, 1897, to November 2, 1898. No longer in existence, it was named for Stephen M. Rasor, first postmaster.

RATHBONE. In southwestern Custer County, 6 miles west of Clinton. A post office from March 3, 1893, to December 31, 1904. No longer in existence.

RATLIFF CITY. In northwestern Carter County. Post office established January 1, 1953. Named for Ollie Ratliff, local garage proprietor.

RATTAN. In southern Pushmataha County. Post office established December 12, 1910. Its name comes from Rattan, Texas.

RAVIA. In Johnston County, 3 miles west of Tishomingo. Post office established March 30, 1894. Named for Joseph Ravia, early-day resident.

RAWDON. In southwestern Woodward County, 11 miles northwest of Vici. A post office from May 18, 1901, to July 15, 1905. Named for John Rawdon, rancher and cattleman.

RAY. In western Cherokee County, 15 miles west of Tahlequah. A post office from September 30, 1904, to November 30, 1927. Named for Ray Huston, local resident.

RAYDON. Formerly Guertie. In Hughes County, 8 miles southeast of Allen. Post office name changed to Raydon, December 16, 1907, and changed to Gerty, June 29, 1910. Named for James S. Raydon, first postmaster.

RAYMOND. In Dewey County, 9 miles southeast of Camargo. A post office from April 5, 1894, to August 14, 1905. No longer in existence, it was named for Raymond Frazee, grandson of Hezekiah Frazee, first postmaster.

READOUT. In western Harper County, 7 miles north of Laverne. A post office from September 19, 1902, to June 30, 1913. Its name comes from Redoubt Creek, a tributary of the Cimarron River.

REAGAN. In Johnston County, 9 miles north of Tishomingo. A post office from June 25, 1894, to May 15, 1931. Named for John H. Reagan of Texas, Confederate postmaster general.

REAMS. In Pittsburg County, 9 miles northeast of McAlester. A post office from March 6, 1901, to December 31, 1915. Named for Robert L. Ream, prominent local resident and nephew of Vinnie Ream Hoxie, the sculptress whose studio was in the national Capitol.

REASON. In Ellis County, 12 miles southeast of Arnett. A post office from July 26, 1902, to February 28, 1919. No longer in existence. Took its name from *Appeal to Reason*, a widely-read populist journal of the time published by Fred Warren.

RECK. In southwestern Carter County, 5 miles southwest of Wilson. A post office from January 25, 1892, to June 21, 1919.

RECYL. In western Latimer County, 7 miles southeast of Hartshorne. A post office from December 16, 1916, to October 15, 1935.

RED BIRD. In Wagoner County, 5 miles southeast of Coweta. Post office established June 20, 1902.

REDDEN. In Atoka County, 13 miles northeast of Stringtown. A post office from June 1, 1903, to October 31, 1954. Named for John A. Redden, first postmaster.

RED EAGLE. In Osage County, 12 miles northwest of Bartlesville.

A post office from August 18, 1920, to October 15, 1930. Named for Paul Red Eagle, Osage chief.

RED FORK. In Tulsa County, adjoining Tulsa on the southwest and now within the city limits. Post office established January 3, 1884, and discontinued July 31, 1928, to become Red Fork Station of the Tulsa Post Office. Took its name from the Red Fork of the Arkansas River.

REDLAKE. In southern Bryan County, 18 miles southeast of Durant. A post office from January 25, 1895, to April 16, 1897. No longer in existence. Took its name from a nearby oxbow lake along Red River.

REDLAND. In Sequoyah County, 7 miles southwest of Muldrow. A post office from May 17, 1883, to June 30, 1937. Took its name from the color of the surrounding soil.

REDMOON. In northwestern Roger Mills County, 9 miles northwest of Cheyenne. A post office from October 14, 1893, to October 15, 1918. Named for Red Moon, Cheyenne chief.

RED OAK. In eastern Latimer County, 14 miles east of Wilburton. Post office established March 11, 1868. Took its name from a well-known red oak tree standing for many years in the center of town.

REDPOINT. In Texas County, 9 miles northwest of Guymon. A post office from April 25, 1896, to February 28, 1915. Took its name from a nearby land feature along Beaver River known as Red Point.

RED RIVER. A county in Apukshunnubbee District, Choctaw Nation.

REDRIVER. In southwestern Jefferson County, 6 miles southwest of Waurika. A post office from June 20, 1904, to September 15, 1904. No longer in existence, it took its name from nearby Red River.

REDROCK. Present Otoe in Noble County. Post office established November 8, 1881, and name changed to Otoe, May 3, 1892. Took its name from nearby Red Rock Creek, a tributary of the Arkansas River.

RED ROCK. In Noble County, 6 miles south of Marland. Post office established June 9, 1892. The name is a continuation of that of the former post office, which had been located 6 miles south.

REDWOOD. In Washita County, 7 miles southeast of Cordell. A post office from August 28, 1903, to May 15, 1905. No longer in existence.

REED. In western Greer County, 11 miles west of Mangum. Post office established September 16, 1892. Named for John Reed Graham, first postmaster.

REEDING. In eastern Kingfisher County, 10 miles southeast of Kingfisher. A post office from August 27, 1900, to September 14, 1935. Named for John Reed, townsite owner.

REGNIER. In northwestern Cimarron County, 9 miles northeast of Kenton. A post office from February 27, 1920, to March 31, 1948. The post office was a continuation of an earlier office of the same name located in Colorado, and was named for Dr. Felix Regnier, local resident and physician.

REICHERT. Formerly Kolb. In Le Flore County, 8 miles south of Wister. Post office name changed to Reichert, May 7, 1892, and discontinued February 15, 1927. Named for William Reichert, first postmaster.

REMINGTON. In Osage County, 5 miles south of Burbank. A post office from January 18, 1905, to March 15, 1912. Its name comes from the Remington rifle.

REMUS. In Pottawatomie County, 4 miles northwest of Maud. A post office from July 3, 1893, to February 15, 1906. It was named for one of the traditional founders of Rome who was slain by his twin brother, Romulus. A post office named Romulus was located 5 miles southwest of Remus, and, consistent with the tradition, it survived Remus as a post office.

REMY. In eastern Sequoyah County, 4 miles northeast of Muldrow. A post office from October 15, 1891, to November 30, 1909. No longer in existence.

RENFROW. In northern Grant County, 9 miles northeast of Medford. Post office established May 25, 1894. Named for W. C. Renfrow, third governor of Oklahoma Territory.

RENO CITY. In Canadian County, 5 miles northeast of El Reno. A post office from June 15, 1889, to October 30, 1899. The site was abandoned because of flooding from the North Canadian River. Took its name from nearby Fort Reno.

RENTIE. In Tulsa County, located at present 91st and Harvard in the Tulsa city limits. A post office from January 21, 1904, to May 31, 1909. Named for Stephen Rentie, townsite owner.

RENTIESVILLE. In northern McIntosh County, 5 miles north of Checotah. Post office established May 11, 1904. Immediately north of Rentiesville is the site of the Battle of Honey Springs, fought July 17, 1863, the most important Civil War battle in present-day Oklahoma. Named for William Rentie, townsite developer.

RETROP. In southwestern Washita County, 10 miles west of Sentinel. A post office from January 12, 1900, to February 28, 1905. The name is an anagram of Ira J. Porter, first postmaster.

RETTA. In western Kay County, 5 miles southwest of Blackwell. A post office from April 3, 1902, to February 15, 1908. No longer in existence, it was named for Retta Richmond, daughter of Thomas Richmond, early-day resident.

REX. Present Okay, in southeastern Wagoner County. Post office established November 16, 1900, and its name changed to North Muskogee May 1, 1911. In 1893 a post office named Coretta had been discontinued at this same site.

REYDON. Formerly Rankin. In western Roger Mills County, 14 miles northwest of Cheyenne. Post office name changed to Reydon, October 1, 1929. Its name comes from Reydon, Suffolk County, England.

REYNOLDS. In northern Atoka County, 3 miles south of Kiowa. A post office from February 19, 1895, to July 31, 1909. Named for H. C. Reynolds, townsite owner.

RHEA. In southwestern Dewey County, 7 miles east of Leedey. A post office from November 7, 1895, to February 28, 1954.

RHOADS. In Roger Mills County, 6 miles southwest of Cheyenne. A post office from April 26, 1904, to July 14, 1905. No longer in existence, it was named for Albert H. Rhoads, first postmaster.

RICE. In western Texas County, 15 miles northwest of Texhoma. A post office from March 2, 1906, to December 14, 1925.

RICH. In Atoka County, 11 miles northeast of Stringtown. Post office established November 2, 1910, and name changed to Chockie, August 3, 1916. Named for Elmer O. Rich, merchant and early-day resident.

RICHARDS. In northern Comanche County, 12 miles north of Lawton. A post office from November 5, 1901, to February 15, 1913. Richards Spur is a railroad loading switch several miles south. Named for William A. Richards, commissioner of the General Land Office and governor of Wyoming.

RICHARDVILLE. In McIntosh County, 9 miles west of Checotah. The community is usually known as Richardsville. A post office from November 7, 1917, to October 15, 1919. Named for Eastman Richard, planter and gin operator.

RICHBURG. In southern Noble County, 7 miles southeast of Perry. A post office from April 10, 1894, to October 31, 1904. No longer in existence, it was named for Ernest G. Richardson, first postmaster.

RICHLAND. In eastern Canadian County, 6 miles northwest of Yukon. A post office from February 29, 1904, to August 15, 1937. Took its name from the character of the surrounding countryside.

RICHLAND. In western Kay County, 10 miles west of Blackwell. Post office established May 25, 1894, and its name changed to Guiley, September 10, 1894. Took its name from the character of the surrounding countryside.

RICHMOND. In southeastern Woodward County, 7 miles northwest of Seiling. A post office from November 6, 1893, to February 15, 1923. Its name comes from Richmond, Kentucky, the home of John W. White, first postmaster.

RICKS. In northeastern Jackson County, 8 miles northwest of Headrick. A post office from May 27, 1902, to December 31, 1904. No longer in existence, it was named for John H. Ricks, first postmaster.

RIDDLE'S STATION. Site in Latimer County, 3 miles east of Wilburton. A stage stop on the Butterfield Overland Mail route to California which crossed southeastern Oklahoma, 1858–61. Named for John Riddle, local merchant and trader.

RIDGE. In northwestern Muskogee County, 7 miles west of Taft. A post office from December 29, 1884, to October 15, 1908. Its name comes from the high terrain on which the site was located.

RIDGETON. In northwestern Roger Mills County, 12 miles west of Roll. A post office from December 19, 1904, to December 31, 1907. No longer in existence. Named by Mrs. Grant McColgin for its location on "a rise of ground where we could see miles and miles."

RILEY. In Dewey County, 6 miles west of Taloga. A post office from November 23, 1892, to April 30, 1903. No longer in existence, it was named for James Riley, early-day rancher.

RINGLING. In eastern Jefferson County. Post office established June 9, 1914. Named for John Ringling, circus owner.

RINGO. In Washington County, 3 miles east of Ramona. A post office from December 12, 1889, to February 15, 1900. No longer in existence. Named for Jimmie Ringo, early-day resident.

RINGOLD. Formerly Burwell. In western McCurtain County, 10 miles northwest of Wright City. Post office name changed to Ringold, May 10, 1911. Its name comes from Ringold, Texas.

RINGWOOD. In northern Major County, 22 miles west of Enid. Post office established March 23, 1894. The name was coined, and comes from the circumstance that the townsite was ringed with trees.

RIPLEY. In southern Payne County, 7 miles west of Cushing. Post office established February 23, 1900. Named for William P. Ripley, president of the Santa Fe Railway.

RITTER. In Hughes County, adjoining Calvin. A post office from September 28, 1912, to September 15, 1919. No longer in existence, it was named for E. B. Ritter, first postmaster.

RIVERSIDE. In Beaver County, 6 miles east of Beaver. A post office from March 20, 1888, to July 15, 1927. So named because of its location along the south side of Beaver River.

RIVERSIDE. Original townsite name for Ralston in Pawnee County. Townsite plat filed July 31, 1894. So named because of its location along the Arkansas River.

RIVERVIEW. Present Calvin, in Hughes County. Post office established March 21, 1895, and name changed to Calvin, June 24, 1895. Its name came from its location on the south bank of the Canadian River.

ROARK. In Greer County, 7 miles northwest of Mangum. A post office from December 15, 1903, to January 15, 1905. No longer in existence, it was named for William M. Roark, first postmaster.

ROBBERSON. In southwestern Garvin County, 8 miles southwest of Elmore City. A post office from June 11, 1890, to April 19, 1924. Named for William F. Robberson, merchant and early-day settler.

ROBBERSROOST. In Bryan County, 3 miles north of Mead. A post office from February 26, 1897, to May 15, 1909.

ROBBINS. In Creek County, 7 miles southeast of Bristow. Post office established April 2, 1903, and name changed to Tabor, December 12, 1903. It was named for Tom Robbins, early-day resident.

ROBERTA. In Bryan County, 5 miles southeast of Durant. A post office from March 23, 1894, to February 15, 1930. Named for James Roberts, first postmaster, but through error the Post Office Department adopted the name Roberta instead of the intended name Roberts.

ROCK FALLS. In northwestern Kay County, 2 miles northwest of Braman. A post office from February 12, 1894, to June 25, 1898. The site of the publication of *Oklahoma*

War-Chief in 1884, first newspaper printed in the Cherokee Outlet. Took its name from the nearby falls on the Chikaskia River.

ROCKFORD. In Blaine County, 10 miles north of Watonga. A post office from April 10, 1894, to March 15, 1902. No longer in existence. Took its name from Rockford, Illinois.

ROCK ISLAND. In Canadian County, 7 miles southeast of Okarche. Post office established April 20, 1889, and name changed to Clermont, April 30, 1892. On October 5, 1892, another post office of the same name was established west of the former site and continued in operation until July 21, 1898. Its name comes from the Rock Island Railroad.

ROCK ISLAND. In northeastern Le Flore County, 2 miles northeast of Cameron. A post office from February 1, 1905, to May 12, 1961. Presumably named for Rock Island, Illinois.

ROCK MARY. In Caddo County, 3 miles west of Hinton. A prominent land feature used for many years as a landmark for travelers on the California Trail. Named in 1849 for Mary Conway, daughter of the governor of Arkansas.

ROCKPIN. In Pittsburg County, 5 miles northeast of Crowder. A post office from May 15, 1909, to August 31, 1914. Intended to be named Rockpen, the name was from a stock pen made of natural rock bluffs and closed on the open side with a rock wall.

ROCKSPUR. In Tulsa County, 3 miles northeast of Tulsa. A post office from June 25, 1901, to June 30, 1902, and now within Tulsa city limits. Named for a quarry siding on the Frisco Railroad.

ROCKY. In southern Washita County, 6 miles east of Sentinel. Post office established July 12, 1898. Took its name from a rock store building of W. F. Schultz, early-day merchant.

ROCKY POINT. Present Lebanon, in Marshall County. Post office established October 22, 1878, and name changed to Lebanon, February 17, 1882.

RODNEY. In Pushmataha County, 5 miles north of Antlers. A post office from June 30, 1890, to July 5, 1899. Named for Rodney Moyer, early-day resident.

ROENA. In Coal County, 5 miles southwest of Tupelo. A post office from November 3, 1903, to June 15, 1907.

ROFF. In Pontotoc County, 12 miles southwest of Ada. Post office established June 14, 1890. Named for Joseph T. Roff, rancher and cattleman.

ROGER MILLS COUNTY. A county in western Oklahoma, different in extent and area from Roger Mills County, Oklahoma Territory. Named for Roger Q. Mills of Texas, member of Congress.

ROGERS. In Custer County, 5 miles southwest of Thomas. A post office from June 25, 1892, to June 15, 1903. No longer in existence, it was named for Willis E. Rogers, first postmaster.

ROGERS. In southwestern Mayes County, adjoining Chouteau. A post office from June 21, 1910, to July 11, 1911. Named for William C. Rogers, principal chief of the Cherokee Nation, 1903–17.

ROGERS COUNTY. A county in northeastern Oklahoma, created at statehood. Named for Clem V. Rogers, elder member of the Oklahoma Constitutional Convention and father of famed Will Rogers.

ROGERS STATION. In northeastern Atoka County, 1 mile north of Wesley. A post office from July 1, 1874, to October 13, 1878. Until October 18, 1877, the official name of the post office was incorrectly spelled Rodgers Station. Named for John P. Rogers, prominent early-day merchant.

ROLAND. Formerly Garrison. In eastern Sequoyah County, 8 miles northwest of Fort Smith. Post office name changed to Roland, May 18, 1904.

ROLL. In Roger Mills County, 14 miles north of Cheyenne. A post office from December 9, 1903, to August 31, 1920.

ROMAN NOSE. Former rural community settled about 1900 in Blaine County, 6 miles north of Watonga. Now location of Roman

208

Nose State Park. Named for Henry C. Roman Nose, Cheyenne leader.

ROME. In northern Roger Mills County, 8 miles east of Roll. A post office from May 5, 1899, to September 30, 1909. No longer in existence.

ROMIA. In southern Bryan County, 15 miles southeast of Durant. A post office from August 30, 1915, to June 30, 1934. Named for Romia Lewis, daughter of Ollie E. Lewis, first postmaster.

ROMULUS. In Pottawatomie County, 4 miles south of Macomb. A post office from June 25, 1892, to October 15, 1918. It was named for one of the traditional founders of Rome who slew his twin brother Remus. A post office named Remus was located 5 miles northeast of Romulus, and, consistent with the tradition, Romulus survived Remus as a post office.

ROOSEVELT. In central Kiowa County. Post office established October 31, 1901. Named for President Theodore Roosevelt.

ROOSTER. In Choctaw County, 7 miles northeast of Soper. Post office established May 19, 1920, and name changed to Zinway, January 18, 1921. In 1915 a post office named Kent had been discontinued at this same proximate location.

ROSCOE. In Major County, 5 miles northwest of Fairview. A post office from April 17, 1900, to May 15, 1909. No longer in existence, it

was named for Roscoe Smith, a local lad and a favorite of L. J. Roberts, first postmaster.

ROSE. In southeastern Mayes County, 9 miles east of Locust Grove. Post office established March 13, 1891. Its name comes from nearby Rowe's Prairie, which had been named for David Rowe, early-day resident.

ROSEDALE. In McClain County, 7 miles east of Wayne. A post office from August 25, 1908, to January 6, 1961. Named for Rose Hopping, townsite allotee.

ROSELAND. In southeastern Dewey County, 10 miles northwest of Thomas. A post office from February 1, 1900, to January 31, 1908.

ROSSTON. In western Harper County, 7 miles north of Laverne. Post office established January 28, 1914. Original townsite name was Ross, by plat filed July 15, 1912. The name was coined from the name of two prominent residents, R. H. Ross and A. R. Rallston.

ROSSVILLE. In Lincoln County, 6 miles south of Wellston. A post office from October 7, 1895, to February 15, 1907. Named for Ross Thomas, early-day resident.

ROSSVILLE. Formerly Jay. In eastern Oklahoma County. Post office name changed to Rossville, February 21, 1895, and discontinued August 19, 1895. No longer in existence.

ROUNDGROVE. In Alfalfa County, 7 miles southwest of Goltry. A post office from September 17, 1894, to June 15, 1901. No longer in existence.

ROUND POND. Original town-site name for Pond Creek, Grant County.

ROW. In southern Delaware County, 9 miles northeast of Kansas. Post office established April 8, 1905; on February 1, 1930, the post office was moved 1 mile south and its name changed to Colcord. Named by James R. Wilson, first postmaster, because of the number of local "drunken brawls and killings."

ROXANA. In northwestern Logan County, 4 miles southwest of Marshall. Townsite plat filed July 21, 1927. No longer in existence. Its name came from Roxana Petroleum Corporation.

ROY. In northern Sequoyah County, 6 miles north of Vian. Post office established March 6, 1911, and name changed to Box, July 7, 1911.

ROY. In southern Texas County, 14 miles south of Guymon. A post office from July 25, 1894, to December 31, 1902. No longer in existence, it was named for Roy Westmoreland, son of Clara Westmoreland, first postmaster.

ROYAL. In northeastern Stephens County, 10 miles southwest of Elmore City. A post office from March 8, 1904, to January 15, 1932. Name selected by Rev. G. B. Hughes, first postmaster, to portray the royal manner with which he intended to give service.

RUBOTTOM. In western Love County, 18 miles west of Marietta. Post office established August 14, 1902. Named for William P. Rubottom, prominent landowner and gin operator.

RUBY. In eastern Nowata County, 11 miles northeast of Nowata. A post office from June 2, 1894, to October 15, 1921. Named for Ruby A. Nelson, daughter of John Nelson, local Cherokee.

RUCKER. In Comanche County, 7 miles east of Lawton. Post office established August 25, 1902, and name changed to Letitia, November 28, 1903.

RUFE. In western McCurtain County, 9 miles northwest of Wright City. Post office established February 13, 1903. Named for Rufus Wilson, son of Mattie Wilson, first postmaster.

RUGGLES. A rural community in Pottawatomie County, 5 miles south of Tecumseh. Named for W. A. Ruggles, county judge prior to statehood. The town fell into disuse about 1920.

RUSH SPRINGS. Formerly Parr. In southern Grady County. Post office name changed to Rush Springs, May 13, 1892. It took its name from well-known springs on the Chisholm Trail, which were the headwaters of Rush Creek.

RUSK. In Major County, 6 miles east of Fairview. A post office from March 21, 1894, to October 31, 1912.

RUSKIN. In eastern Beaver County, 10 miles west of Laverne. A post office from March 17, 1906, to September 15, 1909. No longer in existence. Named for Ruskin Spohn, son of Dee Spohn, first postmaster.

RUSSELL. In southwestern Greer County, 12 miles southwest of Mangum. A post office from January 29, 1901, to July 31, 1915. On November 1, 1934, the post office at Blake, 2 miles north, was moved to this site and its name changed to Russell. Discontinued November 15, 1955.

RUSSELL. A switch and loading point on the Santa Fe in Logan County, 6 miles north of Guthrie. Took its name from nearby Camp Russell.

RUSSELLVILLE. In northeastern Pittsburg County, 4 miles northwest of Quinton. A post office from June 19, 1890, to December 30, 1933. Named for I. N. Russell, local merchant.

RUSSETT. In southwestern Johnston County, 6 miles east of Mannsville. A post office from October 3, 1894, to September 15, 1924.

RUTH. In southern Dewey County, 4 miles southeast of Putnam. A post office from June 20, 1895, to July 30, 1904. No longer in existence.

RUTHDALE. In Nowata County, 5 miles northwest of Delaware. A post office from November 28, 1910, to July 31, 1931. Named for Ruth Downing, local Indian girl.

RYAN. County seat of Jefferson County from statehood to February 24, 1912. Record Town for Recording District No. 20, Indian Territory. Post office established June 19, 1890. On October 31, 1893, the name of the post office at Baldwin was changed to Ryan, and the two separate offices were consolidated. Named for Stephen W. Ryan, early-day resident.

S

SABO. In Creek County, 2 miles northeast of Kiefer. A post office from October 25, 1907, to April 30, 1913. Named for C. R. Sabo, local resident.

SAC AND FOX AGENCY. In Lincoln County, 4 miles south of Stroud. A post office from October 25, 1875, to December 31, 1910. The post office for the Sac and Fox Indian Agency, it was at the site of the agency and boarding school established in 1872.

SACRED HEART MISSION. In southeastern Pottawatomie County, 6 miles east of Asher. Post office established January 30, 1879; name changed to Sacred Heart, May 24, 1888, and discontinued August 31, 1954. The post office for Sacred Heart Mission, established in 1876 by Father Isidore Robot as a major Catholic missionary effort in western Indian Territory.

SADDLE MOUNTAIN. In eastern Kiowa County, 15 miles south of Mountain View. A post office from January 22, 1902, to May 31,

1955. Took its name from nearby Saddle Mountain Indian Mission, which had been so named because of the distinctive peak of the Wichita Mountains.

SADIE. In Sequoyah County, 6 miles southwest of Sallisaw. A post office from March 1, 1906, to April 30, 1928. Named for Sadie Q. Frye, wife of Charles Frye, local resident.

SAGE. In southern Tillman County, 5 miles south of Grandfield. A post office from January 20, 1908, to October 30, 1909. No longer in existence. Took its name from a plant of the sunflower family, sagebrush, growing along the north bank of Red River.

SAGEEYAH. In Rogers County, 5 miles northwest of Claremore. A post office from December 7, 1900, to June 30, 1930. The word is the Cherokee rendering of Zaccheus, and the site was named for Sageeyah Saunders, early-day resident.

ST. ALBANS. In southern Payne County, 5 miles north of Coyle. A post office from March 21, 1894, to March 4, 1895. No longer in existence. Its name comes from St. Albans, Hertfordshire, England.

ST. JO. A rural community in southern Pottawatomie County, 1 mile southwest of Wanette. Townsite plat filed January 11, 1897. No longer in existence. Named for Joe Brown, local resident.

SAINT LOUIS. In Ottawa County, 5 miles east of Picher. Post of-

fice established July 2, 1917, and name changed to Zincville, June 12, 1919.

SAINT LOUIS. In southern Pottawatomie County, 8 miles southwest of Maud. Post office established March 22, 1928. Its name comes from St. Louis, Missouri.

SALEM. In western McIntosh County, 5 miles southeast of Henryetta. A post office from October 3, 1908, to April 27, 1918.

SALEM. In Washita County, 3 miles north of Sentinel. Post office established December 28, 1892, and name changed to Portland, May 16, 1904. Named for Salem, Massachusetts.

SALINA. In Mayes County, 10 miles east of Pryor. Former post office name was Cherokee Orphan Asylum, which was changed to Salina, March 10, 1884. The name is a variant of Saline, and was given to the site because of nearby salt works.

SALINE. A district of the Cherokee Nation, established November 6, 1840.

SALLISAW. A district of the Cherokee Nation. Established prior to 1831 and abolished November 6, 1840. Took its name from Sallisaw Creek. The word is from the French *salaison*, meaning "salt meat" or "salt provisions."

SALLISAW. County seat of Sequoyah County. Record Town for Recording District No. 11, Indian Territory. Post office established

September 29, 1873. In 1888, the post office bearing the name Sallisaw was moved some 15 miles south. The name of the former Sallisaw was changed to Mays on June 7, 1888, and on December 8, 1888, the name of the post office at Childer's Station was changed to Sallisaw.

SALT CREEK. Present Grainola, in northwestern Osage County. Post office established November 26, 1906, and name changed to Grainola, March 28, 1910. Took its name from nearby Salt Creek, a tributary of the Arkansas River.

SALT FORK. Formerly Elmpark. In Grant County, 5 miles south of Lamont. Post office name changed to Saltfork, February 4, 1902, and discontinued April 30, 1951. Took its name from the nearby Salt Fork of the Arkansas River.

SALT SPRINGS. In eastern Harper County, 11 miles west of Freedom. A post office from June 3, 1920, to April 30, 1928.

SALTON. In western Harmon County, 7 miles north of Madge. A post office from July 12, 1898, to December 31, 1914.

SAM. In Le Flore County, 3 miles north of Heavener. A post office from July 22, 1903, to December 15, 1908. Named for Samuel Wilson, early-day resident.

SAMPSEL. In Cimarron County, 16 miles southeast of Boise City. A post office from May 23, 1906, to November 15, 1929. Named for Aaron D. Sampsel, first postmaster.

SAMSVILLE. In Custer County, 3 miles northwest of Butler. A post office from January 16, 1893, to January 10, 1906. No longer in existence, it was named for Mattie Sams, first postmaster.

SAN BERNARDO. Site on the north bank of the Red River in southeastern Jefferson County. An important French trading post that flourished during the middle of the eighteenth century. Named for Governor Bernardo de Gálvez.

SANDBLUFF. In northwestern Choctaw County, 9 miles northeast of Boswell. A post office from June 23, 1919, to December 15, 1934. Took its name from a sandy bluff along the east bank of the Muddy Boggy River.

SAND CREEK. In western Grant County. A post office from June 5, 1895, to November 26, 1971. Took its name from nearby Sand Creek, a tributary of the Salt Fork of the Arkansas River.

SANDERS. In eastern Nowata County, 11 miles northeast of Nowata. A post office from July 9, 1909, to March 31, 1914. Named for Alice G. Sanders, first postmaster.

SANDS. Original townsite name for Knowles in Beaver County. Townsite plat filed February 15, 1907. Named for Dr. A. J. Sands, prominent early-day resident.

SAND SPRINGS. In western Tulsa County. Post office established September 5, 1911. Took its name from nearby springs along the north bank of the Arkansas River.

SANDY. In Garvin County, 7 miles east of Pauls Valley. Post office established January 12, 1889, and name changed to Walker, September 14, 1897. Took its name from nearby Sandy Creek, a tributary of the Washita River.

SANDY. In northwestern Harmon County, 9 miles north of Hollis. A post office from March 8, 1905, to August 31, 1910.

SANFORD. In southern Tillman County, 6 miles east of Davidson. Named for Sanford N. Gosnell, first postmaster at present Frederick.

SANS BOIS. A county of Moshulatubbee District, Choctaw Nation. The name is the French phrase meaning "without wood."

SANS BOIS. In Haskell County, 9 miles south of Stigler. A post office from September 1, 1879, to October 31, 1916. Took its name from nearby Sans Bois Creek, a tributary of the Canadian River. The name is the French phrase meaning "without wood."

SANTA FE. Present Newkirk, in Kay County. Post office established October 5, 1893, and name changed to Newkirk, January 18, 1894. Took its name from the Santa Fe Railway.

SANTA FE. In eastern Stephens County, 15 miles northeast of Co-

manche. A post office from March 19, 1921, to October 15, 1943.

SANTOWN. In western Sequoyah County, 5 miles south of Vian. Post office established September 22, 1904, and name changed to Mabelle, July 3, 1907. The name is a variant of Sand Town, the original name of the community located in the sandy flats along the Arkansas River.

SAPULPA. County seat of Creek County. Record Town for Recording District No. 8, Indian Territory. Post office established July 1, 1889. Named for the Creek leader Sus-pul-ber, whose son, James Sapulpa, lived near where a railroad construction camp was located.

SARATOGA. In northwestern Woods County, 7 miles northwest of Plainview. A post office from May 5, 1906, to June 15, 1918. Its name comes from Saratoga, New York.

SARDIS. In northern Pushmataha County, 6 miles northwest of Clayton. Post office established February 20, 1905. Took its name from nearby Sardis Indian Mission Church.

SASAKWA. In southeastern Seminole County. Post office established January 14, 1880. The name is a Creek Indian word meaning "goose" or "brant."

SAVANNA. In Pittsburg County, 10 miles southwest of McAlester. Post office established May 5, 1876. Took its name from the private railroad car of the general manager of the Katy Railroad, Robert Stevens.

SAWOKLA. Present Haskell, in Muskogee County. Post office established June 17, 1902, and name changed to Haskell, June 20, 1904. Its name comes from a small band of Muskhogean stock in Alabama, which was later absorbed into the Creek tribe. The word means racoon town and is often spelled Sawokli. Sawokla is best remembered as the name of the home of Alice R. Robertson, Oklahoma's first Congresswoman. Built on Agency Hill at Muskogee in 1910, its name was intended by the owner to mean "gathering place." The renowned structure was destroyed by fire in 1925.

SAWYER. Formerly Miah. In Choctaw County, 8 miles east of Hugo. Post office name changed to Sawyer, April 1, 1903. Named for Charles H. Sawyer, attorney for the Dawes Commission.

SAYLOR. In northern Haskell County, 8 miles north of Keota. A post office from September 13, 1901, to December 31, 1920.

SAYRE. County seat of Beckham County. Post office established October 23, 1901. Named for Robert H. Sayre, railroad developer.

SCALES. In Tulsa County, adjoining Tulsa on the east and now within the city limits. A post office from June 10, 1904, to March 31, 1909. Named for Henry Scales, local coal operator.

SCHEIDEL. In northwestern Washita County, 4 miles south of Foss. A post office from January 5, 1899, to March 15, 1903. No longer in existence, it was named for Frank J. Scheidemantel, first postmaster.

SCHLEGEL. A rural community in eastern Payne County, 4 miles northeast of Cushing. Townsite plat filed December 18, 1914. Named for Mathias Schlegel, townsite owner.

SCHLEY. In southwestern Pawnee County, 5 miles west of Quay. A post office from December 24, 1898, to April 30, 1903. Named for Admiral Winfield S. Schley, hero of the Battle of Santiago de Cuba, July 3, 1898.

SCHOFIELD. In northeastern Tillman County, 10 miles east of Manitou. A post office from January 11, 1902, to January 31, 1906. No longer in existence, it was named for Robert J. Schofield, first postmaster.

SCHOOLTON. In northeastern Seminole County, 6 miles south of Boley. A post office from December 19, 1907, to June 30, 1917. Until November 28, 1907, a post office named Irene had been located at this same proximate location. The name was selected by William P. Weston, local educator, in recognition of plans for a fine school system.

SCHROCK. In northwestern Woods County, 10 miles northeast of Plainview. A post office from October 15, 1906, to August 31,

1909. No longer in existence, it was named for Ephrian Schrock, first postmaster.

SCHULTER. In Okmulgee County, 6 miles north of Henryetta. Post office established August 20, 1903. Named for Matt Schulter, St. Louis jurist.

SCIPIO. In northwestern Pittsburg County, 12 miles northwest of McAlester. Post office established January 24, 1890. Took its name from nearby Scipio Creek, a tributary of the Canadian River. The name is from the Roman general who defeated Hannibal at the Battle of Zama.

SCOTT. In northern Caddo County, 7 miles east of Lookeba. A post office from January 11, 1902, to October 31, 1935. Named for Scott Vance, son of James A. Vance, first postmaster.

SCRAPER. A rural community in Cherokee County, 13 miles northeast of Tahlequah. Named for Captain Archibald Scraper of the Union Indian brigade of the Civil War.

SCULLIN. Formerly Vaughn. In Murray County, 7 miles east of Sulphur. Post office name changed to Scullin, March 25, 1901, and discontinued October 31, 1954. Named for John Scullin of St. Louis, railroad engineer.

SCULLYVILLE. The post office name for the Choctaw agency from August 16, 1860, to December 14, 1860, located at Skullyville, Choctaw Nation.

SEAY. In eastern Blaine County, 7 miles southeast of Okeene. A post office from June 25, 1892, to January 15, 1901. On October 25, 1901, a post office named Stearns in western Kingfisher County was moved into Blaine County and its name changed to Seay. Discontinued January 30, 1904. Named for Abraham J. Seay, second governor of Oklahoma Territory.

SEDALIA. In Roger Mills County, 7 miles east of Cheyenne. A post office from May 7, 1903, to December 31, 1907. Its name comes from Sedalia, Missouri.

SEDAN. In eastern Kiowa County, 8 miles south of Mountain View. A post office from December 29, 1902, to March 15, 1935. Its name comes from Sedan, Kansas.

SEGER. In Washita County, 4 miles west of Colony. A post office from September 16, 1892, to April 14, 1906. Named for John H. Seger, founder of the Seger Colony.

SEILING. In northern Dewey County. Post office established May 4, 1894. Named for Louis A. Seiling, townsite owner.

SELMAN. In Comanche County, 3 miles northeast of Cache. A post office from October 17, 1902, to May 31, 1907. Named for Arthur Selman Clark, son of the first postmaster.

SELMAN. Formerly Charleston. In Harper County, 9 miles southeast of Buffalo. Post office name changed to Selman, August 24,

1923. Named for J. O. Selman, townsite owner.

SEMINOLE. Formerly Tidmore. In central Seminole County. Post office name changed to Seminole, February 6, 1907. Its name comes from the Seminole Nation.

SEMINOLE COUNTY. A county in south-central Oklahoma, created at statehood, conforming generally to the area of the Seminole Nation, Indian Territory. Took its name from the Seminole tribe of Indians. The word is Creek for runaway.

SENORA. In southern Okmulgee County, 3 miles south of Dewar. Post office established April 20, 1896, and name changed to Hoardsville, February 8, 1909. Named for Senora Likowski, mother of Frank Likowski, first postmaster.

SENTINEL. In southwestern Washita County. Post office established March 6, 1899. Townsite name was Barton, by plat filed September 23, 1901. Took its name from the *Herald Sentinel*, a newspaper published at Cloud Chief.

SEQUO. In Sequoyah County, 9 miles northeast of Sallisaw. A post office from July 19, 1916, to October 31, 1917. No longer in existence. The name is a word coined from the name of the county.

SEQUOYAH. A district of the Cherokee Nation, established November 4, 1851. Formerly Skin Bayou District. Named for George Guess, or Sequoyah, inventor of the Cherokee alphabet. The word means shut in or away.

SEQUOYAH. In Rogers County, 6 miles northeast of Claremore. Post office established August 10, 1871, and changed to Beulah, March 9, 1909. Named for Sequoyah, inventor of the Cherokee alphabet.

SEQUOYAH COUNTY. A county in eastern Oklahoma, created at statehood. Took its name from Sequoyah District, Cherokee Nation.

SERGEANT MAJOR CREEK. A creek in Roger Mills County, a tributary of the Washita River and adjoining the site of the Battle of the Washita. Named for Sergeant Walter P. Kennedy, who was killed at the battle, November 27, 1868.

SEVENOAKS. In northern Custer County, 7 miles northwest of Thomas. A post office from January 17, 1894, to October 31, 1904. No longer in existence.

SEWARD. In Logan County, 6 miles southwest of Guthrie. A post office from May 15, 1889, to July 11, 1969. Named for William H. Seward, secretary of state under President Lincoln.

SEWELL. In Pottawatomie County, 5 miles southwest of Tecumseh. A post office from June 17, 1905, to December 31, 1905. Usually known as Brooksville. Named for Dr. N. Sewell, prominent local resident.

SEYMOUR. A traveling post office at the railhead during construction of the Santa Fe Railway, and in operation from November 15, 1886, to May 13, 1887.

SHADE. In northeastern Texas County, 3 miles south of Tyrone. A post office from August 19, 1890, to September 15, 1902. Took its name from nearby Shade Well, a water well named for J. N. Shade, an official of the Rock Island Railroad.

SHADY POINT. Formerly Harrison. In Le Flore County, 6 miles north of Poteau. Post office name changed to Shadypoint, December 11, 1894.

SHAFTER. In eastern Payne County, 4 miles southeast of Yale. A post office from November 1, 1898, to August 31, 1905. Named for Major General William R. Shafter, commander of the United States forces in Cuba and victor at the Battle of Santiago de Cuba.

SHAKESPEARE. In northeastern Sequoyah County, 11 miles northeast of Muldrow. A post office from September 4, 1903, to March 31, 1905. Named for William Shakespeare, English bard and man of letters.

SHAMROCK. In Creek County, 5 miles south of Drumright. Post office established July 9, 1910. Named by J. M. Thomas, first postmaster, for his home town in Illinois.

SHANER. In Garfield County, 4 miles south of Covington. A post office from April 27, 1894, to March 15, 1904. No longer in existence, it was named for William H. Shaner, first postmaster.

SHAPPAWAY. A county in Pushmataha District, Choctaw Nation.

Named for noted Choctaw leader. Later Atoka County, Choctaw Nation.

SHARON. Formerly Hackberry. In Woodward County, 12 miles south of Woodward. Post office name changed to Sharon, February 24, 1912. Named for Alexander Sharon, townsite owner.

SHARP. In Okmulgee County, 5 miles southwest of Okmulgee. A post office from May 9, 1903, to May 31, 1915. Named for Joseph W. Sharp, first postmaster.

SHATTUCK. In Ellis County, 9 miles northwest of Arnett. Post office established November 17, 1893. Named for George O. Shattuck, a director of the Santa Fe Railway.

SHAWNEE. County seat of Pottawatomie County from February 26, 1909, to February 13, 1913, and since December 19, 1930. Post office established April 2, 1892. A post office named Shawneetown was in operation at this same site from January 6, 1876, to February 25, 1892. Took its name from the Shawnee tribe of Indians, who shared a reservation with the Pottawatomie tribe. The name is an Algonquian word *shawon*, meaning "southerner."

SHAWNEETOWN. Formerly Kulli Inla. Post office name changed to Shawneetown, August 16, 1892, and discontinued October 15, 1929. Shawneetown was the approximate site of Miller Court House, the first post office in present-day Oklahoma. In McCurtain County, 5 miles southwest of Idabel.

218

SHAY. In Marshall County, 8 miles south of Kingston. A post office from April 23, 1901, to May 31, 1955. Took its name from nearby Shay Prairie.

SHEDD. A switch and loading point on the Rock Island Railroad in Oklahoma County, 10 miles east of Oklahoma City. Named for Louis F. Shedd, official of the Choctaw Coal and Railway Company.

SHELL. In Caddo County, 6 miles north of Fort Cobb. A post office from June 19, 1902, to April 16, 1906. Named for Charles E. Shell, Cheyenne and Arapaho Indian agent.

SHELLY. In Washita County, 7 miles northeast of Cordell. A post office from September 7, 1892, to July 14, 1906. No longer in existence.

SHELTON. In western Texas County, 2 miles north of Eva. A post office from May 16, 1906, to November 30, 1912. No longer in existence.

SHERIDAN. In northeastern Kingfisher County, 10 miles east of Hennessey. A post office from June 28, 1890, to June 30, 1904. No longer in existence, it was named for General Philip H. Sheridan.

SHERMAN. Original townsite name for Union City in Canadian County. Townsite plat filed February 27, 1891. Named for General William T. Sherman.

SHERMAN. In Major County, 10 miles northwest of Phroso. Former post office name was Hoopville, and the name was changed to Sherman January 29, 1913, and discontinued as a post office August 15, 1949. Named for Joseph Sherman, legislator and long-time local resident.

SHERWOOD. In northern McCurtain County, 4 miles southeast of Bethel. Post office established March 20, 1912. Named for Sherwood Davis, early-day settler.

SHIDLER. In Osage County, 21 miles northwest of Pawhuska. Post office established February 23, 1922. Named for E. S. Shidler, townsite developer.

SHILOH. In eastern Logan County, 6 miles southeast of Meridian. A post office from May 5, 1899, to October 31, 1908. Its name comes from the Battle of Shiloh, Tennessee, April 6–7, 1862.

SHINEWELL. In McCurtain County 9 miles northeast of Haworth. A post office from April 20, 1927, to October 31, 1955. The name was assigned arbitrarily by the Post Office Department instead of the requested name of Henry, intended by the community to honor Jack Henry, popular local resident.

SHIPMAN. A rural community in Pottawatomie County, 3 miles west of Saint Louis. Townsite plat filed May 6, 1927. Named for Sallie Shipman, townsite owner.

SHIRK. A railroad switch and loading point on the Frisco Railroad, across the Arkansas River south of Sand Springs in Tulsa County. Named for Ben Shirk, Frisco Railroad official.

SHIRLEY. In northeastern Roger Mills County, 9 miles northwest of Leedey. A post office from June 9, 1900, to October 31, 1912. Named for Edward E. Shirley, first postmaster.

SHOALS. In southern Choctaw County, 8 miles southeast of Grant. A post office from July 2, 1904, to August 31, 1916. Took name from shoals along the Red River.

SHORT. In northeastern Sequoyah County, 3 miles from the Arkansas State line. A post office from December 5, 1908, to November 30, 1954. The name comes from a contrast with the name of a post office nearby, Long.

SHORT SPRINGS. In western Alfalfa County, 9 miles east of Alva. Post office established March 19, 1895, and name changed to Ashley, September 24, 1897. Named for George Short, first postmaster.

SHREWDER. In Harmon County, 7 miles north of Gould. A post office from May 12, 1902, to May 31, 1911. Named for Thomas Shrewder, pioneer resident.

SHULTS. In McCurtain County, 6 miles east of Idabel. A post office from February 9, 1905, to June 30, 1926. Named for George W. Shults, early-day resident.

SHUMPKER. In southwestern Okfuskee County, adjoining Pa-

den. Post office established January 3, 1905, and name changed to Trenton, May 16, 1905.

SIBONEY. In northern Tillman County, 2 miles north of Manitou. A post office from October 4, 1902, to September 31, 1907. Took name from Siboney, Cuba, captured by United States forces under Brigadier General Henry W. Lawton, June 23, 1898.

SICKLES. In Caddo County, 5 miles northwest of Binger. A post office from October 14, 1901, to April 30, 1919. Named for Frank C. Sickles, registrar of the El Reno land office.

SID. In Delaware County, 6 miles northwest of Colcord. A post office from June 23, 1920, to October 15, 1935. Named for Sidney Runyon, son of Fred Runyon, first postmaster.

SIEG. In southwestern Kiowa County, 7 miles southwest of Roosevelt. A post office from September 4, 1902, to August 31, 1904. No longer in existence, it was named for Joseph A. Sieg, early-day resident.

SIGNET. In Payne County, 8 miles east of Stillwater. A post office from June 6, 1921, to April 30, 1935. The name was assigned arbitrarily by the Post Office Department in lieu of the name Ingalls, proposed by the local residents.

SILLER. In Pottawatomie County, at the proximate site of present St. Louis. A post office from March 4,

1903, to December 31, 1905. Named for Siller Tarter, daughter of the first postmaster.

SILO. In western Bryan County, 8 miles northwest of Durant. A post office from November 4, 1893, to January 31, 1946. Named for Albert B. "Silo" Gates, early-day resident.

SILVER CITY. In Grady County, on the south bank of the Canadian River north of Tuttle. A post office from May 29, 1883, to June 17, 1890. An important town on the Chisholm Trail, it now has entirely disappeared. Named for nearby Silver Creek.

SIMON. In northwestern Love County, 9 miles south of Wilson. A post office from November 19, 1888, to October 15, 1927. Took its name from nearby Simon Creek, a tributary of Red River.

SIMPSON. Formerly Gunton. In Marshall County, 10 miles northwest of Madill. Post office name changed to Simpson, March 23, 1904, and discontinued October 31, 1959.

SIMPSON. In Pittsburg County, 8 miles northeast of McAlester. A post office from August 22, 1894, to February 15, 1900. Named for John Simpson, rancher and cattleman.

SIMS. In Kiowa County, 7 miles southwest of Roosevelt. A post office from February 17, 1902, to June 31, 1904. No longer in existence, it was named for William P. Sims, long-time resident.

SINNETT. In southeastern Pawnee County, 5 miles north of Mannford. A post office from September 27, 1894, to January 15, 1906. No longer in existence, it was named for William P. Sinnett, first postmaster.

SIX BULLS. The original name, in vogue prior to about 1830, for the Neosho, or Grand, River.

SKEDEE. In Pawnee County, 6 miles northeast of Pawnee. A post office from February 10, 1902, to August 2, 1963. Took its name from the Skidi, or Wolf, tribe of the Pawnee Confederacy.

SKELLETON. In Garfield County, 8 miles southeast of Enid. Post office from June 11, 1894, to June 14, 1904. No longer in existence. Took its name from nearby Skeleton Creek, a branch of Ephriam Creek, a tributary of the Cimarron River.

SKIATOOK. On the county line between Tulsa and Osage counties, 13 miles north of Tulsa. Post office established March 12, 1880. Until April 11, 1892, the official spelling of the post office was Ski-a-took. Named for Skiatooka, a prominent Osage, the community around his home having been known as Skiatooka's Settlement.

SKIN BAYOU. A district of the Cherokee Nation. Name changed to Sequoyah District by act of the Cherokee Council, November 4, 1851.

SKIN BAYOU. In Sequoyah County near Muldrow. A post office from October 27, 1873, to September 1, 1875. No longer in existence. Took its name from nearby Skin Bayou, a tributary of the Arkansas River.

SKULLYVILLE. A county in Moshulatubbee District, Choctaw Nation. The name is a Choctaw word meaning "money town" and comes from the circumstance that annuities were paid out at the nearby Choctaw Agency.

SKULLYVILLE. In Le Flore County, 2 miles northeast of Spiro. An important trade and political center among the early Choctaws. The spelling of the post office was Scullyville. The name, a Choctaw word meaning "money town," comes from the fact that annuities were paid out at the nearby Choctaw Agency. Former capital of the Choctaw Nation.

SLAPOUT. In southeastern Beaver County, 20 miles west of May. The name comes from the circumstance that the local storekeeper would always reply that he was "slapout" of whatever item was requested for purchase.

SLEDGEVILLE. In Texas County, 7 miles north of Guymon. A post office from May 5, 1906, to February 28, 1907. Named for Bob and Ben Sledge, local ranchers.

SLEEPER. In western Cherokee County, 8 miles northeast of Wagoner. A post office from May 10, 1904, to September 30, 1916. Named for Gid Sleeper, rancher and cattleman.

SLICK. In eastern Creek County, 9 miles southeast of Bristow. Post office established April 28, 1920. Named for Thomas B. Slick, prominent oil producer.

SLIM. In western McCurtain County, 6 miles north of Valliant. A post office from January 15, 1916, to July 31, 1933. Named for Slim Herndon, prominent early-day resident.

SLUSHER. In the northeastern corner of Cleveland County. A post office from June 13, 1894, to August 14, 1905. No longer in existence, it was named for William P. Slusher, first postmaster.

SMITH VILLAGE. An incorporated municipality in Oklahoma County adjoining Del City, organized in November, 1952. Named for Rose H. Smith, townsite owner.

SMITHVILLE. Formerly Hatobi. In northeastern McCurtain County, 16 miles northeast of Bethel. Post office name changed to Smithville, May 1, 1890. Named for Joshua M. Smith, intermarried Choctaw, and long-time local resident.

SNEED. In Carter County, 7 miles northeast of Healdton. A post office from May 29, 1901, to February 29, 1912. Named for Colonel R. A. Sneed, later secretary of state and state treasurer.

SNOMAC. In Seminole County, 4 miles southeast of Bowlegs. A post office from October 11, 1928, to December 31, 1955. The name was coined from Snowden and Mc-Sweeney, the developers who drilled the nearby discovery well.

SNOW. In northern Nowata County, south of Coffeyville, Kansas. A post office from November 3, 1903, to September 15, 1904. No longer in existence. Took its name from nearby Snow Creek, which had been named for G. C. Snow, Indian agent.

SNOW. In Pushmataha County, 18 miles northeast of Antlers. Post office established July 21, 1930. Named for George Snow, local resident and merchant.

SNYDER. In southeastern Kingfisher County, 9 miles southwest of Cashion. Post office established August 28, 1890, and name changed to Nagle, March 18, 1896. Named for Margaret A. Snyder, first postmaster.

SNYDER. In southern Kiowa County. Post office established May 26, 1902. Named for Bryan Snyder, railroad official.

SOBOL. In extreme southeastern Pushmataha County. Post office established January 21, 1911. Named for Harry Sobol, Fort Towson merchant.

SOFKA. In Creek County, 3 miles west of Bristow. A post office from August 27, 1894, to December 14, 1897. No longer in existence. Took its name from *sofka*, a thin Indian gruel popular with the Creek Indians.

SOLDANI. A switch and loading point on the Santa Fe Railway in western Osage County, adjoining Burbank. Named for Sylvester Soldani, prominent Osage.

SOLDIER CREEK. Popular resort area along the northwestern shores of Lake Texoma. Took its name from nearby Soldier Creek, which had been named for a bivouac of Union soldiers in the vicinity at the close of Civil War.

SOLON. In northern Ellis County, 10 miles southwest of Fort Supply. A post office from May 10, 1902, to May 31, 1908. No longer in existence.

SOONER. Formerly Haley. In northeastern Grady County, 5 miles south of Tuttle. Post office name changed to Sooner, April 9, 1913, and discontinued July 15, 1914.

SOONERVILLE. In Lincoln County, 3 miles northeast of Agra, founded at the time of the Sac and Fox opening in September, 1891. Flynn post office re-located there in 1895. The Soonerville school was in operation until 1958.

SOPER. In Choctaw County, 11 miles west of Hugo. Post office established April 2, 1903. Named for P. L. Soper, United States attorney.

SOPHIA. In southern Beaver County, 6 miles southeast of Elmwood. A post office from March 4, 1903, to June 30, 1916. Named for Sophia Miller, first postmaster.

SOUTER. In western Osage County, 3 miles from Cleveland. A post office from May 19, 1914, to September 29, 1917. Named for George W. Souter, prominent local resident.

SOUTHARD. Formerly Cherryvale. In Blaine County, 6 miles east of Canton. Post office name changed to Southard, September 6, 1905. Named for George H. Southard, developer of a local gypsum mill.

SOUTH CANADIAN. In southeastern Dewey County, 6 miles northwest of Fay. Post office established December 9, 1907, and name changed to Nobscot, October 26, 1915. Took its name from nearby Canadian River, now usually known as the South Canadian River.

SOUTH CANADIAN. In northern Pittsburg County, 10 miles southwest of Eufaula. Post office established May 29, 1873, and name changed to Canadian, December 11, 1899. Took its name from nearby South Fork of the Canadian River, now usually known as Gaines Creek.

SOUTH COFFEYVILLE. Formerly Etchen. In northern Nowata County, on the state line south of Coffeyville, Kansas. Post office name changed to South Coffeyville, April 29, 1909. Original townsite name was Polson.

SOUTH McALESTER. Post office established February 5, 1890; so named to distinguish the post office from McAlester, now North McAlester, located 2 miles north. Post office name changed to McAlester May 10, 1907.

SPARKS. In Lincoln County, 7 miles southeast of Chandler. Post office established August 30, 1902. Named for George T. Sparks of Fort Smith, director of the Fort Smith and Western Railway.

SPARTA. In northwestern Dewey County, 3 miles south of Vici. A post office from April 16, 1901, to March 15, 1912. No longer in existence. Its name comes from the renowned city in southern Greece, long a rival of Athens.

SPAULDING. In Hughes County, 6 miles southwest of Holdenville. A post office from December 29, 1902, to May 20, 1966.

SPAVINA MILLS. Formerly Lynch's Prairie. In Mayes County, 4 miles northwest of Spavinaw. Post office name changed to Spavina Mills, October 10, 1878, and discontinued January 6, 1879. Spavina is an earlier spelling of Spavinaw.

SPAVINAW. In Mayes County, 10 miles north of Salina. Post office established March 14, 1892. The name is a corruption of two French words, *cépée* and *vineux*, meaning "shoots" or "young growth" of trees.

SPEED. Formerly Hardin. Present Hobart, in Kiowa County. Name changed to Speed, February 20, 1901, and post office name changed to Hobart, July 9, 1901. Named for Horace Speed, United States attorney for Oklahoma Territory.

SPEER. In Choctaw County, 9 miles northwest of Hugo. A post office from January 20, 1910, to April 30, 1959. First known locally as Cooksville.

SPEER. In Lincoln County, 6 miles north of Chandler. Post office established March 29, 1892, and name changed to Lowe, December 15, 1903. Named for Joseph L. Speer, first postmaster.

SPEERMORE. In extreme southwest Harper County. A post office from September 4, 1901, to December 31, 1940. Named for William H. Speer, townsite owner.

SPENCER. Formerly Munger. In Oklahoma County, 5 miles northeast of Oklahoma City. Post office name changed to Spencer, February 25, 1903. Named for A. M. Spencer, railroad developer.

SPENCER ACADEMY. In Choctaw County, first at Spencerville and later at Nelson. Well-known boys school established by the Choctaw Nation in 1841. Operated by the Presbyterian Board of Missions. Here Negro slave Uncle Wallace composed "Swing Low, Sweet Chariot." A post office named Spencerville operated at original site from January 22, 1844, to July 22, 1847. Named for John C. Spencer, secretary of war.

SPENCERVILLE. In northern Choctaw County, 12 miles northeast of Hugo. Located at first site of Spencer Academy. Post office established May 17, 1902, and took name from Spencer Academy.

SPERRY. In Tulsa County, 8 miles north of Tulsa. Post office established May 17, 1902; in 1907, the post office was moved to Buehler, which was known thereafter as Sperry. Sperry is an English adaptation of Henry Spybuck's last name.

SPIRO. In northern Le Flore County. Post office established September 21, 1898. Although there are several versions on the origin of the name, it is generally believed to have been named for Abram Spiro of Ft. Smith, Arkansas.

SPIRO MOUND. Famous Indian mounds located in northern Le Flore County. Partially excavated, the mounds have revealed artifacts indicating a high culture existing about 1000 A.D. Took its name from nearby Spiro.

SPOKOGEE. Formerly Watsonville. In northeastern Hughes County, 12 miles east of Wetumka. Post office name changed to Spokogee, June 27, 1902, and changed to Dustin, May 9, 1904. The name is believed an Indian word for prairie town.

SPRINGBROOK. Formerly Viola. In Johnston County, 3 miles south of Bromide. Post office name changed to Springbrook, July 17, 1906, and discontinued November 15, 1910.

SPRINGER. In northern Carter County. Post office established September 1, 1890. Named for W. A. Springer, pioneer rancher and cattleman.

225

SPRINGFIELD. In northwestern Comanche County, 5 miles south of Saddle Mountain. A post office from February 18, 1902, to May 15, 1908. No longer in existence. Took its name from Springfield, Ohio.

SPRINGFIELD. In Okfuskee County, 3 miles southeast of Okemah. Post office established April 16, 1884, and name changed to McDermott, March 10, 1894.

SPRINGS. In northeastern Alfalfa County, 6 miles northeast of Amorita. A post office from May 18, 1895, to May 31, 1904. Took its name from the springs along Sandy Creek, a tributary of the Salt Fork of the Arkansas River.

SPRINGVALE. In Logan County, 3 miles southwest of Meridian. A post office from February 21, 1890, to April 30, 1903. No longer in existence.

SPROUT. In northwestern Caddo County, 5 miles north of Eakly. A post office from March 25, 1902, to February 28, 1906. No longer in existence, it was named for Edward P. Sprout, first postmaster.

STAFFORD. In Custer County, 8 miles west of Clinton. A post office from August 2, 1911, to February 28, 1954. Named for Grant Stafford, attorney for the Clinton and Oklahoma Western Railroad.

STANDARD. In northwestern Logan County, 7 miles north of Crescent. A post office from June 30, 1890, to March 31, 1904.

STANDING ROCK. In north-

western Atoka County. A post office from February 6, 1914, to October 31, 1918. No longer in existence. Took its name from a prominent nearby land feature.

STANLEY. In northern Pushmataha County, 8 miles southwest of Clayton. A post office from August 20, 1906, to November 5, 1965. Named for William E. Stanley, member of the Dawes Commission.

STANTON. A rural community in Payne County, 1 mile south of Perkins. First known locally as Main. Townsite plat filed March 27, 1900; now known generally as Vinco. Named for Jesse E. Stanton, townsite owner.

STAPP. In Le Flore County, 10 miles south of Heavener. A post office from January 16, 1918, to January 31, 1944.

STAR. In eastern Haskell County, 5 miles northeast of Keota. A post office from March 14, 1892, to July 31, 1925.

STARVILLA. In southern Muskogee County, 3 miles northeast of Porum. A post office from January 16, 1895, to June 30, 1905. Named for Fannie Starr, early-day local resident.

STAUNTON. In southwestern Carter County. A post office from September 24, 1914, to April 30, 1921. Its name comes from Staunton, Virginia.

STEARNS. In western Kingfisher County, 6 miles northwest of Loyal. Post office established April 28,

1894; name changed to Seay, and post office moved to Blaine County, October 25, 1901. Named for Charles O. Stearns, first postmaster.

STECKER. In Caddo County, 9 miles southwest of Anadarko. A post office from April 2, 1909, to September 30, 1954. Named for Lieutenant Ernest Stecker, Kiowa Indian superintendent.

STEEDMAN. Formerly Blackrock. In Pontotoc County, 11 miles northeast of Ada. First known locally as Ford Switch. Post office name changed to Steedman, January 19, 1910, and discontinued February 15, 1932. Named for E. L. Steed, Ada business leader.

STEELEY. In Delaware County, 8 miles southwest of Jay. A post office from April 20, 1915, to March 27, 1924. Named for Mamie Steeley, first postmaster.

STELLA. In extreme northeastern Cleveland County. A post office from November 23, 1892, to February 14, 1906. Named for Stella Guilliams, mother of William D. Guilliams, early-day resident.

STEPHENS COUNTY. A county of south-central Oklahoma, created at statehood from portions of Comanche County, Oklahoma Territory, and the Chickasaw Nation. Named for John H. Stephens, member of Congress from Texas.

STERLING. In northeastern Comanche County. Post office established October 17, 1901. Named for Captain Charles Sterling of the Texas Rangers.

STERLING. Present Capron, in Woods County. Post office established March 21, 1894, and name changed to Virgel, October 24, 1895.

STERRETT. Present Calera, in southwestern Bryan County. Formerly Cale. Post office name changed to Sterrett, January 30, 1897, and name changed to Calera, November 21, 1910. Named for Dr. John A. Sterrett of Troy, Ohio, member of Choctaw Townsite Commission.

STIDHAM. In McIntosh County, 8 miles northwest of Eufaula. Post office established January 30, 1897. Named for George W. Stidham, prominent Creek leader.

STIGLER. County seat of Haskell County. Formerly Newman. Post office name changed to Stigler, May 3, 1893. Named for Joseph S. Stigler, townsite developer.

STILLWATER. County seat of Payne County. Post office established August 28, 1889. Took its name from nearby Stillwater Creek, a tributary of the Cimarron River.

STILWELL. Designated county seat of Adair County, March 1, 1910, by proclamation of the governor. Formerly Flint. Post office name changed to Stilwell, May 12, 1896. Named for Arthur E. Stilwell, developer of the Kansas City Southern Railway.

STINETON. In Dewey County, 8 miles east of Putnam. A post office from November 3, 1898, to February 15, 1908. No longer in existence. Named for William B. Stine, first postmaster.

STOCKHOLM. In Harper County, 10 miles northeast of Laverne. A post office from July 6, 1901, to April 15, 1915. Its name comes from Stockholm, Sweden.

STONE. In southeastern Ellis County, 7 miles west of Camargo. A post office from February 2, 1894, to November 30, 1914.

STONE BLUFF. In southwestern Wagoner County, 6 miles northwest of Haskell. A post office from May 28, 1897, to August 31, 1955. Took its name from nearby stone bluffs formed by the north face of Conjada Mountain, overlooking the Arkansas River.

STONER. In Stephens County, 7 miles southeast of Duncan. A post office from June 13, 1906, to March 31, 1912. Named for Charles H. Stoner, first postmaster.

STONEWALL. In eastern Pontotoc County, 13 miles southeast of Ada. Original site was at the location of present-day Frisco. Post office established December 30, 1874. Named for General T. J. "Stonewall" Jackson, Confederate hero.

STORY. In northwestern Garvin County, 2 miles north of Maysville. A post office from October 11, 1899, to July 15, 1914. Named for William Story, local Chickasaw.

STOUT. Formerly Boggy. Present Bessie, in Washita County. Post office name changed to Stout, June

14, 1899, and changed to Bessie, May 22, 1903. Named for Benjamin W. Stout, first postmaster.

STRAIN. In northwestern Dewey County, 5 miles southwest of Vici. A post office from February 23, 1904, to September 29, 1906. No longer in existence, it was named for Samuel C. Strain, first postmaster.

STRANG. Formerly Lynch. In northeastern Mayes County, 5 miles northwest of Spavinaw. Post office name changed to Strang, March 18, 1913. Named for Clarita Strang Kenefic, wife of William Kenefic, railroad developer.

STRATFORD. In northeastern Garvin County. Post office established October 23, 1906. Named for Stratford-on-Avon, England.

STRINGTOWN. In Atoka County, 7 miles northeast of Atoka. Post office established August 17, 1874. For a few weeks in July, 1877, the official name of the post office was Sulphur Springs. The name is a modification of Springtown, the original name of the locality.

STROHM. In Osage County, 7 miles northeast of Fairfax. Named for Charles B. Strohm, Santa Fe Railway official.

STRONG CITY. In Roger Mills County, 5 miles northeast of Chey-County. Post office established September 26, 1912. Named for Clinton R. Strong, railroad developer.

STROUD. In eastern Lincoln County. Post office established September 16, 1892. Named for James W. Stroud, prominent early-day trader.

STUART. Formerly Hoyuby. In Hughes County, 10 miles southeast of Calvin. Post office name changed to Stuart, April 14, 1896. Named for Charles B. Stuart, territorial jurist.

STURGIS. In northeastern Cimarron County, 11 miles northeast of Keyes. A post office from March 18, 1926, to December 15, 1936. Named for F. K. Sturgis, Santa Fe Railway director.

STURM. In western Caddo County, 7 miles north of Fort Cobb. A post office from February 10, 1902, to August 31, 1920; site now inundated by waters of Fort Cobb Reservoir. Named for Dr. Jacob J. Sturm, pioneer physician.

SUAGEE. In Delaware County, 6 miles south of Grove. A post office from June 25, 1892, to September 14, 1898. No longer in existence, it was named for Wilson Suagee, prominent Cherokee. Location of courthouse for Delaware District, Cherokee Nation.

SUGAR LOAF. County in Moshulatubbee District, Choctaw Nation. Its name comes from Sugar Loaf Mountain. Sugar Loaf is a corruption of the French *Point de Sucre.*

SUGDEN. In Jefferson County, 6 miles south of Waurika. A post office from November 14, 1893, to November 30, 1955. Named for Carl and Ikard Suggs, local ranchers and cattlemen.

SUGG. The post office name for Ryan in Jefferson County from March 14, 1888, to January 23, 1890. The name has the same origin as Sugden.

SULLY. In eastern Washita County, 6 miles south of Colony. A post office from April 17, 1902, to April 14, 1906. No longer in existence, it was named for Brigadier General Alfred Sully, commander of troops in the western portion of present-day Oklahoma following the Civil War.

SULPHUR. County seat of Murray County. Post office established October 2, 1895. The name is an adaptation of Sulphur Springs, well-known local feature.

SULPHUR SPRINGS. The post office name for Stringtown, in Atoka County, from July 9, 1877, to July 23, 1877.

SUMMERFIELD. In western Le Flore County, 6 miles east of Le Flore. A post office from October 13, 1888, to September 11, 1964. Named for local sawmill operator, whose full name appears lost.

SUMMIT. In Muskogee County, 6 miles southwest of Muskogee. A post office from May 18, 1896, to November 15, 1915. The site is the highest point on the Katy Railroad between the Arkansas and the North Canadian rivers.

SUMNER. In Noble County, 10 miles northeast of Perry. A post office from May 23, 1894, to July 27, 1957. Named for Henry T. Sumner, Perry business leader.

SUMPTER. In Kay County, 6 miles north of Blackwell. A post office from March 23, 1901, to February 29, 1908. No longer in existence, it was named for John R. Sumpter, first postmaster.

SUNKIST. In northwestern Choctaw County, 8 miles north of Boswell. A post office from February 14, 1925, to September 30, 1953. The name is a coined word made popular by the California orange industry.

SUNSET. In southeastern Beaver County, 4 miles southwest of Logan. A post office from April 22, 1905, to September 30, 1908. No longer in existence.

SUPPLY. Present Fort Supply, in northwestern Woodward County. Formerly Fitzgerald. Post office name changed to Supply, May 12, 1903, and name changed to Fort Supply, May 1, 1943. Took its name from nearby Fort Supply.

SUTTER. In Le Flore County, 8 miles northwest of Poteau. Post office established October 18, 1899, and name changed to Calhoun, March 7, 1914.

SVOBODA. A rural community in Kiowa County, 3 miles north of Snyder. Named for Frank Svoboda, long-time local resident.

SWAN. In Custer County, 7 miles southeast of Thomas. A post office from June 23, 1902, to May 15, 1909. Name selected by the Post Office Department from a list of birds submitted by Minnie Cagg, first postmaster.

SWANSON COUNTY. Proposed county in southwestern Oklahoma, created from parts of Kiowa and Comanche counties by executive order of the governor, August 23, 1910. Dissolved by the state Supreme Court, August 9, 1911. Named for Claude A. Swanson of Virginia, governor of that state, 1906–10, and secretary of the navy, 1933–39.

SWEENEY. Present Harrah, in eastern Oklahoma County. Formerly Pennington. Name changed to Sweeney June 22, 1896, and post office name changed to Harrah, December 22, 1898. Named for E. W. Sweeney, early-day settler.

SWEETWATER. On the line between Roger Mills and Beckham counties, 18 miles northwest of Sayre. Post office established September 27, 1894. Took its name from nearby Sweetwater Creek, a tributary of the North Fork of the Red River.

SWIMMER. In Sequoyah County, 14 miles north of Muldrow. A post office from July 24, 1890, to September 9, 1897. No longer in existence. Named for George W. Swimmer, first postmaster.

SWINK. In eastern Choctaw County, 4 miles east of Fort Towson. Post office established August 14, 1902. Named for D. R. Swink, local merchant. One mile northeast of Swink stands Oklahoma's oldest house.

SYCAMORE. In Delaware County, 6 miles east of Jay. A post office from October 7, 1908, to February 1, 1929. Took its name from a tree of the plane family found extensively in Oklahoma.

SYLVAN. In southwestern Johnston County, 8 miles north of Mannsville. A post office from May 18, 1895, to February 28, 1905. The name is from the Latin word *silva*, meaning "forest."

SYLVIAN. In Seminole County, 6 miles west of Cromwell. A post office from February 2, 1907, to April 30, 1935. Name selected by the wife of the first postmaster, W. T. Stavely, because the site was "surrounded by a wonderful wooded area."

SYRIA. In southeastern Woods County, 10 miles west of Aline. A post office from May 25, 1898, to July 31, 1907. Named by George Shahdy, first postmaster, for the country of Syria.

T

TABLER. In Grady County, 5 miles east of Chickasha. A post office from February 2, 1909, to October 31, 1954. Named for Ike Tabler, foreman of a crew laying railroad track.

TABOR. Formerly Robbins. In Creek County, 7 miles southeast of Bristow. Post office name changed to Tabor, December 12, 1903, and discontinued March 31, 1928. Named for Edward A. Tabor, first postmaster.

TACK. In Beckham County, 2 miles southwest of Sayre. Townsite plat filed January 19, 1924. Named for Tack Hodgson, son of townsite owner.

TACOLA. Original townsite name for Cloud Chief, Washita County. Townsite plat filed April 15, 1892.

TAFT. Formerly Twine. In Muskogee County, 8 miles west of Muskogee. Post office name changed to Taft, November 18, 1904. Named for William H. Taft, secretary of war and later President.

TAHLEQUAH. County seat of Cherokee County. Record Town for Recording District No. 6, Indian Territory. Capital of the Cherokee Nation. Post office moved from Park Hill and name changed to Tahlequah, May 6, 1847. The name is a Cherokee word *Talikwa* or *Tellico*, an old Cherokee town.

TAHLEQUAH. A district of the Cherokee Nation.

TAHLONTEESKEE. Site in western Sequoyah County, 2 miles east of Gore. The first capital of the Western Cherokees, established 1829. Named for Tahlonteeskee, prominent Cherokee chief.

TAHONA. In Le Flore County, 3 miles east of Panama. A post office from December 21, 1918, to December 30, 1951. Named for Hatona Morris, wife of A. G. Morris, prominent early-day resident.

TALALA. In northwestern Rogers County, 6 miles north of Oologah. Post office established June 23, 1890. Named for Captain Talala, well-known Cherokee and an officer of the Third Indian Home Guard Regiment during the Civil War.

TALIHINA. In western Le Flore County. Post office established November 30, 1887. The name is the Choctaw word for railroad.

TALLANT. In Osage County, 3 miles northwest of Barnsdall. A post office from March 26, 1921, to March 8, 1957. Named for Ralph K. Tallant, executive of Cities Service Oil Company.

TALLAVILLE. Formerly Ora. In northwestern Stephens County, 6 miles west of Marlow. Post office name changed to Tallaville, June 24, 1905, and discontinued April 14, 1906. Named for John W. Talla, first postmaster.

TALLEY. In western Cherokee County. A post office from September 25, 1913, to July 15, 1915. Named for John H. Talley, first postmaster.

TALOGA. County seat of Dewey County. Post office established March 22, 1892. Although there are several versions of the origin of the name, it is probably from the Creek word meaning "rock in water" and has reference to the original boundary of the Creek nation.

TAMAHA. In northern Haskell County, 13 miles northeast of Stigler. A post office from April 17, 1884, to April 15, 1954. Once a steamboat landing on the Arkansas River, it was the site of the capture by the Confederates, on June 15, 1864, of an armed steamboat, *J. R. Williams.* The name is a Choctaw word meaning "town."

TANDY. In southern Hughes County, 5 miles southeast of Calvin. A post office from September 17, 1894, to November 14, 1903. In 1910, a post office named Hilltop was established at this approximate site. Named for Tandy Walker, Choctaw leader.

TANEHA. In Creek County, 4 miles north of Sapulpa. A switch on the Frisco, the name fell into disuse when a post office named Bowden was established in 1909 at the site. The word is Creek meaning "oil is below."

TANGIER. In Woodward County, 7 miles west of Woodward. A post office from May 18, 1901, to August 31, 1941. Its name comes from the seaport city in northwestern Africa.

TANK. In southern Mayes County, 8 miles southwest of Locust Grove. A post office from September 3, 1920, to July 31, 1935. Its name comes from the fact that it was the site of a water tank on the Kansas, Oklahoma and Gulf Railway.

TANNAR. Formerly Burgor. In Harper County, 13 miles east of Laverne. Post office name changed to Tannar, October 25, 1904, and changed to Carroll, July 10, 1906. Named for Dr. S. W. Tannar, townsite owner.

TAR RIVER. Present Cardin, in Ottawa County. Post office established December 21, 1915, and name changed to Cardin, January 28, 1920. Took its name from nearby Tar Creek, a tributary of the Neosho River.

TATE. In eastern Seminole County, 6 miles south of Wewoka. A post office from June 1, 1903, to November 30, 1906. Named for H. M. Tate, attorney and United States commissioner.

TATUMS. In northern Carter County, 4 miles northeast of Ratliff City. Post office established May 9, 1896. Named for Lee B. Tatum, first postmaster.

TAUPA. In Comanche County, 8 miles west of Lawton. A post office from January 28, 1902, to January 31, 1913. Named for Tau-pa, a Comanche.

TAYLOR. In southern Cotton County, 5 miles southwest of Temple. A post office from November 30, 1907, to May 31, 1911. Named for John Taylor, local early-day merchant.

TAYLOR. In southeastern Custer County, 5 miles northwest of Weatherford. A post office from July 26, 1895, to May 4, 1899. No longer in existence, it was named for Jeremiah H. Taylor, first postmaster.

TEACROSS. In Harmon County, 12 miles northeast of Hollis. A post office from November 29, 1899, to November 15, 1911. Took its name from T+ ranch.

TECUMSEH. County seat of Pottawatomie County from statehood to February 26, 1909, and from February 13, 1913, to December 19, 1930. Post office established September 18, 1891. Named for the renowned Shawnee Indian chief.

TEDDA. In Canadian County, 5 miles southwest of El Reno. A post office from August 30, 1904, to April 30, 1913. No longer in existence, it was named for President Theodore "Teddy" Roosevelt, with the final letter changed by the Post Office Department.

TEGARDEN. In Woods County, 7 miles northeast of Freedom. A post office from October 15, 1909, to March 31, 1958.

TEMPLE. Formerly Botsford. In Cotton County, 8 miles southeast of Walters. Post office name changed to Temple, August 8, 1902. Named for Temple Houston, son of Sam Houston.

TENKILLER. A well-known ferry across the Illinois River 6 miles northeast of Webber's Falls. It was named for Tenkiller, a Cherokee who farmed nearby. His widow and children all received allotments on the west side of the River, adjoining the ferry site. Present Tenkiller Dam, located 1 mile north, takes its name from the crossing.

TEPEE. In Cimarron County, 12 miles southeast of Keyes. Post office established August 16, 1906; date discontinued not available. Took its name from nearby Tepee Creek.

TERESITA. In northern Cherokee County, 11 miles southeast of Locust Grove. A post office from January 6, 1911, to July 15, 1954. Its name comes from Teresita, North Carolina.

TERLTON. In Pawnee County, 4 miles east of Jennings. Post office established November 30, 1894. Named for Ira N. Terrell, member of first territorial legislature.

TERRAL. In Jefferson County, 8 miles south of Ryan. Post office established August 9, 1892. Named for John H. D. Terral, first postmaster.

TEXANNA. In eastern McIntosh County, 9 miles northeast of Eufaula. A post office from June 27, 1888, to July 16, 1940. The name was coined with reference to a nearby settlement of Texas Cherokees.

TEXAS COUNTY. A county of the Oklahoma Panhandle, created at statehood from the central one-third of Beaver County, Oklahoma Territory. Its name comes from the state of Texas.

TEXHOMA. In southwestern Texas County. Post office established March 18, 1902. The name was coined from the words Texas and Oklahoma.

TEXMO. In eastern Roger Mills County, 7 miles north of Hammon. A post office from December 12, 1901, to August 15, 1912. The name was coined from the words Texas and Missouri.

TEXOKLA. Original townsite name for Texola in western Beckham County. Townsite plat filed January 17, 1902.

TEXOLA. In western Beckham County, 7 miles west of Erick. Post office established December 12, 1901. Earlier townsite names were Texokla and Texoma. The name was coined from the words Texas and Oklahoma.

TEXOMA. An earlier townsite name for Texola in western Beckham County. Townsite plat filed August 5, 1902. An earlier townsite plat had been filed January 17, 1902, showing the name Texokla.

TEXOWA. Original townsite name for Davidson in Tillman County. The name was coined from the words Texas and Kiowa.

THACKERVILLE. In southern Love County, 10 miles south of Marietta. Post office established January 31, 1882. Named for Zachariah Thacker, pioneer settler.

THACKERY. A rural community of greatest importance about 1905 in Pottawatomie County between Shawnee and Tecumseh. Named for Frank A. Thackery, an official at the Sac and Fox Indian Agency.

THOMAS. In northeastern Custer County. Post office established February 12, 1894. Named for William W. Thomas, prominent early-day attorney.

THOMAS. In western Johnston County, 6 miles northwest of Ravia. A post office from November 18, 1890, to October 6, 1891. No longer in existence, it was named for John Thomas, prominent early-day resident.

THOMASVILLE. In Le Flore County, 9 miles south of Heavener. Post office established January 25, 1896, and name changed to Zoe, June 14, 1915. Named for Marcus L. Thomas, first postmaster.

THOMPSONVILLE. A rural community in Creek County, 6 miles south of Kellyville. Townsite plat filed July 7, 1922. Named for J. W. Thompson, townsite owner.

THORNTON. In Washington County near Ramona. A post office from March 7, 1895, to October 25, 1895. No longer in existence, it was named for Thomas J. Thornton, first postmaster.

THRACE. In Seminole County, 8 miles south of Seminole. A post office from May 22, 1906, to February 15, 1911. Its name comes from that of ancient country adjoining Macedonia.

THREE FORKS. The traditional name applied to the region immediately north of Muskogee at the confluence of the Neosho, or Grand, Verdigris, and Arkansas rivers.

THREE SANDS. In Noble County, 6 miles east of Billings. A post office from May 4, 1923, to February 22, 1957. Until April 24, 1942, the post office was located in southern Kay County. Its name comes from the circumstance that nearby oil wells were producing from three sands.

THURMAN. In Pittsburg County, 5 miles west of Indianola. Post office established March 20, 1888, and name changed to Garner, July 1, 1902. Named for Samuel Thurman, local merchant.

THURSTON. In southeastern Canadian County, 4 miles northwest of Mustang. A post office from June 25, 1890, to December 31, 1902. No longer in existence. Named for John M. Thurston, United States senator from Nebraska.

THURSTON. In Latimer County, 6 miles northwest of Wilburton. Post office established December 23, 1904, and name changed to Patterson, October 31, 1906.

TI. In southeastern Pittsburg County, 11 miles southwest of Haileyville. A post office from March 6, 1896, to November 30, 1953. The name was coined from the initials of Indian Territory spelled backwards.

TIAWAH. In Rogers County, 5 miles southeast of Claremore. A post office from August 24, 1903, to December 31, 1938. Took its name from Tiawah Mound in Georgia.

TIDMORE. Present Seminole, in Seminole County. Post office established May 17, 1902, and name changed to Seminole, February 6, 1907. Named for Joe Tidmore, a contractor for the erection of Mekasukey Mission.

TIFFIN. In Beaver County, 10 miles southeast of Beaver. A post office from April 24, 1907, to January 31, 1918. Named for John Tiffin, first postmaster.

TIGER. In northwestern Creek County, 2 miles north of Drumright. A post office from June 30, 1910, to March 31, 1913. Named from Tiger Township, organized 1896, which, in turn, had been named for Billy Tiger, prominent Creek Indian.

TIGER. In Okmulgee County, 6 miles northwest of Okmulgee. A post office from December 3, 1890, to September 14, 1891. Named for Moty Tiger, Creek Chief.

TIGER SPRING. A county in Pushmataha District, Choctaw Nation. Later Blue County, Choctaw Nation.

TILLMAN. A rural community in Tillman County, 6 miles north of Grandfield. Townsite plat dated April 5, 1920. Took its name from Tillman County.

TILLMAN COUNTY. A county in southwestern Oklahoma, organized at statehood from a portion of Comanche County, Oklahoma Territory. Named for Benjamin W. Tillman of South Carolina.

TIMBER. In Hughes County, 5 miles south of Holdenville. Post office established December 15, 1902, and name changed to Wecharty, August 2, 1904.

TIMBERLAKE. In southeast Alfalfa County, 4 miles northeast of Helena. A post office from February 7, 1895, to January 14, 1905. No longer in existence.

TINKER AIR FORCE BASE. Adjoining southeastern Oklahoma City. Named for Major General Clarence L. Tinker, killed in action at the Battle of Midway as a member of the Army Air Corps.

TINNEY. In Comanche County, 6 miles southwest of Lawton. A post office from December 20, 1902, to August 15, 1922. Named for John Tinney, early-day resident and merchant.

TIP. In Mayes County, 6 miles east of Pryor. A post office from June 19, 1906, to June 30, 1951. Tip was the nickname of William H. H. Mayes, prominent Cherokee.

TIPTON. In Tillman County, 10 miles northwest of Frederick. Post office established September 18, 1909. Named for John T. Tipton, conductor on the Kansas City, Mexico and Orient Railway.

TISHOMINGO. County seat of Chickasaw Nation. Named for Chief Tishomingo, the great Chickasaw leader.

TISHOMINGO. County seat of Johnston County. Record Town for Recording District No. 22, Indian Territory. Post office established June 29, 1857. Named for Chief Tishomingo.

TITANIC. In Adair County, 12 miles northwest of Stilwell. A post office from January 3, 1916, to December 31, 1927. Its name comes from the Cunard liner, *Titanic*, sunk during the night of April 14–15, 1912.

TIVOLI. In southern Major County, 12 miles northwest of Canton. A post office from January 2, 1896, to June 15, 1913. No longer in existence. The name is from the Tivoli Gardens, Copenhagen, Denmark.

TOBOXKY. In Pittsburg County, about 10 miles north of present McAlester. A post office from September 18, 1857, to May 8, 1871, and an important settlement prior to the Civil War. From May 14, 1872, to March 22, 1878, another post office was in operation at this site and named Toboxy. The name is an adaptation of the Choctaw word for coal and comes from the name of nearby Coal Creek, a tributary of the South Fork of the Canadian River, now known as Gaines Creek.

TOBUCKSY COUNTY. A county of Moshulatubbee District, Choctaw Nation. The name is adapted from the Choctaw word for coal.

TODD. In Blaine County, 5 miles southeast of Okeene. A post office from August 22, 1893, to June 1, 1895. Named for Austin H. Todd, local rancher.

TODD. Formerly Albia. In eastern Craig County, 6 miles southwest of Afton. Post office name changed to Todd, June 9, 1909, and discontinued February 15, 1930. Named for Lee Todd, local early-day resident.

TOGO. In northwestern Major County, 14 miles southeast of Way-noka. A post office from June 23, 1905, to February 15, 1921.

TOHEE. Formerly Jackson. In southeastern Logan County, 5 miles northwest of Luther. Post office name changed to Tohee, November 13, 1890, and discontinued January 31, 1906. Named for Tohee, well-known Iowa Indian chief.

TOKIO. In Kiowa County, 6 miles southeast of Gotebo. A post office from September 27, 1901, to January 31, 1905. No longer in existence. The name is from the Kiowa word *towkyowy*, meaning "long building," and was given because the building housing the post office was a store over 125 feet long.

TOLAN. In western Okmulgee County, 3 miles northwest of Nuyaka. A post office from April 12, 1917, to June 15, 1926. Named for Oscar Tolan, first postmaster.

TOLOKA. In Haskell County, 6 miles north of Stigler. A post office from May 17, 1902, to January 31, 1903. No longer in existence. The name is from the Choctaw words *itola oka*, meaning "place where water remains," such as water formed by a dam or shoal of a stream.

TOM. In extreme southeastern McCurtain County. The farthermost southeastern post office in Oklahoma was established August 15, 1916. Named for Tom Stewart, early-day settler.

TOMY TOWN. In central Adair County. A post office from December 5, 1936, to March 15, 1938. Named for Thomas Townes, first postmaster.

TONKAWA. In southwestern Kay County. Post office established March 9, 1894. Took its name from the Tonkawa tribe of Indians. The name is a Waco term meaning "they all stay together."

TOPEKA. In Noble County, 6 miles east of Billings. A post office from March 30, 1894, to August 23, 1895. No longer in existence. Its name comes from Topeka, Kansas.

TOWNSLEY. In northeastern Johnston County, 5 miles west of Wapanucka. A post office from February 7, 1905, to January 31, 1907. No longer in existence, it was named for James M. Townsley, first postmaster.

TOWSON. A county in Apukshunnubbee District, Choctaw Nation. Took its name from Fort Towson.

TRACY. In Texas County, 15 miles northwest of Guymon. First known locally as Muncy. Townsite plat filed May 1, 1931. Named for Fred Tracy, member of the Oklahoma Constitutional Convention.

TRAHERN'S STATION. Site at Latham, in Le Flore County. A stage stop on the Butterfield Overland Mail route to California which crossed southeastern Oklahoma, 1858–61. Named for James N. Trahern, merchant and stage agent.

TRAIL. In western Dewey County, 7 miles north of Leedey. A post of-

fice from June 18, 1898, to January 31, 1929. Took its name from the Trail Store, a stopping place on the Western, or Dodge City, cattle trail.

TRAMMELL. In Roger Mills County, 6 miles northeast of Cheyenne. A post office from August 20, 1903, to February 28, 1907. No longer in existence, it was named for James Trammell, first postmaster.

TRENTON. Formerly Shumpker. In southwestern Okfuskee County, south of Paden. Post office name changed to Trenton, May 16, 1905, and discontinued August 15, 1910.

TRIBBEY. In Pottawatomie County, 3 miles southwest of Macomb. A post office from February 4, 1905, to September 30, 1958. Named for Alpheus M. Tribbey, townsite owner.

TRIPP. Present Covington, in Garfield County. Post office established July 1, 1902, and name changed to Covington, February 24, 1903. Its name comes from Tripp, South Dakota.

TROTTER. Present Vinson, in Harmon County. Formerly Francis. Post office name changed to Trotter, April 25, 1902, and name changed to Vinson, August 20, 1903.

TROUSDALE. In southwestern Pottawatomie County, 7 miles northwest of Asher. A post office from March 7, 1904, to June 16, 1967. Named for William A. Trousdale, townsite owner.

TROY. In western Johnston County, 7 miles southeast of Mill Creek. A post office from September 14, 1897, to November 15, 1954. Its name comes from Troy, New York.

TRUAX. In Johnston County, 5 miles southeast of Tishomingo. Post office from June 1, 1901, to May 31, 1908. Named for Dr. G. G. Truax, local rancher.

TRYON. Formerly Fouts. In northern Lincoln County. Post office name changed to Tryon, March 15, 1899. Named for Fred S. Tryon, townsite owner.

TUCKER. In northwestern Le Flore County, 9 miles northwest of Spiro. A post office from March 30, 1895, to June 15, 1922. Named for Rev. Hartwell Tucker, Presbyterian minister to the Choctaw Indians.

TUCKER. Present Comanche, in Stephens County. Post office established April 28, 1887, and name changed to Comanche, January 26, 1893.

TUKLO. In southern Bryan County, 12 miles east of Achille. A post office from May 14, 1892, to April 25, 1893. No longer in existence. The name is the Choctaw word meaning "two."

TULLAHASSEE. In southern Wagoner County, 5 miles northwest of Muskogee. Post office established January 26, 1899. Took its name from nearby Tullahassee Mission. The name is a Creek word meaning "old town."

TULSA. County seat of Tulsa County. Post office established March 25, 1879, and now the state's second largest city. Its name comes from Tulsey Town, an old Creek town in Alabama.

TULSA COUNTY. A county in northeastern Oklahoma, created at statehood. Took its name from Tulsa, the county's most populous city.

TUPELO. In Coal County, 9 miles northwest of Coalgate. Formerly Jeffs. Post office name changed to Tupelo, January 13, 1904. Its name comes from Tupelo, Mississippi, which, in turn, had been named for the tupelo gum tree.

TURKEY FORD. In northern Delaware County, 6 miles northeast of Grove. A post office from December 14, 1904, to April 15, 1955. Took its name from nearby Turkey Ford over Elk River.

TURLEY. In Tulsa County, 5 miles north of Tulsa. A post office from January 13, 1897, to August 23, 1957. Named for James Turley, local merchant and blacksmith.

TURN. In Pottawatomie County, 2 miles southeast of Earlsboro. A post office from January 25, 1892, to October 29, 1895. No longer in existence, it was named for Christopher C. Turner, first postmaster.

TURNER. In Wagoner County, 15 miles east of Broken Arrow. A post office from April 23, 1901, to October 15, 1908. Named for Clarence W. Turner, hardware dealer and rancher.

TURNER FALLS. Distinctive

and well-known scenic feature on Honey Creek, located 6 miles south of Davis, in Murray County. Named for Mazeppa T. Turner of Virginia, credited with its discovery.

TURNEY. In western Texas County, 6 miles southeast of Eva. A post office from April 26, 1907, to October 31, 1910. No longer in existence, it was named for Charles B. Turney, first postmaster.

TURPIN. Formerly Lorena. In northwestern Beaver County, 18 miles east of Hooker. Post office moved 3 miles southeast and name changed to Turpin, April 8, 1925. Named for C. J. Turpin of Oklahoma City, railroad developer.

TUSCANIA. In Cherokee County, 6 miles northeast of Tahlequah. A post office from June 12, 1919, to November 30, 1929. The name is an adaptation of Tuscany, the name of a region in Italy.

TUSHKA. Formerly Dayton. In Atoka County, 5 miles south of Atoka. Post office name changed to Tushka, June 9, 1909. The name is the Choctaw word for warrior.

TUSKAHOMA. In northern Pushmataha County, 4 miles east of Clayton. Last capital of the Choctaw Nation. Post office established February 27, 1884. Until October 28, 1891, the official spelling of the post office was Tushka Homma, and until December 6, 1910, the official spelling of the post office was Tushkahomma. The name is the

Choctaw word meaning "red warrior."

TUSKEGEE. In southeastern Creek County, 15 miles northwest of Okmulgee. A post office from April 6, 1872, to September 30, 1957. Its name comes from a Creek town in Macon County, Alabama. The word is probably a corruption of the Creek word *taskialgi*, meaning "warrior."

TUSSY. In northwestern Carter County, 5 miles northwest of Ratliff City. Post office established March 1, 1890. Named for Henry B. Tussy, rancher and cattleman.

TUTTLE. In northern Grady County, 9 miles east of Minco. Post office established August 14, 1902. Named for James H. Tuttle, local rancher.

TWIN OAKS. In southern Delaware County, 4 miles west of Kansas. Post office established August 29, 1946.

TWINE. Present Taft, in Muskogee County. Post office established March 28, 1902, and name changed to Taft, November 18, 1904. Named for W. H. Twine, early-day resident.

TYLER. In Marshall County, 10 miles west of Madill. A post office from January 31, 1899, to July 31, 1919.

TYLERTON. A rural community in Washington County, adjoining Dewey and now part of the townsite of Dewey. Plat filed November

28, 1906. Named for Frank E. Tyler, townsite owner.

TYROLA. In northern Pontotoc County, 10 miles north of Ada. A post office from May 4, 1896, to April 15, 1922. The name was coined with reference to the Tyrol, a region in Austria.

TYRONE. In Texas County, 10 miles northeast of Hooker. Post office established July 26, 1902. A former Tyrone had been established in Texas County on May 5, 1892; its name was changed to Barcross and the post office moved to Kansas, September 20, 1898. Its name comes from county Tyrone, Ulster, Ireland.

U

UDORA. In southeastern Blaine County, 7 miles northeast of Geary. A post office from February 20, 1895, to September 30, 1911. The name was coined from New Dora, referring to Dora, Alabama.

ULAN. In northwestern Pittsburg County, 14 miles northwest of McAlester. A post office from July 3, 1917, to November 30, 1953. Named for Ulan Jones, son of Joe Jones, local ranch foreman.

ULM. Present Leach, in Delaware County. Post office established March 1, 1890, and name changed to Leach, February 20, 1897. Took its name from nearby Ulm Prairie. The word is a corruption of the original name of Elm Prairie.

UNCAS. In Kay County, 6 miles west of Kaw. A post office from June 21, 1895, to May 31, 1956. Named for Uncas, Mohegan chief. The word is from *wonkus*, meaning "fox."

UNCHUKA. In Coal County, 5 miles northeast of Coalgate. A post office from August 9, 1907, to July 30, 1910. The name is from the Choctaw words *an chuka*, meaning "my house."

UNGER. In Choctaw County, 5 miles east of Boswell. A post office from December 8, 1910, to October 18, 1922. Named for Mike Unger, deputy United States marshal.

UNGLES. In central Pittsburg County. A post office from August 21, 1897, to March 3, 1898. Named for Wolford Ungles, rancher and cattleman.

UNION. In Canadian County, 6 miles north of Minco. Original townsite plat name was Sherman. Post office established August 28, 1889. Known popularly as Union City.

UNION MISSION. Site in Mayes County, 5 miles east of Mazie. A mission to the Osages, opened September 1, 1821, by the United Foreign Mission Society. Site of the oldest marked grave in Oklahoma, dated June 7, 1825, and the location of the first printing press in Oklahoma.

USNA. In eastern Cimarron County, 9 miles southeast of Keyes. A post office from January 9, 1917, to July 31, 1920. The name was coined from the initials of United States North America.

UTICA. In southeastern Bryan County, 11 miles southeast of Durant. Post office established February 14, 1894. Its name comes from Utica, New York.

V

VALERIA. On the county line, 5 miles west of Pawnee. The post office name for Lela from October 3, 1904, to March 18, 1905.

VALLEY. In Pawnee County, 10 miles southeast of Pawnee. A post office from July 26, 1894, to October 15, 1934.

VALLEY BROOK. In Oklahoma County, a separate municipality incorporated May 21, 1956, and adjoining Oklahoma City on the southeast.

VALLIANT. Formerly Fowlerville. In western McCurtain County, 10 miles east of Fort Towson. Post office name changed to Valliant, June 23, 1902. Named for F. W. Valliant, chief engineer for the Arkansas and Choctaw Railroad.

VALOROUS. In Ellis County, 9 miles southeast of Gage. A post office from January 4, 1904, to September 30, 1905. No longer in existence, it was named for Valorous Cole, first postmaster.

VAMOOSA. In southern Seminole County, 7 miles east of Konawa. A post office from May 19, 1906, to March 20, 1918. The word is a variant of the subjunctive form of the Spanish verb *ir*, and has come to mean "move along."

VANCE. In western Alfalfa County, 4 miles northwest of Lambert. A post office from June 17, 1895, to January 29, 1898. No longer in existence, it was named for Carrie C. Vance, first postmaster.

VANCE. In northeastern Wagoner County, 7 miles northeast of Broken Arrow. A post office March 28, 1902, to April 30, 1904. No longer in existence, it was named for Malinda Vance, first postmaster.

VANCE AIR FORCE BASE. In Garfield County, 1 mile south of Enid. Named for Major Robert L. Vance of Enid. He was awarded posthumously the Congressional Medal of Honor for services in Europe during World War II as a member of the United States Army Air Corps.

VANN. In southern Muskogee County, 6 miles south of Porum. A post office from July 11, 1894, to September 7, 1898. Named for Herman Vann, Cherokee jurist.

VANOSS. In western Pontotoc County, 10 miles west of Ada. Post office established January 2, 1908. Named for S. F. Vanoss, The Hague, Holland, a director of Oklahoma Central Railroad.

VASSAR. In northwestern Dewey County, 5 miles west of Vici. A post office from July 6, 1901, to July 31, 1913. Its name comes from Vassar College, Poughkeepsie, New York.

VAUGHN. In Murray County, 7 miles east of Sulphur. Post office established December 21, 1896, and name changed to Scullin, March 25, 1901.

VEAK. In Custer County, 5 miles east of Butler. A post office from May 14, 1900, to December 31, 1908. No longer in existence, it was named for Charles A. Veak, first postmaster.

VELMA. In eastern Stephens County. Post office established September 25, 1886. Named for Velma Dobbins, daughter of a local merchant and long-time resident.

VERA. In southern Washington County, 6 miles southeast of Ramona. Post office established December 15, 1899. Named for Vera Duncan, daughter of James Duncan.

VERBECK. Original railroad name for Moore, Cleveland County. The name was coined from the telegraphic call "VK."

VERDEN. On the county line, 10 miles west of Chickasha. Post office established May 5, 1899. Site of Camp Napoleon. Named for A. N. Verden, townsite developer.

VERDI. In southwestern Woodward County, 10 miles southeast of Fargo. A post office from December 22, 1902, to March 15, 1904. No longer in existence, it was named for Giuseppe Verdi, Italian composer.

VERDIGRIS. In southwestern Rogers County, 7 miles southwest of Claremore. A post office from March 12, 1880, to November 15, 1954. Took its name from nearby Verdigris River.

VERDIGRIS RIVER. An important feature of the drainage system of northeastern Oklahoma. Originally known as Persimmon River. The name is from two French words, *vert*, meaning "green," and *gris*, meaning "grey."

VERNE. In southeastern Cimarron County, 5 miles north of Griggs. A post office from May 9, 1907, to May 31, 1910. No longer in existence, it was named for Jules Verne, author.

VERNON. In southwestern McIntosh County, 10 miles southeast of Dustin. Post office established March 20, 1912. On April 13, 1914, the post office was moved 5 miles east. Named for Bishop William T. Vernon, registrar of the treasury.

VERNON. In northwestern Roger Mills County, 12 miles west of Roll. A post office from December 5, 1904, to March 30, 1908. No longer in existence.

VETO. In southern Jefferson County, 5 miles east of Terral. A post office from December 24, 1882, to April 8, 1893. No longer in existence.

VIAN. In western Sequoyah County, 10 miles west of Sallisaw. Post office established May 6, 1886. The name is a corruption of the French word *viande*, meaning "meat."

VICARS. In Creek County, 13

miles north of Bristow. A post office from April 8, 1900, to September 15, 1903. No longer in existence, it was named for John R. Vicars, first postmaster.

VICI. In northwestern Dewey County. Post office established February 15, 1900. Named by Burt Vincent in jest from the Latin phrase *veni, vidi, vici.*

VICMURDOCK. In eastern Caddo County, 7 miles east of Gracemont. A post office from May 21, 1904, to September 30, 1905. No longer in existence, it was named for Victor Murdock, publisher of the *Wichita Eagle.*

VICTOR. In Pontotoc County, 5 miles south of Harden City. A post office from February 21, 1894, to April 4, 1899. No longer in existence, it was named for Alfred Victor, early-day resident.

VICTOR. In Le Flore County, 5 miles west of Wister. A post office from May 1, 1901, to October 15, 1925.

VICTORY. In Jackson County, 6 miles west of Altus. A post office from April 22, 1892, to October 31, 1906. The name was adopted by the local residents to denote their victory in obtaining a post office.

VILAS. In southeastern Major County, 5 miles northeast of Okeene. A post office from March 8, 1894, to April 30, 1903. No longer in existence, it was named for William F. Vilas, postmaster general and secretary of the interior.

VILLA. A former rural community in eastern Payne County, 7 miles northeast of Cushing. Townsite plat filed November 16, 1914. No longer in existence.

VILLAGE, THE. A separate municipality incorporated in 1950 and adjoining Oklahoma City on the northwest. Its name comes from Euclid Village, a suburb of Cleveland, Ohio.

VILOTT. Present Nardin, in Kay County. Post office established February 2, 1894, and name changed to Nardin, April 12, 1898. Named for Charles W. Vilott, first postmaster.

VINCO. In Payne County, 1 mile south of Perkins. A post office from March 5, 1903, to October 15, 1940. First known locally as Main; original townsite name was Stanton. The name is from the Latin word meaning "I conquer."

VINING. In Alfalfa County, 12 miles east of Cherokee. A post office from August 10, 1894, to May 14, 1930. So named because of a local abundance of trumpet vines.

VINITA. County seat of Craig County. Record Town for Recording District No. 2, Indian Territory. The name was coined by E. C. Boudinot as a diminutive of Vinnie Ream, the name of a well-known sculptress.

VINSON. Formerly Trotter. In Harmon County, 20 miles west of Mangum. Post office name changed to Vinson, August 20, 1903. Named for Henry B. Vinson, townsite owner.

VIOLA. In Johnston County, 3 miles south of Bromide. Post office established June 30, 1890, and name changed to Springbrook, July 17, 1906. Named for Viola Jackson, daughter of W. H. Jackson, territorial jurist.

VIOLET. In southeastern Pottawatomie County, 2 miles northwest of Konawa. A post office from April 6, 1899, to September 29, 1906. Townsite name was Violet Springs. Took its name from nearby springs of that name.

VIRGEL. Present Capron, in Woods County. Formerly Sterling. Post office name changed to Virgel October 25, 1895, and changed to Capron, February 20, 1899. Named for Virgel Gregg, son of B. S. Gregg, first postmaster.

VIRGIL. In Choctaw County, 7 miles north of Sawyer. A post office from July 10, 1914, to September 14, 1940. Named for Virgil Lewis, son of E. F. Lewis, first postmaster.

VIRGINIA. Townsite name for Autwine in Kay County. Townsite plat filed June 21, 1899.

VISTA. In Pottawatomie County, 5 miles east of Asher. A post office from December 22, 1900, to December 14, 1905. The name has reference to the exceptional view afforded from the site.

VIVIAN. In McIntosh County, 8 miles west of Eufaula. A post office from January 13, 1910, to September 30, 1947. Named for Vivian Wilhite, local resident.

VOCA. In southern Atoka County, 5 miles northeast of Kenefic. A post office from January 16, 1906, to June 30, 1913. The name is the Latin word for mouth or voice.

VONTON. In Woodward County, 8 miles southeast of Woodward. A post office from December 2, 1902, to July 16, 1906. The name was coined from the middle name of Wesley Von Kneisley, first postmaster.

VRONA. In northeastern Sequoyah County, 12 miles north of Muldrow. Post office established July 11, 1912, and name changed to Nicut, December 16, 1925.

VROOMAN. In western Caddo County, 11 miles north of Carnegie. A post office from March 4, 1902, to July 31, 1903. No longer in existence, it was named for Vrooman Hyde, first postmaster.

W

WACO. Present Chickasha, in Grady County. Post office established October 20, 1890, and name changed to Pensee, September 11, 1891. Its name comes from the Waco tribe of Indians. The word is from the French name, *Houechas.*

WACO. In western Pottawatomie County, 10 miles west of Shawnee. A post office from June 12, 1900, to February 13, 1904. Took its name from the Waco tribe of Indians.

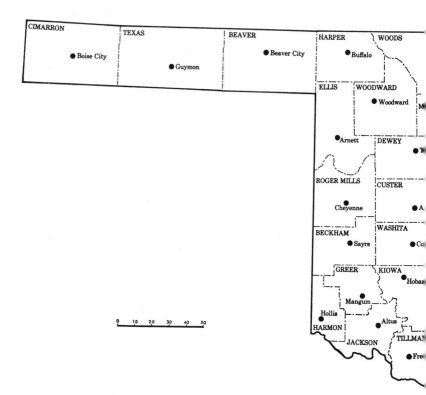

Oklahoma Counties, Today
Reproduced from *Historical Atlas of Oklahoma,* by John W. Morris and
Edwin C. McReynolds. Copyright 1965 by the University of Oklahoma
Press.

Oklahoma Place Names

WADDELL'S STATION. Site in Atoka County, 3 miles west of Wesley. A stage stop on the Butterfield Overland Mail route to California which crossed southeastern Oklahoma, 1858–61. Later known as Rogers Station.

WADE. A county in Apukshunnubbee District, Choctaw Nation. Named for Alfred Wade, prominent Choctaw.

WADE. In Bryan County, 11 miles south of Bokchito. A post office from October 24, 1890, to November 30, 1971. Named for Alfred Wade, prominent Choctaw.

WADEVILLE. In western Le Flore County, several miles east of Talihina. A post office from November 19, 1877, to January 2, 1884. No longer in existence, it was named for Alfred Wade, first postmaster.

WAGONER. County seat of Wagoner County. Record Town for Recording District No. 7, Indian Territory. Post office established February 25, 1888. Named for "Big Foot" Wagoner of Parsons, Kansas, train dispatcher.

WAGONER COUNTY. A county in northeastern Oklahoma, created at statehood. Took its name from the principal town of the county.

WAGOZA. In Pottawatomie County, 9 miles west of Asher. Formerly Oberlin. Post office name changed to Wagoza, July 18, 1881, and discontinued June 9, 1884.

WAU-TI-AU-CAH. In Osage County, 6 miles northwest of Skiatook. A post office for a short period in 1880. Named for Wau-ti-au-cah, an Osage sub-chief.

WAINWRIGHT. In western Muskogee County, 18 miles east of Okmulgee. Post office established October 20, 1905. Named for W. H. Wainwright, local banker.

WAKITA. In northwestern Grant County. Post office established November 14, 1893. The name is a Cherokee word indicating water collected in a depression, such as a buffalo wallow.

WALDON. In northeastern Grady County, 8 miles northwest of Newcastle. A post office from November 23, 1892, to February 15, 1905. No longer in existence, it was named for Hosea Waldon, early-day merchant.

WALKER. Formerly Sandy. In Garvin County, 7 miles east of Pauls Valley. Post office name changed to Walker, September 14, 1897, and discontinued January 31, 1912. Named for Dr. T. Walker, early-day physician. The popular local name for the community was Sevenshooter.

WALKER'S STATION. Site at Skullyville in Le Flore County. A stage stop on the Butterfield Overland Mail route to California, which crossed southeastern Oklahoma, 1858–61. Named for Tandy Walker, Choctaw chief.

WALLACE. In southern Okfuskee County, 7 miles south of Okemah. A post office from January 10, 1911, to April 30, 1919. Named for Joseph Wallace, first postmaster.

WALLS. In western Le Flore County, 7 miles north of Fanshawe. A post office from April 17, 1894, to March 15, 1934. Named for Benjamin F. Wall, first postmaster.

WALLVILLE. In northwestern Garvin County, 5 miles southwest of Maysville. A post office from March 7, 1891, to May 15, 1919. Named for Noah Wall, early-day resident.

WALNER. Present Wynnewood, in Garvin County. Post office established January 8, 1886, and name changed to Wynnewood, April 6, 1887. Named for John H. Walner, early-day settler.

WALNUT. In Mayes County, 6 miles northwest of Spavinaw. A post office from March 25, 1890, to March 31, 1905. On October 30, 1905, a post office named Lynch was established nearby.

WALTERS. County seat of Cotton County. Post office established September 27, 1901. Until July 23, 1917, the official name of the post office was Walter. Named for William R. Walter, prominent local resident.

WALTHALL. In Major County, 5 miles southwest of Ringwood. A post office from April 23, 1894, to January 31, 1906. No longer in existence. The name was coined from that of Walter Hall, local resident.

WANAMAKER. In Kingfisher County, 7 miles east of Dover. A post office from March 25, 1890, to December 31, 1911. Named for John Wanamaker, postmaster general under President Benjamin Harrison.

WANDEL. In eastern Kingfisher County, 10 miles northeast of Kingfisher. A post office from May 5, 1890, to March 15, 1904. No longer in existence, it was named for Benjamin M. Wandel, first postmaster.

WANETTE. In southern Pottawatomie County, 7 miles west of Asher. Post office established March 19, 1894. The name is a variant of "Juanita," a song popular at the time.

WANN. Formerly Coon. In northwestern Nowata County, 7 miles east of Copan. Post office name changed to Wann, October 13, 1899. Named for Robert F. Wann, prominent local Cherokee.

WAPANUCKA. In northeastern Johnston County, 17 miles west of Atoka. Site of the Chickasaw Rock Academy, a girls school established by the Chickasaw Nation in 1852. A post office established March 5, 1883, at the academy was in operation until 1911. The name is a Delaware word, referring to the Delaware Indians and meaning "eastern people." On December 17, 1888, the post office was moved 4 miles east to its present location.

WARD. In northern Le Flore County, 4 miles west of Spiro. A post office from June 20, 1892, to July 31, 1909. Named for a prominent Choctaw family of Spiro. Jefferson B. Ward was town mayor and J. H. Ward was county judge of Skullyville County.

WARDSPRINGS. In western Pittsburg County, several miles east of Stuart. A post office from July 10, 1914, to April 15, 1920. Named for Sam Ward, long-time resident.

WARDVILLE. Formerly Herbert. In northern Atoka County, 14 miles northeast of Coalgate. Post office name changed to Wardville, July 18, 1907. Named for H. P. Ward, territorial jurist.

WARNER. Formerly Hereford. In southern Muskogee County. Post office name changed to Warner, April 22, 1905. Named for William Warner, United States senator from Missouri.

WARR ACRES. Municipality located adjacent to, and northwest of Oklahoma City. Incorporated in 1948; named for C. B. Warr, Oklahoma City developer and civic leader.

WARREN. In northeastern Jackson County, 3 miles east of Blair. A post office from February 25, 1888, to March 31, 1920. Named for William Warren, early-day settler.

WARWICK. In Lincoln County, 8 miles west of Chandler. Post office established October 26, 1892. Its name comes from the county in England.

WASH. In Beckham County, 7 miles southeast of Sayre. A post office from July 6, 1898, to January 31, 1908. No longer in existence.

WASHINGTON. In McClain County, 10 miles northwest of Purcell. Post office established May 10, 1904. Named for George Washington, Caddo chief.

WASHINGTON COUNTY. A county in northeastern Oklahoma, created at statehood. Named for George Washington.

WASHITA. In Caddo County, 6 miles west of Anadarko. Site of the Wichita Indian Agency prior to the Civil War. Location of a Civil War engagement, October 23, 1862. Post office established April 16, 1910. Took its name from nearby Washita River.

WASHITA. In Murray County, 3 miles north of Davis. A post office from August 11, 1887, to October 31, 1900. No longer in existence, it took its name from nearby Washita River.

WASHITA COUNTY. A county in west-central Oklahoma, identical in area to Washita County, Oklahoma Territory. Took its name from the Washita River.

WASHITA RIVER. The principal drainage system for south-central Oklahoma, and a tributary of the Red River. The French form of the word is Ouachita and the English is Washita. The name is from two Choctaw words, *owa* and *chito*, meaning "big hunt."

WASHUNGA. In eastern Kay County, 1 mile north of Kaw. A

post office from November 15, 1902, to November 15, 1918. Until September 25, 1906, the official spelling of the post office was Washungo. A post office named Kaw Agency was located at the site from June 28, 1880, to October 15, 1892. Named for Chief Washunga, well-known Kaw leader. The word means bird.

WASSON. In northeastern Craig County, 6 miles north of Welch. A post office from May 24, 1892, to August 15, 1906. The community was also known as Russell Creek. Named for F. H. Wasson, local merchant.

WATCHORN. In western Pawnee County, 11 miles northwest of Pawnee. A post office from April 4, 1925, to July 15, 1926. Named for Dr. Robert Watchorn, of Redlands, California, oil producer.

WATERLOO. In southern Logan County, 5 miles north of Edmond. A post office from April 9, 1892, to June 6, 1930. The original townsite name was Brayton. Because of a steep grade near the site, a Santa Fe Railway engineer almost "met his Waterloo," and the place was so named.

WATKINS. In southwestern Love County. Post office established May 17, 1883, and name changed to Courtney, August 17, 1886. Named for William R. Watkins, prominent early-day rancher.

WATONGA. County seat of Blaine County. Post office established March 23, 1892. Named for Wa-ton-gha, Arapaho chief. The word means black coyote.

WATOVA. In southern Nowata County, 6 miles south of Nowata. A post office from April 9, 1892, to February 29, 1956. Named for Chief Watova, Osage leader. The word means spider.

WATSON. In northeastern McCurtain County, 6 miles southeast of Smithville. Post office established January 25, 1908. Named for Larsen D. Watson, townsite owner.

WATSONVILLE. In northeastern Hughes County, 12 miles east of Wetumka. Post office established April 18, 1898, and name changed to Spokogee, June 27, 1902.

WATTS. In northeastern Adair County. Post office established March 30, 1912. Named for John Watts, or Young Tassle, chief of the Chickamauga Cherokees.

WAUHILLAU. In western Adair County, 10 miles northwest of Stilwell. A post office from February 13, 1879, to March 15, 1935. The name is from the Cherokee word *awa'hili*, meaning "eagle."

WAUKOMIS. In Garfield County, 5 miles south of Enid. Post office established November 25, 1893. The name is generally believed to be a modification of "walk home us," arising from the circumstance that at one time certain railroad officials were required to walk back to Enid.

WAURIKA. Designated county seat of Jefferson County on Febru-

251

ary 24, 1912, by proclamation of the governor. Post office established June 28, 1902. Named by M. A. Lowe of the Rock Island Railroad as an adaptation of an Indian word meaning "pure water."

WAYNE. In McClain County, 6 miles south of Purcell. Post office established December 11, 1890. Took its name from Wayne, Pennsylvania.

WAYNOKA. Formerly Keystone. In southwestern Woods County. Post office name changed to Waynoka, April 10, 1889. The name is from a Cheyenne word meaning "sweet water."

WEALAKA. In southeastern Tulsa County, 2 miles northwest of Leonard. A post office from April 8, 1880, to August 31, 1910. Site of Wealaka Mission, established 1881. The name is a Creek word meaning "rising water."

WEATHERFORD. In southeastern Custer County. A post office from August 25, 1893, to September 26, 1898. On October 28, 1898, a nearby post office named Dewey changed its name to Weatherford, thus continuing the name. Named for William J. Weatherford, deputy United States marshal.

WEATHERS. In southeastern Pittsburg County, 12 miles south of Hartshorne. A post office from May 14, 1914, to August 31, 1944. Named for John L. Weathers, first postmaster.

WEAVERTON. In Marshall County, 6 miles southwest of Ma-

dill. A post office from April 4, 1898, to December 31, 1908. No longer in existence, it was named for James E. Weaver, first postmaster.

WEBB. In Dewey County, 8 miles southeast of Camargo. A post office from April 17, 1902, to June 30, 1955. Took its name from Webb Township, which had been named for Henry J. Webb, pioneer resident.

WEBB. In Payne County, 3 miles southeast of Stillwater. A post office from April 12, 1895, to March 14, 1896. No longer in existence, it was named for John T. Webb, pioneer resident.

WEBB CITY. In northwestern Osage County. Post office established December 16, 1922. Named for Horace Webb, townsite owner.

WEBBERS FALLS. In southeastern Muskogee County. Post office established July 15, 1856. Named for Walter Webber, Cherokee chief.

WEBSTER. In Muskogee County, 3 miles northeast of Taft. A post office from September 26, 1908, to November 15, 1926. Named for Charles Webster, first postmaster.

WECHARTY. Formerly Timber. In Hughes County, 5 miles south of Holdenville. Post office name changed to Wecharty, August 2, 1904, and discontinued January 15, 1912. Located at the site of old Fort Holmes, it had been named Bilby by the railroad. Wecharty is from the Creek word *we-care-tu*, meaning "to make sparks," and has reference to a blacksmith shop.

WEEKS. In southwestern Ellis County, 16 miles southwest of Arnett. A post office from January 13, 1906, to April 30, 1910. No longer in existence, it was named for John Weeks, first postmaster.

WEER. On the county line, 6 miles south of Broken Arrow. A post office from February 21, 1894, to November 30, 1906. No longer in existence, it was named for John E. Weer, local gin operator.

WEKIWA. In western Tulsa County, 1 mile west of Sand Springs. A post office from April 21, 1906, to June 30, 1931. The name is from the Creek words *uewe kiwa*, meaning "spring" or "well of water," and has the same origin as the name Sand Springs.

WELCH. In Craig County, 13 miles west of Miami. Post office established July 13, 1892. Named for A. L. Welch, railroad official.

WELCOME. In Tulsa County, 6 miles southeast of Tulsa. Post office established May 17, 1905, and name changed to Alsuma, February 12, 1906.

WELDON. Present Copan, in Washington County. Formerly Lawton. Post office name changed to Weldon, July 10, 1901, and name changed to Copan, February 27, 1904.

WELEETKA. In southern Okfuskee County, 10 miles southeast of Okemah. Post office established March 14, 1902. The name is the Creek word meaning "running water."

WELLING. In Cherokee County, 5 miles southeast of Tahlequah. Post office established April 19, 1899. Named for Mrs. L. E. Welling, sister of Margaret McCarrell, prominent Park Hill resident.

WELLINGTON. In western Muskogee County, 3 miles northwest of Boynton. Post office established June 3, 1890, and name changed to Lee, July 22, 1892.

WELLS. A former rural community in Kiowa County, 7 miles southwest of Gotebo. Townsite plat filed August 20, 1910. No longer in existence, it was named for Robert B. Wells, townsite owner.

WELLSTON. In western Lincoln County. Post office established September 19, 1884. Named for Christian T. Wells, licensed Indian trader.

WELTY. In northern Okfuskee County, 8 miles west of Okfuskee. Post office established October 12, 1905. Named for Edwin A. Welty, townsite developer.

WESLEY. In northern Atoka County, 10 miles south of Kiowa. A post office from October 2, 1903, to May 15, 1955.

WESNER. In Harper County, 10 miles northwest of Buffalo. A post office from May 7, 1903, to March 30, 1907. Named for A. F. Wesner, local resident.

WEST. In southwestern Logan County, 4 miles southeast of Cashion. A post office from January 9, 1893, to August 30, 1902. No longer in existence, it was named for Charles West, first postmaster.

WESTBROOK. In Pawnee County, 1 mile south of Hallett. Townsite plat filed October 10, 1902. No longer in existence, it was named for Daniel West, townsite owner.

WESTON. In southeastern Woodward County, 6 miles east of Mutual. A post office from May 22, 1899, to April 18, 1907. No longer in existence.

WESTPOINT. In northeastern Payne County, 4 miles southeast of Glencoe. A post office from March 13, 1894, to March 15, 1904. No longer in existence. Its name comes from West Point, New York.

WEST TULSA. Now a part of Tulsa, in Tulsa County. Post office established October 4, 1907, and discontinued December 31, 1917, to become West Tulsa Station.

WESTVILLE. In northeastern Adair County. Post office established November 18, 1895. County seat of Adair County from statehood to March 1, 1910. Named for Samuel D. West, local resident.

WETUMKA. In northern Hughes County, 15 miles northeast of Holdenville. Post office established February 1, 1881. Its name comes from a Creek town on Coosa River, Elmore County, Alabama. The name is a Creek word meaning "tumbling water."

WEWOKA. County seat of Seminole County. Record Town for Recording District No. 13, Indian Territory. Capital of the Seminole Nation. Post office established May 13, 1867. The name is an ancient place name in Elmore County, Alabama, and is a Creek word meaning "roaring water."

WEWOKA SWITCH. Not a site or place, but Oklahoma's own unique contribution to the English language. Meaning "caught in a dilemma" or to "be in a tight," the phrase originated shortly before 1900 when freight was often lost or misplaced due to the congested condition of the newly laid railroad switch to Wewoka.

WHEATLAND. In southwestern Oklahoma County. Post office established February 10, 1902. Took its name from the principal local agricultural product.

WHEELER. In western Carter County, 7 miles north of Wilson. Post office established May 8, 1896, and name changed to Oil City, October 15, 1909. Named for Martin Wheeler, early-day hotel proprietor.

WHEELESS. In western Cimarron County, 21 miles west of Boise City. A post office from February 12, 1907, to September 27, 1963. Named for William Wheeless, first postmaster.

WHEELING. In western Comanche County, 6 miles north of Indiahoma. A post office from December 17, 1903, to November 15, 1907.

Took its name from Wheeling, West Virginia.

WHEELOCK. In western McCurtain County, adjoining present Millerton. A post office from March 21, 1845, to May 3, 1895, located at the site of Wheelock Academy. On December 15, 1902, a post office named Parsons was established at this same site. Named for Eleazar Wheelock, first president of Dartmouth College.

WHISLER. In northwestern Oklahoma County, 6 miles west of Edmond. A post office from June 9, 1890, to July 30, 1904. No longer in existence, it was named for W. L. Whisler, first postmaster.

WHITE. In Garfield County, 5 miles southwest of Garber. A post office from April 14, 1894, to January 15, 1903. No longer in existence, it was named for H. D. White, first postmaster.

WHITE. In Le Flore County, 11 miles west of Heavener. A post office from August 27, 1906, to April 30, 1921. Named for Livingston B. White, local resident.

WHITEAGLE. Formerly Ponca. In southern Kay County, 5 miles south of Ponca City. Post office name changed to Whiteagle, August 21, 1896, and discontinued June 15, 1926. Site often known as White Eagle Agency. Named for White Eagle, prominent Ponca Indian chief.

WHITEBEAD. Formerly White Bead Hill. In Garvin County, 5 miles northwest of Pauls Valley.

Post office name changed to Whitebead, April 26, 1895, and discontinued June 15, 1912. The name is a continuation of that of the former post office.

WHITE BEAD HILL. In Garvin County, 5 miles northwest of Pauls Valley. Post office established May 5, 1876, and name changed to Whitebead, April 26, 1895. Named for Chief White Bead of the Caddos.

WHITEFIELD. Formerly Oklahoma. In northwestern Haskell County, 6 miles west of Stigler. Post office name changed to Whitefield, November 27, 1888. Named for Bishop George Whitefield, early-day Methodist leader.

WHITEHEAD. In northeastern Ellis County, 13 miles southwest of Woodward. Post office established October 14, 1893, and name changed to Oleta, August 24, 1901. Named for E. E. Whitehead, early-day druggist.

WHITEOAK. In Craig County, 7 miles west of Vinita. A post office from October 31, 1898, to October 31, 1957.

WHITEROCK. Formerly Arnold. In northwestern Noble County, 4 miles southeast of Billings. Post office name changed to Whiterock, December 14, 1894, and discontinued September 30, 1915. The name was coined from that of Richard M. White, townsite owner.

WHITESBORO. In western Le Flore County, 10 miles southeast of

Talihina. Post office established April 14, 1909. Named for Paul White, early-day settler.

WHITE WATER. In northeastern Delaware County, about 10 miles southeast of Grove. A post office from April 1, 1873, to July 9, 1886. No longer in existence. Took its name from nearby Whitewater Creek, a tributary of Grand River.

WHITING. In northeastern Ottawa County. A post office from October 3, 1882, to May 6, 1885. No longer in existence, it was named for Ida Whiting, first postmaster.

WHITMIRE. In northeastern Cherokee County, 7 miles south of Oaks. A post office from September 23, 1897, to September 30, 1913. Named for J. R. Whitmire, proprietor of an early-day general store.

WHIZBANG. Local name for Denoya in Osage County. Took its name from *Captain Billy's Whizbang*, a magazine popular at the time.

WICHITA. A county in Chickasaw District, Choctaw Nation. Later part of Chickasaw Nation.

WICHITA. In Comanche County, a few miles northwest of Fort Sill. A post office from December 5, 1901, to March 31, 1902. Took its name from nearby Wichita Mountains.

WICHITA MOUNTAINS. A prominent land feature in southwestern Oklahoma, lying from central Comanche County to southern Kiowa County. Took its name from the Wichita tribe of Indians. The word is from the Choctaw *wia chitoh*, meaning "big arbor." In Spanish the tribe is known as *Jumano*, and in that language the mountains are known as the *Sierra Jumano*.

WIGWAM NEOSHO. Site in southeastern Wagoner County, 2 miles east of Okay. The name of a trading post operated by Sam Houston from 1829 to 1833.

WILBER. In northern Kay County, 8 miles west of Chilocco. A post office from May 9, 1894, to November 30, 1908. No longer in existence, it was named for Decie L. Wilber, first postmaster.

WILBURTON. County seat of Latimer County. Post office established January 2, 1891. Named for Elisha Wilbur, president of the Lehigh Valley Railroad.

WILCOX. In Garfield County, 7 miles west of Enid. A post office from February 27, 1895, to August 31, 1903. No longer in existence, it was named for George C. Wilcox, early-day resident.

WILDCAT. In southeastern Okmulgee County, 11 miles southeast of Okmulgee. Post office established May 19, 1897, and name changed to Grayson, February 20, 1902.

WILDMAN. In southern Kiowa County, 4 miles southeast of Roosevelt. A post office from May 3, 1901, to November 15, 1904. Named for Frank R. Wildman, banker and mining developer.

WILDWOOD. In southwestern Garfield County, 4 miles east of Ames. A post office from December 4, 1894, to May 31, 1905. No longer in existence. The name is a combination of *Wiley*, the last name of James P. Wiley, first postmaster, and *timber*, referring to a nearby timber grove.

WILKINS. In southern Cimarron County, 16 miles southwest of Boise City. A post office from May 19, 1905, to January 31, 1930.

WILLARD. In northern Harper County, 10 miles northwest of Buffalo. A post office from February 27, 1902, to January 31, 1924.

WILLIAMS. In Le Flore County, 3 miles east of Panama. A post office from October 14, 1904, to July 31, 1954. Named for Rev. Alexander S. Williams, prominent Choctaw.

WILLIS. In Marshall County, 15 miles south of Madill. Post office established March 15, 1886. Named for Britt Willis, long-time local resident.

WILLOW. In Greer County, 10 miles north of Mangum. Post office established October 17, 1899. The name was adapted from that of William O'Connell, first postmaster.

WILLOWBAR. Present Keyes, in Cimarron County. Post office established October 5, 1906, and name changed to Keyes, October 15, 1926. The Willowbar post office was in several different locations, all several miles southwest of Keyes. Its name comes from nearby Willow Bar Crossing on the Cimarron River.

WILLOWVALE. In southern Jackson County, 5 miles southwest of Olustee. A post office from April 18, 1890, to November 30, 1903. No longer in existence.

WILLZETTA. Formerly Guild. In southeastern Lincoln County, 4 miles northwest of Prague. Post office name changed to Willzetta, July 2, 1904, and discontinued June 30, 1909. The name was coined from the names of William and Emma Johnson, townsite owners.

WILSCOT. In Le Flore County, 13 miles south of Heavener. A post office from August 19, 1930, to March 31, 1934. The name was coined from the name of William T. Scott, first postmaster.

WILSON. In southeastern Carter County, 7 miles southeast of Ardmore. A post office from April 4, 1888, to August 15, 1907. No longer in existence. Named for J. H. Wilson, local merchant.

WILSON. Formerly New Wilson. In Carter County, 17 miles west of Ardmore. Post office name changed to Wilson, January 28, 1920. Named for Charles Wilson, secretary to John Ringling, circus owner.

WILSON. In Pushmataha County, 12 miles north of Antlers. A post office from October 15, 1908, to August 15, 1910. No longer in existence, it was named for Benjamin D. Wilson, first postmaster.

WIMER. In Craig County, 12 miles northeast of Lenapah. A post office from December 20, 1899, to May 31, 1933. Named for Dr. James Wimer, early-day resident.

WINCHESTER. In northern Woods County, 13 miles northwest of Alva. A post office from June 5, 1894, to August 31, 1939. Took its name from the Winchester rifle.

WINDING STAIR. A mountain range in eastern Oklahoma serving as a divide between the Arkansas and Red rivers. Name first applied by early-day army personnel when a military road surveyed through the mountains gave the appearance of "winding stair steps."

WINDOM. In Payne County, 6 miles southwest of Stillwater. A post office from January 18, 1890, to October 15, 1892. No longer in existence, it was named for William Windom of Minnesota, secretary of the treasury.

WINGO. In western Beckham County, 12 miles west of Sayre. A post office from April 14, 1902, to July 31, 1906. No longer in existence, it was named for James Wingo, early-day resident.

WINN. In southern Lincoln County, 5 miles west of Meeker. A post office from February 5, 1902, to February 13, 1904. No longer in existence, it was named for John C. Winn, first postmaster.

WINNVIEW. In Blaine County, 8 miles northeast of Watonga. A post office from June 23, 1892, to April 29, 1905. No longer in existence. Named for Joseph B. Winn, first postmaster.

WIRT. In Carter County, 2 miles west of Healdton. Post office established December 12, 1914. Named for Wirt Franklin, oil producer.

WISTER. In Le Flore County, 9 miles southwest of Poteau. Post office established June 30, 1890. Named for an official of the Choctaw, Oklahoma and Gulf Railroad.

WITCHER. In northeastern Oklahoma County. A post office from January 31, 1903, to May 31, 1914. Named for Daniel J. Witcher, townsite owner.

WITT. In Harmon County, 2 miles west of Hollis. A post office from April 28, 1892, to February 28, 1903. No longer in existence, it was named for John L. Witt, first postmaster.

WITTEVILLE. In Le Flore County, 4 miles northwest of Poteau. A post office from August 22, 1894, to April 30, 1908. No longer in existence, it was named for Gerhard H. Witte, first postmaster.

WOLCO. In eastern Osage County, 5 miles east of Barnsdall. A post office from December 16, 1922, to March 31, 1957. The name was coined from that of the Wolverine Oil Company.

WOLF. In Seminole County, 2 miles south of Bowlegs. A post office from February 25, 1903, to September 14, 1907. No longer in existence.

WOLF COUNTY. *See* Nashoba County, Choctaw Nation.

WOMACK. In western McClain County, 2 miles southeast of Blanchard. A post office from August 6, 1900, to August 14, 1909. Named for John C. Womack, proprietor of general store.

WOOD. In southwestern Washita County, 6 miles northwest of Sentinel. A post office from November 17, 1892, to January 31, 1906. Named for James W. Wood, early-day resident.

WOODDALE. In Major County, 11 miles southwest of Fairview. A post office from February 9, 1909, to June 15, 1926.

WOODFILL. In Comanche County, 6 miles east of Fort Sill. A post office from March 4, 1902, to February 15, 1908. No longer in existence, it was named for Lewis C. Woodfill, first postmaster.

WOODFORD. In northern Carter County, 9 miles west of Springer. Post office established February 4, 1884. Named for Woodford Smith, local intermarried Chickasaw.

WOODLAWN PARK. In Oklahoma County, a separate municipality incorporated July 28, 1952, and adjoining Oklahoma City on the northwest.

WOODROW. In Nowata County, 6 miles west of Nowata. A post office from March 27, 1913, to January 31, 1916. No longer in existence, it was named for President Woodrow Wilson.

WOODS COUNTY. A county in northwestern Oklahoma, created at statehood from a portion of Woods County, Oklahoma Territory. Flynn was also considered as the name for this county. Named for Sam Wood, Kansas political leader.

WOODVILLE. Formerly Harney. In Marshall County, 5 miles southeast of Kingston. Post office name changed to Woodville, July 9, 1888. Named for L. L. Wood, prominent Chickasaw.

WOODWARD. County seat of Woodward County. Post office established February 3, 1893. Named for Brinton W. Woodward, Santa Fe Railway director.

WOODWARD COUNTY. A county in northwestern Oklahoma, organized at statehood from a portion of Woodward County, Oklahoma Territory. Took its name from Woodward, the county's principal city.

WOOLAROC. In Osage County, 14 miles southwest of Bartlesville. Well-known ranch of the late Frank Phillips and now a game preserve and museum. The name was coined from the words woods, lakes, and rocks.

WOOLSEY. In Stephens County, 7 miles southeast of Comanche. A post office from January 21, 1891, to May 15, 1912. Named for N. B. Woolsey, early-day resident.

WOULDBE. On August 27, 1919, a post office by such name was established in Creek County near Gypsy, and on March 12, 1920, another post office by the same name was established in Noble County near Billings. Both were discontinued October 15, 1921.

WRIGHT. In Lincoln County, 7 miles southeast of Coyle. A post office from June 30, 1892, to October 15, 1904. Named for F. H. Wright, local resident.

WRIGHT CITY. Formerly Bismark. In western McCurtain County. Post office name changed to Wright, September 13, 1918, and to Wright City, May 18, 1920. Named for William W. Wright, the first soldier from McCurtain County killed in World War I. The name was changed because of Bismark's association with Germany.

WYANDOTTE. Formerly Grand River. In Ottawa County, 11 miles southeast of Miami. Post office name changed to Wyandotte, October 3, 1894. Took its name from the Wyandotte tribe of Indians. The word is Iroquoian, *wendot,* meaning "islanders."

WYANET. In western Harper County, 6 miles south of Laverne. A post office from March 24, 1902, to August 15, 1912. No longer in existence.

WYATT. In Carter County, 7 miles east of Gene Autry. A post office from September 6, 1895, to June 30, 1906. Named for Pickney F. Wyatt, first postmaster.

WYATT. In northwestern Harper County, 10 miles north of Rosston. Post office established August 25, 1905, and name changed to McKim, July 18, 1907.

WYBARK. In northern Muskogee County, 4 miles north of Muskogee. A post office from January 18, 1890, to June 30, 1940. The name is a modification of Verdark, the railroad name for the town which was coined from the names of the Verdigris and Arkansas rivers.

WYNNEWOOD. Formerly Walner. Post office name changed to Wynnewood, April 6, 1887. Took name from Wynnewood, Pennsylvania. In southern Garvin County.

WYNONA. In Osage County, 8 miles south of Pawhuska. Post office established December 17, 1903. The name is a Sioux word meaning "first-born daughter."

Y

YAHOLA. In northwestern Muskogee County, 3 miles west of Taft. A post office from October 8, 1906, to January 15, 1940. Named for Yahola Harjo, Creek allotee.

YALE. In Payne County, 17 miles east of Stillwater. Post office established October 4, 1895. Name selected by Sterling F. Underwood, first postmaster, because of a Yale lock on the post office door.

YANT. In extreme southwestern Lincoln County, 3 miles northeast of Harrah. A post office from March 12, 1901, to February 29,

1904. The name was assigned inadvertently by the Post Office Department instead of Jaunt, the name requested because the site was only a short jaunt from Oklahoma City.

YANUSH. In southern Latimer County, 6 miles north of Tuskahoma. A post office from February 6, 1911, to October 15, 1925. The name is a Choctaw word meaning "buffalo," and the post office took its name from nearby Buffalo Creek.

YARNABY. In Bryan County, 8 miles southeast of Achille. A post office from January 22, 1883, to June 31, 1957. The name is a Choctaw word meaning "to go and kill."

YARROW. In Okmulgee County, 5 miles northeast of Beggs. A post office from April 25, 1898, to October 15, 1900. Took its name from Yarrow, County Selkirk, Scotland.

YATES. In western Payne County, 7 miles east of Orlando. A post office from May 21, 1890, to December 15, 1908. Named for Yates Smith, first postmaster.

YEAGER. In Hughes County, 6 miles northeast of Holdenville. Post office established February 6, 1902. Named for Hattie Yargee, local Creek allotee, with the spelling altered by the Post Office Department.

YELDELL. In southeastern Jackson County, 2 miles northwest of Hess. A post office from May 28, 1892, to December 31, 1904. Named for the Yeldell brothers, Edd, Frank, Fenner and James, proprietors of the general store.

YELLOW HILLS. In Carter County, 7 miles east of Ardmore. Post office established November 25, 1890, and name changed to Durwood, September 11, 1891.

YELLOWSTONE. In northern Woods County, 17 miles northwest of Alva. A post office from May 22, 1909, to October 31, 1913.

YELTON. In northern Harper County, 3 miles west of Willard. A post office from February 6, 1902, to June 13, 1919. Named for Theodore A. Yelton, first postmaster.

YEWED. In Alfalfa County, 6 miles southwest of Cherokee. A post office from December 24, 1898, to April 30, 1952. Named for Admiral George Dewey, hero of the Battle of Manila Bay, Yewed is Dewey spelled backwards.

YOHO. In central Beckham County. A post office from June 4, 1901, to May 31, 1905. No longer in existence, it was named for Thomas J. Yoho, first postmaster.

YONKERS. In Wagoner County, 10 miles south of Locust Grove. A post office from January 31, 1913, to September 30, 1953. In October, 1924, the post office was moved from Cherokee County to Wagoner County. Named by William Kenefic, railroad developer, for Yonkers, New York.

YORK. In southwestern Pontotoc

County, 6 miles east of Hickory. A post office from August 17, 1894, to April 30, 1914. No longer in existence, it was named for Joseph F. York, first postmaster.

YOUNG. In Le Flore County, 5 miles south of Heavener. A post office from September 7, 1911, to November 15, 1915. Named for Clarence Young, first postmaster.

YOUNG'S CROSSING. In Pottawatomie County, 3 miles west of the southeast corner of the county. A community at the site of a principal crossing of the Canadian River. Named for George Young, townsite owner. The town fell into disuse by the time of statehood.

YOUST. In Payne County, 5 miles northeast of Stillwater. A post office from January 29, 1901, to July 14, 1905. Railroad name was Yost. Named for John Youst, Stillwater hotel proprietor.

YUBA. In southern Bryan County, 12 miles east of Achille. A post office from September 14, 1898, to November 30, 1932. On October 1, 1950, the name of the post office of Karma, located 1 mile south, was changed to Yuba and thus the name was continued.

YUKON. In eastern Canadian County. Post office established March 28, 1891. Took its name from the Yukon River in Alaska.

Z

ZAFRA. In extreme southeastern Le Flore County. A post office from June 9, 1917, to March 31, 1942.

ZANGWILL. In southwestern Garfield County, 10 miles west of Bison. A post office from January 28, 1897, to May 31, 1905. No longer in existence, it was named for Israel Zangwill, English author and man of letters.

ZEB. In Cherokee County, 10 miles southwest of Tahlequah. A post office from July 13, 1918, to October 31, 1929. Named for Zeb Keahea, local resident.

ZELMA. In northeastern Beaver County, 3 miles southeast of Knowles. A post office from April 17, 1903, to October 31, 1917. No longer in existence. Named for Zelma Hostetter, sister of first postmaster.

ZENA. In Delaware County, 12 miles northwest of Jay. A post office from April 11, 1896, to January 31, 1956. Named for Asenith Wood, whose nickname was Zeen, wife of William H. Wood, first postmaster.

ZENDA. In Ellis County, 6 miles north of Shattuck. A post office from February 28, 1903, to June 30, 1905. No longer in existence. Its name comes from *Prisoner of Zenda*, a novel by Anthony Hope.

ZENOBIA. Formerly Juanita. Present Bromide, in northeastern Johnston County. Post office name changed to Zenobia, April 27, 1906, and changed to Bromide, June 8, 1907. Named for Zenobia Jackson, daughter of W. H. Jackson, territorial jurist.

ZINCVILLE. Formerly St. Louis. In northern Ottawa County, 5 miles east of Picher. Post office name changed to Zincville, June 12, 1919, and discontinued October 31, 1954. Took its name from a local mining product.

ZINWAY. The post office name for Rooster in Choctaw County from January 28, 1921, to December 31, 1921.

ZION. In eastern Kingfisher County, 5 miles west of Crescent. A post office from July 20, 1891, to May 31, 1906. No longer in existence.

ZOE. Formerly Thomasville. In Le Flore County, 9 miles south of Heavener. Post office name changed to Zoe, June 14, 1915, and discontinued May 31, 1956. Named for Zoe Thomason, local resident.

ZORAYA. In western Pushmataha County, 5 miles northwest of Kosoma. A post office from April 22, 1905, to October 31, 1919.

ZULA. In Woods County, 12 miles southeast of Alva. Post office established June 8, 1894, site and name changed to Dacoma, October 31, 1904.

ZYBRA. In southern Garfield County, 7 miles east of Bison. A post office from April 23, 1898, to August 31, 1903. No longer in existence. The name was a colloquial word, popular in the 1890's, meaning "a moving settler."

CONTRIBUTORS

Turner Alfrey
Curtis Alpers
Mrs. H. P. Anderson
Cleve Andrew
Myron E. Andrews
Marjorie Appelman
Hazel M. Apple
W. B. Armstrong
Walter Arnote
Atchison, Topeka
   and Santa Fe
   Railway Company
Mrs. Robert L. Atkins
Bertha B. Bailey
Mary Balantine
Mrs. Frank C. Ball
Clyde Ballard
Bryce Ballinger
F. H. Balyeat
Mrs. J. Z. Barker
David A. Bartlett
C. S. Bassler
Velma Becker
Bonnie Belcher
J. I. Belford
C. R. Bell
Mrs. Robert J. Bell
Cody Bennett
Mrs. Mildred F. Bethel
R. H. Birkhead
O. K. Bivens
Mrs. Nelda Bonner
John D. Boswell
Elwood K. Bowden
Edna Bowman
H. J. Bowman
Edward M. Box
Mrs. Ina S. Boyle
Mrs. J. R. Brady

Bob Breeden
B. F. Breeding
Mrs. Pearl Briles
A. C. Brodell
Frances Rosser Brown
Ivan D. Brown
Jean Brown
Montagu K. Brown
Mrs. Victor Brown
Mrs. Ellie Bryant
Mrs. L. A. Burgess
Mrs. Frank L. Busch
Joe Bush
G. R. Butcher
Mrs. F. E. Butts
Mrs. Walter Cagg
LaRoy Caldwell
Charles J. Cansler
Mrs. Bessie Carpenter
William E. Carry
James M. Carseloway
Tom Carson
Mary Carter
Wilburn Cartwright
Fern Cassel
Mrs. Leo D. Chamberlin
Mrs. T. H. Channell
Ben P. Choate
Finis Clark, Jr.
John W. Clark
Frank Cleckler
Fred R. Clement
Glade Clemons
J. G. Clift
Orra E. Cockrell
Van D. Coffman
A. B. Cohn
Roscoe Cole
Jerome Coling

Mrs. Katherine E. Collins
Jeanne Cook
Mrs. O. J. Cook
James F. Cooper
Jack T. Conn
Robert Cotton
Edna M. Couch
J. T. Courts
Ellis A. Cowan
Bill Cox
Mrs. Myrtle Creason
Mrs. George W. Crosnoe
Mrs. Ivan Cunningham
Mrs. Aaron Curtis
Joe W. Curtis
Mrs. B. E. Darby
Mrs. William Daugherty
J. Carter Davis
Nelda Davis
Alvina Davison
Francis Davison
Mrs. Roy Decker, Jr.
George F. Defiel
Mrs. Lou Denton
Harry L. Deupree, M.D.
Mrs. Mottie Dodson
Claude Donald
Robert H. Dott
Kelly E. DuBusk
Joe L. Duer
J. H. A. Dumas
E. T. Dunlap
Joe Durham
Ruby Easley
Mrs. Seth Edwards
Lee K. Emenhiser, M.D.
Mrs. A. S. Erwin
David L. Estes
Hattie W. Evans

Mrs. Ray Farley
Harold R. Farrar
Clyde Felix
Irene Ferguson
Mrs. James H. Finley
Frank F. Finney
Ava Nell Fisher
Dorothy Fite
Mrs. Clifton Fleming
Carolyn T. Foreman
Robert S. Fox
Elmer L. Fraker
John French
Martin L. Frerichs
Mabel C. Fry
E. D. Fudge
J. G. Gaddy, Jr.
Mrs. Fannie T. Gale
Marie Garland
E. L. Garnett
G. R. Gear
A. E. Gibson
Ed Gill
Noble Glenn
Mrs. G. H. Godwin
Lahoma H. Goldsmith
Charles Good
Mrs. E. E. Gore
John S. Gould
Lona Neff Graham
C. W. Grant
Frank Greier
Robert G. Griffith
Mrs. O. L. Green
Len Green
Weldon Guest
Mrs. Hayden Guild
H. C. Hackney
A. D. Haddox, M.D.
Mrs. R. L. Hale
Alpha D. Hall
Noah W. Hall
Stuart B. Halley
Mrs. N. H. Hamilton
Wilburn Hampton

B. Frank Hance
Claude Hanna
Mrs. Jewel L. Hardy
J. L. Hargett
Joe Harp
Jean E. Harper
Mrs. Charley Harris
James A. Harris
Mrs. Nellie R. Hartsaw
Edna G. Hatfield
Mrs. Elma Heffley
Mrs. Joe Hatcher
Carl W. Held
J. H. Hendrex
Roy E. Hendricks
Guy Hensley
J. E. Heuston
Mildred Heuston
W. A. Heuston
Leon Hibbs
Mrs. W. A. Hicks
M. O. Hilderbrand
A. J. Hinkle
Frances H. Holway
Lidia Hook
Mrs. Thelma Hornbaker
T. J. Horsley
Mrs. Guy P. Horton
Eva Howard
Gladys W. Howard
Mrs. John Howard
Neil S. Howell
Wendell E. Howell
Harold Hubbard
W. H. Hudson
Helen M. Hudspeth
Mrs. J. W. Huff
Georgie Hughart
Adelle Hunt
Clark Hurd
Jack Immell
Mrs. W. L. Ivester
Gladys J. James
Mrs. Berenice Jackson
Marie W. Jamieson

Mrs. Velma Jayne
O. T. Jennings
Wynona Job
Arlain Johnson
Foster F. Johnson
Jack Johnson
Mrs. Kern Johnson
D. P. Karns
Lee Keck
Tom Keef
W. H. H. Keltner, Jr.
Wallace Kidd
Jack S. King
A. Martin Kingkade
Lula M. Klein
Leo Koetter
Georgia Kraft
Mrs. J. D. Lambert
Plessie LaMunyon
D. E. Lanham
Mrs. A. R. Larason
Clark Lawrence, Jr.
Roy Leas
E. P. Ledbetter
Robert E. Lee
Mrs. Della Lenox
Ila Lewis
Mrs. C. E. Long
Mrs. Willis McCabe
C. A. McCall
Mrs. Bessie McColgin
Richard N. McGuinn
W. E. McIntosh
W. S. McKelvy
Cliff C. McKown
George G. McMillan
Patricia McNaughton
Herbert Mann
Mrs. Lucy Markham
C. C. Martin
J. Frank Martin
Leonard Martin
O. W. Mead
Mrs. John F. Melton
Maurice H. Merrill

265

Mrs. Mary E. Merry
Thomas Metcalf
Emma G. Miller
Mary Mills
Mrs. F. W. Millwee
Norma E. Minnett
Fannie B. Misch
Hugh H. Monroe, M.D.
Lena M. Moore
Virgil W. Morris
E. Walter Morrison
L. A. Morton
R. M. Mountcastle
Clara A. Mudd
Helen Muller
Irvin W. Munn
Jerry Newby
Ruth B. Nickle
Vema Nieberding
Joann Nitzel
Mrs. F. W. Nuckolls
Carl B. O'Daniel
Dorothy J. Orton
G. L. Packer
Fred L. Patrick
B. B. Patterson
Linnie E. Patton
Frazier Pierce
John Ploszay
Mrs. Flora B. Porter
Mrs. C. V. Poteet
Roy R. Potter
W. E. Pryor
Henry A. Quillin
Mrs. A. M. Quinby
H. D. Ragland
John H. Rains
E. M. Rector
Clarence Reeds
Mildred Reeds
Cecil Rhoades
Lester R. Rhoades
Mrs. Roy A. Richardson
Nola Rigdon
M. S. Robertson

Frances Rodgers
B. O. Roop
Ralph G. Rose
M. C. Rouse
Florence B. Rowland
George Rowland
Joe Ruffin
Kent Ruth
Nellie M. Ryan
J. A. Sackett
St. Louis–San Francisco
   Railway Company
Sara Salmon
Erma F. Schmalzried
Mrs. W. V. Schoonover
Perry Scoggins
Mrs. Penn Scott
A. H. Seigfried
Grace M. Seitler
Mrs. Lou Selby
Mrs. Grace Sersain
Tom Seymour
Ben Sharp
Ira C. Shimp
L. L. Shirley
Mrs. Myrtle Short
Delbert Shugars
C. R. Sibley
Gaspare Signorelli
Lydia M. Simpson
Mrs. Cecil Sims
Mrs. E. H. Smallwood
J. M. Smith
Julia B. Smith
Lee Todd Smith
Mrs. R. J. Smith
Mrs. Virgil Snell
Helen W. Snow
H. G. Spivey
Don E. Sporleder
Jack Stone
C. E. Sturgeon
Mrs. J. W. Sullins
Sam Sullivan
Mrs. D. S. Talbot

Bill Tharp
Bonnie P. Thomas
Jesse Thomas
Wade M. Thomas
Myrtle Thompson
Mrs. Marvin Ton
George Townsend
Mae Turner
Mary Jo Turner
Mrs. C. E. Wade-Dalton
Mrs. George Walker
J. C. Walker
George W. Wallace
John R. Wallace
Sam A. Wallace
Theda Wammack
Mrs. Edward Ward
William Wauhop
Ann Weathers
Mrs. M. B. Webb
A. L. Weber
Edgar E. Weston
W. O. Wethington
Mrs. E. T. Wheeler
Mrs. Frank A. White
Virgie White
Mrs. Jewell Wilcox
Roger Wilcox
Arnold E. Williams
Evelyn F. Williams
Mrs. Henryetta Wills
Constance J. Willson
Clarence H. Wilson
Steve Wilson
Gary Witcher
Mary S. Witcher
Herman O. Wolfe
John Womack
Mrs. Frances Wood
Isabel Work
Mrs. H. P. Wornstaff
Mrs. J. M. Wyrick
Mrs. A. L. Yeager
Mary Yeager
Jeffie Young
Ruth Zinnecker

BIBLIOGRAPHY

Alley, John. *City Beginnings in Oklahoma Territory.* Norman, 1939.

Brackett, Walter L. "Place-Names of Five Northeast Counties of Oklahoma." Unpublished Master's Thesis, University of Tulsa, 1943.

Brewington, Eugene H. *Place Names in Oklahoma.* Oklahoma City, 1956.

Carter, W. A. *McCurtain County and Southeast Oklahoma.* Idabel, 1923.

Eisele, Fannie L. *Covington and Community.* Privately printed, 1952.

Gannett, Henry. *Gazetteer of Indian Territory.* Washington, 1905.

Gould, Charles N. *Oklahoma Place Names.* Norman, 1933.

Gould, Charles N. "Oklahoma Place Names." Unpublished revisions. MS collection, University of Oklahoma Library, Norman.

Holland, C. Joe, and Bruce Palmer. *A Pronunciation Guide to Oklahoma Place Names.* School of Journalism, Norman, 1950.

Hodge, Frederick W., ed. *Handbook of American Indians.* Smithsonian Institution *Bulletin No. 30.* 2 vols. Washington, 1907.

Marshall, James. *Santa Fe, The Railroad That Built an Empire.* New York, 1945.

McCarrell, Fred. "History of the Names of Oklahoma County Seats." *Progress,* Vol. I, Nos. 8 and 9, May and June, 1912.

Mooney, Charles W. *Localized History of Pottawatomie County, Oklahoma to 1907.* Midwest City, 1971.

O'Beirne, H. F., and E. S. *The Indian Territory: Its Chiefs, Legislators and Leading Men,* St. Louis, 1892.

Peck, Henry L. *The Proud Heritage of LeFlore County.* Van Buren, 1963.

Rainey, George. *The Cherokee Strip.* Guthrie, 1933.

Read, William A. *Indian Place-Names in Alabama.* Baton Rouge, 1937.

Ruth, Kent, ed. *Oklahoma: A Guide to the Sooner State.* Norman, 1957.

Rydjord, John. *Indian Place-Names.* Norman, 1968.

Sealock, Richard, and Seely, Pauline. *Bibliography of Place-Name Literature.* Chicago, 1967.

Shirk, George H. "First Post Offices Within the Boundaries of Oklahoma" Indian Territory. *The Chronicles of Oklahoma,* Summer, 1948. Vol. XXVI, No. 2.

———. "First Post Offices Within the Boundaries of Oklahoma" Oklahoma Territory. *The Chronicles of Oklahoma,* Spring, 1952. Vol. XXX, No. 1.

————. "First Post Offices Within the Boundaries of Oklahoma" The State of Oklahoma. *The Chronicles of Oklahoma,* Spring, 1966. Vol. XLIV, No. 1.

Starr, Emmet. *Encyclopedia of Oklahoma.* Claremore, 1912.

Stewart, George R. *American Place-Names,* New York, 1970.

Tarpley, Fred. *Place Names of Northern Texas.* Commerce, 1969.

Wilson, Raymond R. "Place-Names of Six Northeast Counties of Oklahoma." Unpublished Master's Thesis, University of Tulsa, 1940.